Henning Groenda

**Certifying Software Component
Performance Specifications**

The Karlsruhe Series on Software Design and Quality
Volume 11

Chair Software Design and Quality
Faculty of Computer Science
Karlsruhe Institute of Technology

and

Software Engineering Division
Research Center for Information Technology (FZI), Karlsruhe

Editor: Prof. Dr. Ralf Reussner

Certifying Software Component Performance Specifications

by
Henning Groenda

Dissertation, Karlsruher Institut für Technologie (KIT)
Fakultät für Informatik
Tag der mündlichen Prüfung: 11. Juli 2013

Impressum

 Scientific
Publishing

Karlsruher Institut für Technologie (KIT)
KIT Scientific Publishing
Straße am Forum 2
D-76131 Karlsruhe

KIT Scientific Publishing is a registered trademark of Karlsruhe
Institute of Technology. Reprint using the book cover is not allowed.

www.ksp.kit.edu

Print on Demand 2013

ISSN 1867-0067
ISBN 978-3-7315-0080-3

Karlsruhe Institute of Technology

Certifying Software Component Performance Specifications

Zur Erlangung des akademischen Grades eines

Doktors der Ingenieurwissenschaften

von der Fakultät für Informatik
des Karlsruher Instituts für Technologie (KIT)

genehmigte
Dissertation
von

Henning Karl Horst Groenda
aus Starnberg

Tag der mündlichen Prüfung: 11. Juli 2013
Erstgutachter: Prof. Dr. Ralf H. Reussner
Zweitgutachter: Prof. Dr. Lars Grunske

KIT – Universität des Landes Baden-Württemberg
und nationales Forschungszentrum der Helmholtz-Gemeinschaft

www.kit.edu

Abstract

Component-based Software Engineering of business information systems on the architectural level is supported by performance prediction approaches. These approaches allow quantitative evaluations of architectural decisions throughout the lifecycle from the early design to the maintenance phase.

The evaluations rely on performance behavior specifications of the composed components. These specifications are abstract descriptions of the performance-relevant behavior and can contain probabilistic as well as deterministic parts. The accuracy of a prediction depends on the accuracies of the composed specifications. Current specification languages support specification reuse through loose coupling and separation of influence factors like the hardware environment or the propagated usage profile. However, these degrees of freedom increase the required effort and chance to make errors during the evaluation of the accuracy of specifications with respect to the behavior of implementations.

Evaluating the accuracy requires high effort even with limited degrees of freedom and parameter space. The evaluation requires deep knowledge in the areas performance testing and evaluation. Additionally, the separation of roles and concerns increases the chance for whitewashed specifications due to different aims of the participants. Whitewashed specifications endanger their meaningful use in predictions, especially if only specifications are offered on marketplaces. Inaccurate and whitewashed specifications endanger objective and trustworthy predictions for composed systems as well as subsequent architectural decisions.

Existing approaches for performance prediction on the architectural level assume that the accuracy of specifications for the composed components 1) is adequate for the selected influence factors and usage profile, 2) does not put decisions at risk by their influence on the overall prediction, and 3) is not whitewashed.

This thesis aims to evaluate the appropriate use of performance specifications in predictions. It mitigates the listed assumptions and provides benefits for the roles in the development process as follows. The thesis defines a language for the specification and processing of accuracy statements. This eases the specification and access for performance engineers, software architects, and analysis tools. The thesis defines coverage criteria for validating the accuracy of specifications. This eases the goal-oriented definition of tests and reduces the required testing knowledge for performance engineers and software architects. The thesis allows the automated validation of specifications. Performance engineers are relieved from a tedious task and the coverage of all selected aspects is ensured. The thesis defines a certification process, which addresses trust in specifications and their use in internal component repositories as well as marketplaces. Software architects and performance engineers profit from trustworthy specifications and can evaluate the appropriateness of a (re-)used specification.

The contributions are the formalized specification of the accuracy of specifications, the automated validation of specifications against the behavior of implementations as well as their integration into the engineering process with considerations of their trustworthiness. The contributions span several areas and are as follows.

Meta-model for Accuracy Statements. The presented formalization allows to specify the accuracy of performance specifications. The developed language for the statements takes into account the different influence factors as well as concurrent and probabilistic specifications. This generic language was additionally tailored for Palladio Component Model (Palladio) specifications.

Heuristic for Estimating the Accuracy of Overall Predictions.
The required effort for taking into account all inaccuracies including combinations of inaccuracies is prohibitive even for small specifications. The heuristic allows to cut the effort for estimating the effect that the inaccuracies of specifications have on an overall prediction. The heuristic was integrated into the Palladio prediction approach.

Accuracy Statement Validation. The presented coverage criteria ease the evaluation of covered aspects of specifications. Mutually coverage analysis as well as algorithms for test set size estimation, coverage creation, and coverage evaluation support criterion selection. The developed framework allows an automated validation of platform-independent Palladio specifications with implementations taking into account concurrent as well as probabilistic specification parts.

Specification Certification. Trustworthy specifications allow component evaluation and selection on the architecture level. The risks for the trustworthiness of specifications and the protection of intellectual property in implementations were identified. The presented certification approach addresses these risks and supports the appropriate use of specifications in internal repositories as well as on open marketplaces. The approach requires adaptations of the used development process. This adaptation is demonstrated for a variant of the Rational Unified Process (RUP).

The evaluation of the applicability, the benefits, and the contribution is based on three systems for experimentation. The first uses a complex deterministic specification from the Common Component Modelling Example (CoCoME). CoCoME is a benchmark for the comparison and evaluation of prediction approaches. The other two highlight the handling of probabilistic and concurrent specifications. The effect of inaccuracies on an overall prediction and the certification as part of an development process is evaluated based on CoCoME.

The results confirm the completeness of the accuracy statement language with respect to the influence factors. They show the benefits of estimating the accuracy of an overall prediction. The results show that the deviation varies heavily and the 90% quantile of a prediction is about 17% off even if a constant and low deviation of the resource demand of 10% in the specifications is assumed. The results for the accuracy statement validation show that all failures in the specifications are identified correctly, no false positives were found, and the results are verifiable by independent parties. The results for the certification show that component sharing, evaluation and selection on the architecture level can be successfully applied using protected repositories as well as open marketplaces.

Kurzfassung

Der Entwurf von komponenten-basierten betrieblichen Informationssystemen kann auf Software-Architekturebene durch Performance-Vorhersageverfahren unterstützt werden. Diese Ansätze erlauben die quantitative Bewertung von Architekturentscheidungen während des gesamten Lebenszyklus ausgehend vom Grobentwurf bis in die Wartungsphase.

Die Bewertung basiert auf Performance-Spezifikationen der beteiligten Komponenten. Diese stellen abstrakte Beschreibungen des Verhaltens dar und können sowohl probabilistische als auch deterministische Anteile enthalten. Die absolute Genauigkeit einer Vorhersage hängt dabei von der Genauigkeit der Beschreibung eingesetzter Implementierungen ab. Aktuelle Sprache zur Spezifikation unterstützten ferner die Wiederverwendung von Spezifikationen durch lose Kopplung und getrennte Berücksichtigung von Einflussfaktoren wie der Hardware-Umgebung, dem propagierten Nutzungsprofil und den Eingabe- und Komponentenparametern. Diese Freiheitsgrade erschweren jedoch im gleichen Zug die Bewertung der Übereinstimmung und Genauigkeit von Perfomance-Spezifikationen und Implementierungen.

Die Bewertung der Übereinstimmung und Genauigkeit erfordert selbst für eingeschränkte Parameterbereiche einen hohen Aufwand und tiefgreifendes Fachwissen in den Bereichen Performance-Tests und -Bewertung. Die Rollen- und Aufgabentrennung bei der Arbeit mit der gleichen Komponente erhöht die Wahrscheinlichkeit unterschiedlicher Ziele der Beteiligten und die Bereitstellung geschönter Spezifikationen. Insbesondere bei Nutzung von Marktplätzen erfordert die Verwendung von Spezifikationen das Vertrauen in deren Korrektheit. Nur in diesem Fall ist eine objektive und vertrauenswürdige Vorhersage unter Berücksichtigung der Kompositi-on und der gewählten Einflussfaktoren möglich und eine solide Grundlage für Entscheidungen.

Existierende Ansätze zur Performance-Vorhersage auf Architekturebene verwenden die Annahmen, dass die Genauigkeit der Performance-Spezifi-kationen der beteiligten Komponenten 1) für deren Wiederverwendung mit den aktuell gewählten Einflussfaktoren geeignet ist, 2) die Gesamtvorhersa-ge und darauf basierende Entscheidungen nicht gefährdet werden sowie 3) nicht absichtlich ein besseres als das tatsächliche Verhalten vorgeben wird.

Die Dissertation verbessert die Bewertbarkeit der Eignung von Spezifi-kationen für deren Wiederverwendung. Sie adressiert die Abschwächung der genannten Annahmen und unterstützt Rollen im Entwicklungsprozess wie folgt. Eine Sprache zur Angabe der Genauigkeit erlaubt die Beschrei-bung und maschinelle Verarbeitung von Qualitätsaussagen zu Spezifikatio-nen. Performance-Ingenieure, Software-Architekten und Analysewerkzeu-ge können einfacher auf dieses Wissen zugreifen. Die Dissertation definiert Abdeckungskriterien zur Bewertung der validierten Aspekte einer Spezifi-kation. Performance-Ingenieure und Software-Architekten können Testfäl-le gezielter entwerfen und mit geringerem Fachwissen als bisher anhand der Kriterien bewerten. Die Dissertation erlaubt die automatisierte Prüfung von Performance-Spezifikationen. Performance-Ingenieure werden entlas-tet und zielgerichtete Tests sichergestellt. Der definierte Zertifizierungspro-zess nutzt die ermittelten Informationen zur Vertrauensbildung in die Spezi-fikationen, die darauf aufbauenden systemweiten Analysen und erleichtert deren Verwendung in Marktplätzen.

Die Beiträge meiner Dissertation sind die formalisierte Beschreibung der Qualität von Performance-Spezifikationen, deren automatische Prüfung sowie die Integration in den Entwurfsprozess unter Berücksichtigung von Vertrauensfragestellungen. Sie können wie folgt zusammengefasst werden:

Metamodell zur Angabe der Genauigkeit von Performance-Spezifikationen. Die entwickelte Formalisierung erlaubt die Angabe der Genauigkeit von Spezifikationen. Diese berücksichtigt den unterschiedlichen Einfluss und die Trennung der Einflussfaktoren sowie Nebenläufigkeit und Plattform-unabhängige Spezifikationen.

Heuristik zur Abschätzung der Genauigkeit von Gesamtvorhersagen. Der Umfang der möglichen Parameter und Ungenauigkeiten führt zu prohibitivem Aufwand bei deren vollständiger Berücksichtigung. Die entworfene Heuristik stellt einen Kompromiss zwischen Analyseaufwand und Genauigkeit der Abschätzung dar. Sie wurde mittels Modell-Transformationen für Palladio-Spezifikationen exemplarisch umgesetzt.

Validierung von Aussagen zur Genauigkeit. Für die Bewertung der durch eine Bewertung abgedeckten Aspekte einer Spezifikation wurden Abdeckungskriterien entworfen. Die gegenseitige Überdeckung wurde analysiert. Algorithmen zur Erzeugung und Prüfung der Kriterien sowie der Abschätzung des notwendigen Testaufwands wurden ermittelt und umgesetzt. Diese berücksichtigen probabilistische sowie parametrische Spezifikationsanteile und Besonderheiten der nebenläufigen Verarbeitung. Das darauf aufbauend entwickelte Rahmenwerk erlaubt eine automatische Validierung für Plattform-unabhängige Palladio-Spezifikationen.

Zertifizierung von Spezifikationen. Vertrauenswürdige Spezifikationen erlauben die Bewertung und Auswahl von Komponenten auf der Architekturebene. Gefahren für die vertrauenswürdigen von Spezifikationen und den Schutz geistigen Eigentums in Implementierungen wurden ermittelt. Der erforschte Ansatz zur Zertifizierung erlaubt die Adressierung dieser Gefahren und deren Nutzung in Komponenten-Lagern und auf Marktplätzen. Die notwendigen Anpassung des komponenten-basierte Entwicklungsprozesse wurden ermittelt und exemplarisch für eine Variante des Rational Unified Process (RUP) umgesetzt.

Die Evaluation der Anwendbarkeit und Vorteile erfolgt anhand dreier Fallbeispiele. Das erste enthält eine komplexe rein deterministische Spezifikation aus dem Common Component Modelling Example (CoCoME). CoCoME ist ein Benchmark zum Vergleich und zur Bewertung unterschiedlicher Modellierungsansätze. Die weiteren veranschaulichen gezielt einzelne Aspekte: Das zweite Fallbeispiel enthält eine Spezifikation mit probabilistischen Anteilen und das dritte Fallbeispiel eine Spezifikation mit Elementen zur expliziten Modellierung von Nebenläufigkeit innerhalb einer Spezifikation. Der Einfluss auf eine Gesamtvorhersage und die Verwendung der Zertifizierung im Entwurfsprozess werden am komplexen ersten Beispiel aufgezeigt.

Die Ergebnisse zeigen die Vollständigkeit des Metamodells zur Beschreibung der Genauigkeit für alle Einflussfaktoren. Sie zeigen ferner die Vorteile der Abschätzung der Genauigkeit einer Gesamtvorhersage, welche selbst bei gleichmäßiger und geringer Abweichung der Resourcenlast in den Spezifikationen von 10% stark variiert und im 90% quantil bei über 17% liegen kann. Die Ergebnisse zur automatischen Bewertung von Aussagen zur Genauigkeit zeigen, dass alle Fehler in den Spezifikationen korrekt gefunden wurden, keine Falsch-Positiv-Meldungen erfolgt sind und durchgeführte Bewertungen von unabhängiger Seite überprüft werden können. Die Ergebnisse zur Zertifizierung von Spezifikationen zeigen, dass sowohl die Bereitstellung als auch die Auswahl von Komponenten auf der Architekturebene anhand vertrauenswürdiger Spezifikationen unter Nutzung von geschützten Komponenten-Lagern und offener Marktplätze erfolgreich angewendet werden kann.

Acknowledgements

A lot of people supported me during the creation of this thesis and i want to thank each of them deeply for sharing their views, providing valuable comments, and many fruitful discussions. First of all, i want to thank my supervisor Prof. Dr. Ralf Reussner who inspired, guided, and supported me throughout my dissertation. His pursued scientific ideal, wealth of ideas, and lived best practices shaped the working group and provided an excellent and commendable working atmosphere. His management style is an inspiration. I am privileged to be a part of his group. I also want to thank my second supervisor Prof. Dr. Lars Grunske for his constructive suggestions, insightful questions, and valuable comments, which helped me to improve my work.

I want to express my gratitude to my former and current managers, Jun.-Prof. Dr.-Ing. Steffen Becker, Dr.-Ing. Mircea Trifu, and Dr.-Ing. Klaus Krogmann. Their continuous and unwavering support ensured an pleasant working atmosphere, the ability to conquer challenging tasks and deadlines, and their guidance and leadership continues being an inspiration.

I also want to thank my former and current colleagues at the FZI as well as the university and the group SDQ for their interest in my work, sharing their ideas, providing me new insights, working collaboratively, and many fruitful discussions. I am honored to know you and treasure our shared experiences. They are (in alphabetical order): Sascha Alpers, Dr. Christian Bartsch, Christoph Becker, Dr.-Ing. Franz Brosch, Fabian Brosig, Ph.D. Barbora Bühnova, Erik Burger, Martin Blersch, Oliver Denninger, Zoya Durdik, Esmahan Eryilmaz, Michael Faber, Viktoria Firus, Dr. Giovanni Falcone, Dr.-Ing. Thomas Goldschmidt, Dr.-Ing. Jens Happe, Dr.-

Ing. Lucia Happe, Michael Hauck, Christoph Heger, Dr. Stefan Hellfeld, Jörg Henß, Nikolas Herbst, David Hlavac, Matthias Huber, Nikolaus Huber, Jun.-Prof. Dr. Oliver Hummel, David Karlin, Benjamin Klatt, Ph.D. Jan Kofron, Dr.-Ing. Samuel Kounev, Dr.-Ing. Anne Koziolek, Dr.-Ing. Heiko Koziolek, Max E. Kramer, Rouven Krebs, Steffen Kruse, Martin Küster, Dr.-Ing. Michael Kuperberg, Dr.-Ing. Volker Kuttruff, Michael Langhammer, Philipp Merkle, Prof. Dr. Marco Mevius, Aleksandar Milenkoski, Seyed Vahid Mohammadi, Dr.-Ing. Christof Momm, Qais Noorshams, Fouad ben Nasr Omri, Michal Papez, Ph.D. Pierre Parrend, Dr.-Ing. Christoph Rathfelder, Andreas Rentschler, Piotr Rygielski, Patrik Scheidecker, Thomas Schuster, Simon Spinner, Johannes Stammel, Gabor Szeder, Peter Szulman, Dr.-Ing. Adrian Trifu, Ph.D. Catia Trubiani, Dr. Ralf Trunko, Robert Vaupel, Alexander Wert, Dennis Westermann, and Jan Wiesenberger.

I owe my sincere gratitude to all of my students, especially Dominik Ernst, Martin Krogmann, Pavel Nikolov, and Adam Taras, who deserve credit for implementing many of my ideas. I also want to thank the people working in the background and keeping everything running for their constant support: Susanne Agwaze, Heike Döhmer, Elena Kienhöfer, Vanessa Martin Rodriguez, Tatiana Rhode, and Elke Sauer.

My special gratitude goes to my parents, Ilse and Hartmut. Their love, encouragement, sacrifices, and care allowed me to make my way and pursue my dreams. None of my achievements would have been possible without them and their guidance as well as constant and unconditional support. Finally, I want to thank Marina Gary for her love, support, encouragement, and understanding especially in the final stage of writing.

Contents

Contents

1. Introduction

1.1. Motivation

Component-based Software Engineering on the architectural level is supported by performance prediction approaches enabling the prediction of effects cause by the chosen architecture. This allows considering composition alternatives already in early design stages and selecting the appropriate architecture for a system. However, these approaches are not restricted to the initial architecture design. They allow ensuring desired system properties throughout the entire lifecycle of systems. For example, their use in the development phase enables software engineers to predict the performance of different architecture design alternatives and hence select the best alternative. In the deployment phase, these specifications guide the selection and sizing of an appropriate execution environment and on the deployment of components within this environment. During operation, the specifications can be used to reason about effects caused by different usage profiles and ensure meeting service levels in advance. In the maintenance or evolution phase, performance predictions allow examining the effects of modifications on the performance, reduce the probability of discovering unwanted behavior in live systems, or identify bottlenecks in running systems.

The paradigm of component-based development breaks down complexity, emphasizes separation of concerns, and targets application scenarios in which roles from different and independent parties cooperate in the development of systems. Thus, it has a strong separation of roles for the definition, development, and assembly of components. The separation of roles can span multiple independent organizations. The definitions for de-

1

veloped components are shared and offered in component repositories or marketplaces. Sharing only the definition of components allows protecting the implementation itself and contained intellectual property but still allows selecting a component for evaluation and assembly. Augmenting the definitions by performance specifications can ease and improve the selection process. The different organizations and roles may have different individual goals. These goals may lead to inaccurate specifications which do not describe the implementation or are a very positive interpretation of the real behavior. The potential conflicts must be addressed in order to use specifications in this scenario and rely on prediction results. The conflict cannot be solved by appropriateness assessments of each role participating in the process as not every role has the required expertise and artifacts. The effort for such an assessment depends on the complexity of the specification and can be quite high as it includes the instrumentation and measurements of implementations as well as deep knowledge in validating performance specifications.

Current performance prediction approaches allow describing the influencing factors of a system independently. This means that the usage profile, configuration parameters, the behavior of external services, the runtime environment for components, and the performance-relevant behavior of each component can be specified and validated independently. This separation fosters reuse of each of these specifications in different contexts.

The accuracy of an overall prediction for a system is the result of the accuracy of the behavior specifications of the components and the accuracy of the prediction approach itself. The accuracy of a behavior specification depends on 3 factors: 1) on the stage in the design process, e.g. if it is an early estimation or consists of performance properties measured in the targeted environment on a real implementation, 2) the abstraction level of the specification, and 3) the effort spent to create and validate the specification. This leads to the situation that several behavior specifications for the same

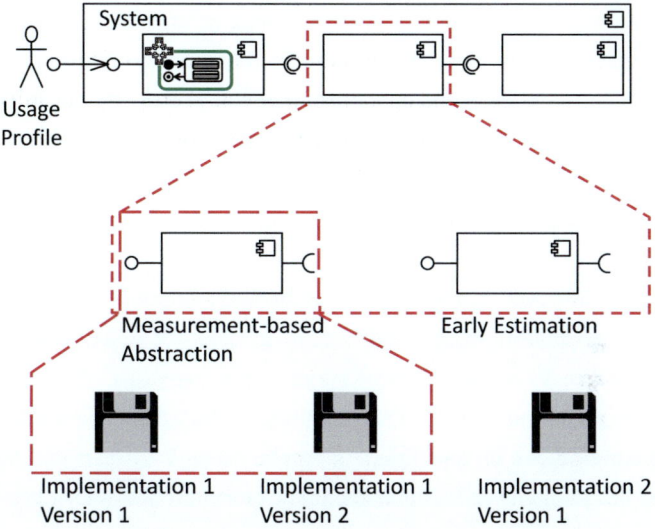

Figure 1.1.: Example of Relation between Implementations and System Architecture for Performance Predictions in the Lifecycle

component, which commonly differ in accuracy, are available during the lifecycle of a system.

Figure 1.1 provides an example for the relations of behavior specifications and implementations during the lifecycle of a system. The dashed lines visualize the relations and possible substitution of artifacts within the lifecycle of a system. These artifacts and their relations are described in the following.

In the example, a system is composed of three components and used according to the Usage Profile shown in the top left in the figure. The behavior of one of the composed components (top, in the middle) has been estimated to optimize the system's architecture in an early design stage. This estimated specification is shown in the middle on the right side. After an initial version of the system was implemented and deployed a specification based on measurements was created, which is shown in the middle on the left side. The measurements were made on `Version 1` of `Implementation 1` for the parameter range of the `Usage Profile`. `Version 1` contained errors in the functionality, which were identified and fixed. This results in `Version 2`. After a while, `Implementation 2` was developed with new features and another data management framework. There is no behavior specification (yet) describing this new implementation.

The accuracy and appropriateness of the early estimation depends heavily on the estimating expert and is hard to quantify objectively. Nevertheless, its use in an early design stage is advantageous. In later design stages, the deviation between the measurement-based specification and the implementation can be quantified. It can be assured by tests and observations of the implementation that accuracy threshold are not violated. The same specification can describe different implementations. For example the measurement-based specification can be an appropriate description of `Version 1` and `Version 2` if the acceptable deviation is big enough to cover the differences between the versions. In the described scenario,the measurement-based specification is validated for the parameter range of the `Usage Profile`. There is the question if the specification can be appropriately re-used for a modified usage profile or for `Implementation 2` without endangering the quality of the overall prediction or decisions based on prediction results. Furthermore, if a specification is not appropriate then how can users of a prediction be notified of this fact.

The goal of the approach presented in this thesis is to evaluate the appropriate use of performance specifications. This requires stating the accuracy, evaluating the trustworthiness of accuracy statements and analyzing how the accuracy of individual specifications effects the overall prediction results. This leads to the research questions listed in table 1.1. If these questions remain unanswered then overall predictions will provide seemingly accurate predictions but their relation to the real behavior remains unknown. There is the danger of becoming a victim of the 'garbage in

Table 1.1.: Questions Regarding the Trustworthiness of Single Specifications and the Overall Prediction with Respect to Inaccuracies of Specifications

Identifier	Question
Goal: Evaluate Appropriate Use of Performance Specifications	
Q1	Are the targeted implementations appropriately described by the specifications?
Q2	Which accuracy does each specification have?
Q3	Is the accuracy of each specification valid for the propagated usage profile?
Q4	How trustworthy are the statements about targeted implementation and accuracy?
Q5	What is the effect of the accuracies of the composed components on the overall prediction?

implies garbage out'-principle without being aware because the prediction approach still delivers seemingly good predictions. If they are only partially answered there remain uncovered risks. These risks pose a danger to the validity of the prediction and the prediction result as sound base for a decision on the architectural level. Section 1.3 points out how this thesis addresses the questions.

Unfortunately, current prediction approaches address these questions only implicitly or not at all. They assume that accurate specifications are created and used by performance engineers and ensure that the overall prediction is accurate if this assumption holds. They support the use of prediction approaches at distinct points in the development process. They do not focus on their continuous use and the reuse of specifications in the long run, especially the reuse by different or independent parties. Even if quality statements exist and are coupled with specifications then it often remains unclear which aspects are tested and how thorough the accuracy has been tested. This includes the reproducibility of results and which inaccuracies may remain uncovered. This issue is aggravated by the complexity of parameterized specifications which allow statements independent of usage profiles, used external services, or hardware environments.

The continuous use of performance prediction approaches during the whole lifecycle, the re-use of specifications, and broad use on the architectural level is impaired by this limitation. The potential and advantage of protecting intellectual property by providing specifications instead of implementations in marketplaces without endangering the evaluation of components is currently not exploited.

1.2. Application Scenario

The application area targeted by the approach presented in this thesis is a component-based software engineering process, which uses predictions on the architectural level to reason about performance properties of the composed system. It additionally targets distributed development. This distribution can either be in space or in time. The approach can be applied at every stage in the life-cycle and takes reuse of specifications in the long-term into account. Reasoning about the trustworthiness of specifications with respect to their relation to implementations (Q1 and Q4) requires implementations by design and can only be applied after implementations are available. It targets usage profile and platform independent, parameterized, and complex specifications. Answers to the questions Q2, Q3, and Q5 are possible in all stages. The specifications can contain probabilistic and non-probabilistic elements as well as concurrent behavior.

It specifically addresses trust issues and supports the separation of work and different parties for developing, offering and using components. The reuse of specifications in the long run and therefore maintenance and further development is addressed as well. This enables the broad use of specifications in component repositories and component marketplace scenarios. Its support is provided by a general description which activities and steps are necessary to implement the presented approach in own development processes as well as a tailored version of Palladio's component-based reference development process described in [RBB+11a]. It supports exploiting the potential of intellectual property protection by sharing specifications instead of implementations for evaluation purposes. Furthermore, a guideline shows which trust issues occur in different scenarios and how trustworthiness can be addressed.

This thesis supports performance engineers in storing and validating the accuracy of specifications on the component level. A high degree of automation of the validation ensures easy applicability, covered issues, and reproducibility of results. It provides feedback to performance engineers and software architects if specifications are used outside the range in which their accuracy is specified (e.g. because the usage profile leads to input parameters of the specifications in which it is not valid) as well as shows the effect of accuracies on the component level on overall predictions. This knowledge aids in determining if a prediction is a sound base for a decision or the inherent inaccuracy make it too risky without further evaluation.

1.3. Aim and Contributions

The aim of this thesis is the certification of the accuracy of specifications and using these certified statements for evaluating and ensuring the appropriate (re-)use of specifications in prediction approaches. The certificate must state which aspects of the specification have been tested and ensure complete testing of each aspect. This sound and trustworthy assessment advances (cross-party) component-based engineering and increases the trustworthiness in predictions of composed systems, especially if specifications are reused in the lifecycle of a system or in different systems. The objectives followed to reach this goal and how this thesis answers the questions shown in Table 1.1 are addressed in the following for each area of work.

The thesis itself spans four areas of work: Accuracy Statements, Accuracy Effects on Overall Prediction, Accuracy Statement Validation, and

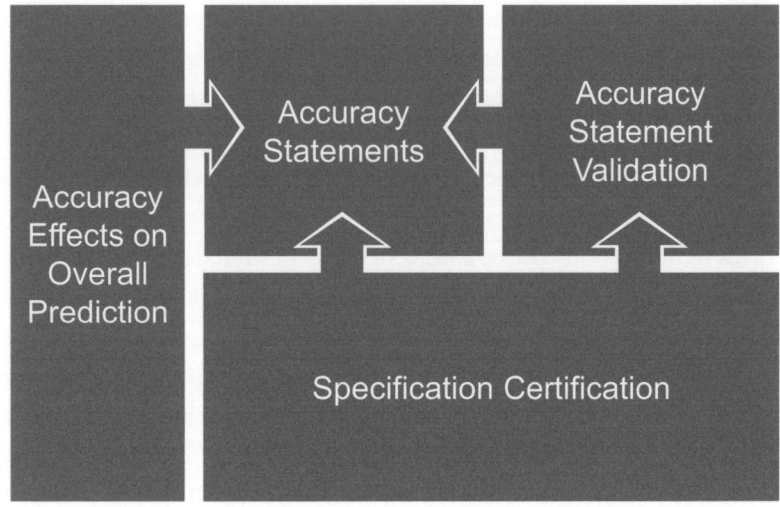

Figure 1.2.: Areas of Work and Dependencies between Areas

Table 1.2.: Work Areas and Addressed Questions (X: directly, x: indirectly)

	Q1	Q2	Q3	Q4	Q5
Accuracy Statements		X			
Accuracy Effects on Overall Prediction		x	X		X
Accuracy Validation	X	x,X		X	
Specification Certification	x	x		x,X	

Specification Certification. The first is the core in which a language to make accuracy statements and attach them to behavior specifications is addressed. The second uses these statements and infers the effects on the overall prediction approach. The third addresses the automated validation of accuracy statements for given specifications and implementations. The final area uses the accuracy statements and the validation information to ensure trust in the specifications. All areas of work and their mutual dependencies are depicted in Figure 1.2. Their relation to the questions is depicted in Table 1.2.

1.3.1. Accuracy Statements

The accuracy of a specification can be stated for different abstraction levels and with different level of details. Furthermore, the accuracy is often restricted to certain parameter ranges for parameterized specifications as validation in the whole potential parameter space requires unjustified high effort. The source of a specification, e.g. required, estimated, or measured performance, has implications on the accuracy but only measured performance can be compared on a sound basis. The elements contained in a specification providing details on the performance can all differ in accuracy. Both, absolute and relative thresholds may apply for the same element depending on the degree of abstraction and capturing precision. The statements depend on the specification language as the accuracy of elements of that language is described.

This thesis provides an annotation meta-model for attaching accuracy information to performance specifications. It allows stating the accuracy of specifications for current prediction approaches and is a common language for automated processing of the contained information. The customization of the meta-model for Palladio-based specifications is shown and this thesis demonstrates how the customization to a specification language can be realized.

These contributions provide answers to question Q2 as they provide formalized means to state and access the accuracy of a specification for humans as well as programs.

Open and addressed scientific challenges in this area are:

1. Formalization of accuracy information for performance specifications. Devise a customizable meta-model to state accuracy for specifications which separate the influencing factors into different models and allow stating absolute and relative thresholds for the elements of the specification.

2. Demonstration of the customization process.

1.3.2. Accuracy Effects on Overall Prediction

The degree of the influence on an overall prediction caused by the accuracy of a component's specification depends on its composition within the overall system and the propagated usage profile. Inaccuracies in other component specifications can alter the propagation of the usage profile and hence indirectly influence the overall influence size. Furthermore, the propagated usage profile may lead to the use of specifications in areas in which no accuracy information is available and the specification has not been validated.

Worst-case scenarios of this influence point out the margins around predicted values and allow judging if a prediction will most likely provide a sound basis for a specific evaluation goal. This makes these scenarios the most valuable for users of an accuracy analysis. It is possible that inaccuracies in one model hide inaccuracies in another rather than accumulate but only the accumulation demonstrates the worst-case effect where all models are still used within their accuracy statements ranges.

In general, determining worst-cases or graduations of them requires a full exploration of the parameter space, which implies parameter modification and a subsequent analysis run. Full exploration means each model in a composition must be modified individually and all combinations must be tested to be sure any possible effect has been identified. For example, increasing a parameter, which influences the priority of certain jobs could increase the throughput for these jobs at the expense of the performance of other jobs. Even smaller resource demands in parts of the model do not necessarily imply faster processing as the changed situation could lead to contention where there has been none before and hence increased response times.

This thesis provides a discussion about trade-off decisions for influence analyses and realizes an influence analysis for Palladio-based specifications. It shows how software architects and performance engineers benefit from accuracy information and how it supports their decisions. The accuracy effects analyses and reasoning can stay on the architecture level.

These contributions provide answers to question Q3 and Q5. The use of the area accuracy statements allows to indirectly provide the answers for that area as well. If a prediction uses specifications in parameter ranges for which no accuracy information is available this situation and the propagated usage profile leading to this situation are reported to the user by the approach presented in this thesis. The realized influence analysis provides answers to Q5. The thesis demonstrates how the feedback helps in judging on the appropriateness of specifications for an evaluation goal.

Open and addressed scientific challenges in this area are:

1. Provide an influence analysis realizing a trade-off between analysis effort and quality of the analysis showing the effects of the accuracies of composed specifications on the overall prediction.

1.3.3. Accuracy Statement Validation

Even today, Parkes identified in the survey [Par12] with 200 participants with executive jobs in large North American companies that quality assurance is still a major issue in software development and improvements would help companies:

> 75% of companies anticipate they would realize faster release times by removing connection complexities; 'Technical constraints during the development process, particularly around managing data and a sufficiently robust infrastructure for component, system and performance testing is a major issue. [Par12]

> Advanced development and testing solutions can resolve the most common challenges in the software delivery lifecycle (SDLC). North America respondents admitted that having this

> kind of technology would help them increase quality (81%), shorten development cycles (75%) and reduce costs (71%). [Par12]

Quality assurance is carried out by validation and verification activities. Validation focusses on users needs and verification on the fulfillment of specified requirements (see section 2.1 for detailed definitions). In model-based testing, validation addresses if a model conforms to the user requirements. In the applied case, validation addresses if a performance specification is appropriate for making the architectural decision at hand. Verification addresses the comparison between a given model and implementation based on testing.

The user requirements for performance specifications regard their use in prediction approaches and the suitability of the overall prediction for their questions. Validating their fulfillment requires verifying their correctness. The verification can be made by formal proofs or testing. Verifying the accuracy of performance specifications is usually carried out by testing. The application of formal techniques and proving their correctness is limited by the high degrees of freedom between the abstraction level of specification and implementation, certain dependencies which are only observable at runtime, and the parameter space taking into account all influencing factors.

Test-based assessments of the soundness of specifications require deployed and appropriately instrumented instances of the corresponding implementation and deep knowledge in validating specifications. Selecting appropriate tests is especially challenging for models allowing both, probabilistic as well as deterministic transitions. Exhaustive testing requires prohibitively high effort for state-of-the-art specifications. Trade-off decisions involve restricting the validation to certain parameter ranges and to focus on certain elements or aspects of the specification. The resulting restrictions must be stored together with the model for proper (re-)use.

Existing approaches often rely on the expertise of performance engineers to infer test sets for models. Without hard evaluation criteria, it is challenging for performance engineers and third parties to assess the quality and thoroughness of the validation or the aspects covered by the tests. This requires high effort for the test set creation and renders the evaluation of existing test sets cumbersome and comparisons between different test sets hard. Quantitative and objective evaluation criteria would allow reasoning about covered aspects with less performance engineering background knowledge, ease comparisons of test sets, and allow creating test sets tailored to cover selected aspects. Formalized criteria tailored for specification languages would allow taking into account their expressiveness, constraints, and assumptions while enabling the automation of test set creation. Automated test set creation would increase reproducibility and reduce the required effort of performance engineers. Automated test execution would further decrease the required effort of performance engineers. It can be enhance to dynamic test set creation in order to cover and adapt to probabilistic modeled decisions within specifications. Additional estimation algorithms for test set sizes linked with a criterion and a selected specification would allow reasoning about the required validation effort beforehand and support trade-off decisions.

This thesis provides coverage criteria definitions for Palladio-based specifications and test set size estimators for each criterion. The criteria take into account execution platform independent specifications, the parameters supported by Palladio as well as the influencing factors for specifications. An implemented validation framework provides automated test set creation and test execution. This framework eases testing and addresses the issues identified by Parkes and shown at the beginning of this section.

These contributions provide answers to question Q1, Q2, and Q4. The use of the area Accuracy Statements provides provides answers to the questions linked with that area as well. The criteria allow answering which aspects are covered and the automated validation with dynamic test set creation ensures that these aspects are appropriately verified for a given implementation and specification. It enriches the accuracy statements themselves by a method to check if these statements are valid and hence provides more information to Q2. The automation and formalized criteria definition as well as knowledge about pairwise relation of criteria allow reasoning about the trustworthiness of accuracy statements and which error might still remain.

Open and addressed scientific challenges in this area are:

1. Define performance-oriented component coverage criteria for specifications taking into account the parameters and influencing factors

2. Analyze pairwise relation and mutual covered aspects for the defined criteria

3. Create algorithm for dynamic test set creation and handling of probabilistic elements of specifications

4. Analyze which information is necessary to automate the validation of specifications

5. Support validation of execution platform-independent specifications

1.3.4. Specification Certification

There are several approaches to ensure that different parties trust the soundness of the statements made by a specification.

The offering party of a component providing the specification can agree to contractual penalties if the statements are not sound. However, its hard to evaluate in advance for all available components if the offering party is able to cover the penalties. Furthermore, this does not work well with Free/Libre Open Source Software (FLOSS) components in which there is no single responsible company behind a component.

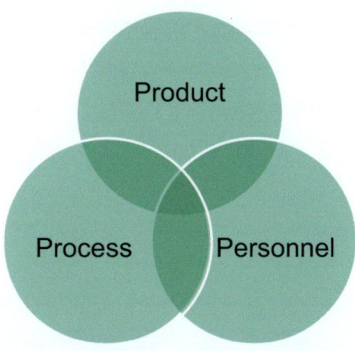

Figure 1.3.: Software Quality Triangle [Voa99]

Other approaches are based on the certification of specifications. In general, there are three basic types of approaches to certification: personnel, product and process certification as Voas showed in [Voa99]. All of these aspects affect how well a piece of software or the description for that software has been engineered. These types are described in the following and their relation is visualized in Figure 1.3.

Process certificates focus on the management aspect of development, e.g. that estimates match real effort and development processes are repeatable and serve reaching defined goals. However, the best process cannot guarantee that a system has a good quality or a specific specification is sound [MW08].

Personnel certificates focus on the knowledge and expertise of individuals. Such a certificate can ensure that the training of a person matches the requirements for assigned tasks. It cannot ensure that the knowledge is properly applied. It does not provide evidence which aspects of a specification have been validated to which extent.

Product certificates focus on the artifact, in this case the specification, itself. They can provide evidence which aspects of a specification have been validated to which extent.

The analysis of immaturities of marketplaces by Overhage and Thomas in [OT04] showed the following threats to the (re-)use of specifications and components.

> Being unable to predict and assess component behavior often leads to extreme difficulties in software reuse. [OT04]

> Component marketplaces today often support the distribution of special component test versions that can be assessed by the respective buyers prior to the acquisition of a fully functional component version. However, test versions are usually restricted to a reduced functionality and often show different extra-functional characteristics compared to the fully functional version, which makes it difficult to take over assessment results. Moreover, forcing buyers to gain information (e.g. to compare alternative components) solely on the basis of exhaustive component testing burdens them with significant additional efforts and thus severely violates the postulation of minimal transaction costs. [OT04]

This shows that trustworthy specifications help mitigating the issue as they support the assessment of components and prediction of their properties. The conformance of the information offered in marketplace and the behavior of the implementation of the component must hold in order to fulfill minimal transaction costs.

This thesis follows a product certification approach as it is the only way to ensure that each individual specification is providing sound statements while maintaining the component-based development paradigm. A certificate covers the successful validation of criteria defined in the Accuracy Statement Validation area. If followed, it ensures that only sound inputs are used by software engineers to reason about performance on the architectural level. These trustworthy specifications can be provided on marketplaces ensuring the conformance to the implementation as well as minimal transaction costs. This thesis also defines the workflows necessary to tailor an own certification-aware component-based development process and shows this tailoring for the Palladio development process. It follows the separation of concerns of the component paradigm and extends the existing Palladio development process by distinguishing the capabilities required for the roles of performance engineers and developers.

These contributions provide answers to question Q4. The use of the areas Accuracy Statements and Accuracy Statement Validation indirectly provides answers to questions Q1, Q2, and Q4 as well. The sound statements about the validity of accuracy statements for specifications validated by a product certification approach comparing implementation and specification ensures trustworthy statements. The process ensures that this information can be supplied successfully and the certification of specifications is conform with component-based development and architectural level performance engineering.

Open and addressed scientific challenges in this area are:

1. The formulation of certification criteria used to define the aspect of performance specifications, which have to be covered in the validation and the extent to which these aspects have to be covered.

2. The creation of a workflow for performance specification certification usable in scenarios with repositories or marketplaces used by several independent parties.

3. The specification of an adapted component-based development process incorporating certified specifications.

1.4. Contribution

Existing performance prediction approaches rely on the capability of software engineers to select suitable performance specifications of a component and do not address trust issues in specifications and their use by independent parties. Research focused on validating prediction approaches under the assumption that the specifications were suitable for the situation at hand. Validating performance specifications is seen as manual activity during the generation of the specifications. Explicit statements about the quality and the thoroughness of the specification's validation are uncommon. Especially if specifications should be reused in different context, for example because of late composition, then missing validity statements increase overall efforts as specifications have to be recreated and revalidated before each use.

The combined contributions addressing the scientific challenges listed for each area fulfill the aim to advance cross-party component-based engineering in the following points:

C1 Performance engineering can be used in scenarios with cross-party component repositories or marketplaces. The trustworthy specifications allow exploiting the benefits of architecture level performance predictions without reducing the quality of the evaluation and selection of components.

C2 Reproducible and more reliable validation results. Automated validation and formalized coverage criteria reduce human validation errors and ensure a sound validation.

C3 Faster validation by higher degree of automation.

C4 Reduced effort for specification creation by lowering bar for correct reuse of existing specifications.

C5 Better architectural decisions, especially on the selection of components, based on the knowledge of error margins of predictions due to specification inaccuracies.

C6 Reduced effort of performance engineers required for validation and evaluation of specifications.

C7 Software architects need less performance engineering interpretation knowledge when using architecture level predictions. Results are easier to interpret, inappropriate specifications are easier identified and the understanding of validated aspects is more precise with the criteria.

These advantages are available during the whole lifecycle of a software system and its different stages.

1.5. Structure

The thesis is structured as follows. Chapter 1 presented the motivation, introduced the approach, presented how the aim of the thesis is refined into questions, and how the questions relate to the four different areas of work.

Chapter 2 presents the foundations used in the presented approach. It provides basic definitions for different types of mismatches between specification and implementations. It discusses the comparison between a specification and implementation in general and its meaning in particular for specifications with probabilistic parts. It provides an introduction to the use of performance analyses on the architecture level in software engineering. It explains performance modeling with the Palladio approach used for the evaluation of the presented approach and introduces the relevant parts of its meta-model. Finally, it introduces the pre-existing component-based software engineering process of Palladio, which is based on the Rational Unified Process (RUP).

Chapter 3 discusses related work. It provides an overview on supported accuracy statements and influence analysis techniques in current performance engineering approaches. It discusses the state of the art in test-based validation and model-based testing as well as the application of coverage criteria. It concludes with an overview on certification approaches applicable to component-based software engineering for business information systems.

Chapters 4, 5, 6, and 7 are the core of this thesis and present the contributions for each area of work.

Chapter 4 presents the developed meta-model for stating the accuracy of performance specifications. It explains the skeleton for language-independent statements for performance specifications on the architecture level. Furthermore, it presents the tailoring to Palladio and shows the extension for the Palladio language.

Chapter 5 presents the influence analysis of inaccuracies of specifications on overall predictions of composed systems. It discusses the trade-off decision between analysis effort and quality of the analysis in general. It presents the developed heuristic and discusses the made trade-off decision.

Chapter 6 presents the approach for an automated test-based validation of performance specifications against the behavior of implementations. It introduces a meta-model for stating the configuration options for a validation and presents a validation process, which defines the necessary process steps and flow of artifacts. The chapter defines coverage criteria for Palladio performance specifications taking into account the semantics of the elements in that language. The criteria allow focussing the validation on selected aspects and ensure that these aspects are covered. Examinations of the mutual coverage and algorithms for test set size estimation complement the definition and support the selection of validation criteria. The validation requires the specification of a mapping between the specification and the implementation. The chapter presents the corresponding link meta model as well as the meta-model for reporting validation results. Finally, the chapter presents the tool part of the validation framework, which is responsible for executing the validation automatically.

Chapter 7 discusses risks for the trustworthiness of performance specifications and analyzes how certification can mitigate these risks. It shows that trust depends heavily on the participating roles and parties and that these relations influence what kind of certification ensures trustworthiness. The chapter introduces a guideline for the selection, which allows tailored solution for different application scenarios. Furthermore, the chapter presents the process steps required for the integration of certification into a development process. The chapter shows how these steps can be integrated into the development process used by Palladio and defines a certificate for Palladio specifications.

Chapter 8 describes the evaluation of the contributions presented in the chapters 4, 5, 6, and 7. It describes the refinement of research questions to experiments for each area of work. Then, it introduces the overall three systems for experimentation covering a realistic industrial use case as well as technology demonstrators. The chapter discusses the results of each experiment individually and provides a summarizing discussion of all results including an examination of internal and external validity.

Chapter 9 concludes the thesis. It summarizes the contributions and validation results for each area of work and shows the benefits. A detailed discussion of the assumptions and limitations follows. Finally, a perspective on short-term and long-term future work closes the thesis.

2. Foundations

This section introduces the foundations used throughout this thesis. Definitions for the certification, cause, manifestation and identification of mismatches between specification and implementation are provided. The comparison of specification and implementation is discussed in general and in particular for specifications with probabilistic branches. An introduction to performance analyses on the architecture level is provided and for Palladio specifications in particular. At the end, the component-based software engineering process of Palladio is presented, which is extended in chapter 7.2.1.

The International Organization for Standardization (ISO) defines certification in [DIN05] as "third-party attestation related to products, processes, systems, or persons" [DIN05, definition 5.5] and attestation as "issue of a statement, based on a decision following review, that fulfillment of specified requirements has been demonstrated" [DIN05, definition 5.2]. In this thesis, a more focussed definition is used:

Certification Attestation that a product fulfills specified requirements.

This definition does not require third-party attestation but allows it. The third-party is only required to ensure trust in the attestation in certain scenarios but has no effect on the attestation and product review. This topic and the assignment of the certificate issuing party is discussed in detail in section 7.1.2. The used definition only addresses the attestation of products as this thesis follows a product certification approach (see section 3.3 and chapter 7 for a detailed discussion). Chapter 7 defines the reviewed artifacts and used processes based on the specified requirements for performance specifications and the corresponding (automated) review process introduced in chapter 6.

The comparison between specification and implementation requires terms denoting the correctness of specifications with respect to a stipulated accuracy or quality. This thesis uses the following definitions tailored for the comparisons. They are based on the vocabulary used in the industry norm ISO 26262 for functional safety of electrical and/or electronically systems [ISO11b] and Meulen's definitions for software reliability engineers[Meu95].

Error Detected deviation between specification and implementation.

Failure Manifestation of an error resulting in the inability to perform as required by the specification. Case or condition in which the deviation between specification and the implemented behavior is outside of the stipulated quality bounds.

Fault Cause of an error. Incorrect specified behavior, which is an inherent weakness of the specification. A fault can be present without being identified.

If the conditions for experiencing a fault are met then the implementation is erroneous and a failure occurs. The test-based validation presented in this thesis reports validation failures if an error is detected and provides additional information to identify the fault.

This chapter is structured as follows. Section 2.1 discusses the issues of comparing specifications and implementations. Section 2.2 shows the foundations for statistical hypothesis testing and branch probability validation. Section 2.3 introduces the concept of performance analyses on the architecture level. Section 2.4 introduces how performance is specified in Palladio. Finally, section 2.5 introduces the component-based software engineering process respecting analyses on the architecture level, which is also used in Palladio.

2.1. Comparing Implementation and Specifications

The comparison between implementations and specifications is part of the validation and verification activities carried out during quality assurance. Annex B of ISO 9126-1[ISO01] provides the definition of validation and verification based on ISO 8402:1994[ISO94] with additional notes. These definitions are still used as can be seen for example in the glossary[vV10] of the International Software Quality Testing Board (ISTQB).

Validation is defined as

> Confirmation by examination and provision of objective evidence that the particular requirements for a specific intended use are fulfilled. [ISO01, B.33]

> Confirmation by examination and through provision of objective evidence that the requirements for a specific intended use or application have been fulfilled. [vV10]

Verification is defined as

> Confirmation by examination and provision of objective evidence that specified requirements have been fulfilled. [ISO01, B.34]

> Confirmation by examination and through provision of objective evidence that specified requirements have been fulfilled. [vV10].

Validation focusses on users needs and verification on the fulfillment of specified requirements. Pretschner and Philipps map these terms to model-based testing in [PP05]. They define model-based validation as checking

25

whether a model conforms to the user requirements and using tests generated based on these model as verification. These definitions are used in this thesis.

Specification are abstract descriptions of the behavior of an implementation. They focus on the relevant behavior and reduce the complexity of the implementation. Otherwise, the implementation could be used itself. However, the level of abstraction means that the behavior described by the specification and observations on the implementation will differ to a certain degree. Furthermore, the mathematical function describing the specified behavior can be completely different from the implemented behavior, as long as the deviation between specification and implementation does not exceed given acceptance thresholds. For example exponential resource demands can be approximated with linear functions in limited sections. This has the advantage that simple abstractions can be used instead of complex functions but has the disadvantage that the assumptions that the specification and implementation show the same resource demand distribution does not hold. This implies that the judgement on remaining errors after testing a specification is limited to the ratio of covered input parameter space of the implementation if no further assumptions on the behavior of the implementation are made. This is true because even a single remaining point in the parameter space might be the one point for which acceptance thresholds are violated. The approach presented in this thesis does not make any assumptions on implementations and uses the following definition for comparing the deviation between specification and implementation:

Accuracy A specification is an accurate description of the behavior of an implementation if the observable behavior of the implementation does not deviate beyond given accuracy threshold. These can be absolute as well as relative thresholds with reference to the specification.

The identification of failures between specification and implementation (inaccuracies) can be regarded as an information retrieval task aiming at retrieving all failures. In information retrieval, the standard terms precision and recall are used for the classification of approaches:

Precision Ratio of correctly identified cases to the identified cases of an approach. Precision is a measure for classifying the quality or correctness of the identified cases.

Recall Ratio of correctly identified cases of an approach to the overall existing cases. Recall is a measure for classifying the completeness of the identified cases.

The precision of comparing implementation and specification based on tests and the observations of their behavior is influenced by noise disturbing the measurements and if probabilistic decisions are specified. Bytecode instruction-based measurements of resource demand are not influenced by noise and there is no measurement error. This means the corresponding measurements and the validation approach presented in this thesis have a precision of 1. Otherwise, compensations for warm up or tear down may improve the situation or an estimate of the measurement can be calculated based on statistical reasoning with a given confidence. Compensations or measurements are not required in the presented approach. However, there is a single exception. Comparing probabilistic decisions based on observations is only possible with a given confidence by definition. Precision and recall for that case are discussed in section 2.2.

2.2. Statistical Hypothesis Testing

Statistical hypothesis testing addresses testing probability distribution assumptions based on observations. It is used in this thesis to check the probabilities of branches in Palladio specifications. Two alternative hypotheses

27

must be chosen before testing. They must be mutually exclusive and as soon as one hypothesis can be accepted, the other one is rejected.

The null hypothesis is denoted with H_0 and the alternative hypothesis is denoted with H_1. The hypothesis are tested using a sample size, denoted with n. The sample size determines how many outcomes are observed and integrated into a statistic. The statistic summarizes the outcomes, for example how often a branch was taken. The value of the statistic is compared to the expectations if H_0 or H_1 hold. The probabilistic nature means that the value of the statistic varies between repetitions for the same setting. The acceptance or rejection of a hypothesis is therefore only possible with a degree of certainty. There are two types of error, which can appear.

Errors of Type I, also known as significance level or false positives, are denoted with α and describe the probability of falsely rejecting a hypothesis. They determine the confidence level, which is $1 - \alpha$. Errors of Type II, also known as false negatives, are denoted with β and describe the probability of falsely accepting a hypothesis. They determine the power of a test, which is $1 - \beta$. The acceptable error probabilities determine the thresholds, also known as critical values, delimiting the acceptance and rejection range for values of the statistic. The resulting expected precision for a sufficiently large number of tests for the same hypothesis is $\frac{1-\alpha}{1-\alpha+\beta}$ and the resulting expected recall is $1 - \alpha$.

A Bernoulli experiment is an experiment with two different outcomes for a sample X (e.g. success $X = 1$ and failure $X = 0$) and a probability p for each outcome. The statistic $S = \sum_{k=1}^{n} X_k$ has a Binomial distribution $B(n, p)$ for the sample size n and if X is an independent, identically distributed random variable. The probability of exactly k successes is $P(S = k) = f(k, n, p) = \binom{n}{k} p^k (1-p)^{n-k}$. The cumulative distribution function is $P(S <= k) = F(k, n, p) = \sum_{i=0}^{k} \binom{n}{i} p^i (1-p)^{n-i}$ and its inverse $F^{-1}(q, n, p)$, where q is the quantile. Using the Moivre-Laplace theorem, the resulting distribution can be approximated with the normal distribution $N(np, np(1-p))$ for a sufficiently big n. For hypothesis testing, $np(1-p) \geq 9$ is often used as limit for a good approximation.

2.3. Architecture-Level Performance Analyses

This section introduces performance specifications and their use for analyses on the architecture level in general. Specifications can be parameterized and independent of influence factors like the usage profile or execution environment. This separation and decoupling allows late composition and re-use of the specifications. The specifications can be on different levels of abstractions and represent concurrent as well as probabilistic behavior. The influencing factors are presented, which are taken into account in current specification languages. See the surveys of Becker et al. [BGMO06] and Koziolek [Koz10] for an overview on the languages.

In general, the influence factors at composed system level (see figure 2.1(a)) are the Usage Profile, the Configuration or State of the system, the Hardware Environment, and the behavior of External Services. The usage profile describes how the system is used from the outside. This includes human users as well as machine to machine communication. The configuration or state represent the transient or persistent settings within the system, which influence the performance on system or component level. The hardware environment determines the capability and rate of handling resource demands issued by components in the architecture. External services do not compete for resources with components in the architecture but their Quality of Service (QoS)-properties influence the experienced behavior of the composed system. All influencing factors and the architecture or component behavior itself can be specified independent of each other, for example in different models. As mentioned before, a higher degree of separation goes along with a higher degree of re-use of the specifications in different contexts.

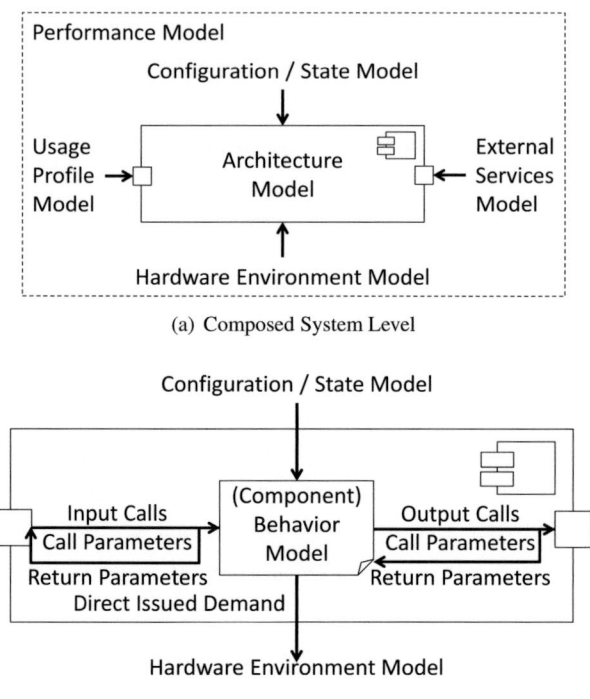

(a) Composed System Level

(b) Component Level

Figure 2.1.: Influence Factors and Performance Model Partitioning

The four influence factors can be mapped to the component level (see figure 2.1(b)) as follows. The Usage Profile propagated through the composed system is reflected by the number of input calls and the parameters used in the calls as well as the performance-relevant returned parameters. Configuration or State of a component is the same as for the whole system only on a lower level. The influence of External Services maps to component-external calls with given parameters and the performance-relevant parameters returned by these calls. The Hardware Environment determines the capability and handling of resource demand issued by the component to its environment.

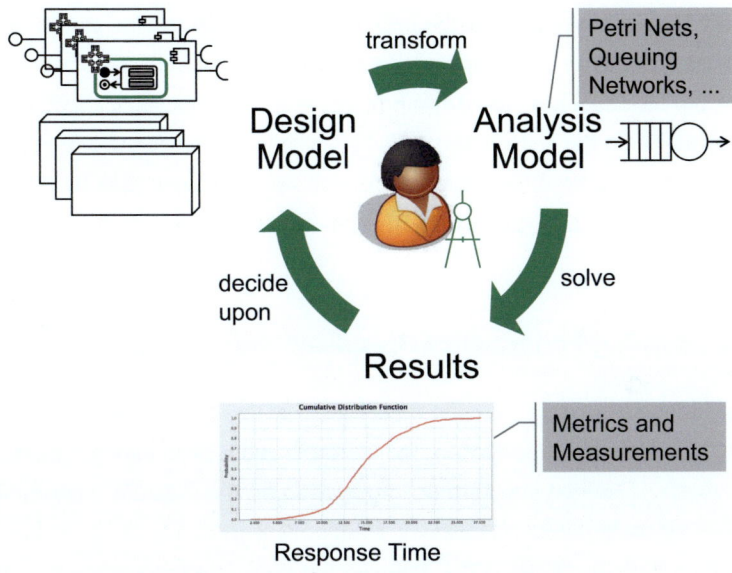

Figure 2.2.: Architecture-level Performance Engineering Cycle

These specifications are all part of the QoS engineering cycle on the architecture level, which is depicted for performance in figure 2.2 and described in the following. At the beginning, there is an architecture and a QoS-related question, which should be answered based on quantitative analyses. An example for such a question is the selection decision between two design alternatives based on the response time for the main usage scenario. The architecture design models covering the influence factors listed in the last paragraph are represented by the drawing board on the top left in the figure and are the main artifacts. They can be combined into a system's QoS model. This integrated QoS model can be transformed into analysis models, for example Petri Nets, Queuing Networks, or Stochastic Process Algebras. The transformation is already part of the prediction approach, for example Palladio for performance analyses. The prediction approach is then used to solve the model and gain quantitative measurement for the metrics important to answer the initial question. This solving can be realized analytically or via Monte-Carlo simulations. Analytical solutions are typically faster but have more assumptions and limitations than simulations, for example on the distribution of values or mutual interference of request processing. The resulting metrics and measurements can then be used to reason about the QoS-properties of the composed system and answer the question.

2.4. (Palladio) Performance Specifications

The presentation of the Palladio meta-model in this section focusses on the aspects, which are important for the concepts and realizations discussed in this thesis. Detailed and further information on the Palladio meta-model and on all meta-model elements and relations is available in the technical report on Palladio [RBB+11b]. Palladio has built-in solvers using a Monte Carlo simulation [BKR09, MH11] as well as analytical solver, for example based on Petri Nets [MKK11] or Layered Queuing Networks [KR08a].

In Palladio, the usage profile, the behavior of external services and the hardware environment are separated and specified in independent models. Palladio supports behavior specifications, which specify their resource demand in terms of invocations of intermediate language instructions, for example bytecode instructions for Java. Performance predictions based on bytecode instructions have been developed and successfully evaluated by Kuperberg in his PhD thesis [Kup10]. Configuration or state is modeled together with the behavior of components. Composition and deployment of components within a system on the hardware environment is specified separately and allows easy evaluation of design alternatives.

Components and interfaces are first class entities in Palladio and specified in repositories. Their specification is described in the following and the respective Palladio meta-model elements are provided. A running example is used to visualize the way Palladio specifications look like. The

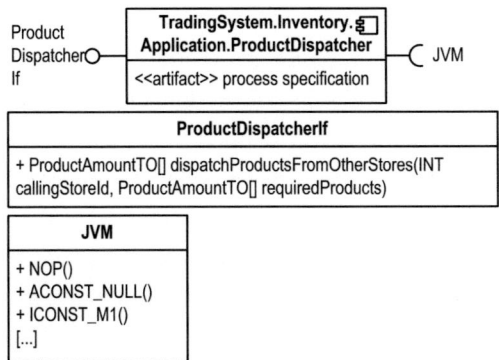

Figure 2.3.: Example for Component and Interface Specification in UML

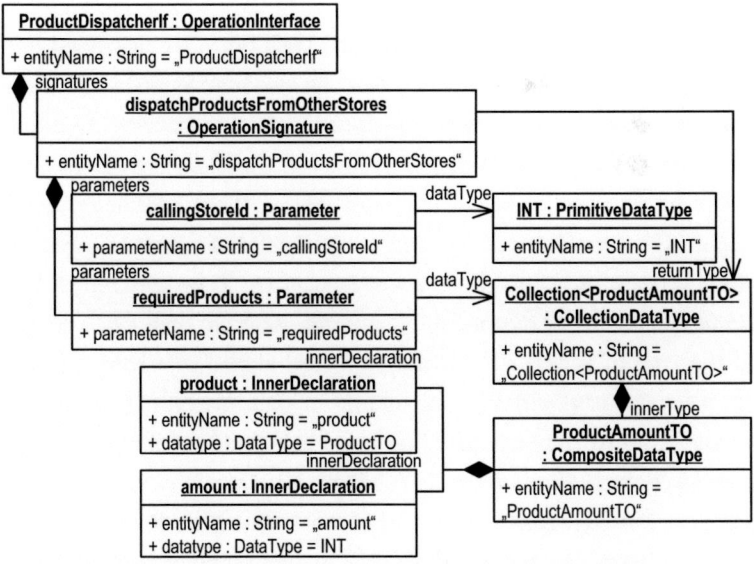

Figure 2.4.: Example for Interface Specification in Palladio

component and interfaces of the example are depicted in UML in figure 2.3. The Palladio representation of the `ProductDispatcherIf` interface and its operation is shown in figure 2.4.

In general, there are business interfaces (`OperationInterface`), infrastructure interfaces (`InfrastructureInterface`), and resource interfaces (`ResourceInterface`). The business interfaces are responsible for the interface of the system themselves. An example is the `ProductDispatcherIf` interface. The infrastructure interfaces are responsible for libraries and non-business related infrastructure, for example Java bytecode instructions. An example is the `JVM` interface. Resource interfaces are responsible for the access to resources in the environment, for example hard disk drives.

The different types of interfaces do not only differ in their semantics but also in their support for parameters. Business interfaces can have any number of operations. Each operation is described with an `OperationSignature`. This specifies the parameters including their names and data types and the return data type of the operation. Data types are discussed in the next paragraph. Infrastructure interfaces can also have any number of operations. Each operation is described with an `InfrastructureSignature`. In contrast to the business operations, the infrastructure operations do not allow returning data to behavior specifications. Their parameters are not limited. Resource interfaces can have any number of operations. Each operation is described with a `ResourceSignature`. They have only a single parameter and do not return data. They represent the access to a resource and the type of access. For example a read-access to a hard disk drive with a parameter describing the amount of data to read. The interfaces are connected to components using provided (`OperationProvideRole`, `InfrastructureProvidedRole`) and required roles (`OperationRequiredRole`, `InfrastructureRequiredRole`, `ResourceRequiredRole`). Resource interfaces can only be required but not provided by components.

Palladio supports data specifications using three different types: `PrimitiveDataType`, `CollectionDataType`, and `CompositeDataType`. The first are primitives and specifications for BOOL, BYTE, CHAR, INT, DOUBLE, and STRING are provided. Their semantics is comparable to such data types used in programming languages like Java. An usage example is available for parameter callingStoreId in figure 2.4. CollectionDataType represents a collection of a single data type (see Collection<ProductAmountTO> in figure 2.4 as an example). This data type must be set via the innerType containment link. CompositeDataType are data types composed from other ones. The innerDeclaration containment link allows to define the names and data types for a composition (see ProductAmountTO in figure 2.4 for an example).

The value for a data type instance is not specified directly in Palladio but its performance-relevant aspects are characterized. Palladio supports the characterizations VALUE, BYTESIZE, NUMBER_OF_ELEMENTS, STRUCTURE, and TYPE. They are explained in the following. The technical report of Reussner et al. [RBB+11b, p.59ff] provides additional examples and descriptions. The PhD thesis of Koziolek [Koz08] provides the theoretical background.

VALUE allows specifying the value of a given variable. The specification can be either made directly as a primitive numeric or string type, describe how the value is calculated based on parameters, or a probabilistic distribution function can be stated. The first option allows to set a fixed value for a parameter, for example a parameter for a component call or a component parameters. An example for such a call parameter is provided in figure 2.5(c). The second option is commonly used in behavior specifications to state the resource demand depending on the processed input. The third and last option is commonly used to specify the usage profile, for example a distribution of how many products are sold to customers using a shop solution in a single purchase. These specifications can be made for each characterization. The next paragraphs explains the semantics of the characterizations.

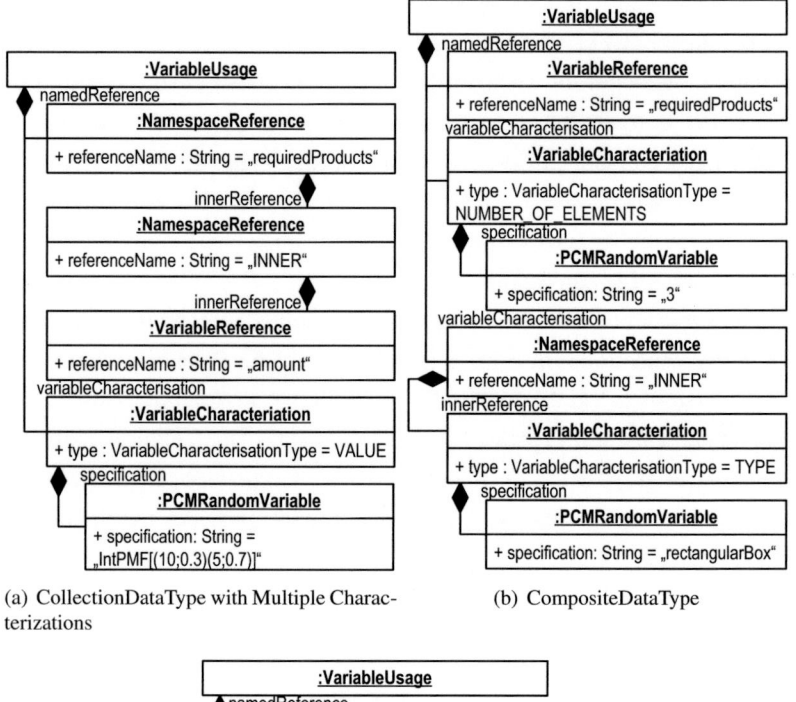

(a) CollectionDataType with Multiple Characterizations

(b) CompositeDataType

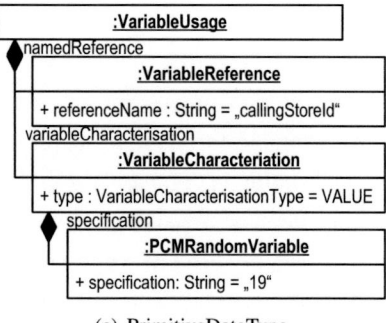

(c) PrimitiveDataType

Figure 2.5.: Data Type Instance Characterization Examples

BYTESIZE allows specifying the size of the data type instance in bytes.

NUMBER_OF_ELEMENTS allows specifying how many other data type instances are contained in a data type instance and is important for collections.

STRUCTURE allows specifying performance-relevant properties of the data type instance. For example if a collection is sorted or the compression rate of a file.

TYPE allows specifying properties of the data type instance from a business perspective. For example, if the shape of the packaging of a product is cylindrical or a rectangular box.

PrimitiveDataTypes can be characterized by VALUE, BYTESIZE, and TYPE. An example is given in figure 2.5(c). There, the VALUE of the parameter callingStoreId is set to 19, for example when a call to dispatch-ProductsFromOtherStores is made.

CollectionDataType are usually characterized by the NUMBER_OF_E-LEMENTS, but VALUE, BYTESIZE, and TYPE are possible as well. VALUE characterizations are rare and must describe all contained elements appropriately, for example with a distribution function denoting the individual values. An example is available in figure 2.5(a). There, the NUMBER_OF_E-LEMENTS of the collection behind the parameter requiredProducts is set to 3 and the TYPE of all contained data instances is set to rectangularBox. Specifications, which are true for all elements in a collection use the keyword INNER as referenceName. Palladio does not allow the specification of single elements independently.

The data type instances used in the composition of CompositeDataType are characterized in order to specify composite instances. figure 2.5(b) provides an example. There, the VALUE of the composed instance amount for all elements in the collection of the parameter requiredProducts is set to have the probability mass distribution with a value of 10 in 30% of all cases and 5 in 70% all cases. This represents that in 30% of all cases 10 products are required, 5 otherwise. Such a specification would usually be part of

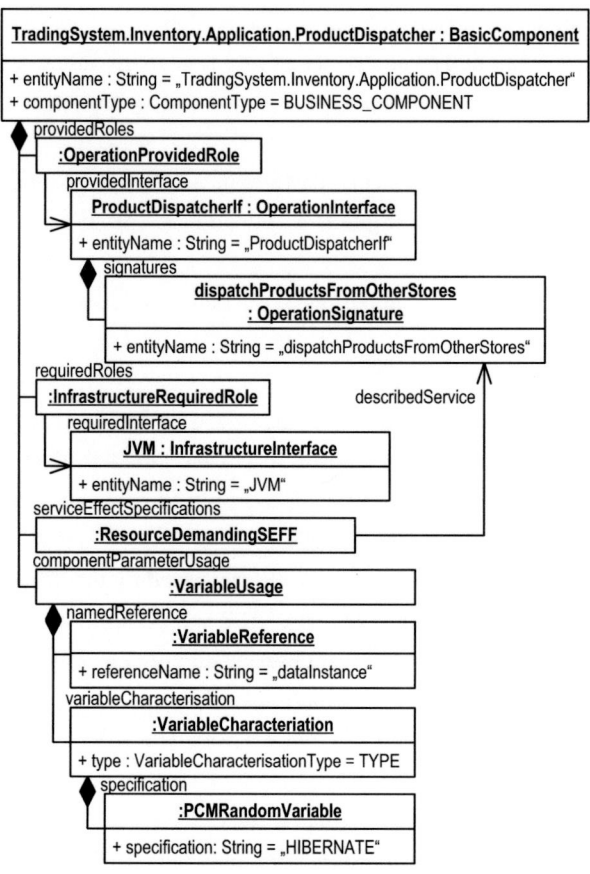

Figure 2.6.: Example for Component Specification in Palladio

the usage profile if the operation `dispatchProductsFromOtherStores` would be part of the interface of the composed system.

Components are specified in Palladio as depicted in figure 2.6. The figure represents that the business component `TradingSystem.Inventory.Application.ProductDispatcher` provides the business interface `ProductDispatcherIf` and requires the infrastructure interface `JVM`. Furthermore, it has a behavior specification for the operation `dispatchPro-`

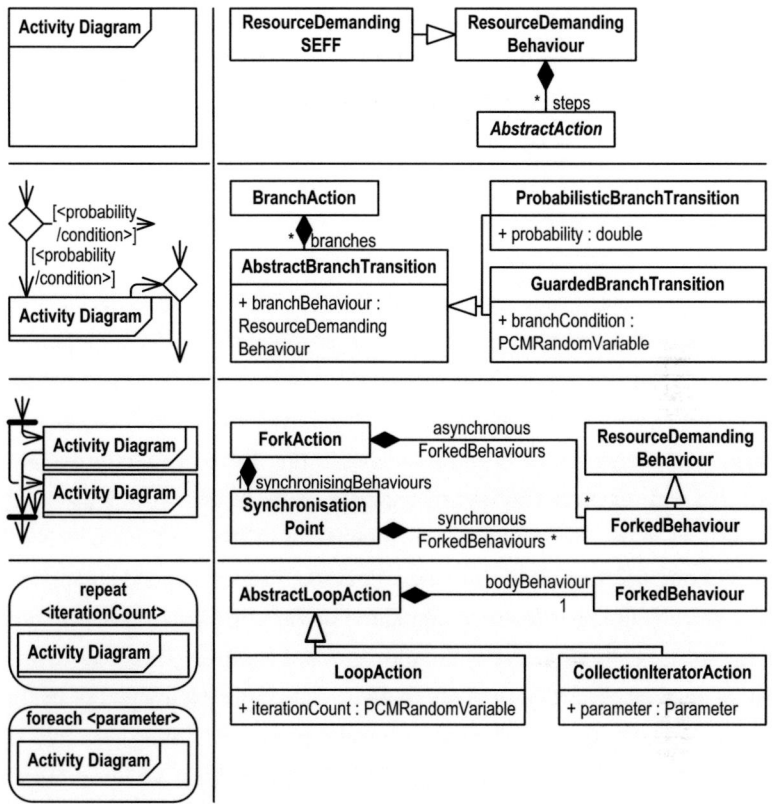

Figure 2.7.: Behavior Specifications - UML Notation and the Palladio Meta-Model

ductsFromOtherStores and defines the component parameter dataInstance. Component parameters do not have a static type in Palladio. This component parameter is initialized with a TYPE set to HIBERNATE. This represents that the persistence framework Hibernate is used as setting for the component. Behavior specifications are shown in the following.

Behavior specifications in Palladio are comparable to UML Activity Diagrams and can be represented in a UML-based notation. The commonalities and differences are pointed out in the following and the semantic of Palladio meta-model elements in behavior specifications is discussed in the following. Figures 2.7, 2.8, and 2.9 provide an overview on the UML notation as well as the Palladio meta-model.

The behavior of an operation is specified as `ResourceDemandingSEFF` (see figures 2.6 and 2.7), which is a `ResourceDemandingBehaviour`. It is an abstraction of the control-flow for that operation from a performance perspective and separates resource demands from calls to loosely coupled business components. The control-flow is represented using `AbstractAction` instances, which are comparable to activities in the UML. Each `Abstract-Action` is a single step in the control-flow. A step can have at most one predecessive control-flow step and at most one successive step. Object Constraint Language (OCL) constraints ensure that there is exactly one start and one end for each `ResourceDemandingBehaviour`. The idea behind the actions is that they cover as much behavior of the component as possible without violating their semantics. For example, subsequent component-internal calculations should be contained in the same `InternalAction` if there are no calls to business-components in between. This may include component-internal loops and alternatives. The input parameters of the operation linked with the behavior are available for calculating resource demands or call parameters throughout the behavior. Certain actions represent decisions in the control-flow. These are presented in the following.

Decisions are represented with `BranchAction` elements (see figure 2.7). They are comparable to decision and merge nodes in the UML. They define the behavior of all possible `branches` via the `branchBehaviour` containment link. One of those branches is selected either probabilistically or based on parameter conditions. Probabilistic branches are represented with `ProbabilisticBranchTransisiton` elements, which specify the `probability` of taking that branch as real number. Parameter-based deterministic decisions are represented with `GuardedBranchTransistion`. The condition is specified in `branchCondition`. A branch with probabilistic decisions can only contain those and vice versa. Exactly one branch must be selected for each visit to the `BranchAction`.

Concurrent behaviors are represented with `ForkAction` elements (see figure 2.7). They are comparable to fork and join nodes in the UML. They define asynchronously started behaviors via the `asynchronousForkedBehaviours` containment. Additionally, they define spawned behaviors, which are synchronized at a barrier. This barrier is represented by a `SynchronisationPoint`. The barrier is comparable to a join node in the UML. The barrier contains the specifications of synchronized concurrent behaviors via the `synchronousForkedBehaviours` containment.

Loops are represented with `AbstractLoopAction` elements (see figure 2.7). They define the behavior of the body of the loop via the `bodyBehaviour` containment. Palladio defines two semantics for loops. Either, parameters accessed within the body are evaluated stochastic independently (`LoopAction`) or dependently (`CollectionIteratorAction`). The number of loop iterations is fixed when the control-flow enters the action from the previous step. The fixed number is denoted as frequency of the loop. The number of iterations is specified via the `iterationCount` attribute of `LoopAction` or a reference to a collection parameter via the `parameter` attribute of `CollectionIteratorAction`. In the latter case, the `NUMBER_OF_ELEMENTS` characterization of that parameter is used to determine the number of iterations and all characterizations for that parameter are evaluated stochastically dependent during a single iteration.

In general, `AbstractAction` are represented by an UML activity (see figure 2.8). The actions have an attribute `entityName`, which is a human readable name describing the control-flow step. This name is also used for the activity. All other actions are also `AbstractActions`, which is not depicted in the figures. There are three special cases besides the presented control-flow decision actions. They are described in the following.

The first control-flow of a behavior is a `StartAction` and it is represented by an UML initial node (see figure 2.8). The last control-flow ele-

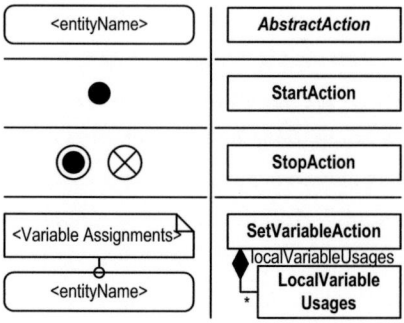

Figure 2.8.: Special Actions in Specifications - UML Notation and the Palladio Meta-Model

ment of a behavior is a StopAction. The control-flow of a behavior ends after processing its StopAction. Consequently, it is semantically represented by an UML activity final or flow final node (see figure 2.8). The mapping depends on the hierarchic nesting of activities and the existence of concurrent behavior in an activity diagram. Examples for both alternatives are provided in the figures 2.10(b) and 2.10(c).

Handling performance-relevant characteristics of parameters requires defining the parameter values returned by an operation. SetVariableAction specifies the information on returned data in Palladio. The characterizations of the returned data type are assigned via the localVariableUsages containment. The keyword RETURN is used in these specifications to refer to the returned data type. The assignments are represented in a note attached to the activity representing the SetVariableAction.

Specifying the performance impact of a behavior requires stating the resource demand and calls within that behavior. Figure 2.9 provides an overview on these parts of the Palladio meta-model. Palladio does not impose any order on handling requests within the same action. All actions but ExternalCallAction allow resource demand specifications, which goes along with inheriting from AbstractInternalControlFlowAction. StartAction, StopAction, BranchAction, ForkAction, SetVari-

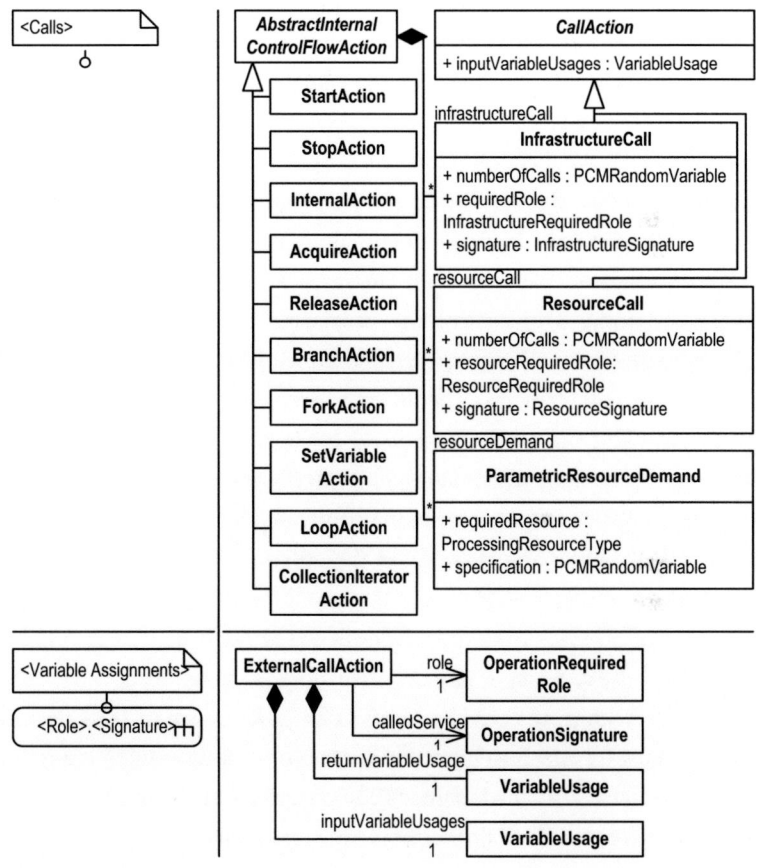

Figure 2.9.: Resource Demand and Call Specifications - UML Notation and the Palladio Meta-Model

`ableAction`, `LoopAction` and `CollectionIteratorAction` have been presented above. `InternalAction` has the semantic of any successional component-internal calculation without calls to business components. `AcquireAction` and `ReleaseAction` have the semantic of acquiring or releasing a single software token. They support modeling exclusive access to software partitions. A common way for ensuring exclusive access is the use of monitors. An example is the `synchronized` statement in Java, which is mapped to the `MONITORENTER` and `MONITOREXIT` bytecode instructions. The tokens can be defined for `BasicComponents` in the repository and access is allowed only in the defining component. `AcquireAction` and `ReleaseAction` are separate from `InternalActions` to specify the synchronization point in the control-flow precisely.

The resource demand can be specified for all `AbstractInternalControlFlowAction` elements. The different options are shown in figure 2.9. Palladio provides different mechanisms for specifying resource demand: requests of processing units via implicit interfaces, explicit parameterized processing requests to resources in the hardware environment, and explicit parameterized processing requests in the software environment. All requests are represented with a note in the UML notation. For example, the request of 50 units from the processor via implicit interfaces could be noted as `50x CPU`, a single request of reading 20 bytes from a hard disk via an explicit interface could be noted as `1x HDD.read(BYTESIZE=20)`, and the request for 219 Java bytecode instructions via an explicit hardware-independent Java Virtual Machine (JVM) interface as `219x IADD`. These mechanisms are explained further in the next paragraphs.

`ParametricResourceDemand` represents the request of units via an implicit interface (see figure 2.9). The required type, for example a processor, is referenced via the `requiredResource` attribute. The amount of requested units is specified via the `specification` attribute.

`ResourceCall` represents explicit parameterized processing requests to resources in the hardware environment (see figure 2.9). The required role of the resource's interface is referenced via the `resourceRequiredRole` attribute. The signature within the interface is referenced via the `signature` attribute. The parameters of the call can be set via the `inputVariableUsages` containment link inherited from `CallAction`. Multiple calls with the same parameter values in the same action are specified via the `numberOfCalls` attribute.

`InfrastructureCall` represents explicit parameterized processing requests in the software environment (see figure 2.9). This allows modeling hardware-independent specifications issuing demand in bytecode instructions or modeling calls to infrastructure libraries. The required role of the infrastructure component's interface is referenced via the `requiredRole` attribute. The signature within the interface is referenced via the `signature` attribute. The parameters of the call can be set via the `inputVariableUsages` containment link inherited from `CallAction`. Multiple calls with the same parameter values in the same action are specified via the `numberOfCalls` attribute.

Calls to business components are represented by `ExternalCallAction` (see figure 2.9). A call behavior represents this action in UML. The name of the call behavior activity is set based on the role and signature used by this call. An attached note describes the variable or parameter assignments. The `role` references the role of the required business component' interface. The `calledService` references the signature within that interface that is called. The `returnVariableUsage` specifies the assignment of the return value of the call to behavior-local variables. The `inputVariableUsages` specifies the assignment of input parameters.

The most simple valid Palladio performance behavior specification consists of a single `StartAction` and a single `StopAction`. It is depicted in figure 2.10(a) and its textual description as sequence is `StartAction`, and `StopAction`. Figure 2.10(b) provides an example for an empty concurrent behavior started within a loop. Please note the use of flow final nodes instead of activity final nodes to express that all concurrent behaviors termi-

45

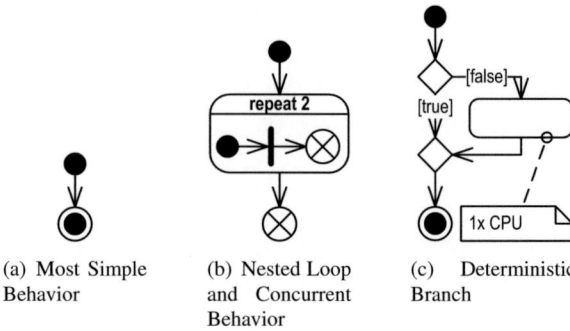

(a) Most Simple Behavior

(b) Nested Loop and Concurrent Behavior

(c) Deterministic Branch

Figure 2.10.: Example Palladio Model Instances

nate and none is aborted if one of them finishes before the others. The textual specification of the sequence is StartAction, Loop(frequency=2: ForkAction(Asynchronous(StartAction, StopAction))), and StopAction. Figure 2.10(c) provides an example for a decision within a control-flow. The textual specification of the sequence is StartAction, BranchAction(GuardedBranchTransition(true, StartAction, StopAction), GuardedBranchTransition(false, StartAction, InternalAction (Resource Demand (1, CPU)), StopAction), and StopAction.

2.5. Component-Based Software Engineering Process

This section provides details on the process used for component-based software engineering. The development process of Palladio is presented to demonstrate the general workflows for component-based development. Its capability of taking non-functional requirements and architecture level decision making into account are shown. Non-functional requirements or properties of a system are denoted as QoS properties in the process definition. Furthermore, this section presents details of the Palladio workflows for architecture design and QoS assurance. The workflows do not take into account certified specifications.

The Palladio reference development process was first introduced by Koziolek and Happe in [KH06]. It is based upon the component-development process introduced by Cheesman and Daniels in [CD03], which in turn is based on the RUP defined by Jacobson et al in [JBR99] and introduced by Kruchten in [Kru00]. The adaptation of Koziolek and Happe addresses QoS-related process tasks and roles. Its current version is described in [RBB+11a]. Its applicability in practice remains to be validated. The process is generic and can be applied to QoS properties other than performance, for example reliability or availability. The participating roles are shaped with respect to knowledge and experience needed for the influence factors on a system.

The technical report on Palladio defines five different roles [RBB+11a]: Software Architect, Component Developer, System Deployer, Domain Expert, and QoS Analyst. These roles and their main responsibilities are summarized in the following.

Software Architects are responsible to design and implement a component-based system. They decompose the envisioned system into components and make or buy these components. They are responsible for the development of components but the development itself is delegated to Component Developers. Software Architects specify the assembly of the components and supervise testing and deployment. They can set the Configuration or State for the system and its components.

Component Developers are responsible for the implementation and the QoS specifications of a component. They must provide Component Behavior Models to specify the QoS. In Palladio, these are the specifications presented in section 2.4, which allow their use in different contexts. Component Developers can develop components on their own for offering it on the market or on demand from Software Architects.

System Deployers are responsible for specifying the properties and capabilities of the Hardware Environment and the deployment of components according to the architecture. They can also have maintenance responsibilities for the deployed system, for example configuration and start or stop.

Domain Experts are familiar with the business domain and potential use of systems. They are responsible to state requirements and the Usage Profile.

QoS Analysts have detailed knowledge and experience in a QoS properties and its modeling. They support the translation of business requirements into QoS properties and model them accordingly. They support the assessment of the behavior of External Services. They assist Component Developers in modeling the behavior. They assist Software Architects in the interpretation of prediction results.

The separation of concerns allows relating the roles with the presented influencing factors. This eases understanding the responsibilities and possible interactions. The relations are shown in figure 2.11 for composed system level and in figure 2.12 for the component level. The QoS Analyst is not shown besides the Software Architect on the system level as the aid is restricted to result interpretation and there is no active creation involved. The role is shown besides the Component Developer on component level as they create the behavior specification together.

The process model is structured as the RUP. The development phases are Inception, Elaboration, Construction, and Transition. [JBR99] describes the phases in detail. The process model consists of seven core workflows, which are iterated for the four development phases. A development cycle consists of the four development phases and leads to a (new) release of a system. Workflows consist of activities, which create or modify artifacts. Depending on the phase and iteration, the effort spent for the activities of the workflow differs. For example, system testing has a bigger share towards the end of a cycle.

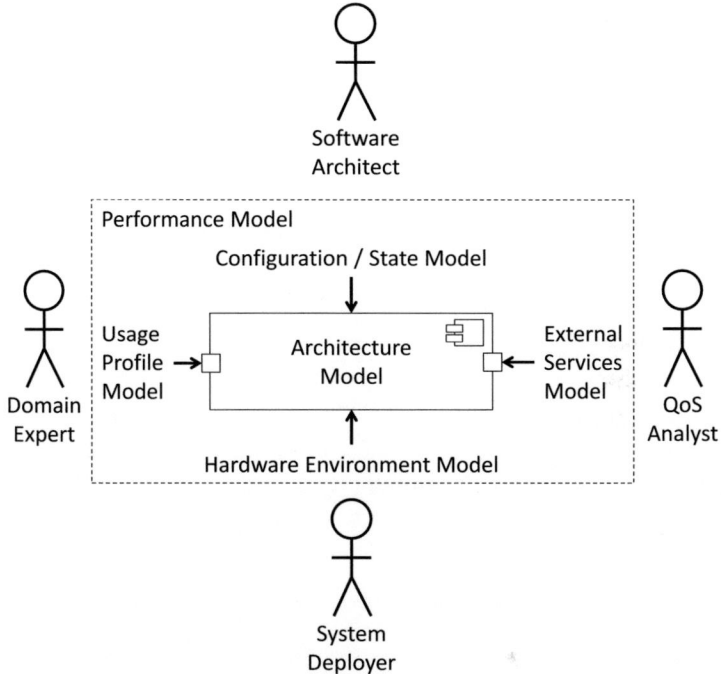

Figure 2.11.: Relation of Influence Factors and Roles: Composed System Level

Figure 2.13 shows the workflows for the Palladio process model. It uses the notation of [CD03] and describes the flow of artifacts between the different workflows. The iterative development aspect is visualized by the Change of Activity transition, which allows transitions even in the same iteration. The process model consists of the workflows for Requirements, Specification, QoS Analysis, Provisioning, Assembly, Test, and Deployment. The workflows Requirements and Test are described in detail in [JBR99], Deployment in [Kru00], the Specification and QoS Analysis in [KH06], and the Provisioning, Assembly and Deployment in [CD03]. The workflow steps are summarized in the following.

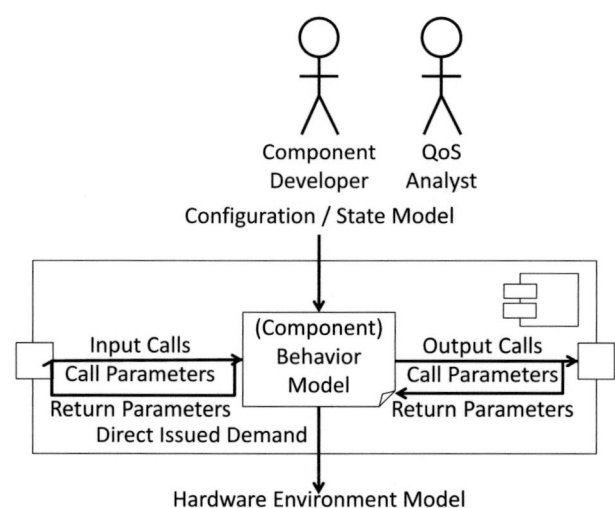

Figure 2.12.: Relation of Influence Factors and Roles: Component Level

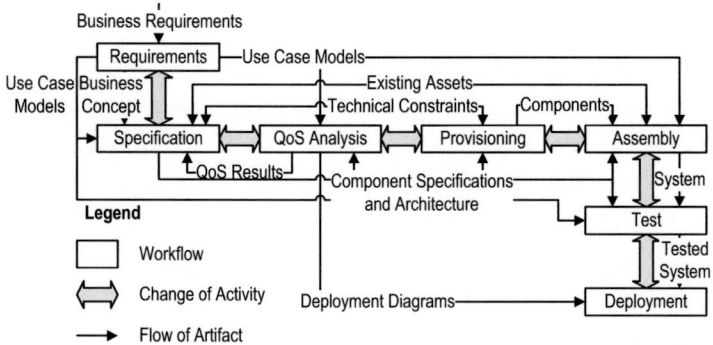

Figure 2.13.: Process Model for the Palladio Development Process [RBB+11a]

The Requirements workflow creates the functional and QoS requirements for a system. The Specification workflow leads to the system architecture, which fulfills the requirements and technical restrictions. The architecture contains the composed components and their functional and QoS requirements. The QoS Analysis workflow ensures that QoS-related information required for predictions is available and consists of predictions and their interpretation for possible architecture adjustments. The Provisioning workflow ensures the availability of the implementation for the components in the architecture. They can be bought or developed. The Assembly workflow involves configuring and wiring the components. They are deployed in the test environment. The Test workflow ensures that all functional and QoS requirements are fulfilled and the system is ready for deployment. The Deployment workflow ensures that the system is installed in and configured for its target environment.

The Specification workflow is depicted in figure 2.14. In the workflow, existing and new components are identified, which can be composed in order to build the envisioned system. The identified components are selected in several stages, which usually involves going forth an back between the activities. The result of this stepwise process is the system's architecture. The Specification of a component contains information on the functional and QoS behavior of the component. It is stored in the Component Repository after the development of a component. The Behavior Specifications of Palladio are presented in section 2.4. The Software Architect is the main role. The Software Developer participates only indirectly but is included to show the relation of artifacts. That role has its major part in the Provisioning workflow.

The QoS Analysis workflow is depicted in figure 2.15. The workflow targets the provisioning of information for QoS analyses and the analyses themselves. It does not include the subsequent process steps of making decisions or identifying alternatives based on the analyses. The System Deployer must specify the QoS properties of the environment for the given

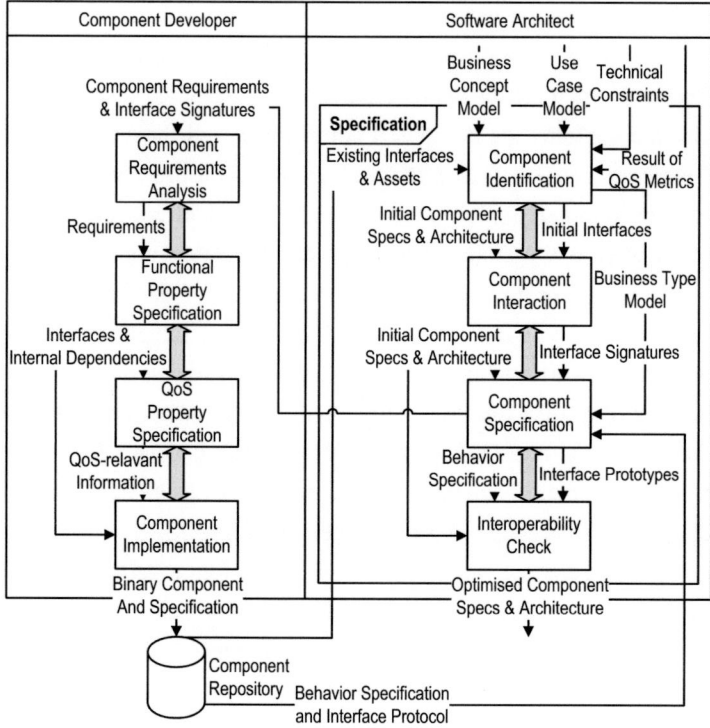

Figure 2.14.: Specification Workflow [RBB$^+$11a]

architecture. The QoS Analyst uses this information for analyses. The Domain Expert specifies the expected usage of the system from an external view point. The QoS Analyst requires this information for analyses. The information on the QoS properties and behavior of the components is included in the component specifications. It is originally provided by the Component Developer and stored in the component repository (see also Specification workflow). The QoS Analyst ensures that the QoS requirements for the system are connected with suitable metrics and that the analyses provide measurements for these metrics. The QoS Analyst selects metrics and thresholds based on the requirements for the software.

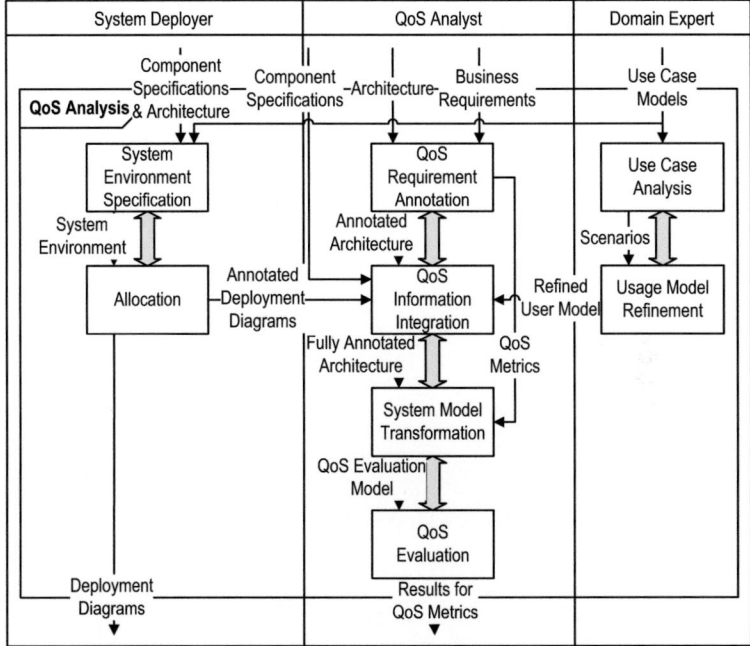

Figure 2.15.: QoS Analysis Workflow [RBB$^+$11a]

The QoS Analyst ensures the soundness of the available QoS information and integrates it as preparation of the evaluation. The evaluation itself
provides the measurements of the QoS Metrics. These measurements influence the Component Identification and architecture of the system
as part of the Specification workflow.

3. Related Work

This section discusses the related work. Smith introduced the idea and concepts of Software Performance Engineering (SPE) in [Smi90]. Menascé et al. provide a more recent general introduction in [MAD04].

This chapter is structured as follows. Section 3.1 provides an overview on accuracy statements and influence analysis in current performance engineering approaches. Section 3.2 provides an overview on test-based validation approaches. Section 3.3 concludes with an overview on certification approaches.

3.1. Specification Accuracy

Existing prediction approaches focussed on making good predictions for accurate specifications and allow making sound design decisions in this case. Performance engineers are responsible for providing such accurate specifications and ensuring that they are appropriate for the parameter values induced by the propagated usage profile.

The existing support of accuracy in current prediction approaches and specification languages is discussed first. Second, the question how to get accuracy information is addressed. Parts of the discussion have also been published in [Gro11a, Gro12a]. A general overview on current prediction approaches is available in the surveys [BDIS04, BGMO06, Koz10].

Accuracy Statements Analytical solvers for performance specifications often require strong assumptions on the input and used specification constructs but provide results fast. They provide parametric distribution functions and statistical point estimators like the mean, which are insensitive to many types of accuracy. Using only parametric distribution functions and point estimators provides valuable insights but does not allow to identify performance peaks or clusters in predicted arbitrary distribution functions. The accuracy does influence non-analytical predictions for arbitrary distribution functions. This makes it worthwhile to take it into account and specify the accuracy of the specifications themselves.

Furthermore, the assumption that inaccuracies in one specification are evened out by the inaccuracies in others is often made. This compensation of inaccuracies might happen but each specification may be exactly at its deviation limits for a composed system and usage of the system. The definition of accuracy allows any deviation up to the limits without being more or less likely. This is due to the level of abstraction of the specification, which implies a corresponding degree of deviation and that no further assumptions on the proximity to the limits can be made. Hence, taking into account accuracy for a prediction provides valuable insights on the actual limits of the overall prediction. The following presents existing approaches for specifying performance and points out their capability to specify resource demands and take into account accuracies.

The performance modeling language UML Profile for Modeling and Analysis of Real-Time Embedded Systems (UML-MARTE) defined by the Object Management Group (OMG) in [OMG13, Obj11b] is derived from the UML Profile for Schedulability, Performance, and Time (UML-SPT) [Obj05]. The profile supports expressing QoS requirements, characteristics, and measurements for specifications. Statements can be made for required, assumed, estimated, and measured values. It supports statistical measures like minimum, maximum, average, mean, and percentiles [Obj11b, p. 49]. UML-MARTE augmented this by attributes for measurement sources, precision, and time expressions [Obj11b, p. 37, p. 517]. The precision is represented by a single floating point number and defined as follows:

> Degree of refinement in the performance of a measurement operation, or the degree of perfection in the instruments and methods used to obtain a result. Precision is characterized in terms of a Real value, which is the standard deviation of the measurement.

The standard deviation implies a probability of deviation, which does not allow considering the following semantics. The approach presented in this thesis considers a specification valid as long as the deviation of an implementation is below a given deviation threshold. The specification is likely to deviate because of the specification's level of abstraction. This difference is most probably due to the difference in considered systems — embedded versus business information — and questions, for example schedulability analysis for real-time systems versus cumulative response time distribution functions for an Service Level Agreement (SLA). An example for a UML-MARTE based approach is provided by Tribastone et al. in [TMW10], which uses Layered Queuing Networks and an analytical solver. Other approaches are listed in the following.

Compared to the approach presented in this thesis, UML-MARTE does not take into account accuracy in detail. UML-MARTE has a strong focus on measurements and statistical point estimators, which is often found in the analysis of embedded systems. The standard deviation describes the deviation of the values of a statistic from its mean but its expressiveness for arbitrary distribution functions is limited. UML-MARTE focusses on the description of measurements and does not support stating relative deviations above an absolute threshold for specified values natively. It defines the Value Specification Language (VSL) in [Obj11b, Annex B], which allows the definition of data types, variable, operators and expressions. This general language provides the mean to realize such descriptions and is comparable to the specification language of Palladio. However, the VSL is not used by the existing approaches for taking into account accuracy. Furthermore, the deviation is very likely to depend on specific parameter values, which could be specified using the VSL. Unfortunately, existing approach do not take into account these complex dependencies.

Bertolino and Mirandola's approach Component-Based Software Performance Engineering (CB-SPE) [BM04] is based on an older version of the language UML-SPT and uses the analytical Queuing Network-based solver Rapid Analysis of Queuing Networks (RAQS) [RAQ04]. In this version of UML-SPT, resource demands can be specified via one of the four sources required, assumed, predicted, or measured and one of the six types mean, variance, k^{th}-moment, percentile, or probability distribution [Obj05, p. 7-21]. The accuracy of specified values is not considered.

Distefano et al. introduce and provide an overview on the Performance Context Model (UML-PCM) in [DPPS04, DPS11, DSP11]. It is based directly on UML-SPT and provides a mapping to Petri Nets for predictions. Accordingly, resource demands can be specified via one of the four sources required, assumed, predicted, or measured and one of the six types mean, variance, k^{th}-moment, percentile, or probability distribution [Obj05, p. 7-21]. The resource demands in the reported case studies with predictions were based on experts measuring generated implementations and creating accurate performance specifications. The accuracy of specified values is not considered.

Marzolla describes an approach oriented at UML-SPT in [Mar04]. Resource demands are specified similar to UML-SPT with the exception that only probability distribution functions can be specified. The corresponding simulation provides information on the utilization of resources and the mean execution times. The accuracy of specified values is not considered.

Wu and Woodside [WW04] defined the approach Component-Based Modeling Language (CBML) based on an own XML-based specification language in [Woo05]. This approach uses a Layered Queuing Network from the toolset presented by Franks et al. in [FHM$^+$95]. Resource demands can be specified with a mean value and the number of repetitions of that demand. The accuracy of such a specified value is not considered.

Wallnau and Ivers defined the Construction and Composition Language (CCL) [WI03], which is used in the approach Prediction-Enabled Component Technology (PECT) and Predictable Assembly from Certifiable Components (PACC) developed at the Software Engineering Institute (SEI). These approaches are described in more detail in section 3.3. The CCL is focused on real-time embedded systems. Resource demand is specified in fixed time units. An accuracy cannot be specified.

The approach of Göbel et al. [GPRZ04] is called COMponents with QUantiative properties and ADaptivity (COMQUAD) and uses the language Component Quality Modeling Language+ (CQML+) defined by Röttger and Zschaler in [RZ03]. CQML+ allows the specification of required or provided QoS for intervals of self-defined quality characteristics. For example a memory requirement for 200 kilobytes with the quality characteristic "size" handled in kilobytes is writen as "size (resource).minimum > 200". The language allows the specification of invariants, which should hold for a successful execution of components at run-time. For example, this allows expressing that the execution time should be less than a specified processing threshold. However, the language does not allow to specify the dependencies between required and provided QoS for a component. The theoretical extension of the language by Zschaler and Meyerhöfer [ZM03] allows to specify such dependencies between input and output values if only one parameter is used in the calculation. This extension allows the specification of lower and upper bounds for a resource demand instead of a single value. An accuracy cannot be specified.

Compared to the approach presented in this thesis, CQML+ including its extension does not allow explicitly accuracy specifications or taking into account relative and absolute deviations. The level of abstraction of a specification cannot be taken into account explicitly. However, the lower and upper bounds of the extended version could be used to store the accuracy bounds. However, CQML+ does not provide a precise definition of the semantics of such an interval and how it should be handled in analyses for average cases. The defined dependency language does not support taking into account the order of component-external calls, probabilistic branches or concurrent behavior. The approach presented in this thesis is more general, supports control-flow oriented specification languages, allows taking into account multiple parameter dependencies, and making the accuracy of a specification explicit.

Grassi et al. defined the Kernel LAnguage for PErformance and Reliability analysis (KLAPER) [GMS07]. Model transformations from design models to KLAPER and from KLAPER to analysis models should make it easier to combine predictions and design models. A single value can be specified for resource demands, for example the execution time of a step within a behavior. The source of values cannot be specified, for example if the value is estimated, measured, or has a certain deviation. It is explicitly assumed that parameters and values represent a suitable abstraction. The accuracy cannot be specified.

Petriu and Woodside defined the Core Scenario Model (CSM) [PW04] with a focus on scenario and resource descriptions. CSM is also a kernel language and based on UML-SPT. The same focus on measurements and statistical point estimators for resource demand specifications applies as for UML-MARTE. CSM is used in the Performance by Unified Model Analysis (PUMA) approach. The foundations are presented by Woodside et al. in [WPP+05] and the current version including two case studies by Petriu et al. in [PAT12]. The accuracy of resource demands in specifications or implications of it are not addressed in CSM, PUMA, or the case studies.

The ITEA project Robust Open Component Based Software Architecture for Configurable Devices Project (ROBOCOP) defined an own specification language. This language is sketched by Bondarev et al. in [BMdW+04] and described in detail by Laverty in [Lav03]. Resource demands can be specified as single value in integer resource units. The case studies in [Lav03] contained manually measured resource demands from real implementations or worst case estimate. Bondarev et al. present the corresponding Component Architectures Analysis Tool (CARAT) in [BCdW07]. They state as limitations that "it does not enable analysis of the components whose execution times are specified by probability distribution curves. Finally, the simulation techniques do not guarantee finding boundary conditions: worst- and best-case response times." The accuracy of resource demands or specifications cannot be specified.

The approach of Liu et al. uses a combination of Queuing Networks and UML diagrams as input language and is introduced in [LGF05]. They focus on separating the performance of a Enterprise Java Bean (EJB) component from its EJB container. Their approach describes resource demand as the required time for certain activities using mathematical functions. The functions have variables, which are set according to measured values on a real implementation of the system. Each variable is represented with a constant value and the variable is calibrated based on samples until the standard deviation is below 3 percent of the mean. This technique allows reducing noise on measurements of constant values. Statements about the accuracy of resource demands or specifications are not supported. The propagation of inaccuracies is not considered.

Sitamaran et al. propose the use of asymptotic resource demand specifications in [SKK$^+$01], which is comparable to a small and big O notation. They support describing the order of growth and approximate upper and lower bounds for infinite input spaces. Their definitions do not take into account limitations on the parameter space. Their theoretical elaborations are demonstrated in a case study specifying a stack. They do not consider the validation or prediction based on their specifications. The lower and upper asymptotic bounds could be considered absolute lower and upper accuracy thresholds. However, the definitions do not ensure that these accuracy threshold hold in all cases — only for sufficiently big parameter values. Although the asymptotic behavior is interesting on a theoretical level their use for performance predictions and accuracy considerations is seen as minimal.

Hamlet provides an analysis approach for components in [Ham09]. He assumes that component have only single floating-point value domains for the input and output, the state of components is local and represented with a single floating-point value domain, and there is no concurrency. The component specification is a mathematical function defined in several intervals, which states for each interval the exact calculation of the output value based on the input values and the runtime for the computation. The composition of such components allows to identify all intervals which should show the same performance. These intervals can then be used in a validation framework to test if the behavior is equal. The specified value for an interval can also be determined based on random tests within the interval on an implementation resulting in either step-wise or linear approximations. The accuracy of specifications cannot be stated or used for analyzing the effect on a composite.

The Analysis and Prediction of Performance for Evolving Architectures (APPEAR) approach by Eskenazi et al. was presented in [EFH02] and an extension for the composition in [EFH04]. It supports different types of specifications for the behavior of a components. This supports covering different levels of detail from statistical and probabilistic to complete control-flow graph specifications with data-flow information. The approach uses observations on implementations as training data to create the statistical specifications. The test set must be provided manually. The performance is approximated using techniques like linear regression and multivariate adaptive regressive splines. The accuracy of specifications is only considered in the training stage as quality criterion for the regression approach. The accuracy is not stored in combination with the specification. The accuracy is not taken into account for the prediction itself.

The Component Performance Assurance Solutions (COMPAS) approach by Mos et al. is presented in [MM02, DMM04]. It is based on monitoring execution times of EJB components and storing measurements in a given performance specification. It is focussed on identifying performance hot spots. A later version with a stronger focus on run-time management of components is named Automatic Quality Assurance (AQuA) and presented by Diaconescu and Murphy in [DM05]. It focusses on the dynamic adaptation of systems according to load changes. Parsons and Murphy describe the extension Performance Antipattern Detection (PAD) in [PM08]. It uses predefined rules to determine misconfigurations of EJB components and provide feedback how to change the parameters for the current system and load. The resource demand is measured on a coarse level in execution time or as aggregated utilization value on a resource. In all of these approaches, accuracy is not considered.

Meyerhöfer and Neumann present another EJB component measurement framework with the name TestEJB in [MN04]. It uses the COMQUAD approach discussed above and has the same power with respect to resource demand and accuracy specifications. It focusses on measuring and storing resource demand in form of the response times for the calls to components.

Approaches based on process algebras are impaired by the state space problem as described by Balsamo et al. in [BDIS04] and have problems in taking into account acquiring and releasing resources. Analytical solvers usually provide statistical point estimators and confidence intervals. The accuracy of the specifications is not explicitly considered and it is usually assumed that point estimators like the mean are not affected by these inaccuracies. The approach presented in this thesis does not have these limitations or need such strong assumptions.

The OMG defined the Systems Modeling Language (SysML) in [Obj12] for modeling systems beyond software and provide a unified language. The language supports the specification, analysis, design, verification, and validation of systems. Its widely used in the automotive industry and for electric and electronic systems. The language is a UML profile and its tight integration with UML supports considerations of software and non-software parts likewise. SysML allows the use of UML timing diagrams and the specification of performance constraints [Obj12, p.92]. The performance constraints should support analysis and are based on mathematical expressions. However, SysML provides only a rough framework not a precise and analyzable definition:

> SysML identifies and names constraint blocks, but does not specify a computer interpretable language for them. The interpretation of a given constraint block (e.g., a mathematical relation between its parameter values) must be provided. An expression may rely on other mathematical description languages both to capture the detailed specification of mathematical or logical relations, and to provide a computational engine for these relations. In addition, the block constraints are noncausal and do not specify the dependent or independent variables. The specific dependent and independent variables are often defined by the initial conditions, and left to the computational engine. [Obj12, p.83f]

Resource demands cannot be specified directly but the use of UML-SPT or UML-MARTE is possible as described by Jarraya et al. in [JSDH07]. Accuracy is not considered in SysML.

Meedeniya et al. present an approach in [MAG12] for the automated design space exploration with respect to reliability optimization taking into account input parameter inaccuracies. The authors identified that inaccurate input parameter estimates influence the ranking of design decisions and with it the design decisions on the non-dominated Pareto frontier. The approach takes an architecture and accuracy statements for certain values in the architecture as input. It runs a large number of Monte-Carlo simulations for each design candidate until the difference in the percentile of the distribution of predicted reliability values from each simulation is below a given threshold. The last value of the percentile is then used as reliability value of the design candidate. A genetic algorithm is used to create design candidates and finally leads to the identification of design candidates on the

Pareto frontier. The case study of the approach is a good visualization of how inaccurate input parameters can lead to an inappropriate decision basis if inaccuracies are not taken into account. The approach presented in this thesis does not optimize the architecture. It requires a significantly less number of analyses to determine the influence of accuracy. It supports arbitrary distribution functions as prediction results and it is does not require to summarize the prediction as a single value. No information is lost but the influence of accuracy is additionally pointed out.

Sensitivity analysis aims at quantifying the relation of changes in the input domain to the output domain. Knowledge on these relations allows inter- and extrapolation of expected values in the target domain. Satelli et al. give a general introduction in [SRA+08]. In the area of performance prediction, sensitivity analysis allows reasoning on the impact of parameters and considering the most relevant first but has to take into account that performance predictions are usual non-linear. The value in the output domain is usually approximated by a mathematical function with values in the input domain as parameters. However, this approximation does not replace a prediction with these values as certain factors are usually ignored. Sensitivity analysis requires multiple points for comparison as the correlation of input to output values must be examined in order to identify a fitting function. This resulting effort can be quite high, especially if multiple dimensions or parameters are taken into account. There are several sampling strategies for reducing the required effort, for example (multivariate) stratified sampling, one-at-a-time sampling, fractional factorial sampling, or latin hypercube sampling. However, they usually require at least 2 times the number of parameters as comparisons [SRA+08, p.89]. Satelli notes on the same page, that this restriction on the minimum numbers can severely effect the capability to handle complex models. Applying sensitivity analysis on the component level leaves the handling of a composition in the open. Applying sensitivity analysis on the system level allows to reason only for the selected composition and influence factors. The latter one is also closely related to design space exploration and automated architecture optimization.

In contrast to the approach presented in this thesis, sensitivity analysis tries to determine effect sizes of input values on output values for inter- and extrapolation instead of taking into account given accuracy limits. Sensitivity analysis itself does not replace predictions but can provide additional insight on the most influential parameters for a specific composition at the cost of additional effort. The heuristic for influence analysis presented in this thesis is based on a factorial sampling for each specification, which allows to take into account the non-linearity of the prediction for the composition.

Specifications guaranteeing a lower or upper bound are required for Worst-Case Execution Time (WCET) analyses. Accuracy or the usual behavior is not of interest, as it must be formally proven that the bounds are adhered in all cases. The guarantee is usually an overestimated bound in order to ensure properties of the component, which are safety-relevant in most cases. However, using WCET approaches for specifications and prediction is not feasible for real-world business information systems due to their size. Harmon and Klefstad identified in their survey in [HK07] that state-of-the-art approaches are still restricted to a per-method base and often require additional information on loop bounds for their analysis. Return-value dependencies within single methods are also not supported in general. Kirner et al. surveyed WCET approaches in [KKP$^+$11] and found that each approach supports a specific set of constructs, no approach supports all constructs, and no approach is superior to the others. They conclude that each approach has its own individual strengths and limitations.

Compared to the approach presented in this thesis, WCET specifications state absolute performance bounds and not an abstraction of the performance-relevant behavior itself. Making design decisions for business information systems benefits stronger from average case considerations than from overestimated worst-case guarantees. Hence, the targets of the approaches differ. Using WCET techniques would restrict the size of treatable components severely and would still have to be adapted to capture the average case and determine the accuracy.

Summarizing, existing approaches do not support explicit accuracy statements for resource demand statements. These inaccuracies are currently not taken into account for an influence analysis on predictions of composed systems. If properties are not proven formally, the documentation of the accuracy of a performance specification is therefore not possible or only very limited.

Creating Accuracy Statements   Accuracy statements can be generated as part of the process of creating a performance specification or they can be determined explicitly for a given specification. If a specification is modified after its initial creation then the accuracy statements have to be re-created or at least re-validated. Determining accuracy statements explicitly requires the knowledge and experience of a performance engineer in order to create appropriate statements, which are neither wrong nor too pessimistic but appropriate for the specification's level of abstraction.

Woodside et al. provide a general introduction to the creation of abstract resource functions based on test sets in [WVCB01]. The authors target a single mathematical function using input parameters to approximate an output parameter. These functions are usually applied on a high abstraction level and do not require additional information on control or data flow.

A discussion of different approximation techniques and a tool set for determining such functions is provided by Westermann et al. in [WHKF12]. These resource functions are still a black box view and may approximate the real behavior only in a limited way, which is a danger for the appropriate reuse of such a specification. If cross validation with its separate calibration and validation test sets is used then the accuracy can be estimated based on the difference between the resource function and the validation test results.

An example for an approach using cross validation is provided by Eskenazi et al. in [EFH02] and described above.

Faber and Happe applied and compared Genetic Programming to other abstract resource function creation techniques in [FH12]. The author identifies that the accuracy depends heavily on the analysis method and test set and that "Most existing methods require prior knowledge about parameter dependencies or their models are limited to only linear correlations". Again, the accuracy is not stated explicitly and reuse of specifications is potential dangerous. The accuracy is estimated based on the difference between the approximated resource function and the validation test results. Cross-validation is used to reason on the accuracy of the different techniques in the validation.

Neuronal Networks can be used instead of mathematical resource functions. Reusing such specifications is dangerous if influence factors change between old and new composition. If cross validation is used then the accuracy can be estimated based on the difference between the approximated resource function and the validation test results.

Monitoring the behavior of running implementations allows capturing the current behavior and management of a deployed system. Examples given above are the approaches of Meyerhöfer and Neumann [MN04] and Diaconescu and Murphy [DM05]. Epifani et al. introduce the Keep Alive Models with Implementations (KAMI) approach in [EGMT09], which uses a Bayesian estimator to update predefined specifications. Zheng et al. introduce an approach based on Kalman filters in [ZWL08]. It support minimally invasive measurements based only on response times and utilization of resources. It uses the observations of the behavior within a given period to set parameters of a performance specification. The filters allow dynamic adaptations of the system but the external validity of the specification, especially after influence factor changes, is minimal. Cardellini et al. introduce the approach MOdel-based SElf-adaptation of SOA systems (MOSES) in [CCG$^+$09]. The approach support QoS-driven adaptation at run-time according to given policies. Brosig et al. introduce an approach in [BHK11], which allows updating specification parameters for Palladio specifications. All of these approaches focus on easy model creation for running systems and dynamic reaction of the software or hardware environment. The accuracy of the specification varies over time if new observations are made and is either unknown or not stated explicitly during run-time. The reuse of the specifications in different contexts is limited.

Reverse engineering approaches can reconstruct the behavior of a component statically and determine remaining unknowns by testing an implementation. An example for such an approach is provided by Krogmann et al. in [KKR10]. Such specifications can be likely reused if influence factors change as they are directly mapped to the implementation. The accuracy of the unknowns determined by testing can be estimated using cross validation.

Summarizing, automated techniques for creating a specification can provide accuracy information if cross validation is applied. The techniques differ with respect to the targeted abstract level and the sensitivity of the created specifications with respect to influence factor changes.

3.2. Validation and Testing

This section provides an overview on related validation and testing approaches. It shortly introduces performance testing in general. It continues with a presentation of model-based testing approaches. It discusses the use and relation of coverage criteria for testing performance specifications. Finally, it discusses the selection of tools for the validation approach and provides a summary. Parts of the discussion on tools and test case generation have been previously published in [Gro09, Gro10, Gro11a, Gro12a]. Parts of the discussion on coverage criteria in [Gro09, Gro12b].

In general, testing of software is as old as software itself. However, the focus and complexity changed over time. Functional testing was there at the beginning and is well introduced in [Bei95]. A good introduction on test management and test automation is provided by Dustin et al. in [DRP99]. The following focusses on performance testing and the validation of performance specifications.

Performance testing has many different types: Load testing determines the behavior of a system in a given scenario, which is expected during the operation of the system. Stress testing determines the capability of a system to handle excessive load and allows scrutinizing the behavior in excessive load conditions. Endurance testing determines the behavior and potential change of behavior if a system is in operation for a long period of time. All of these types of performance testing evaluate the software or component under test. Their purpose is to check the behavior of the system or component and assess if requirements are met.

Testing performance specifications is an own type of testing, as the goal is to validate the specification against the behavior of an implementation beyond a single selected scenario. Load, stress, or endurance testing focus on the behavior in selected scenarios and not on validating a more general specification of the behavior. Testing performance specifications is a form of model-based testing.

Model-Based Testing A general introduction to model-based testing is provided by Broy et al. in [BJK$^+$05] and by Pretschner and Philipps in [PP05]. The terms used by Pretschner and Philipps are also used in the following. Please note that a performance specification is technically a model. The use of the terms in the following depends on the context. They are interchangeable and the terms should ease the identification if the discussed issue is more on the model-based testing side or on the specification validation side.

According to the definition, the approach presented in this thesis uses a Separate Models scenario in which distinct models are used for the development of the implementation and for the generation of tests. The additional notion of performance specification reuse implies that the implementation does not only adhere to the requirements of the developed component but the performance specification itself is also valid if it is composed in other systems. These additional requirements are expressed by the structure and content of the performance specification. This duality is not covered in the work of Pretschner and Philipps but the test cases created with the approach presented in this thesis cover it.

Utting and Legeard defined a process for model-based testing in [UL07, p.26ff]. This waterfall-like process has the five steps: 1) Model the System Under Test (SUT) and/or its environment 2) Generate abstract tests from the model, 3) Concretize the abstract tests to make them executable, 4) Execute the tests on the SUT and assign verdicts, and 5) Analyze the test results. The validation approach presented in this thesis focusses on the steps 2 to 5. The implemented process deviates from the defined process and is as follows.

The approach presented in this thesis assumes that a specification and accuracy statements are provided, which would be part of step 1. However, the order is different due to dynamic test case generation. After step 1, step 3 is required in order to check if all input and output values can be converted between the model and the implementation. Missing converters must be provided in order to generate inputs and compare results. This prepares the later execution. Step 2 and 4 are bundled in the automated validation framework and the steps execute iteratively. Test cases are generated automatically based on model coverage, validation quality settings, and the behavior of the implementation. Reacting on the behavior of the implementation and dynamic creation of test cases is required in order to handle probabilistic specifications and implementations. For example, if a probabilistic branch is taken in the implementation the mapped branch in the specification must be compared for the validation. Statically defined test cases do not support reacting on such alternatives, which are only known at run-time and influence the subsequent test and input and output parameter values. Test results are provided including information on failures. These results and additional information help in the analysis in step 5. As can be seen, the process defined by Utting et al. requires adaptations in order to fit the use case, but the general steps and frame remain the same.

Using the taxonomy defined by Utting et al. in [UPL06], the approach presented in this thesis is classified as follows. The Subject of the Model is the implementation of the component. The Redundancy of the Model is a Separate Test Model. For Palladio specifications, the Characteristics of the Model are Deterministic, Non-Deterministic, Timed, Untimed and Discrete. The Paradigm of the Model is Transition-Based and Operational. The Test Selection Criteria of the Test Generation can be Structural Model Coverage or Random & Stochastic. The Technology of the Test Generation is Random Generation. Finally, the Test Execution is Online, which is equivalent to at run-time. This classification should ease understanding the presented approach.

Coverage Criteria Coverage criteria have become a common technique in quality assurance [Mye04] and are part of the best practices in software engineering and development of code [Som07]. Liggesmeyer provides definitions for well-known control and data flow criteria on the code level in [Lig09]. In general, coverage criteria define the rules how testing requirements are created or which aspects must be covered by existing test sets. However, these rules must be adapted to the semantics of a specification language. The coverage of a specification on one level of abstraction does not imply the coverage of an equivalent specification on a different level as Chilenski and Miller pointed out in [CM94]. Hence, coverage criteria on performance specifications must be explicitly defined and cannot simply be inferred from coverage information on other levels, such as source code, or vice versa. The approach presented in this thesis defines coverage criteria for Palladio specifications.

A coverage criterion has the goal to cover a distinct aspect of a specification. In quality assurance, criteria with a high fault detection probability are preferred in order to identify faults. The fault detection effectiveness also depends on the selection of input parameter samples. The main question is if sampling should be concentrated on certain input space domains or random testing should be applied. Different views on this topic are provided by Hamlet and Taylor in [HT90], Frankl and Weyuker in [FW93], DeMillo et al. in [DMW+95], and Gaston and Seifert in [GS05]. Hamlet and Taylor show that random sampling is at least as effective as subdomain testing if there is no known difference in the fault density of possible input domains.

Covering a criterion requires testing effort. Depending on the criterion, a significant number of tests is required for coverage. This number can even be infinite and testing infeasible if all paths in a program with an open loop are to be covered. Relations between the criteria allow reasoning, which criterion is subsumed by others. However, Frankl and Weyuker show that the subsumption relation does not necessarily imply better effectiveness if aspects not covered by the related criteria cause faults. As a consequence, the covered aspects of a criterion must be known in order to decide if it's coverage would provide valuable additional information. Relations for control flow path criteria on the code level are for example discussion by Yates and Malevris in [YM09]. A sound decision for or against a certain coverage criterion is only possible if information on the required effort and covered aspects is available. The approach presented in this thesis provides effort estimations and information on the relation between criteria.

Gaston and Seifert provide an overview about coverage based testing and the application of coverage criteria in model-based testing in [GS05]. The criteria defined in the approach presented in this thesis are Structural Criteria because the test case specifications depend on structural aspects of the performance specification. However, the verified aspects are Functional and Stochastic as well. The first because output values are verified and the latter because the probability of decisions can be verified. They discuss the fault detection ability of coverage criteria with respect to comparing random with partition/subdomain-based testing. This results in the statement that partition-based testing only provides advantages if a fault distribution is formerly known. There is no fault distribution for the performance specifications validated by the approach presented in this thesis. Hence, random testing is the technique to use.

A criterion may define testing requirements, which are infeasible for a distinct specification. For example, a dead branch in the code can never be covered or implicitly coupled conditions of parameters can exclude some conditions. However, determining that covering a certain testing requirement is not feasible cannot be decided in general. The approach presented in this thesis does not take infeasible testing requirements into account. This issue is part of future work.

Testing probabilistic decisions is rare on the code level but testing probability ratios is common in reliability engineering. Methods with fixed and step-wise evaluated sample plans are available. The class of step-wise evaluated methods is designated as sequential tests. Sequential tests evaluate at every stage of a n-stage trial if a null hypothesis or the alternative hypothesis should be accepted or if the evaluation should continue. The average sample size can be reduced if a hypothesis can be accepted without looking at all n samples. Mature methods are available, for example the Sequential Probability Ratio Test (SPRT), which was initially developed by Wald in 1945 [Wal45, Wal47]. It is used for reliability engineering as described in the military handbook of the Department of Defense [Dep96] and by current approaches on reliability engineering of software systems, for example Younes approach [You05] and the runtime monitoring framework ProMo described by Grunske and Zhang in [GZ09]. SPRT uses two hypothesis to check whether the sequence of samples experienced so far is above an acceptable threshold (H_0), below (H_1), or in the indifference region. The expected probability is in the indifference region and new samples are required until the indifference region is left or a predetermined number of test cases is reached. This allows sampling termination if the samples are better or worse than expected. This technique works very well for reliability analyses in which the evaluated system performs better or worse than specified. It can be applied at run-time and for systems, which can not be brought intentionally to a desired state for analyses.

The approach presented in this thesis works on the assumption that a specified probability is correct. This implies that the benefits of sequential sampling is limited. Furthermore, SPRT requires an upper limit for the samples n in case the probability is in the indifference region and neither hypothesis is acceptable. This limit is the same as for a fixed sample plan. The limit must be provided by the reliability analyst. The approach presented in this thesis automatically determines this limit for given error probabilities of Type I (α) and Type II (β) and executes a fixed sample plan. This sample plan uses the hypothesis $H_0 : p_{impl} = p_{spec}$ and $H_1 : p_{impl} \neq p_{spec}$. It ensures that the power does not fall below $(1 - \beta)$ assuming a deviated probability. The thresholds deviated to lower or upper probability values are p_{lt} and p_{ut} with $p_{lt} < p_{spec} <$ ut.

Tools The market for performance testing has been growing steadily [Ham07] and hence there is a number of commercial and non-commercial performance testing tools available. The tools differ in the type of supported performance testing, the measurable metrics, test case specification languages, supported implementation frameworks, and measurement overhead. Fine-granular measurements of hardware-independent resource demands, for example on bytecode instruction level, are rarely supported. They are supported by the approaches of Meyerhöfer [Mey07] and Kuperberg [Kup10]. The approaches usually have an overhead comparable to profilers and can hence only be applied to systems or components which are not in productive environments. However, this does not impair the validation of specifications.

Belinfante et al. provide a survey and overview on test generation tools in [BFS05]. Test derivation of most tools is based on Constraint Logic Programming (CLP), Labeled Transition Systems (LTS), or Finite State Machines (FSM). The semantics of the Palladio specifications validated by this approach differ from the more closely related FSM and LTS used in the other approaches. Mapping a specification is theoretically possible but the coverage criteria for the mapped specifications are different than for the original specification due to the semantic gap. The required online execution and dynamic generation including a mapping of Palladio parameter specifications reduces the set of possible tools. An evaluation of 10 candidate tools and mapping for the Conformiq tool [Con13] is provided by Ernst in [Ern11]. Additionally, online generation also requires that the resource demand must be properly measured by the approach. The required hardware-independent measurements on a fine-granular level within methods as well as across methods are not provided by the surveyed approaches and would require large integration effort. Hence, the approach presented in this thesis uses an own validation framework.

There is also a number of commercial and non-commercial test execution tools, for example for the Testing and Test Control Notation (TTCN-3) language [Eur13]. A common load testing tool for business information system with various frameworks is Apache JMeter, which is presented representatively. Apache JMeter is a load testing tool for client/server systems and available at [Apa]. It tests the functional behavior and can measure the end-to-end performance as well as access management interfaces of servers for analyzing user-defined load scenarios. Its strengths are managing conditions with concurrent heavy load. The approach presented in this thesis provides an own execution tool in order to support fine-granular, hardware-independent measurements and online generation of test cases. It uses the Bytecode Counter (ByCounter) approach developed by Kuperberg.

Summary The approach presented in this thesis is a model-based testing approach. Online generation of test cases requires an adaptation of the usual model-based testing process. The application of coverage criteria on the code level and in model-based testing has been shown. The need for customized criteria for Palladio specifications was identified and the statistical testing of probabilistic specification elements discussed. An overview on test generation and execution tools was provided and the decision for integrating both into the validation framework of the presented approach was explained.

3.3. Certification

This section provides an overview on the different types of certification targeting the quality of the product and shows related product certification approaches. The definition of certification used in this thesis is available in chapter 2. Parts of the discussion have been previously published in [RGR08, Gro09, Gro12c].

For certification, there are the three different viewpoints process, personnel, and product as described by Voas in [Voa99] and introduced in section 1.3.4. These areas overlap each other but are neither equivalent nor is one completely contained in the others. In order to provide a complete picture, the following gives an overview and presents approaches from all three viewpoints. Product certification oriented approaches are described in more detail and put into context with the approach presented in this thesis.

Process certificates focus on the management aspect of software development within an organization. The general idea is that a defined and controlled process, which may take into account self-improvement, allows managing the quality of a developed or offered component or product. Standards define the requirements for the management processes of an organization. The processes themselves document quality assurance and requirements management. They are tailored to the application domain, company, and developed product. The compliance and adherence of this standard can be certified for an organization. Widespread representatives for this type of approaches are ISO 9001[ISO08a] defined by the International Organization for Standardization and the Capability Maturity Model Integration (CMMI) [SEI] defined by the SEI of the Carnegie Mellon University (CMU). A common infrastructure for software-related processes from business software to firmware is provided by ISO 12207 [ISO08b]. This is extended by the ISO 15504, also referred to as Software Process Improvement and Capability Determination (SPICE), which consists of overall 5 mandatory and 5 optional parts [ISO04] to [ISO11a]. The purpose of ISO 15504 is on process assessment and capability improvement. This relates to the CMMI, which has even detailed guidelines for teams participating in the process with the Team Software Process [Hum99] and individuals with the Personal Software Process [Hum05].

The drawback of process certification despite its use in industry is that even mature processes cannot guarantee a good quality of a developed component or product as identified by Maibaum and Wassyng in [MW08]. The processes can state that experienced performance engineers should reason on the appropriate use of component specifications, validate specifications thoroughly and that software architects should take into account the accuracy of overall predictions. However, this does not guarantee that its done properly nor error probabilities are reduced. The approach presented in this thesis supports software architects and performance engineers in validating and using component specifications for their purposes. The developed certification-aware component-based development process does not focus on the specific process in a company but ensures in general that different parties can use component specifications cooperatively. The adapted process supports the protection of knowledge and Intellectual Property (IP) contained in implementations and allows the use of internal component repositories as well as public marketplaces. It ensures that component evaluation and selection can be successfully applied on the architecture level in such scenarios.

Personnel certificates focus on the knowledge and experience of individuals working with a component or product. A personnel certificate can ensure the competence and proper training for performed tasks. There is a wide range of certificates from academia to industrial product application. Examples for academic certificates with a broad focus are a bachelor or master's degree from an university. Examples for specific application areas are Certified Professionals for Requirements Engineering, Certified Tester, or Certified Software Product Manager from the international Software Quality Institute (iSQI) [iSQI13]. Examples for product application oriented certificates are Enterprise Desktop Support Technician on Windows 7 or Server Administrator on Windows Server 2008 from the Microsoft Certified IT Professional (MCITP) program [Mic13].

The drawback of personnel certification is that knowledge or experience does not address unintentional errors or that a product adheres to a given quality if given constraints on time or budget are ambitious. Validating the accuracy of a specification and an implementation requires knowledge in special areas but the existence of knowledge does not ensure that accuracy statements are created and thoroughly validated. This type of certification does not address the consequences of certifier party selection on trust and attractiveness, and how the knowledge and IP of an implementation can be protected without endangering component evaluation and selection on the architecture level.

Product certificates focus on assessment of the component or product itself. Today, product certification is applied on a broader scale for safety and security critical software, for example for systems in the aviation, automotive, or medical industry. Experience in analyses is often related to safety, as it justifies the additional analysis effort. The certificates can address the compliance with given regulations, that certain analyses have been applied successfully, or the interoperability between applications and the adherence to an Application Programming Interface (API). An example for the compliance with regulations is the standard DO178-B for software in avionics [RTC92]. An example for the type of analyses is a certification according to the Common Criteria [Comer], which focusses on the security of software. Examples for interoperability certifications are provided for Windows device drivers by Ball et al. in [BCLR04] and Balakrishnan and Reps in [BR08a], as well as for the data exchange between field devices between different vendors in the automation industry by the non-profit organization FDT Group [FDT13].

The drawback of product certificates is that only a specific component or product is certified and a new certificate must be issued for comparable products or maintained versions. This type of certification can ensure that a given specification is an accurate description of an implementation, regardless of the development process or documented knowledge of the participating persons. It does address the accuracy and, as shown by the approach, can be integrated into component-based development processes in order to allow component evaluation and selection on the architecture level without endangering the quality of the decision or the protecting of knowledge and IP contained in the implementation.

In the following, product certification oriented approaches are presented and their relation to the approach presented in this thesis is shown.

For the non-functional property safety, the approach of safety cases by Bloomfield and Bishop [BB10] provides a framework to show that arguments are supported by evidence for a system and its environment. The framework is influenced by existing standards and shows preferences for different types of evidence: deterministic is preferred to statistical, quantitative to qualitative, and direct to indirect. Safety cases are a generic framework with a lot of degrees of freedom in its application. Wassyng et al. identified in [WMLB11] that such frameworks are valuable but need to be tailored and more clearly defined for the application domain. Their precision and effectiveness is not high enough yet. Wassyng et al. also take a look at other engineering domains and identify that product focussed assessments should address the four points: completeness and correctness of testing with respect to the specification, the repeatability, and a precise definition of the testing configuration.

The approach presented in this thesis fulfills all preferences, although it is applied to performance rather than safety. It provides deterministic evidence and only falls back to statistical evidence where the probabilistic decision requires it. It provides quantitative and direct information. The four points are addressed as well. The coverage criteria and observation of achieved coverage by the tests address the completeness and correctness of testing a performance specification. The validation framework support the repeatability and independent verification by third parties. The testing configuration is described with the meta-model for accuracy statements, the test-based validation configuration and the link between implementation and specification.

The idea of safety cases was also applied to dependability considerations by Graydon et al. in [GKS07] based on ideas of Strunk and Knight on assurance based development in [SK06]. The authors propose a co-development of these assurance cases with the system in order to guide development decisions. They use functional decomposition to map dependability goals to parts of the system and 7 categories for pruning alternatives, for example functionality, cost, and restrictions on later alternatives.

They do focus on the assurance cases themselves and how decisions may benefit from co-development. They do not provide criteria for the quality of the evidence or for checking certain aspects. Although they consider integrating quality statements on developed parts for future decisions in the development process, they do not address component-based development or different participating parties. Their general ideas could be used to state the performance alternative evaluation goal and the selection between the alternatives.

The use of certificates in component-based software engineering is surveyed by Alvaro et al. in [AdAdLM05]. The authors provide a timeline visualizing the history of the approaches. They show the trend from early approaches focussing on mathematical and purely test-based models towards quality prediction, a stronger degree of reuse, and further means to ensure credibility in quality statements. None of the described approaches addresses the protection of knowledge and IP of implementations or the consequences of certifier party selection. The need for accurate specifications is identified but no means for ensuring the accuracy of specifications was targeted for business information systems. A detailed discussion of specific approaches and their differences follows.

The issue of trust in component specifications was already discussed by Meyer et al. in [MMS98]. They identify that technical as well as sociological aspects influence the perceived trust in a component. Technical aspects include verification and validation techniques and include formal specifications, design by contract, test-driven development, or testing. Social aspects include the use of generally accepted best practices, independent repetition and verification of results, or gut feeling. The authors take into account the correctness of specifications, the quality of analysis or reasoning approaches, and the trust between participants. They provide a thorough discussion of trust issues in general but do not focus on knowledge and IP protection or an applicable process for reasoning on the architecture level on component evaluation and selection.

Meyer coined the complementary terms high road and low road already in 2003 in [Mey03] for the classification of verification approaches, which are still used to distinguish approaches. He defined a Trusted Component as follows:

> A Trusted Component is a reusable software element possessing specified and guaranteed property qualities.

The word guarantee hints at verification techniques based on proving properties for high road approaches formally. In contrast, low road approaches use test-based techniques for the assessment. Today, a combination of high and low road approaches is used. Proofs can be applied for small areas of safety-critical software systems whereas testing on unit and component level is a generally accepted best practice. The quality assurance for safety-critical software is often eased by additional restrictions, for example the MISRA rule set [Mot08] for using C++ in safety-critical automotive software. Formal techniques like contracts on the code level, static code analysis, and symbolic execution can aid in identifying potential faults. According approaches are available in industry for Java, for example by FindBugs [AHM+08], or C++ by QA C/C++ [PRQ09]. The complexity of todays systems lead to the fact that low road approaches are more widespread. The approach presented in this thesis with its test-based validation and heuristic for accuracy influence analysis is classified as low road approach.

Certifiable statements using a high road approach with a focus on real-time or embedded systems were addressed at the SEI by Hissam et al. with their idea on PECT [HMSW02, HMSW03] and by Wallnau with his idea on PACC [Wal03]. They define PECT as "the integration of a component technology with one or more analysis technologies" and strive for a simplification of the composition by bundling specifications with the implementations. The approaches are based on ideas by Crnkovic et al. [CSSW01] towards "active component dossiers" providing a component including test harnesses or benchmarking mechanisms to enable independent verification of properties. They regard a component as certifiable if the properties described in the specification can be quantified and separate assessments of the property show the same outcome. They provide an analysis technology with UML statechart semantics, which uses rate monotonic scheduling for predictions. The performance values for their components are based on point estimators: "What we consider to be the certified latency of a component is the average of a large sample of measurements" [HMSW01]. They use random sampling and a given number of executions to determine the statistical point estimators average and standard deviation for the latency of a single component and compare these between predictions and measurements. The empirical validation of their analysis technology is based on random generation of systems from a given set of components and comparing the mean residual error between the predicted value and a measured values. The authors separate the component evaluation and selection phase from the system composition phase, which support evaluations on the architecture level. They use the term Virtual Assembly for an architecture. Despite their efforts, they state that the approach "fell short in guaranteeing behavioral properties such as those for safety and performance" [SEI13].

The authors of PECT and PACC provide a basis for the approach presented in this thesis. The approaches differ with respect to the targeted group of systems and analytical versus simulation-based predictions. The approach presented in this thesis does neither require nor include a run-time for component execution. The separation between the component evaluation and selection phase and the system composition phase is adopted and extended to support the certification of components and their use in repositories and marketplaces in scenarios across different parties. This requires additional process adaptation for component-bases software engineering processes in order to certify and validate the specifications as well as validate issued certificate ensuring their trustworthiness. The approach presented in this thesis further extends the basis by considering the coverage of specifications during validation, applying statistical reasoning only where necessary and advantageous, supporting arbitrary distribution function in the prediction, and by taking into account the accuracy of specifications and their influence on the overall prediction.

Bøegh describes a formalized theoretical approach for the certification of fine-granular properties of components in [Boe06]. The idea is that any measure used in a quality model or quality characteristic like usability or maintainability can be objectively evaluated and the claim verified. Properties can be on any of these abstraction levels from values for a metric to compliance to a full standard. Independent third parties can evaluate and certify the properties. Multiple independent parties can certify different sets of properties for the same component. The approach ensures trust in quality claims of components, especially if multiple different certification parties are involved. However, Bøegh does not separate the implementation from the component description and does not support that even properties of a specification, for example its accuracy, should be certified in combination with the implementation. The approach presented in this thesis provides the definition of several measures and metrics, describing the quality of a specification. These can be certified according to Bøegh's approach. The guideline for certifier party selection presented in this thesis can be used to decide for different sets of properties how they should be certified. Bøegh does not provide a development process or information on how to integrate his approach into software engineering.

Morris et al. propose a self-certification approach for developers and describe it in [MLP+01]. The authors propose that developers provide tests in a standardized format together with the implementation, which allows the verification of claims and further analysis for component integrators. An alternative and wide-spread language for conformance testing of embedded and communication systems is provided by the European Telecommunications Standards Institute (ETSI) with the TTCN-3 language in [Eur04]. The approach presented in this thesis provides support for certifier party assignment and evaluating if self-certification is appropriate. It does not require to share the implementation or use tests to reason on the covered aspects. Furthermore, test cases are generated automatically by a framework for the validation and manual test case creation is not required.

Alvaro et al. proposed a component quality assurance process in in [AdAM07, AdAdLM07], which focusses on the management aspects of quality assurance and provides a guideline what aspects should be considered when planning the certification of the quality properties of components. Their process has the following four main activities: establish evaluation requirements, specify the evaluation, design the evaluation, and execute the evaluation. It is comparable to a subset of the activities described in the IEEE standard on software verification and validation [IEE05], which is applicable to any software from firmware to business information systems. The process by Alvaro et al. gives additional hints, which quality-related aspects should be considered and which activities are related to certification. The approach presented in this thesis does provide an applicable validation and certification framework and the integration of certification into component-based engineering processes. This integration shows when certification must be considered and which artifacts are transferred. In contrast to Alvaro et al.'s approach, it does not address how an evaluation team is built or evaluation requirements are elicited.

The similarities of component selection and certification and their use in the development process are discussed by Land, Alvaro and Crnkovic in [LAC08, ALC07]. The authors analyze the similarities and differences in a component-of-the-shelf and a product line scenario. Simple waterfall development processes are used in both scenarios to discuss the position of selection and certification activities in the process. The authors envision a two-level selection process. The higher level consist of a pre-selection of components based on publicly available information, the lower level of a prototype of the envisioned system. The acquisition decision is located after the evaluation on the system prototype. The authors provide examples that certifier party selection can influence trust. The authors identify the following challenge:

Standards are needed so that test and analysis results as well as issued certificates are universally recognized and have an agreed-upon meaning. To this end, and also useful for component selection, analysis and test methods need to be designed enabling a meaningful division and packaging of tests and analyses between component vendors, certifiers, certification institutes, system developers and software organizations. [ALC07]

The approach presented in this thesis considers a wider range of development processes and how certification can be integrated and successfully applied in a component-based development process. It supports a separation of the specifications of components and implementations allowing the protection of knowledge and IP even in scenarios with multiple parties. It takes into account that prototypes can only be built after the implementation is acquired and the evaluation on this level requires more effort than on the architecture level. The presented approach addresses the issue of certifier party selection and implications on trust explicitly and provides a guideline for trade-off decisions. Additionally, it points out the flow of artifacts in a development process, the possible separation of information between protected and public repositories and ensure that certificates can be used successfully. The performance-oriented coverage criteria defined in the approach presented in this thesis are a common evaluation base, which can be used to reason about the quality of validations even between independent parties. They allow reasoning on the level of covered aspects instead of single test cases. The automated validation of specifications and implementations is a test-based method and can ensure the coverage of elements. The development process ensures that division and packing is taken into account appropriately. This shows, that the identified challenge is successfully addressed.

4. Accuracy Statements

This chapter presents the developed meta-model for stating the accuracy of performance specifications. It is designed for architecture-level performance specification languages. Its statements provide formalized means to express and access the accuracy of a specification for humans as well as programs. It consists of a generic and language-dependent part. A language dependent part is developed and shown for Palladio.

The requirements for making accuracy statements and how this approach addresses them is described in the following.

1. **Support the influencing factors of architecture-level performance specifications**. This approach allows to specify the accuracy separately for each influencing factor.

2. **Support comparison between architecture-level performance specification languages.** Accuracy statements depend on the specification language. However, architecture-level performance specification languages have common domain-specific denominators. These denominators ease the comparison between specifications of different languages. This approach defines a common meta-model including variation points for customization. It shows the language-specific customization using Palladio as exemplary language. Palladio is chosen as it is one of the most advances languages in terms of parameterization support.

3. **No need to modify specification languages.** This approach defines a meta-model which annotates the specification languages.

4. **Automated processing of accuracy information.** The developed meta-model is accessible using the Eclipse Modeling Framework (EMF). This ensures the conformance with standards and industry-suitable tooling.

5. **Editable by human users.** Human-oriented graphical editors are provided to display and modify model instances. It is ensured by using the EMF.

6. **Support parameter range restrictions.** The confirmed validity of performance specifications is often restricted by their level of abstraction. It is also restricted by the necessary validation and verification effort, especially in conjunction with huge parameter spaces. This approach allows to couple accuracy information with their parameter space restrictions.

7. **Support different deviation threshold types.** Instrumentation and measurement techniques vary in their absolute and relative accuracy. The resulting accuracy influences the verifiable accuracy of a specification. This approach supports taking into account these threshold types.

This chapter is structured as follows. Section 4.1 describes the annotation meta-model for attaching accuracy information to performance specifications. Section 4.2 describes the customization for a specific modeling language and shows its extension for Palladio-based specifications.

4.1. Accuracy Meta-Model

This section shows the language independent meta-model part for stating the accuracy of performance specifications. Previous versions with limited deviation and range support, limited parameter support and customization of it, and without taking probabilistic decisions into account have been published in [Gro10] and [Gro11a].

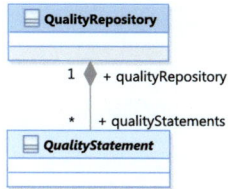

Figure 4.1.: Storing Quality Statements

Figure 4.1 shows how quality statements are stored consistently. The `QualityRepository` contains a set of `QualityStatements`. The annotations are stored in repositories. This allows to store semantically connected annotations combined in one place. There is no need to change the specification languages for statement storage. This solution fulfills requirement 3.

The abstract `QualityStatement` is a place-holder for any statement about quality. It should be specialized through subclasses for the different types of quality statements. The existing subclasses are shown in the following.

Figure 4.2 shows the elements which allow to state the accuracy for exactly one performance specification.

The `QualityAnnotation` is a `QualityStatement` and bundles the necessary information. Its attribute `isValid` provides information if this annotation is considered valid. It allows to take into account the process of creating, modifying and verifying accuracy statements. The attribute may only be true if the accuracy has been successfully verified. The `QualityAnnotation` is linked to the performance specification via the `forServiceSpecification` reference. The restrictions of the parameter space are contained via the `validForParameterPartitions`. There can be any number of restrictions. This solution fulfills requirement 6. The precision of the performance specification with respect to probabilistic decisions is contained via the `probabilisticElements`. The precision of the performance specification with respect to access via required

Figure 4.2.: QualityAnnotation Overview

interfaces is contained via the stipulatedREPrecisions. The precision depends on the required elements stated as part of the specification, for example certain required software components or hardware resources. Therefore, there can be any number of precision statements. If tests are used to verify the accuracy then the internal state of the tested component may influence the results. The difference between results is stored via the internalStateInfluenceAnalysisResults containment. There can be any number of results. There should be no results if the influence is part of a specification language parameter, for example a configuration parameter of the component.

The ServiceSpecification stores the link to a performance specification. A link instead of a direct reference is required to provide the loose coupling and fulfill requirement 3. This abstract class must be customized to the specification language. This fulfills requirement 2. Its checksum attribute stores a calculated hash value of the performance relevant information in the linked specification. This allows to check if the accuracy

Figure 4.3.: `ParameterPartition` Overview

information is valid for the provided version of the specification. The `checksumAlg` attribute stores the name of the algorithm used for the checksum calculation. This allows to have separate algorithms for different languages and take into account meta-model changes of specification languages and changes if weaknesses of one algorithm are recognized.

Figure 4.3 provides an overview about partitions for parameters. `ParameterPartition` stores the parameter space restrictions for exactly one parameter. The link to that parameter is contained via the `parameterReference` reference. This abstract class must be customized to reflect how a partition for a single parameter is specified in the language. This fulfills requirement 2. It allows taking into account additional information on the measured value. Partitions for nominal parameter values can be specified as set of values whereas partitions for ordinal parameter values can be specified using value intervals. If there is more than one value describing the actual performance relevant value a subclass can handle the partitions for all descriptions properly. This fulfills requirement 6.

The `ParameterReference` stores the link to one parameter of the performance specification. Examples are input parameters or component configuration parameters. A link instead of a direct reference is required to provide the loose coupling and fulfill requirement 3. This abstract class must be customized to reflect the parameter types available in the specification language. This fulfills requirement 2.

The description of the elements `InternalStateInfluenceAnalysis` and `RequiredElement` will follow in the paragraphs about stating the influence of internal state and stating the accuracy with respect to accessed resources.

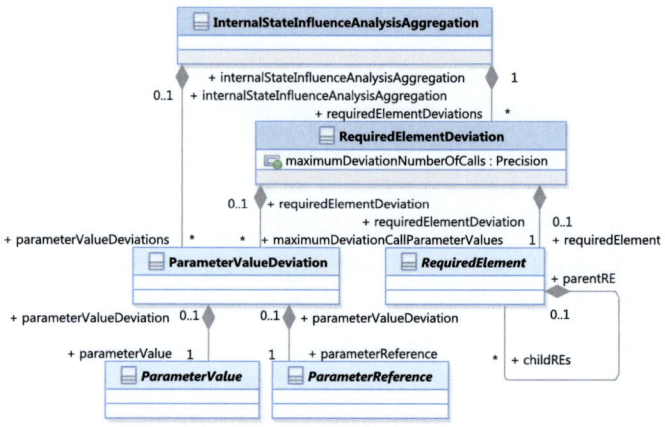

Figure 4.4.: Stating the Influence of Internal State

Figure 4.4 shows the elements for stating the influence of internal state. The internal state of a component can influence the performance although all specified parameters remain the same. Explicit parameters, for example configuration parameters, are not considered as internal state. The information about this unspecified influence allows judging on the stability of a performance specification for long-running components. It allows to identify this type of risk and support decisionmaking based on specifications and predictions.

The `InternalStateInfluenceAnalysisAggregation` stores the information about the deviations caused by internal state. This information is typically gained by repeated measurements. The difference between these repetitions can be stored at this element. The aggregated values of a validation can be stored for the deviation of parameter values using the `parameterValueDeviations` containment. There can be any number of deviations. The number depends on the parameters influencing the specification. The aggregated deviation values for accessed resources can be stored using the `requiredElementDeviations`. There can be any number of deviations depending on the resources accessed by the specification.

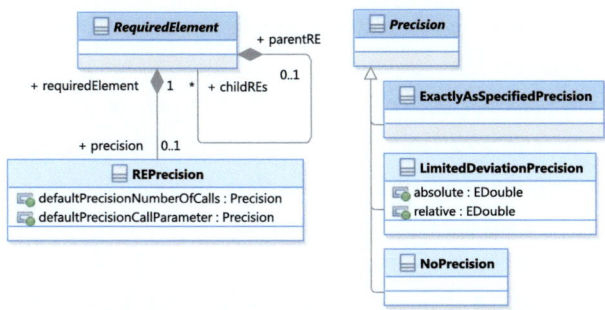

Figure 4.5.: Stating Accuracy with Respect to Accessed Resources

The `ParameterValueDeviation` stores the maximum deviation for one parameter. The value of the deviation is linked via the `parameterValue` containment. The parameter is linked via the `parameterReference` containment.

The `ParameterValue` stores the value for a parameter. It is an abstract class to support potentially different datatypes as well as characterizations indirectly describing the parameter value. An example for such a characterization is to state the number of elements in a collection instead of a detailed data structure. This kind of modeling supports fulfilling requirement 2. The abstract class must be customized for the datatypes and characterization of a specification language.

The `RequiredElementDeviation` stores the deviation caused by internal state for one required element. The aggregated deviation for the number of calls to the required elements is stored via the `maximumDeviationNumberOfCalls` containment. The required element is stored via the `requiredElement` containment. It must be provided. The aggregated deviation for the call parameters is stored via the `maximumDeviationCallParameterValues` containment. There can be one aggregated value for each specified parameter. The description of the element `RequiredElement` will follow in the paragraph about stating the accuracy with respect to accessed resources.

Figure 4.5 shows the elements for stating the accuracy with respect to accessed resources. The resources of a specification are the points which influence the behavior but are not described as part of the specification. Examples are calls to other components, a calculation on a processor, or data requested from a hard disk. The accuracy between such categories can be quite different for the same specification.

The `RequiredElement` stores links to the required elements of a specification. The required elements can be ordered hierarchically. This order is represented by the `parentRE` and `childREs` containment. A `RequiredElement` can be either contained in a `QualityAnnotation`, in a `RequiredElementDeviation`, or in the next higher hierarchical `RequiredElement`. The hierarchy allows a convenient way to specify the precision for a certain resource without having to specify the accuracy for each resource individually. It fulfills requirement 5. An example is if the precision for all hardware resources is set to 1% with the exemption of the processor which is set to 5%. The precision of the most specific match must be used. The accuracy can be stated using the `precision` containment. It must be stated if it is contained in the `stipulatedREPrecisions` containment of a `QualityAnnotation`. This abstract class must be customized for the required elements of a specification language. This solution fulfills requirements 1, 3, and is needed for 7.

`REPrecision` stores the accuracy for required elements accessed by the performance specification. The accuracy with respect to the number of specified calls to the element is stored via the `defaultPrecisionNumberOfCalls` attribute. The accuracy with respect to the parameter values provided during these calls is stored via the `defaultPrecisionCallParameter` attribute. This fulfills requirement 7.

`Precision` is a template for a kind of precision. It is an abstract class. Its subclasses must provide the semantics for the kind.

`ExactlyAsSpecifiedPrecision` denotes that the number of calls and each parameter value used during such a call or a stated decision probability

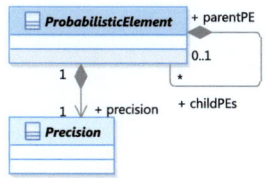

Figure 4.6.: Probabilistic Element Overview

is a perfect match. This means the corresponding implementation behaves exactly as stated in the specification.

`LimitedDeviationPrecision` denotes that a corresponding implementation may deviate from the specification. This deviation is limited. The absolute acceptable deviation must be provided using the `absolute` attribute. The relative deviation with respect to the specified value must be provided using the `relative` attribute. The relative deviation is only considered if the absolute acceptable deviation is exceeded. This enables taking measurement inaccuracies into account. For example, that a certain instrumentation can measure the processor consumption with an accuracy of $\pm$ 1 ms but it's relative error is not above 13%. If the specification states 1 ms but the measured implementation takes 2 s then the specification is still valid although the relative threshold is exceeded. Real-world deviation values are provided by Kuperberg et al. in [KKR11] for different measurement techniques and execution platforms. An example for probabilistic decisions for which it was shown using hypothesis testing that the probabilities are most likely accurate up to $\pm$ 3 % will have an absolute accuracy of 0.03 and a relative accuracy of 0.

`NoPrecision` denotes that there is no ensured precision. Specification and implementation may be completely different. This allows to state that certain required or probabilistic elements have not been validated or verified.

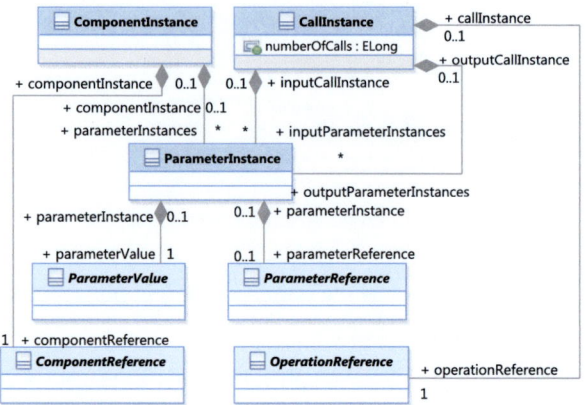

Figure 4.7.: Stating and Using Parameters

Figure 4.6 shows the elements for stating the accuracy with respect to probabilistic decisions. Statements between different sets of decisions can be specified using a hierarchical relationship.

`ProbabilisticElement` stores links to the sets of probabilistic decisions. Comparable to `RequiredElements`, there is a hierarchy. The hieratic order is represented by the `parentPE` and `childPEs` containment. A `ProbabilisticElement` can be either contained in a `QualityAnnotation` or in another `ProbabilisticElement` of the next higher level. The hierarchy provides a convenient way to specify the precision for single decisions as well as all decision. It fulfills requirement 5. An example is if a single decision has a higher allowed deviation than the other ones: the probability for each decision alternative could be modeled with a deviation lower than 3% in most cases and 10% for that single exception. This accuracy of the probabilities must be stated using the `precision` containment. This abstract class must be customized for the decisions of a specification language. This solution fulfills requirements 3, and is needed for 7.

Figure 4.7 shows the elements for stating and using parameters in a specification language-independent way. This kind of modeling supports requirement 2. The designed meta-model is compatible with the Service Architecture Meta-Model (SAMM)[Q-I08]. The SAMM is a common set of the component meta-models KLAPER[GMS07], Palladio[RBB+11b], ProCom[BCC+10], and SOFA[PV02]. The presented model goes beyond SAMM as it supports the native types of the language and does not enforce another XML-based language on top. The shown elements can be used to report verification errors to users including information about invalid values.

ComponentInstance stores the description of a deployed component instance and its component parameters. The component is linked via the componentReference containment. The parameter values for the component parameters are set via the parameterInstances containment. There can be one instance per specified parameter.

The ComponentReference stores the link to one component. A link instead of a direct reference is required to provide the loose coupling and fulfill requirement 3. This abstract class must be customized to reflect the parameter types available in the specification language. This solution fulfills requirements 2 and 3.

ParameterInstance stores the description of one parameter. The value of the parameter is linked via the parameterValue containment. The parameter can be reference via the parameterReference containment. The parameter needs only to be referenced if it would be ambiguous otherwise.

CallInstance stores the information about one or several calls to the same operation or service. The number of calls described by this element must be stated in the numberOfCalls attribute. The call parameters and their values can be provided via the inputParameterInstances and outputParameterInstances containments. The first describes the parameters provided to the operation, the second the parameters received in return after the operation has completed. The operation or service is linked via the operationReference containment.

The `OperationReference` stores the link to one operation or service provided by a component. A link instead of a direct reference is required to provide the loose coupling and fulfill requirement 3. This abstract class must be customized to reflect the parameter types available in the specification language. This solution fulfills requirements 2 and 3.

The presented information allows to state, access, and report the accuracy of specifications in a language-independent way.

4.2. Palladio Customization

This section shows the language dependent meta-model parts for stating the accuracy. The statements are customized for the Palladio specification language.

Figure 4.8 shows the customized parameter references for Palladio. The abstract class `PCMParameterReference` is used to group all parameter types for this language. The types are presented in the following.

`PCMOperationParameterReference` stores the link to an input parameter of an operation. This operation can either be a business operation or an infrastructure operation. The parameter is linked via the `parameter` reference.

`PCMComponentParameterReference` stores the link to a parameter of a component. Identifying the parameter unambiguously requires referencing the component type as well as context definition of the parameter. The component type is linked via the `implementationComponentType` reference. The context definition is linked via the `variableUsage` reference.

`PCMRequiredBusinessOperationReturnParameterReference` stores the link to an output parameter of an operation. This parameter is coupled in Palladio with the signature of the operation. The signature is linked via the `signature` reference. Interfaces and their signatures can be re-used in different context even within the same system. Examples are filters or databases with different content. The context is linked via the

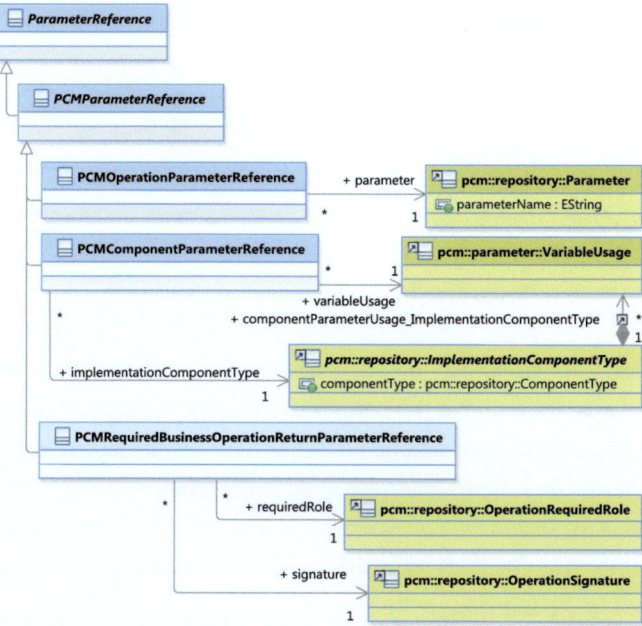

Fully qualified names are provided for external elements. Palladio elements are additionally shown in khaki.

Figure 4.8.: Accuracy Parameter References in Palladio

requiredRole reference. It identifies a deployed instance of a component unambiguously. Both references combined identify the return parameter.

Figure 4.9 shows the customized service specification. There is just one type so there is no explicit abstract grouping class necessary.

PCMServiceSpecification stores the link to a performance specification. The specification is linked via the resourceDemandingSEFF reference. The calculation of the checksum must ensure that the specified order, frequency, parameter types, parameter names, and values of the performance-relevant behavior remain the same. Name and identifier changes as well as formatting changes should not change the checksum if they are not performance-relevant. The names and types of parameters belong-

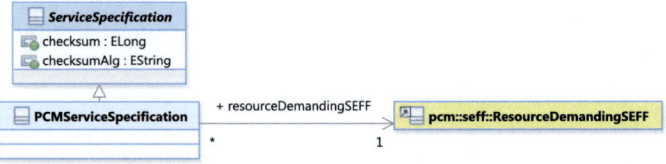

Fully qualified names are provided for external elements. Palladio elements are additionally shown in khaki.

Figure 4.9.: Service Specifications in Palladio

ing to provided or required interfaces and required roles must stay the same. This is due to the fact that parameters are referenced in the meta-model by their name and not their unique identifier. The implemented algorithm is shown in section A and supports these requirements.

Figure 4.10 shows the customized required elements. The abstract class PCMRE is used to group all parameter types for this language. The types are presented in the following.

The enumeration PCMRERequestCategory lists the different accessible resources or required element types of this language. Resource represents resource accesses via a well-defined interface. An example is a hard disk access using a read and write operation. Infrastructure represents accesses of infrastructure operations. Examples are issued Java bytecodes or Java API calls. Component represents accesses of business operations. An example is the request of a file from a database. ResourceDemand represents abstract resource accesses via an implicit interface. Technically, this access is for an ProcessingResourceSpecification of the language. An example is a direct processor access. It is specified in abstract processing units. ComponentInternal represents accesses of a component-internal performance specification which is not provided to the outside. It can be considered as the performance specification of a reusable helper function.

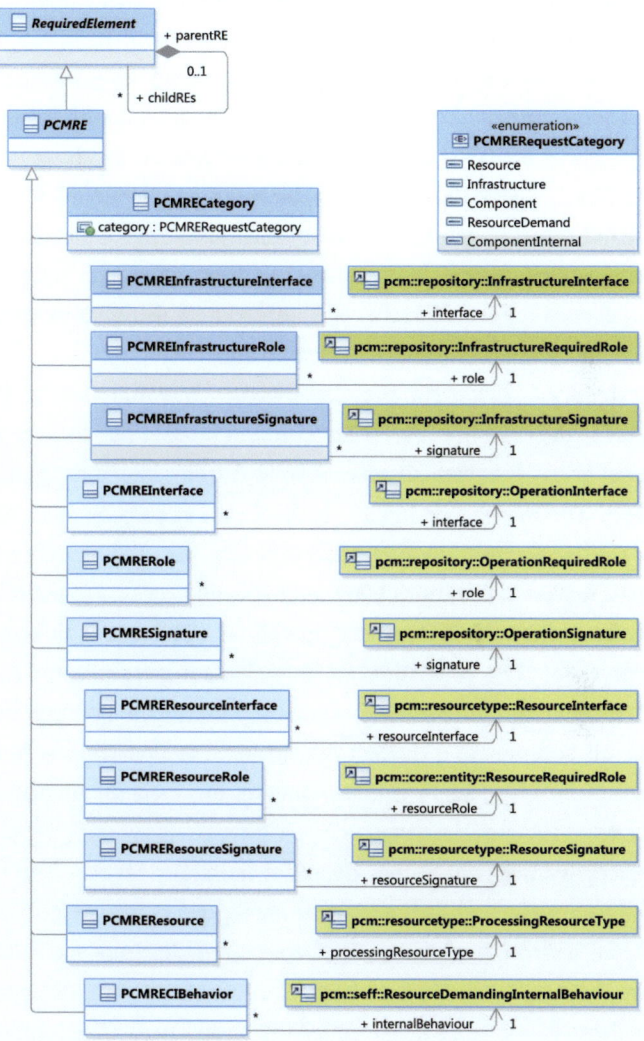

Fully qualified names are provided for external elements. Palladio elements are additionally shown in khaki.

Figure 4.10.: Stating Accuracy with Respect to Accessed Resources in Palladio

`PCMRECategory` stores the link to one category. This category is referenced via the `category` attribute. There must be at least one of these elements for a category if a specification accesses anything within that category. There must not be more than one of these elements for the same category. These elements are the highest elements in the hierarchy. Constraints in OCL ensure the hierarchy. The resulting constraints for this element are presented in listing 4.1. These constraints ensure that there are no ambiguities or conflicts. The hierarchy is different for each category. The different classes for each category are marked with different indentation in the figure. They are presented in the following.

The category `Infrastructure` has overall 4 hierarchy levels. The topmost level is the category. `PCMREInfrastructureInterface` represents the second level. It covers all accesses to a distinct interface regardless of its context. The interface is linked via the `interface` reference. The constraints for this element are presented in listing 4.2. `PCMREInfrastructureRole` represents the third level. It covers all accesses to the role of an interface regardless of the accessed operations. The role is linked via the `role` reference. The constraints for this element are presented in listing 4.3. `PCMREInfrastructureSignature` represents the bottommost level. It covers all accesses to a distinct operation. The operation is linked via the `signature` reference. The constraints for this element are presented in listing 4.4.

The category `Component` has overall 4 hierarchy levels. The topmost level is the category and its hierarchy is analogous to the category `Infrastructure` with adapted names for the required elements and links to the semantic elements `PCMREInterface`, `PCMRERole`, and `PCMRESignature`.

The category `Resource` has overall 4 hierarchy levels. The topmost level is the category and its hierarchy is analogous to the category `Infrastructure` with adapted names for the required elements and links to the semantic elements `PCMREResourceInterface`, `PCMREResourceInterface`, and `PCMREResourceInterface`.

The category `ResourceDemand` has overall 2 hierarchy levels. The topmost level is the category. The only lower level is `PCMREResource`. It links the resource targeted by the abstract resource demand via implicit interfaces. This kind of resource doesn't have additional categories or interfaces in Palladio. The constraints are analogous to listing 4.4.

The category `ComponentInternal` has overall 2 hierarchy levels. The topmost level is the category. The only lower level is `PCMRECIBehavior`. It links the targeted specification of the component internal behavior. These specifications can only be reused within the same specification visible to the outside. They can only be accessed directly. Grouping is not possible.

Listing 4.1: Hierarchy Constraints for `PCMRECategory`. Ensures that the next lower level matches the selected `category` and that each category is not described more than once.

```
 1  context  PCMRECategory
 2  inv  EachCategoryExactlyOnceIfSpecified  :
 3       self.qualityAnnotation.stipulatedREPrecisions
 4       ->select(pcmre | pcmre.oclIsTypeOf(PCMRECategory)
 5       and pcmre.oclAsType(PCMRECategory).category
 6           = self.category)->size() = 1
 7  inv  NextLowerHierarchyLevelIsPCMREInfrastructureInterface
         ForCategoryInfrastructure  :
 8       self.category = PCMRERequestCategory::Infrastructure
 9       implies  self.childREs->forAll(child
10       | child.oclIsTypeOf(PCMREInfrastructureInterface))
11  inv  NextLowerHierarchyLevelIsPCMREResourceInterface
         ForCategoryResource  :
12       self.category = PCMRERequestCategory::Resource
13       implies  self.childREs->forAll(child
14       | child.oclIsTypeOf(PCMREResourceInterface))
15  inv  NextLowerHierarchyLevelIsPCMREInterface
         ForCategoryComponent  :
16       self.category = PCMRERequestCategory::Component
17       implies  self.childREs->forAll(child
18       | child.oclIsTypeOf(PCMREInterface))
```

```
19  inv  NextLowerHierarchyLevelIsPCMREResource
          ForCategoryResourceDemand :
20        self.category = PCMRERequestCategory :: ResourceDemand
21        implies self.childREs –>forAll(child
22        | child.oclIsTypeOf(PCMREResource))
23  inv  NextLowerHierarchyLevelIsPCMRECIBehavior
24  ForCategoryComponentInternal :
25        self.category = PCMRERequestCategory ::
          ComponentInternal
26        implies self.childREs –>forAll(child
27        | child.oclIsTypeOf(PCMRECIBehavior))
```

Listing 4.2: Hierarchy Constraints for `PCMREInfrastructureInterface`. Ensures that the next lower level describes `InfrastructureRoles` and that each interface is not described more than once.

```
1  context PCMREInfrastructureInterface
2  inv EachRETargetMustBeReferencedOnlyFromOneRE :
3       self.parentRE.childREs
4       –>select(pcmre
5       | pcmre.oclAsType(PCMREInfrastructureInterface).
         interface
6          = self.interface)–>size() = 1
7  inv NextLowerLevelMustConsistOfTypePCMREInfrastructureRole
       :
8       self.childREs –>select(pcmre
9       | not pcmre.oclIsTypeOf(PCMREInfrastructureRole))
10      –>size() = 0
```

Listing 4.3: Hierarchy Constraints for `PCMREInfrastructureRole`. Ensures that the next lower level describes `InfrastructureSignatures` and that each role is not described more than once.

```
1  context PCMREInfrastructureRole
2  inv EachRETargetMustBeReferencedOnlyFromOneRE :
3       self.parentRE.childREs –>select(pcmre
4       | pcmre.oclAsType(PCMREInfrastructureRole).role
5          = self.role)–>size() = 1
```

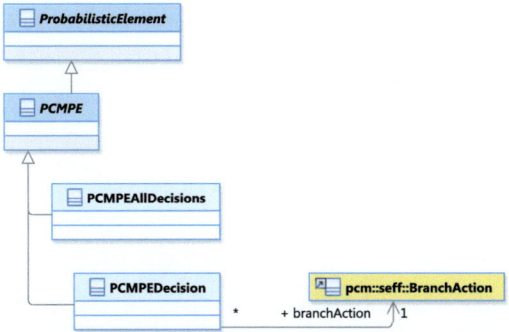

Fully qualified names are provided for external elements. Palladio elements are additionally shown in khaki.

Figure 4.11.: Stating Accuracy with Respect to Accessed Resources in Palladio

```
6  inv NextLowerLevelMustConsistOfTypePCMREInfrastructure
       Signature :
7      self.childREs −>select(pcmre
8      | not pcmre.oclIsTypeOf(PCMREInfrastructureSignature))
9         −>size() = 0
```

Listing 4.4: Hierarchy Constraints for `PCMREInfrastructureSignature`. Ensures that this is the lowest level and that each signature is not described more than once.

```
1  context PCMREInfrastructureSignature
2  inv EachRETargetMustBeReferencedOnlyFromOneRE :
3      self.parentRE.childREs −>select(pcmre
4      | pcmre.oclAsType(PCMREInfrastructureSignature).
       signature
5         = self.signature)−>size() = 1
6  inv ThisIsTheLowestInfrastructureHierarchyLevel :
7      self.childREs −>isEmpty()
```

Figure 4.11 shows the customized probabilistic elements. The abstract class PCMPE is used to group all types for this language. Palladio allows probabilistic decision only at BranchAction elements. Palladio does not have grouping mechanisms for probabilistic decisions besides their position in the specification. Hence, there are 2 hierarchy levels, which are presented in the following.

The level PCMPEAllDecisions is the topmost level. It spans all probabilistic decisions within a specification. This supports setting a default value for all decisions within a specification. The constraints 4.5 and 4.6 ensure the position in the hierarchy. The only lower level is PCMPEDecision. It links the single targeted probabilistic decision via the branchAction reference. The constraint 4.7 ensures the position in the hierarchy.

Listing 4.5: Hierarchy Constraints for PCMPE. Ensures that the highest level consists only of PCMPEAllDecisions.

```
1  context  PCMPE
2  inv  TopmostLevelMustBePCMPEAllDecisions  :
3       self . parentPE . oclIsUndefined ()  implies  self .
         oclIsKindOf ( PCMPEAllDecisions )
```

Listing 4.6: Hierarchy Constraints for PCMPEAllDecisions. Ensures that the next lower hierarchy level consist only of PCMPEDecision.

```
1  context  PCMPEAllDecisions
2  inv  NextLowerHierarchyLevelMustBeDecision  :
3       self . childPEs –>forAll ( child  |  child . oclIsKindOf (
         PCMPEDecision ) )
```

Listing 4.7: Hierarchy Constraints for PCMPEDecision. Ensures that this is the lowest level and that each probabilistic decision is not described more than once.

```
1  context  PCMPEDecision
2  inv  ThisIsTheLowestDecisionHierarchyLevel  :
3       self . childPEs –>size () = 0
4  inv  EachPETargetMustBeReferencedOnlyFromOnePE  :
5       self . parentPE . childPEs –>select ( pcmpe
6       |  pcmpe . oclAsType ( PCMPEDecision ) . branchAction
7           = self . branchAction )–>size () = 1
```

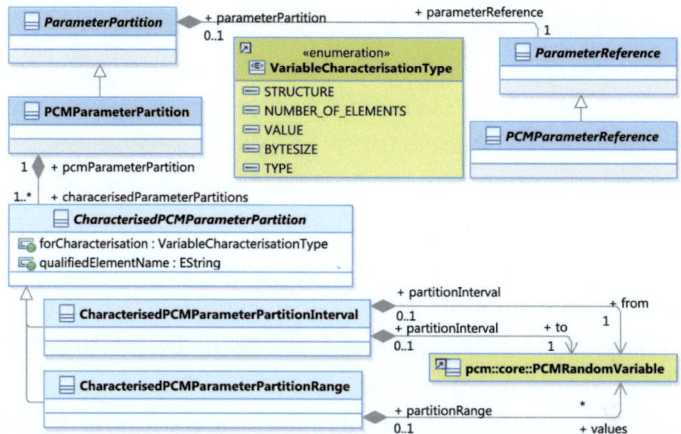

Fully qualified names are provided for external elements. Palladio elements are additionally shown in khaki.

Figure 4.12.: Parameter Partitions in Palladio

Figure 4.12 shows the customized elements for stating parameter partitions.

PCMParameterPartition stores the link to the language-dependent parameter. The constraint 4.8 ensures that only PCMParameterReference instances are referenced via the inherited parameterReference containment. Palladio uses different characterizations describing a parameter. The partition for each characteristic is stored via the characterisedParameterPartitions containment. There must be at least one partition for a characterization of the parameter.

The CharacterisedPCMParameterPartition stores the partition for one data type characterization. The characterization is referenced via the forCharacterisation attribute. Composed or collection data types have named elements within which can be characterized as well. The qualified name for an element must be provided via the qualifiedElementName attribute. It is a textual representation as there is always a distinct textual identifier but the same data type can be used more than once within a data type definition. The textual representation must be the empty string for simple data types. The possible parameter characterization types of Palladio are listed in the `VariableCharacterisationType` enumeration. The technical report on Palladio [RBB+11b] provides further details on the types. Subclasses of this abstract class must define the semantics for the actual partition.

`CharacterisedPCMParameterPartitionInterval` denotes a partition, which consists of a closed interval. It requires an ordinal scale type on the parameter. The lower bound is stored via the `from` containment, the upper bound via the `to` containment.

`CharacterisedPCMParameterPartitionRange` denotes a partition, which consists of a range or set of values. It can be applied to any scale type including nominal or categorical. The values included in the partition are stored via the `values` containment.

The description of the element `PCMParameterReference` is available in the section above about accuracy parameter references in Palladio. All values are stored in Palladio using `PCMRandomVariable`, which is re-used in this context.

Listing 4.8: Constraints for `PCMParameterPartition`. Ensures that only Palladio parameters are referenced.

```
1  context PCMParameterPartition
2  inv APCMParameterPartitionMustReferenceAPCMParameter
     Reference :
3      self.parameterReference.oclIsTypeOf(
4          Quality::Parameters::PCM::PCMParameterReference)
```

Figure 4.13 shows the customized component references. There is just one component type in Palladio, which may contain performance specifications. `PCMComponentReference` stores the link to a component. The component is linked via the `basicComponent` reference.

Figure 4.14 shows the customized operation references. Palladio distinguishes two different types of operations. These types have been described

110

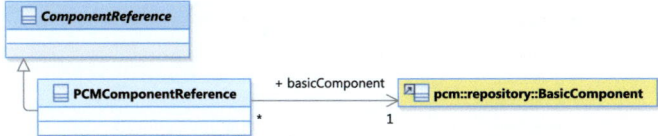

Fully qualified names are provided for external elements. Palladio elements are additionally shown in khaki.

Figure 4.13.: Component References in Palladio

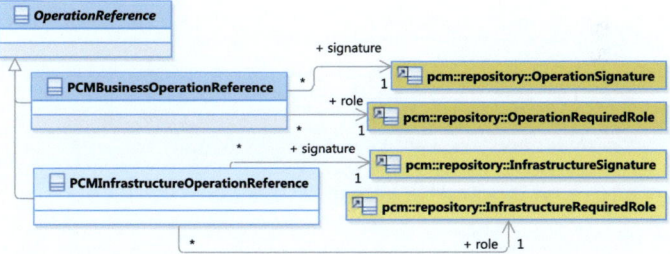

Fully qualified names are provided for external elements. Palladio elements are additionally shown in khaki.

Figure 4.14.: Operation References in Palladio

above in the section about accuracy parameter references. The resulting elements for operation references are presented in the following.

`PCMBusinessOperationReference` stores the link to a distinct business operation. Interfaces are considered first class entities in Palladio. This means that information on the operation as well as the role in which it is used needs to be available for a distinct identification. The operation is linked via the `signature` reference. The role is linked via the `role` reference.

`PCMInfrastructureOperationReference` stores the link to a distinct infrastructure operation. Infrastructure interfaces are considered first class entities and must be handled analogous to business interfaces. The infras-

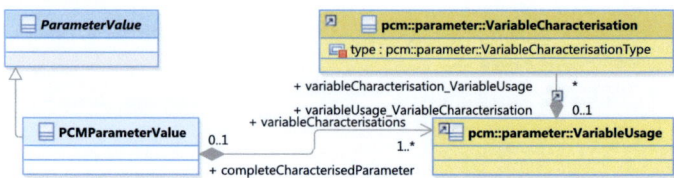

Fully qualified names are provided for external elements. Palladio elements are additionally shown in khaki.

Figure 4.15.: Parameter Values in Palladio

```
▼ ‡ platform:/resource/de.fzi.se.validation.testbased.tests/models/Validation/TestReturnCPExact_NoCExact.quality
    ▼ ◆ Repository _5Ou6YAu7EeKCDdt12qHMAQ
        ▼ ◆ Quality Annotation PCM Service Specification SEFF processBoolean <ResourceDemandingSEFF> [ID: _LvrtYAfoEeK5pcZxZI04Xg]
            ◆ PCM Service Specification SEFF processBoolean <ResourceDemandingSEFF> [ID: _LvrtYAfoEeK5pcZxZI04Xg]
            ▶ ◆ PCMRE Category Infrastructure NoC=(Exactly As Specified) CP=(None)
            ▶ ◆ PCMRE Category ResourceDemand NoC=(None) CP=(None)
            ▶ ◆ PCMRE Category Component NoC=(Exactly As Specified) CP=(Exactly As Specified)
```

Figure 4.16.: User Interface Example for a Customized `QualityAnnotation`

tructure operation is linked via the `signature` reference. The infrastructure role via the `role` reference.

Figure 4.15 shows the customized parameter values. There is just one generic parameter type in Palladio. `PCMParameterValue` stores all characterizations for one parameter. A Palladio parameter value is characterized directly for simple data types. Collection data types are characterized for the collection itself, for example the number of contained elements, and over all elements contained, for example the distribution of their values. Composite data types are characterized via their composed inner elements. The characterized values for a parameter are stored via the `variableCharacterisations` containment. There must be exactly one characterization for a simple data type. Collection and composite data types can have more than one characterization. A `VariableUsage` stores all information about the characterized value for one data type. The possible value characterizations for a single data type are depicted in figure 4.12.

Figure 4.16 provides an example of the user interface for editing quality annotations. It describes a distinct operation *processBoolean* of a Palladio model which is not depicted in the figure. The precision is shown using the shortcuts NoC and CP. NoC stands for the number of calls, CP for call parameters. The number of infrastructure calls and business operation calls and their parameters are exactly as specified. The other categories are not verified and there is no quality information available. This demonstrates fulfilling requirement 5.

The presented customization allows to state, access, and report the accuracy of Palladio specifications without neglecting a specific property of the language.

5. Accuracy Effects on Overall Prediction

This chapter presents the influence analysis of inaccuracies of specifications on predictions of composed systems. This includes effects from inaccurate specifications on the usage profile propagation. The accuracy of specifications is expressed with the statements presented in chapter 4.

Influence analysis points out margins around the performance prediction of a system. Software architects and performance engineers must be aware of these margins. Their awareness prevents becoming a victim of the garbage-in-implies-garbage-out-principle and allows judging the appropriateness of a prediction for an evaluation goal. In general, there is a high chance of becoming a victim of the principle because automated prediction approaches hide a lot of complexity and always provide precise prediction figures. If the prediction does not include the margins from an accuracy influence analysis then the performance of the real system may deviate substantially. This deviation can even happen if all assumption of the prediction approach hold and there is no error in the prediction of the specifications without deviations. Relying only on seemingly precise figures and the quality of the prediction approach does not help if the input of the prediction is not accurate enough for a decision. The confidence in the capability of the prediction to identify actual characteristics rather than specification errors is a critical point for performance engineering. Addressing it is considered a best practice [SW03, practices 2.10 and 5.3]. The approach presented in this thesis allows to distinguish between the actual margins of a prediction due to possible inaccuracies and the prediction accuracy of the approach. It is assumed that the prediction approach makes valid predictions if the used specifications exactly describe the behavior of the implementation.

Accuracy statements (see chapter 4) and specification validation (see chapter 6) address the input part and ensure that individual specifications have a trustworthy and known quality. The remaining threats for the overall prediction and arising effects for composition are discussed in section 5.1.

The exhaustive analyses of these effects for composition can require prohibitive effort for complex systems due to the complexity and parameters for each individual specification and their number of possible combinations. Optimization approaches using (meta-)heuristics like genetic algorithms or simulated annealing usually require several hundreds or thousands of individual predictions. Exemplary approaches for design decision optimization in the areas performance and reliability using Palladio are provided by Koziolek [Koz11] and in the area of reliability taking into account accuracies with the SCOUT approach by Meedeniya [Mee12]. The effort can be reduced as part of a trade-off between effort and the quality of the margins of the overall prediction. The trade-off is discussed for Palladio in section 5.2. The section also points out how the identified trade-off is realized by the presented approach and how the prediction approach is extended to support margin identification.

5.1. Accuracy Propagation Effects

This section presents the threats for overall predictions and effects of propagating inaccuracies of specifications in prediction approaches.

In general, a prediction can contain specifications with and without accuracy information. The accuracy information can be limited to certain intervals or parameter value ranges. There may be more than one specification available for the same component. Examples include specifications which differ in their accuracy or parameter ranges with accuracy information. The separation of a system's usage profile from the specifications supports reuse

Table 5.1.: Threats Depending on Available Accuracy Information and Mitigation Actions

Information	Prediction Threat	Action
Missing	Unknown quality	Feedback for which parts the information is missing.
Existing but not for used parameters	Extrapolation errors	Feedback which parameter values were outside the bounds.
Existing for used parameters, unambiguous	Interpolation or abstraction errors	No action required.
Existing for used parameters, ambiguous, overlapping parameter ranges	Different influences possible	Feedback for ambiguity conflicts and use one arbitrarily.
Existing for used parameters, ambiguous, non-overlapping parameter ranges	Interpolation or abstraction errors	No action required.

and late composition. However, the separation also means that threats can only be identified to their full extent if all information is available in combination. A prediction including influence analysis and margins provides this kind of information.

The threats for a prediction depend on the availability of accuracy information. This context also limits the actions to mitigate the threats. Threats and mitigation actions are summarized in table 5.1 and explained in the following. The threats are illustrated using simplistic specifications determining the CPU load depending on the parameter value x and assume that $f_{\text{real}}(x) = 0.8 + 0.84 * x$ describes the real relation. This allows the demonstration and the principle is valid for complex specifications as well.

If accuracy information is missing for at least one specification used in the prediction then the quality of the resulting prediction is unknown and it should not be used for decisions. For the example, it would be unclear if a

117

specification $f_1(x) = x$ or $f_2(x) = 1 + 0.82 * x$ is an appropriate description. The deviation additionally changes with the value of x: $f_1(5) = 5$ would provide accurate predictions for $f_{real}(5)$ while the deviation for $f_1(10) = 10$ is $\frac{f_{real}(10) - f_1(10)}{f_{real}(10)} = \frac{10 - 9.2}{9.2} \approx 8.7\%$. However, this knowledge is crucial in reasoning about the appropriateness of a prediction for an evaluation goal or identifying if the error is higher than a specified threshold such as the bound of 30% acceptable error proposed by Menasce in [MA01] for predictions in software performance engineering. The accuracy influence analysis allows identifying specifications for which accuracy information is missing. The analysis additionally shows the parameter values for which the information is missing. This additional information eases goal-oriented validation of the specification. In order to mitigate the threat, accuracy information should be added for the respective specification and parameter values. For example by validating the specification with the techniques presented in chapter 6. A new analysis is required after the accuracy information is supplied.

If accuracy information exists but at least one specification is used with parameter values for which no accuracy information is available then the resulting prediction contains extrapolation errors. For the example, if $f_1(x)$ is valid for $x \in [0, 10]$ with an accuracy of ± 1 then the accuracy of $f_1(11)$ or $f_1(100000)$ remains unclear and extrapolations errors can occur. The analysis additionally shows the parameter values for which extrapolation was used. This additional information eases a goal-oriented analysis of the extrapolation error. This extrapolation analysis is the appropriate mitigation action. If the extrapolation error is below the deviations allowed by the stated accuracy then the original analysis and margins remain valid. If the extrapolation error is above the stated accuracy limits then a new analysis is required.

If accuracy information exists for the used parameter values and is un-ambiguous then the resulting prediction is only influenced by interpolation errors. These interpolation errors are due to the abstraction level of the specification. For the example, $f_1(x)$ can be used for $x \in [0, 10]$ with accuracy ± 1 and the interpolation error should be below $1 \ \forall x \in [0, 10]$. Analogously, the interpolation error could be smaller then $\pm 3\%$ for the specification $f_2(x) = 1 + 0.82 * x$ for $x \in [10, 10000]$. There is no mitigation action required. If the margins of the prediction are too big for a sound decision then a modification of the accuracy statements of specifications and a subsequent prediction can aid in determining if the decision could be made with more accurate specifications.

If there is accuracy information for a specification with statements for intersecting parameter value ranges then their influence on the prediction is most probably different. For the example, if $f_1(x)$ is used as specification for $x \in [0, 10]$ with an accuracy of ± 1 and for $x \in [10, 100]$ with an accuracy of $\pm 3\%$ then the accuracy for $x = 10$ is unclear, being limited by either ± 1 or $\pm 3\% * x = 0.3$. The question arises which provides lower margins. Unluckily, it is not decidable in general without making performance predictions which of the alternatives has a smaller influence of the prediction's result. A mitigation action is to provide the accuracy information, which finally leads to lower margins. Another mitigation action is to use one of the specifications arbitrarily. The margins may be good enough for sound decision making.

If there is accuracy information for a specification with statements for non-intersecting parameter value ranges then interpolation errors can occur. These interpolations errors are due to the abstract level of the specification. There is no mitigation action required. If the margins of the prediction are too big for a sound decision then a modification of the accuracy statements of specifications and a subsequent prediction can aid in determining if the decision could be made with more accurate specifications.

The effect of inaccuracies of specifications on an overall prediction depends on the types of allowed deviations and the composition. The resulting effect can be quite different from a specification without deviation even for simple specifications. An example with relative deviation d_r beyond an absolute deviation threshold d_a is given in the following.

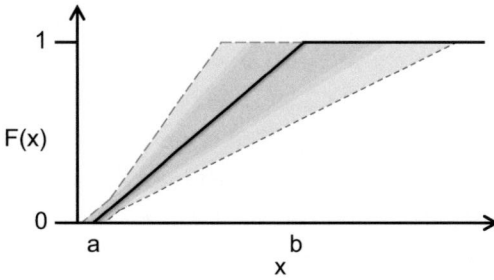

Notation: Black = No Deviation, Dark Grey = $\pm 25\% * d_r(x)$, Lighter Grey = $\pm 50\% * d_r(x)$, Red/Short Dashes = Worst-Case Maximum after Deviation $+100\% * d_r(x)$, Green/Long Dashes = Worst-Case Minimum after Deviation $(-100\% * d_r(x))$

Figure 5.1.: Illustration of Accuracy Influence on the Metric Response Time of a System using Cumulative Distributions

The example in figure 5.1 illustrates this effect for the uniformly distributed function $f(x) = U(a, b)$ and deviation $d(x) = max(d_a, d_r * |x|)$. The figure additionally shows the areas corresponding to modified relative deviations of $\pm$ 25% (dark grey), $\pm$ 50% (lighter grey), and $\pm$ 100% (light grey) of $d_r(x)$.

In general, determining the worst-case influence or graduations of them requires a full exploration of the parameter and deviation space. For example, increasing a parameter influencing the priority of certain jobs could increase the throughput for these jobs at the expense of the performance of other jobs. Even smaller resource demands in parts of the specification do not necessarily imply faster processing as the changed situation could lead to contention where there has been none before and hence increased response times. The composition of specifications means that the inaccuracies of one specification can influence the input of others. This influence on the propagation of the usage profile takes effect in every specification, which the control passes in the system. The full exploration of these interdependencies requires predictions for each possible combination of parameter values and possible deviations. The distribution of the prediction values resulting from all of these analyses allow reasoning about the margins. As shown in the examples, the margins can be different for each predicted value.

Users of an accuracy influence analysis are mostly interested in the effect of worst-case scenarios as they point out the margins around predicted values and allow judging if a prediction will most likely provide a sound basis for a specific evaluation goal. Graduations of the worst case provide additional information on the resulting distribution of the predicted values. It is possible that inaccuracies in some specifications are hidden by inaccuracies in other specifications rather than that they are accumulated. Depending on the proportion between these two options, the predicted values without deviation can deviate stronger and be closer to the margins.

There is a trade-off between the number of required predictions for parameter values and specifications deviations and the quality of the margins. Heuristics allow to prune the parameter and deviation space. The time required for a single prediction should be taken into account when determining an appropriate heuristic for a specification language. Even the simple example shown in figure 5.1 requires 7 predictions for a single specification. This influence assessment requires a prediction for the offsets of $\pm$ 100%, $\pm$ 50%, $\pm$ 25%, and without deviation. Please note that the depicted probability distribution shows how deviation sizes influence the prediction. It does not show the certainty with which a certain value is hit as the allowed deviation of a validated specification could be the minimum or maximum without endangering the validity itself. It should also be noted that the influence on an overall prediction does not necessarily need do be symmetrical as depicted in the provided figure. For example if a prediction includes only very small effects because a composed entity is rarely used for the predicted usage profile, its overall influence is most probably not seen as a symmetrical deviation. A lower accuracy of such models might be acceptable for many decisions, and it might be nearly negligible for extreme cases. However, this depends on the composition and usage profile.

121

5.2. Analyzing Effects on Overall Palladio Predictions

This section discusses the trade-off between the number of analyzed deviation alternatives and the quality of the margins for Palladio specifications. The section additionally points out the realization developed as part of the presented approach.

The time required for performance predictions using Palladio depends on the prediction technique, complexity of the composed system, and depth of the analyzed influencing factors. Infuence factors with heavy run-time impact include fine-grained network transfer analyses. The available analytical solvers provide predictions without heavy impact factors typically in several seconds. Their predicted values are restricted to statistical point estimators and the specifications must meet additional assumptions. For example, synchronization is not supported. The simulation-based solvers have no restrictions and provide arbitrary distribution functions for the predicted values. The run-time for a single prediction is typically from several seconds to minutes. Either the total run-time of an influence analysis must be reduced or the number of considered deviation alternatives must be very low in order to apply the approach successfully on a broad scale.

The time and effort for analyzing the influence in each deviation alternative scales approximately linearly. Drawing conclusions from previous deviation alternatives is limited for Palladio. Modifications of a performance-relevant value in one specification may indirectly influence the performance of other parts. Examples for this influence are resources with contention or the propagation of values as usage profile of assembled required components. Potential optimizations are limited for Palladio. Only performance-relevant information is processed and the prediction itself is the propagation operator. The chance for reducing the total run-time of an influence analysis by taking into account prediction values of previous deviation alternatives is limited.

Business information systems often have linear dependencies of input parameters of a specification to required resource demands. Hence, observing a worst-case deviation for a single specification is most likely at the boundaries of the parameter space for which the quality information is available. Furthermore, case studies from academia [Koz11, RKE11, Bec08, Bro12] as wells from the industry [And08, HBR+10, RBKR12, BKBR12, Bro12] have shown that higher values usually correspond with higher required resource demands. Palladio's focus on business information systems suggests to use these characteristics for deriving a heuristic.

In general, deviation alternatives must be considered separately for each specification. This means the number of necessary deviation alternatives is the product of graduation alternatives and the number of specifications. The added value of having more information for the case that some specifications do not use their allowed deviation does not make up for the required analysis effort for medium or large systems.

The heuristic for Palladio specifications therefore is to focus on the worst-case deviations for all specifications at once. Only two alternatives with the minimum (-100% $d(x)$) and maximum (+100% $d(x)$) deviation have to be considered besides an undeviated prediction. The overall run-time is only three times the run-time of a prediction without accuracy influence analysis. The quality of the margins should be high for business information systems. Errors due to a small number of specifications within a medium or large system, which behave opposite to the assumptions, should be either compensated by the fact that it is unlikely that every specification is at its deviation bounds or by the fact that they have such a big impact on the system's performance that their behavior determines the overall predicted values.

The realization of the heuristic and its implementation in Palladio is described in the following. The description starts with showing the requirements. Additionally, it shows how this approach addresses these requirements and its implementation.

1. **Compatibility with existing prediction approach.** The specifications, which are modified according to the alternatives of the heuristic must remain valid instances of the prediction approach. This allows the application of the prediction directly on the modified specifications. This requirement is fulfilled by creating Operational Query/View/Transformation (QVTO) transformations, which modify the specifications and create valid Palladio specifications. The transformations are presented later in this chapter.

2. **Integration into the existing prediction process.** The accuracy influence analysis must be integrated into the existing prediction process. This eases the application and use by performance engineers and software architects.

The adaptation and extension of the prediction process is depicted in figure 5.2. The three deviation alternatives are designated as Minimum, As Specified, and Maximum.

The for each loop encloses the previously existing activities for a single prediction. A separate prediction is made for each of the alternatives. This allows reusing the existing implementation of the prediction and prevents risks due to prediction adaptation. It supports modifications of the specifications which require adding or removing elements from the specifications. This solution ensures that all specifications in a composition are modified according to the alternative handled in a loop iteration. This separation allows comparing predicted values between the alternatives and pointing out the margins using the existing Palladio tooling. The loop itself is implemented in the workflow class de.fzi.se.accuracy.jobs.AccuracyInfluenceAnalysisJob. It is executed instead of a single prediction in the unextended prediction. A single prediction after the extension is represented by the body of the loop and is split into three steps: Prepare, Transform and Predict. These steps, their activities, and necessary extensions are presented in the next paragraphs.

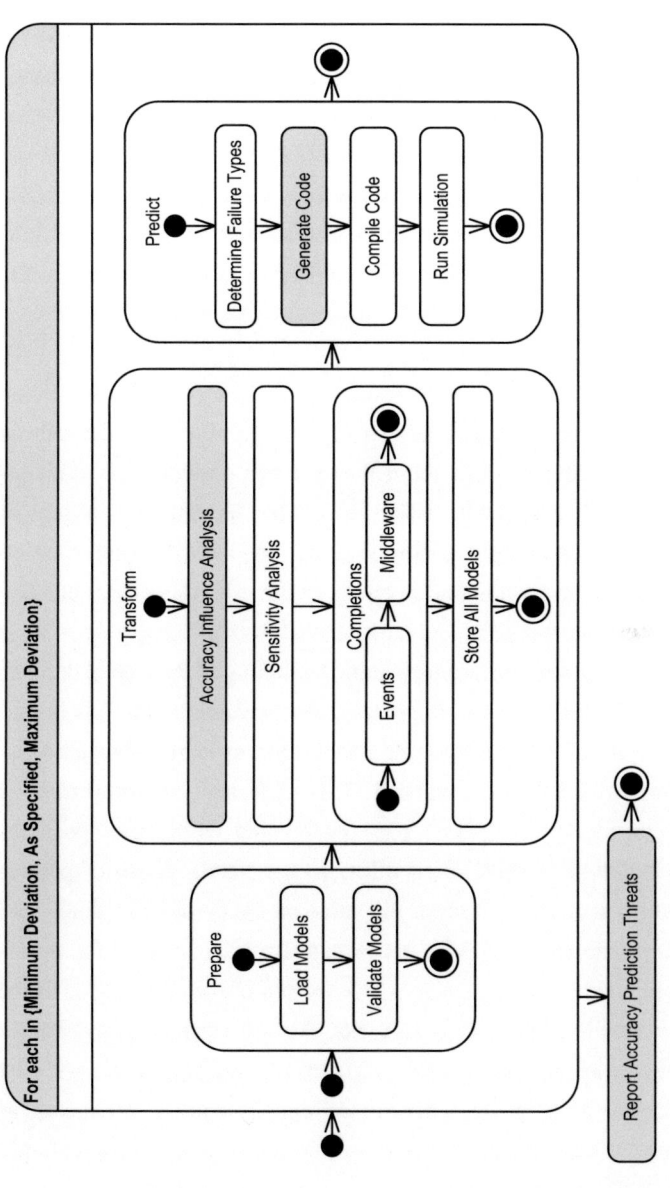

Figure 5.2.: Prediction Process Steps of Palladio

Adaptations for accuracy influence analysis are marked grey.

The `Prepare` step ensures that all models containing the specifications and necessary information on the system for a prediction are available for the subsequent steps. The preparation is split into the activities of loading the models in the `Load Models` activity and validating the loaded models in the `Validate Models` activity. This step is implemented in the abstract workflow class `de.uka.ipd.sdq.codegen.simucontroller.workflow.jobs.AbstractSimulationJob` and executed via the workflow class `de.uka.ipd.sdq.codegen.simucontroller.workflow.jobs.SimuComJob`. The activities and their order remain unmodified by the developed solution.

The `Transform` step modifies the specifications and weaves in additional information, which is not part of the performance specifications themselves but performance-relevant overhead of the system's environment. This includes, for example, the representation in Palladio for different settings of the middleware for the wiring of components. The additional information should not be affected by the modifications of the user's specifications due to accuracy influence analysis. Therefore the additional activity `Accuracy Influence Analysis` is introduced at the beginning of the step in order to modify the specifications according to the influence alternative. It is implemented in the workflow class `de.fzi.se.accuracy.jobs.TransformPCMForAccuracyInfluenceAnalysisJob`. The activity `Sensitivity Analysis` can modify a distinct parameter value within the specification. The sensitivity modifications allow to generate a group of predictions in order to assess the effect of the value on the predicted values. The `Completions` activity weaves in performance-relevant aspect for event-based communications in the `Events` activity and of the middleware in the `Middleware` activity. The `Store All Models` activity ensures that a copy of all models, which are used for the prediction, is stored together with the simulation code. This includes the quality annotations for the specifications. It supports testing and error identification of the modification chain and analysis technique.

The `Predict` step represents a single prediction. `Determine Failure Types` support reliability predictions and creates a set of failure types for the system. The behavior of the `Generate Code` activity was extended using a pre-defined extension point. This extension point allows the definition of custom functions for Palladio's parameter value specification language Stochastic Expression (StoEx). This solution allows the calculation of minimum and maximum values if samples are drawn during run-time from arbitrary distributions. Using this solution, the parameter value evaluation techniques and independence assumptions do not have to be modified. Such a solution is required to fulfill requirement 1. The extension is described directly after the prediction process. The existing model to code transformation for the simulation was extended to include the quality annotations of the specifications. The extension is implemented in the open Architecture Ware Xpand language template at `de.uka.ipd.sdq.pcm.codegen.m2m/templates/m2t_transforms/sim/accuracy.xpt`. The simulation environment was extended to report accuracy prediction threats, which are identified during run-time of the simulation using this added information. The `Compile Code` activity compiles the generated simulation code and creates a simulation package. This package is then transferred to a simulation environment and the prediction is executed in the `Run Simulation` activity.

The `Report Accuracy Prediction Threats` activity reports any prediction threats to the user, which were observed during a prediction. These reported threats help deciding on possible counteractions. See also section 5.1 for a description of threats and actions. This new activity is implemented in the workflow class `de.fzi.se.accuracy.jobs.ShowAccuracyInfluenceAnalysisErrorsJob`.

As shown above, the creation of the three alternatives runs automated and is integrated into the existing prediction process. This integration fulfills requirement 2. By doing so, the comparison between `Minimum`, `As Specified` and `Maximum` shows the exact deviation for the composition, wiring, and usage profile under scrutiny without disregarding any capability of Palladio.

The extension of the parameter value specification language StoEx comprises the two functions `MinDeviation` and `MaxDeviation`. These functions calculate the minimum and maximum deviated values taking into account a relative deviation ($r \in \mathbb{R}^+$) above an absolute threshold ($a \in \mathbb{R}^+$). Their realization as part of the language allows the use of arbitrary distribution functions in the specifications, which require run-time sampling within the simulation environment. The independence assumptions and evaluation characteristic of Palladio can remain unchanged by this approach. The function definitions for sample($s \in \mathbb{R}$)-based evaluations are:

$$MinDeviation(s,a,r) = \begin{cases} (1+r)s & \text{if } s*r < -a, \\ s-a & \text{if } |s*r| \leq a, \\ (1-r)s & \text{if } s*r > a \end{cases}$$

$$MaxDeviation(s,a,r) = \begin{cases} (1-r)s & \text{if } s*r < -a, \\ s+a & \text{if } |s*r| \leq a, \\ (1+r)s & \text{if } s*r > a \end{cases}$$

The transformations of the specifications for the alternatives in `Accuracy Influence Analysis` are realized as model to model transformations in Java using the EMF. The implementations are available in the Subversion (SVN) repository at [Gro11b]. Each alternative requires a different transformation of specification elements according to the specification's precision with respect to the five abstract request categories defined in `PCMRERequestCategory` (see section 4.2). The common transformations are implemented in the strategy `de.fzi.se.accuracy.transformation.AbstractAccuracyInfluenceSEFFTransformationStrategy`. There is one subclass for the behavior of each alternative within the same code package: `AccuracyInfluenceSEFFTransformationStrategy-Minimum`, `AccuracyInfluenceSEFFTransformationStrategyAsSpe-`

cified, and `AccuracyInfluenceSEFFTransformationStrategyMaximum`.

The transformation for a given specification and alternative is demonstrated for the alternative `Minimum`. The transformation is as follows. All call parameter value specifications s are replaced by $MinDeviation(s, a, r)$ with the accuracy values a and r stated for the parameter. The number of calls c to `Infrastructure` components and explicit `Resources` is likewise replaced with the respective $MinDeviation(c, a, r)$. The original specification's elements representing calls to business `Components`, `ComponentInternal` calls, and `ResourceDemand` are replaced by $c = \lfloor MinDeviation(1, a, r) \rfloor$ instances of themselves, again with the stated values for a and r. These call specifications are independent of parameters. Their value is calculated and stored during transformation. The transformation for the alternative `Maximum` works analogously with using the function $MaxDeviation$ and $c = \lceil MaxDeviation(1, a, r) \rceil$ instead of $MinDeviation$. The alternative `As Specified` represents the identity function without transformations and is therefore not described.

This section pointed out why the three alternatives `Minimum`, `As Specified`, and `Maximum` are a good heuristic for accuracy influence analysis of Palladio specifications. The implementation and relation to the existing prediction process was described. The different aspects of the extension and transformation were further described and references to the implementation provided.

6. Accuracy Statement Validation

This chapter explains the test-based validation of accuracy statements for performance specifications.

The selection of appropriate test sets for the validation of specifications is supported by the definition of coverage criteria. The defined criteria support trade-off decisions between the required validation effort, covered aspects of the specification, and trustworthiness to discover invalid specifications. Test set size estimation algorithms are provided for each criterion in order to support this decision making. The criteria consider probabilistic as well as deterministic elements of Palladio specifications. The criteria are formally defined and the coverage of test sets on specifications can be automatically assessed in a quantitative and objective way. The formalization additionally supports the automated generation of test sets.

The validation process and the required information in each process step is described in detail. The process is additionally implemented in a validation framework. The framework allows to validate platform-independent Palladio specifications automatically without limiting the decoupling of influence factors. The framework is a basis for certifying the validity of accuracy statements for performance specifications.

This section is structured according to the sequence in which information is required for the validation process. Section 6.1 describes the meta-model for stating the quality of a test-based validation. This meta-model is used as input for the validation process and is a basis for reasoning about the quality of validation results. Section 6.2 describes the process for the test-based validation itself. Section 6.3 shows means for a goal-oriented validation of specifications and defines goals for test coverage of Palladio specifications.

Section 6.4 describes the meta-models which are required by the process and the developed tooling in order to map specification and implementation, instrument the implementation, and gather measurements at runtime. Section 6.5 presents the meta-model for the validation results and possible validation failures. Section 6.6 provides an overview on the developed tooling for the automated verification and validation of specifications.

6.1. Test-based Validation Meta-Model

This section presents the meta-model developed in this thesis for stating the quality of a test-based validation. Previous versions without coverage-driven stop strategies, without taking probabilistic decisions into account, and without explicit set bytecode interface role have been published in [Gro10] and [Gro11a]. The quality of the validation addresses how thorough a specification was tested and allows reasoning about the confidence in the result. For example, if only one test with random input parameter values was chosen for a complex specification many risks may remain untested. The quality of the test-based validation only affects the trust in the quality statements but not the (potential) correctness of the statements themselves. It is necessary to know the covered aspects of a test-based validation in order to assess the soundness of quality statements. This meta-model is specification language independent and focusses on aspects of test-based validation.

The following are the requirements for making validation quality statements. The list additionally shows how this approach addresses each requirement.

1. **Easy adaptation to new validation algorithms.** Different algorithms need different configuration options to determine the thoroughness of tested aspects. These configuration options should be bundled per algorithm. The developed meta-model will use the design pattern Strategy. This allows to bundle configuration options

and eases distinguishing and replacing different algorithms used in the validation. The general pattern's disadvantage of having to know the strategy for selection does not manifest as you have to know the algorithm anyway in order to reason about its quality or run a validation with configuration settings. The general pattern's disadvantage of more communication overhead between strategy and context is covered by the validation framework developed in this approach. Users of the approach are not affected. The general pattern's disadvantage of having more classes is outweighed by the more precise bundling of configuration options. The overall number of classes still remains low.

2. **Reuse of configuration options as far as possible.** Validations often differ in their assessment about the value of an aspect for the overall quality of the validation. These different viewpoints can be either considered as integral part of the validation or modeled explicitly. The latter eases comparisons between different validations as common viewpoints are easily identified. It also comes at the cost of more meta-model elements. For example, two validations might have the same view on influence analysis but differ in their parameter value generation strategy. The presented approach uses the presented explicit modeling.

Figure 6.1 shows the elements which allow to state the test-based validation quality.

The TBValidationQuality is a QualityStatement and bundles the information on the test-based validation quality. This allows to store all quality information together in one repository. See documentation and figures 4.1 and 4.2 in section 4.1 for a description of QualityStatement and QualityAnnotation. The quality annotations which have been validated using a TBValidationQuality can be linked using the qualityAnnotations reference. This is optional and there can be any number of links.

133

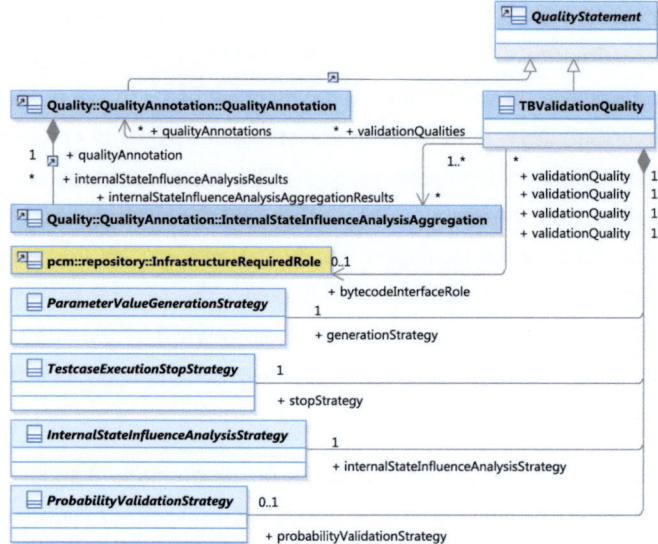

Fully qualified names are provided for external elements. Palladio elements are additionally shown in khaki.

Figure 6.1.: Testbased Validation Quality

If the influence of internal state is analyzed then the aggregated results can be linked via the `internalStateInfluenceAnalysisAggregationResults` reference. This is optional and there can be any number of links. If the validation uses hardware-independent bytecode measurements then a special infrastructure role must be defined. This role references the corresponding Java bytecode interface in the specification language. This explicit definition allows to take different versions of the interface into account. The role connecting the bytecode interface for a component and its contained specifications must be linked via the `bytecodeInterfaceRole` reference. The algorithm and its configuration options for selecting values out of the input parameter space is linked via the `generationStrategy` containment. The algorithm and its configuration options for the stop con-

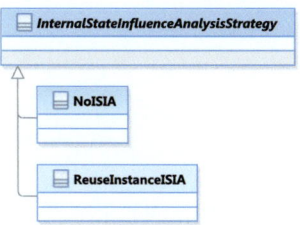

Figure 6.2.: Internal State Influence Analysis Strategies

dition of a validation run are linked via the stopStrategy containment. The algorithm and its configuration for analyzing the influence of internal state is linked via the internalStateInfluenceAnalysisStrategy containment. The algorithm and its configuration options for the decision probability validation is linked via the probabilityValidationStrategy containment. The differentiation between these four classes allows reusing these strategies between different validation algorithms and fulfills requirement 2.

Figure 6.2 shows the different strategies for analyzing the influence of internal state on the validation. The abstract InternalStateInfluence-AnalysisStrategy models the strategy and must be specialized through subclasses to provide the algorithm and its configuration options. The currently available strategies are as follows.

NoISIA models that there is no analysis of the influence of internal state. This strategy has no configuration options.

ReuseInstanceISIA models that one instance is reused for all tests within the validation. Re-running the test suite more than once allows identifying the influence. The aggregated deviation for the different observations for identical test cases is stored via the internalStateInfluence-AnalysisResult containment of a QualityAnnotation. This strategy has no configuration options.

Figure 6.3 shows the different strategies for selecting values out of the input parameter space. Input parameters can be component parameters, oper-

135

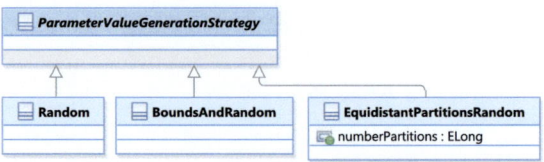

Figure 6.3.: Parameter Value Generation Strategies

ation signature parameters, and returned parameters from calls to other operations. The abstract `ParameterValueGenerationStrategy` is a template for the parameter value generation strategy. It must be specialized through subclasses to provide information on the selection algorithm and its configuration options. The currently available strategies are as follows.

`Random` models that values are selected randomly from the input parameter space of each parameter. This strategy has no configuration options.

`BoundsAndRandom` models that values are selected at the parameter space boundaries and after that randomly from the whole parameter's space. The boundaries are considered per parameter. A full testing of the combinations of all boundary values of all parameters is not required. It ensures that the boundary values are tested at least once. This strategy has no configuration options.

`EquidistantPartitionsRandom` models that the parameter space is split into partitions of equal size. The selected values are considered per parameter. A full testing of the combinations of all partitions of all parameters is not required. This strategy has the configuration option `numberPartitions` which determines in how many distinct partitions the parameter space is split. There must be at least one value per partition. If the parameter space for a parameter is too small for splitting it into the configured number of partitions then the number of partitions for that parameter is reduced until there is at least one value per partition.

Figure 6.4 shows the different strategies for stop conditions of the validation. The abstract `TestcaseExecutionStopStrategy` is a template

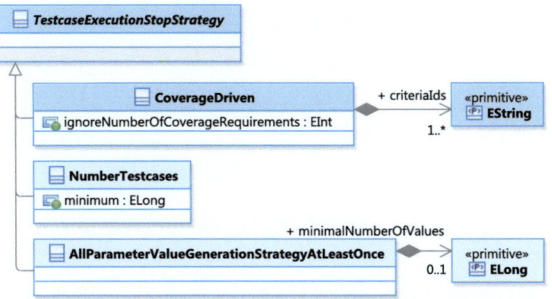

Figure 6.4.: Testcase Execution Stop Strategies

for the test case execution stop strategy. It must be specialized through subclasses to provide information on the stop condition algorithm and its configuration options. The currently available strategies are as follows.

CoverageDriven models that certain aspects of the specification with respect to given coverage criteria have been covered by the tests. The evaluation can be at runtime. At least one criterion must be provided using the criteriaIds containment. The criteria are identified using globally unique textual identifiers (EMF-Type: EString). This decision allows loose coupling and applying the same criteria in programming languages in which an EMF-based meta-model is not available. Furthermore, it allows distributed extensions of criteria repositories without endangering reuse of existing criteria. The criteria defined in this thesis and their identifiers are presented in section 6.3. The attribute ignoreNumberOfCoverageRequirements supports the validation of coverage criteria, which require covering infeasible paths. The feasibility analysis is not supported by the presented approach yet but if the infeasible paths are known it is sufficient to provide their number in order to run an automated validation.

NumberTestcases models that the number of executed test cases determines when to stop. The configuration option minimum allows to set the minimal number of test cases which must be executed in order to fulfill the stop condition.

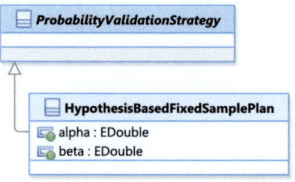

Figure 6.5.: Probability Validation Strategies

`AllParameterValueGenerationStrategyAtLeastOnce` models that all aspects of the strategies used for parameter value generation must be fulfilled. For example if `BoundsAndRandom` is selected then all bounds and at least one random value must be provided for each parameter. A minimal number of generated values for each parameter can be provided. This additional constraint is linked via the `minimalNumberOfValues` containment.

Figure 6.5 shows the different strategies for the validation of decision probabilities. The abstract `ProbabilityValidationStrategy` is a template for the validation strategy. It must be specialized through subclasses to provide information on the decision probability validation algorithm and its configuration options. The currently available strategies are as follows.

`HypothesisBasedFixedSamplePlan` models that statistical hypothesis testing is used to validate decision probabilities. The acceptable Type I error of falsely rejecting a specified probability must be provided via the `alpha` attribute. The acceptable Type II error of falsely accepting a specified probability must be provided via the `beta` attribute. These configuration options determine the required sample size of the test plan taking into account the accuracy statements for the probabilities. The actual algorithm is described in section 6.3.2.5.

The presented meta-model allows stating the quality of a test-based validation. It takes into account hardware-independent bytecode measurements and various algorithm for covered aspects, stop conditions and parameter selection. The meta-model is extensible and new algorithms can be provided easily using the Strategy design pattern.

6.2. Test-based Validation Process

This section describes the automated validation process for performance specifications. The validation is based on model-based testing using the terms coined by Pretschner and Philipps in [PP05]. It is realized by comparing the specification with measurements of the implementation. Coverage information on the specification can be used to reason about the trustworthiness of the validation.

Performance testing usually requires measuring execution time. These measurements are usually error prone due to side effects and inaccuracies of the used internal performance timers. These inaccuracies can be quite large, especially for fine-granular measurements. An overview about different timers is provided by Kuperberg et al. in [KKR11]. In contrast to the pass/fail results in functional testing, the measured results for the identical test case can be different as a consequence. Repetitions of the same test case and statistical analyses are usually applied to determine the most probable value. The presented approach uses the framework ByCounter for measuring the performance. It supports measuring implementations in a hardware-environment and platform-independent way by measuring the resource demand in bytecode instructions. ByCounter avoids measuring side effects or inaccuracies caused by the measurements themselves. Repetitions of the same test case are not necessary to reduce these errors with the developed approach. The decision of using exact measurements, like the ones provided by ByCounter, reduces the required testing effort significantly.

Previous versions of the test-based validation process described in this section were restricted to static validation of non-probabilistic specifications and used prepared test suites as well as other test execution stop strategies. Theses versions have been published in [Gro10] and [Gro11a].

The process uses the accuracy statement descriptions presented in section 4, the validation quality statements presented in section 6.1, the links between implementation and specification presented in section 6.4, and the validation result statements presented in section 6.5.

Figure 6.6 provides an overview of the process in form of an Activity Diagram of the UML. The first and the last activities provide a default behavior but can be replaced without hampering the validation. All shown activities and data object types are described in the following.

The activity `create default RunProtocol` prepares a run protocol for validation. Prerequisites are providing the validation quality via `TB-ValidationQuality` (see section 6.1), the accuracy statements via `QualityAnnotation` (see section 4), and links between implementation and specification via `(GAST)LinkRepository` (see section 6.4.2). Defaults are used for for following attributes of the run protocol. The random seed of the run protocol is chosen randomly based on the current system time. The current time is additionally used for the `creationTime` of the run protocol. This results in a `Prepared Run Protocol`.

A `Prepared Run Protocol` consists of a run protocol, which provides references to the validation quality, the accuracy statements to validate, the links between implementation and specification, a creation time, and a seed for the required random number generator. The validation must not be marked as successful and the number of test case executions must be initialized with 0. Validation begin and end date must not be set. These requirements improve the usability and reduce reasoning failures due to improper reuse and usage of incomplete run protocols.

The activity `instrument` is responsible for providing an instrumented version of the implementation. This implementation provides measurements at runtime. The links in the `(GAST)LinkRepository` are used to generate the input for ByCounter and determine the measured code sections

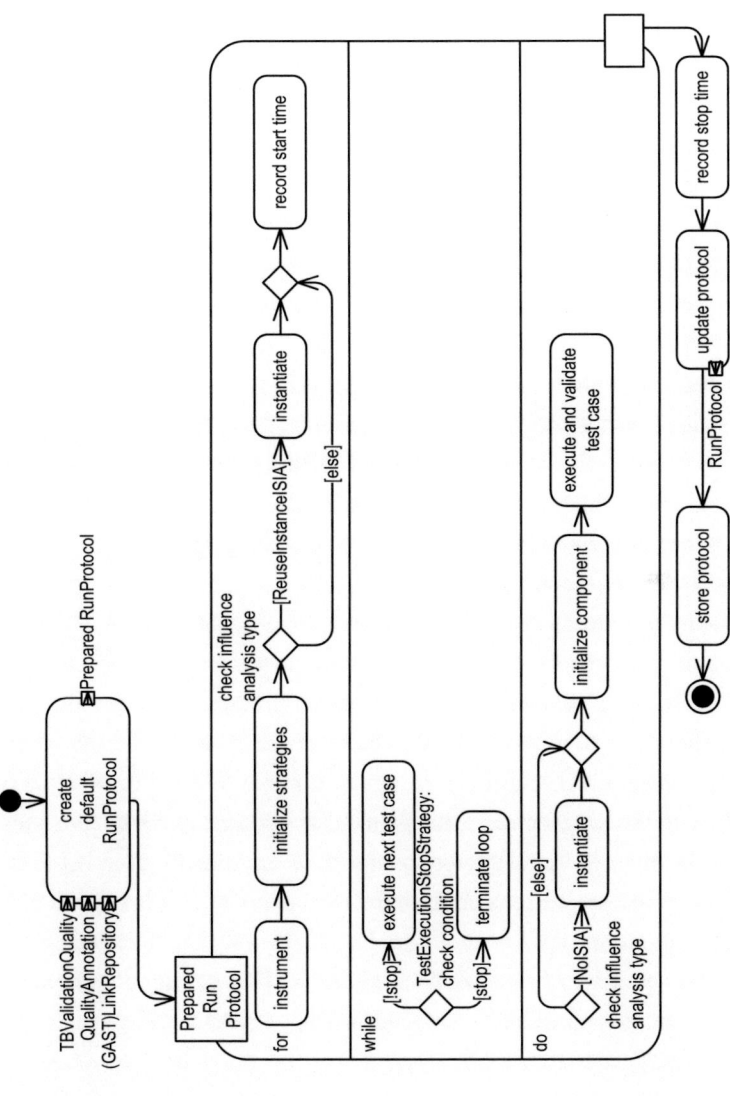

Figure 6.6.: Default Validation Process Overview

141

as well as component boundaries in the implementation. The instrumented implementation is available but not yet deployed or instantiated at the end of this activity.

The activity `initialize strategies` is responsible for initializing the implementation of the selected strategies for parameter value generation and the test case execution stop strategy. This supports parameter value generation strategies for whole test suites crossing single test case boundaries. If a coverage-driven test case execution stop strategy is selected then the required coverage for the specification is calculated in this step and the coverage framework is prepared to measure the specification coverage during the validation at runtime.

The decision `check influence analysis type` depends on the internal state influence analysis strategy selected in the used `TBValidation-Quality` (see descriptions for figure 6.2 in section 6.1 for the available strategies). If one component instance should be reused for all test cases then this instance is created in the `instantiate` activity in the control flow. Otherwise this step is skipped.

The activity `instantiate` is responsible for providing a deployed new instance of the component. The dependencies to required components are resolved. Business components are replaced by proxies. These proxies notify the validation framework of individual component external calls. They allow to generate and return parameters at runtime tailored for the given execution context, parameter value generation strategy, and test case execution stop strategy. Infrastructure components are directly used but their performance impact is excluded from the measurements. This ensures that implementations and specifications can be validated without hampering the provided functionality or intended control flow. This activity does not initialize the component instance with component parameter values.

The activity `record start time` marks the point in the process at which the `validationBegin` timestamp is set. It is included to distinguish which aspects are included in and excluded from the validation time. The definition is required for the metric validation run time.

The decision `TestExecutionStopStrategy: check condition` depends on the runtime state of the implemented test case execution stop strategy, which has been initialized in the `initialize strategies` activity. The available strategies are described in conjunction with figure 6.4 in section 6.1. If the strategy does not require additional test cases then the `stop` branch is taken. Otherwise, the `!stop` branch is taken.

The activity `execute test case` marks that the control flow continues with the next iteration of the loop starting with the second `check influence analysis type` decision.

The second decision `check influence analysis type` depends on the internal state influence analysis strategy. If a new component instance should be used for each test case execution then this instance is created in the `instantiate` activity next in the control flow. Otherwise, this step is skipped.

The activity `terminate loop` marks that the control flow leaves the loop and continues with `record stop time`.

The activity `initialize component` is responsible to set the component state before executing a test case. All component parameters are set using the strategies selected in the link model for the parameters via `ComponentParameterDependencyInjection` elements.

The activity `execute and validate test case` is responsible for the automated validation of a single test case execution. This includes generating parameter values, executing the implementation and the behavior comparison with the specification. The specification is simulated with the same parameter values as the implementation, comparable to a bisimulation. The parameters are dynamically generated on demand for efficient stop coverage strategy fulfillment and according to the selected parameter value generation strategy. Dynamic reaction on the behavior of the implementation is necessary due to probabilistic model elements. Probabilistic

143

elements usually represent the behavior for a certain usage profile of the specification. The implementation's underlying behavior is in most cases deterministic but there is simply no analyzed dependency to input parameters. The implementation's branching choice must be taken into account for the further validation of the specification. At the end of the test suite the probability distribution for the branches is compared with the specified probability. This ensures validating the control flow for each branch as well as for the branch conditions. The hardware-environment independent measurements of ByCounter provide reliable measurements without errors. This renders repeated execution of identical test cases unnecessary. This is a big advantage compared to the number of repetitions required to reason about actual values based on error distribution assumptions and confidence level analysis. It especially allows efficient measurements for specification elements which are mapped to short and fast parts of the implementation.

The activity `record stop time` marks the point in the process at which the `validationEnd` timestamp is set. This definition is required for the metric validation run time.

The activity `update protocol` is responsible to calculate the pass/fail verdict of the validation and the checksum of the validated specification. The checksum allows to check if accuracy statements describe the linked specification or if there have been performance-relevant modifications of the specification. The checksum is only calculated if the validation succeeded.

The activity `store protocol` is responsible to persist the run protocol and additional information for failure assessments. It is ensured that the original models remain unchanged and all information for fault identification is bundled in one place.

The process runs fully automated given the prerequisites. The resulting run protocol denotes success or failure of the validation and provides additional information for subsequent fault identification. Users of the approach only have to provide the stipulated accuracy statements, provide a mapping between specification and implementation, and specify the quality of the validation.

When compared to a manual validation, the accuracy statements have to be provided in both alternatives. The formalized way of stating the quality of a validation and the covered aspects in the automated approach restricts the validation to the defined set of qualities. However, it ensures that these defined aspects are thoroughly and reliably validated. Manual validation on demand requires the same amount of tests but instrumentation, measurement or comparison errors and inaccurate verdicts are more likely. Furthermore, the approach provides a formalized and consistent way of quality assurance and reporting validation failures, which eases fault identification and removal. The mapping of the specification and tailored instrumentation must be ensured in both alternatives. The automated approach requires human interaction only for fault identification of failed validations.

6.3. Performance Specification Coverage

This section presents the developed and implemented testing strategies for validating performance specifications. The coverage of a specification can be regarded from outside or take into account the structure and statements of the specification. The former is denoted as black-box strategy, the latter as white-box strategy. Black-box strategies are advantageous for validation if a uniform distribution of errors is assumed. White-box strategies are advantageous if some errors in the specification are more likely, for example in the behavior sequence or for control-flow decisions.

Black- and white-box strategies can be combined. White-box strategies can ensure that certain aspects of a specification are tested and partition the tested parameter space. Black-box strategies can ensure that the parameter space partitions are covered appropriately. The most complete black-box validation strategy is to cover the whole input parameter space with repeated tests. The most basic black-box validation strategy is a smoke test which executes a single test case. The former requires prohibitively high effort for real-world specifications and implementations. The latter is implausible to identify a valid or invalid specification correctly for a non-trivial parameter space.

The validation effort can be guided systematically by defining validation goals. Such a validation goal can address black-box aspects, for example the number of samples form the input parameter space, or white-box aspects, for example that certain control-flow paths within the specification are covered. The fulfillment of these goals is measurable and two test suites or validations are comparable if they cover the same goals. A thorough definition of the goals allows covering each aspect to its full extent and prevent coverage errors. Knowledge about cross-coverage of different goals can reduce the number of required tests. In general, the goals allow making sound trade-off decisions. The validation and their formalization ensures comparability of validations and reduces the chance for different interpretations. Automated assessment of goal fulfillment addresses human errors and ensures integrity of the validation.

The goals or covered aspects can be oriented at covering the overall parameter input space, structural aspects of the implementation or structural aspects of the specification.

Aspects of the parameter input space are easy to use but there is a high chance that alternatives in the control-flow remain uncovered, especially if there are nested alternatives.

Structural aspects of an implementation are a consequence of providing a functional, stable, and fault tolerant implementation. Covering all aspects of the implementation's structure is important for validating the functionality and fault tolerance. These quality attributes may be critical for the system but a big share of their effects on the structure is later on hidden by the abstraction of a performance specification. Testing the performance with such a goal would give a big weight on rare case handling rather than the usual expected performance behavior.

Table 6.1.: Possible Category Values for Parameter Space Testing Strategies

Partitioning	Sampling	Iterations
One	Random	Overall number $n \in \mathbb{N}^+$ of test cases (OTC-n)
Several	Bounds & Random	Each parameter partition sampled at least $n \in \mathbb{N}^+$ times (PPS-n)

Structural aspects of a performance specification are shaped according to the performance-relevant behavior. Using this information has the advantage that all specified aspects are validated. Incorrectly specified aspects which are contained in one structural block can be identified by test iterations with new parameter values.

Test strategies are defined for parameter space coverage and oriented at covering the structure of performance specifications. Implementation coverage is disregarded because of its abstraction level. This allows focusing the testing effort and using the coverage criteria for the optimization of the number of required test cases. The criteria allow ensuring that all performance-relevant aspects are tested at least once and are a base to apply existing optimization algorithms. The parameter space coverage strategies are shown in section 6.3.1. The structure and control-flow oriented testing strategies are shown in section 6.3.2.

6.3.1. Parameter Space Testing Strategies

This section provides information on the implemented coverage strategies oriented at the parameter space and which model elements are required to use them. The strategies are grouped according to the categories partitioning, sampling, and iterations. The possible values for the categories are shown in table 6.1.

The implemented strategies for partitioning and sampling are merged into the parameter value generation strategies for the validation presented in section 6.1 and shown in figure 6.3. The strategy Random has one partition and samples are taken randomly. The strategy `BoundsAndRandom` has one partition and samples are taken at the stated validation boundaries and randomly within the boundaries. The strategy `EquidistantPartitions-Random` has several partitions and samples are taken randomly within each partition. These three strategies have been selected out of the 2^2 possible ones. The remaining category value combination was not selected as several partitions combined with sampling each internal border from both sides increases the number of overall samples by the number of partitions, if all partitions are samples equally well, but there is no general advantage above randomly chosen values.

The implemented strategies for iterations are represented by the test case execution stop strategies for the validation presented in section 6.1 and shown in figure 6.3.

The strategy `NumberTestcases` maps to OTC-n (see table 6.1). It ensures that a minimal number of tests is used for the validation. The selection of n for the validation is hard because there is no error density model, which can be assumed in general for the parameter space or deviation between implementation and specification. The value of adding another test case for error discovery cannot be judged in general besides the fraction it adds to testing the whole space. Especially if you assume that the specification is correct and failures will occur only in few special cases where the abstractness of the specification and special cases in the implementation do not match as expected. For practical reasons, the overall coverage will remain at a fraction of the whole parameter space for real implementations due to the inherent complexity and huge parameter space. This strategy does not ensure that samples are drawn from all partitions. Case studies using this strategy have been published in [Gro10] and [Gro11a]. These case studies have a very restricted parameter space of only one parameter with possible values ranging from 1 to 1000. They show the validation of an implementation of the algorithm for calculating fibonacci numbers. Overall, 100 test cases with one randomly chosen value in each test case haven been applied.

Even in this very simple case, only about 10% of the parameter space are covered. Testing the remaining percentage will increase the necessary effort tenfold from about 2 to 20 minutes which is not advisable even for such a small example.

The strategy `AllParameterValueGenerationStrategyAtLeast-Once` maps to the strategy PPS-n where n equals to the number provided via the `minimalNumberOfValues` containment of that strategy or one if this additional information is not available. This strategy ensures that samples are drawn from each partition defined by the parameter value generation strategies. Values of n greater than one ensure that parameter values are chosen randomly from within the partitions and prevent repeated tests of boundary conditions. PPS-n is equal to OTC-n if the parameter value generation strategy `Random` is used. It provides an efficient way to test the validity of specifications at the boundaries of accuracy specifications.

Any combinations of the parameter value generation and test case execution stop strategies is possible in theory and supported by the presented approach. Assessing the appropriateness of the number of iterations for parameter space testing strategies is difficult at best. The only aspect standing out of random testing is testing the boundaries of the accuracy statements. At least simple functions or abstraction are likely to have their extreme values at the boundaries.

6.3.2. Structure-Oriented Testing Strategies

Test strategies defines which aspects must be tested and allow goal-oriented validation. The strategies must be adapted for each performance specification language as they differ in their abstraction level, assumptions, and supported features. There are several considerations for coverage criteria regarding (1) their mutual coverage, (2) their error-exposing capability, (3) the complexity to create test sets for a specification, or (4) the ease with which it can be determined if a criterion is satisfied for a given specification and test set.

This section provides definitions for structure-oriented testing strategies for Palladio specifications. These strategies are represented by criteria. Each criterion defines, which aspects of a Palladio specification must be covered. It is shown which criteria cover the same aspects and do not need to be tested if a stronger criterion is covered. This allows the selection of criteria for validation, which promise the best capability of spotting defects. Additionally, information on the number of required test cases for covering the criteria is provided. This supports trade-off decisions between the trustworthiness of the validation and the required effort.

Structure-oriented test strategies are white-box testing techniques. Test sets ensure that the behavior is a valid abstraction for the covered structural aspects and control-flow stated in the specification. The strategies neither aim at creating a new performance model with a black-box assumption from a representative test set nor analyzing the sensitivity of performance demands to input parameters. This information is already available in form of the control-flow and accuracy of the specification. The criteria allow to define test sets in order to validate these stated aspects with test sets.

The next subsection provides definitions for the terms and function used for the definition of the criteria. The following subsections define criteria with respect to covered nodes and edges, the structure of decisions, and the coverage sequence. Section 6.3.2.17 summarizes the relations of the criteria and the effort to create test sets.

6.3.2.1. Definitions

This section provides the developed and used definitions for reasoning on the mutual coverage, error exposing capability, complexity to create test suites, and ease of checking the fulfillment of a given test suite for the coverage criteria. The definitions 6.3.1 to 6.3.7 have been published in [Gro12b].

If a specification contains an element with a probabilistic dependency, e.g. that a branch is taken with a probability of 1%, the question arises how many test cases are necessary to cover this element. The number can only be stated with a confidence level, e.g. a level of 95% certainty due to the probabilistic nature. The number of necessary test cases $n \in \mathbb{N}_0$ to cover the element with a probabilistic parameter of $p \in (0,1]$ at least once for a confidence level α can be specified as follows: $1 - (1 - p)^n \geq \alpha \Leftrightarrow n * log(1 - p) \leq log(1 - \alpha) \Leftrightarrow n \geq \frac{log(1-\alpha)}{log(1-p)}$. Consequently, the element can never be covered if its probabilistic parameter $p = 0$. $\alpha = 1 \Rightarrow n = \infty$. Examples are $n \geq 6$ for $p = 0.01$ and $\alpha = 0.05$ as well as $n \geq 299$ for $p = 0.01$ and $\alpha = 0.95$, which also demonstrates the consequences of high confidence levels.

Specifications without probabilistic dependencies require at least one test for $\alpha \in (0,1]$ and no test at all if $\alpha = 0$. Let $\mathbb{L}$ denote the language defining valid specifications. Let S be a valid specification in the language $\mathbb{L}$. Let t denote a test and T denote a test set for a specification.

Definition 6.3.1 *A test is applicable to S if it can be executed on S. A test set T is applicable to S if all tests $t \in T$ can be executed on S.*

Definition 6.3.2 *The ternary relation $C(S,T,\alpha)$ holds if the test set T for a specification S fulfills all testing requirements for the coverage criterion C with a confidence level of α and T is applicable to S. It is noted that T α-satisfies C for S.*

Definition 6.3.3 *A criterion C is α-applicable if $\forall S \exists T : C(S,T,\alpha)$.*

Definition 6.3.4 *Criterion C_1 subsumes criterion C_2 if $\forall S \forall T \exists \alpha > 0 : C_1(S,T,\alpha) \rightarrow C_2(S,T,\alpha)$.*

Definition 6.3.5 *The size of a test set T is the number of contained tests and denoted $|T|$.*

Definition 6.3.6 *The smallest test set α-satisfying C is T if*
$$C(S,T,\alpha) \wedge \alpha > 0 \wedge \forall T_1 : C(S,T_1,\alpha) \to |T_1| \geq |T|$$

Definition 6.3.7 *The size complexity of a criterion C, a specification S, and a confidence level α is the smallest test set $|C(S,T,\alpha)| = |T|$ such that $C(S,T,\alpha)$ holds, undefined otherwise. The size complexity bounds of a criterion C are as follows. The upper bound $|C(T,\alpha)|_U = \sup\{|C(S,T,\alpha)| : S \in \mathbb{L} \wedge C(S,T,\alpha)\}$. The lower bound $|C(T,\alpha)|_L = \inf\{|C(S,T,\alpha)| : S \in L \wedge C(S,T,\alpha)\}$. $|C|_U$ and $|C|_L$ are used as short forms to denote the bounds of a criterion C instead of $|C(T,\alpha)|_U$ and $|C(T,\alpha)|_L$.*

It is assumed for upper bound calculations that the modeled control-flow can be taken and the conditions leading to alternative flows are independent of each other. These assumptions hold for the upper bound of arbitrary specifications as selectable alternatives and independent conditions can only increase the number of necessary tests. Using the generic upper bound calculation for a specific specification instance however can lead to over approximation of the number of test cases. Infeasible paths within that specification can mean that the specification cannot be covered at all regardless of the number of tests. Hence, the upper bound is only valid if criterion C is α-applicable to the specification.

Definition 6.3.8 *The Test Effectiveness Ratio (TER) is a metric describing the ratio of covered to existing coverage aspects for a criterion C, a specification S, and a test set T. Let $X_C(S)$ denote the number of distinct aspects in S, which should be covered given criterion C. Let $X_C(S,T)$ denote the number of distinct aspects covered by T on S at least once. An empty test set does not cover any aspects: $X_C(S,\emptyset) = 0$.*

$$TER_C(S,T) = \begin{cases} \frac{X_C(S,T)}{X_C(S)} & X_C(S) > 0 \\ 1 & else \end{cases}$$

If T is not applicable to S then $TER_C(S,T) = TER_C(S,T')$ for $T' = \{t | t \in T \wedge t$ applicable to S\}. TER_C is used as short notation to denote the ratio instead of $TER_C(S,T)$.

The TER ensures that coverage results are provided based on the same aspects and that they are comparable. They define what must be measured but does not restrict how it is measured. This enables using different measurement algorithms or algorithm optimizations.

Definition 6.3.9 *An executed test set T satisfies a criterion C for a specification S if $TER_C(S,T) = 1$ for that execution. If criterion C_1 subsumes criterion C_2 then the executed test set T satisfying C_1 also satisfies C_2, which implies $TER_{C_1}(S,T) = 1 \rightarrow TER_{C_2}(S,T) = 1$.*

The $TER_C(S,T)$ can change between test set executions for the same S and T if the behavior is influenced by probabilistic elements. For example a rare branch in the control flow might not be taken if each test in T is only executed once. Observing $TER_C(S,T)$ during execution allows to decide if more executions are required. A confidence level α allows to reason about the average number of required tests to cover each aspect in S for C at least once. If T α-satisfies C for S then there is a number of executions for which $TER_C(S,T) = 1$.

The following notations are used to define the TER for each criterion. The metrics are defined using the elements of the specification language. Let e denote distinct elements, E denote the distinct element types, and $\mathbb{E}$ the set of element types of the language $\mathbb{L}$.

Definition 6.3.10 *The function # provides the number of elements for a given element type and specification:*

$$\# : \mathbb{L} \times \mathbb{E} \rightarrow \mathbb{N}^+$$

$$S, E \mapsto \text{number of elements of type E in S} \qquad (6.1)$$

$$\#(E) \text{ is used as short notation of } \#(S,E)$$

153

Definition 6.3.11 *The function #visits provides the number of visits to an element during execution for a given element type and specification:*

$$\#visits : \mathbb{L} \times \mathbb{E} \to \mathbb{N}^+$$

$$S, E \mapsto \text{number of visits to element of type } E \text{ in } S$$
$$\text{after execution} \tag{6.2}$$

$$\#visits(E) \text{ is used as short notation of } \#visits(S, E)$$

Definition 6.3.12 *The function sum provides the number of elements of a given element type and specification during execution for which a condition holds. Let $\mathbb{C}$ denote the language of conditions and c a condition.*

$$sum : \mathbb{L} \times \mathbb{E} \times \mathbb{C} \to \mathbb{N}^+$$

$$S, E, c \mapsto \text{number elements of type } E \text{ in } S$$
$$\text{for which } c \text{ holds after execution} \tag{6.3}$$

$$sum(E, c) \text{ is used as short notation of } sum(S, E, c)$$

Definition 6.3.13 *The function #visited provides the number of elements visited during execution for a given element type and specification:*

$$\#visited : \mathbb{L} \times \mathbb{E} \to \mathbb{N}^+$$

$$S, E \mapsto sum(E \; e \mid \#visits(e) > 0) \tag{6.4}$$

$$\#visited(E) \text{ is used as short notation of } \#visited(S, E)$$

Definition 6.3.14 *The function MinRequiredTests provides the required number of visits to observe an element at least once with a given confidence level c equal to $1 - \alpha$ if a transition to the element occurs with a given probability p:*

$$MinRequiredTests : \mathbb{R} \cap [0,1] \times \mathbb{R} \cap [0,1] \to \mathbb{N}^+$$

$$p, c \mapsto \begin{cases} 0 & \text{if } c = 0 \\ \lceil \frac{log(1-\alpha)}{log(1-p)} \rceil & \text{if } c > 0 \wedge p > 0 \\ \infty & \text{else} \end{cases} \tag{6.5}$$

The definitions above are used in the following for the definition of the coverage criteria, the definition of their TER, reasoning about pairwise subsumption, and for providing algorithms to estimate the average number of required test executions for a given (probabilistic) specification.

6.3.2.2. Functional Call Coverage

This section describes and defines functional call coverage criteria for Palladio. These criteria belong to the criteria with respect to covered nodes and edges.

Functional coverage requires that all calls to functions have been visited.

Functional call coverage for Palladio is separated into two criteria: One criterion for specified calls, which might have a frequency of 0, and one for specified calls which have a frequency greater than 0. This first allows to uncover unvisited calls, and the second one allows to uncover visited calls which have not been executed by tests.

$C_{\text{call spec}}$ coverage allows to detect call specifications which have not been visited.

$$X_{C_{\text{call spec}}}(S,T) = \begin{aligned} &\#visited(InternalCall) \\ &+\#visited(ExternalCall) \\ &+\#visited(InfrastructureCall) \\ &+\#visited(ResourceCall) \\ &+\#visited(ParametricResourceDemand) \end{aligned}$$

$$X_{C_{\text{call spec}}}(S) = \begin{aligned} &\#(InternalCall) \\ &+\#(ExternalCall) \\ &+\#(InfrastructureCall) \\ &+\#(ResourceCall) \\ &+\#(ParametricResourceDemand) \end{aligned} \tag{6.6}$$

$$TER_{C_{\text{call spec}}} = \frac{X_{C_{\text{call spec}}}(S,T)}{X_{C_{\text{call spec}}}(S)}$$

$C_{\text{call obs}}$ refines $C_{\text{call spec}}$ and allows to identify calls which are specified and visited but no actual call has been observed.

$$X_{C_{\text{call obs}}}(S,T) = \begin{aligned}&\#\textit{visited}(\textit{InternalCall})\\&+\#\textit{visited}(\textit{ExternalCall})\\&+\#\textit{visited}(\textit{InfrastructureCall } c\\&\qquad|c.\textit{frequency} > 0)\\&+\#\textit{visited}(\textit{ResourceCall } c\\&\qquad|c.\textit{frequency} > 0)\\&+\#\textit{visited}(\textit{ParametricResourceDemand } d\\&\qquad|d.\textit{value} > 0)\end{aligned}$$

(6.7)

$$X_{C_{\text{call obs}}}(S) = \begin{aligned}&\#(\textit{InternalCall})\\&+\#(\textit{ExternalCall})\\&+\#(\textit{InfrastructureCall})\\&+\#(\textit{ResourceCall})\\&+\#(\textit{ParametricResourceDemand})\end{aligned}$$

$$TER_{C_{\text{call obs}}} = \frac{X_{C_{\text{call obs}}}(S,T)}{X_{C_{\text{call obs}}}(S)}$$

$C_{\text{call obs}}$ subsumes $C_{\text{call spec}}$ but not the other way around because of the refinement relation.

$|C_{\text{call spec}}|_L$ and $|C_{\text{call obs}}|_L$ equal 0 for the ResourceDemandingBehaviour consisting of StartAction and subsequent StopAction without any calls. $|C_{\text{call spec}}|_U$ is given in listing 6.1. All actions in the control-flow sequence are checked by the loop starting at line 3. Control-flow alternatives with deterministic transition conditions must each be visited often enough to cover the specified calls within that alternative (lines 7 and 8). Alternatives with probabilistic transition conditions also must each be visited often enough to cover the specified calls within that alternative. Addition-

157

ally, the chance of entering the alternative with a given confidence must be taken into account (lines 9 and 10, see also definition 6.3.14). Line 12 ensures that the number of required visits req is updated with the number of visits required for all alternatives of a BranchAction. This update must ensure that req is never reduced and compensates that each visit to the ResourceDemandingBehavior containing the BranchAction implies a visit to one of the branches (min(req, 1)). c actions requiring a single visit do not require c but only 1 visit to the behavior. Line 15 ensures that the body of a loop is visited often enough if it contains any calls. Again, the compensation is applied. Lines 17 to 19 ensure that forked behaviors are visited often enough if they contain calls. The compensation is applied in line 18, as all behaviors are started for each visit to the fork action. Lines 22 to 26 ensure that a behavior and all actions contained in it is visited at least once if one of the actions contains call specifications.

$|C_{\text{call obs}}|_U$ is given in listing 6.2. The difference to $|C_{\text{call spec}}|_U$ is in the lines 21 to 27 in which for each specified call a frequency greater than 0 has to be ensured by tests. Again, the compensation is applied in line 26.

6.3.2.3. Entry / Exit Coverage

This section describes and defines the entry and exit coverage criterion for Palladio. This criterion belongs to the criteria with respect to covered nodes and edges.

Functional entry / exit coverage requires that all possible points in the control-flow of entry and all possible points of exit have been visited.

$C_{\text{entry/exit}}$ coverage for Palladio is defined to check if for each StartAction as entry point the corresponding StopAction as exit point has been visited for a specification. Besides the entry and exit point of the specification (ResourceDemandingSEFF), this includes all ResourceDemandingBehaviour, which are forked asynchronously during execution and are therefore location directly beneath ForkActions. This criterion un-

Listing 6.1: Algorithm for $|C_{\text{call spec}}|_U$

```
1  function CCallSpecTests(ResourceDemandingBehaviour b,
       Confidence alpha) : int
2      int req = 0;
3      do for Action a in b
4          if a hasType BranchAction
5              int breq = 0;
6              do for BranchCondition c in a
7                  if c hasType GuardedBranchCondition
8                      breq += CCallSpecTests(c.behavior);
9                  else //ProbabilisticBranchCondition
10                     breq += CCallSpecTests(c.behavior) *
       MinRequiredTests(c.probability, alpha);
11                 endif
12             enddo
13             req += max(0, breq - min(req,1));
14         elseif a hasType LoopAction
15             req += max(0,CCallSpecTests(a.behavior) *
       MinRequiredTests(probability(a.frequency > 0), alpha)
       - min(req,1));
16         elseif a hasType ForkAction
17             do for ResourceDemandingBehaviour fb in a
18                 req += max(0,CCallSpecTests(fb) - min(req
       ,1));
19             enddo
20         endif
21     enddo
22     if any a in b contains calls
23         if req = 0
24             req = 1;
25         endif
26     endif
27     return req;
28 endfunction
```

159

Listing 6.2: Algorithm for $|C_{\text{call obs}}|_U$

```
1  function CCallObsTests(ResourceDemandingBehaviour b,
       Confidence alpha) : int
2      int req = 0;
3      do for Action a in b
4          if a hasType BranchAction
5              int breq = 0;
6              do for BranchCondition c in a
7                  if c hasType GuardedBranchCondition
8                      breq += CCallObsTests(c.behavior);
9                  else //ProbabilisticBranchCondition
10                     breq += CCallObsTests(c.behavior) *
       MinRequiredTests(c.probability, alpha);
11                 endif
12             enddo
13             req += max(0, breq −min(req,1));
14         elseif a hasType LoopAction
15             req += max(0,CCallObsTests(a.behavior) *
       MinRequiredTests(probability(a.frequency > 0), alpha)
       −min(req,1));
16         elseif a hasType ForkAction
17             do for ResourceDemandingBehaviour fb in a
18                 req += max(0,CCallObsTests(fb) − min(req
       ,1));
19             enddo
20         endif
21         if a contains calls
22             int callreq = 0;
23             do for Calls c in a
24                 callreq += MinRequiredTests(probability(c.
       frequency > 0), alpha);
25             enddo
26             req += max(0, callreq − min(req,1));
27         endif
28     enddo
29     return req;
30 endfunction
```

covers unvisited or only partially visited control-flow partitions within a specification.

$$
X_{C_{\text{entry/exit}}}(S,T) = \begin{aligned}
&\#visits(StartAction\ s| \\
&s.behavior.isKindOf(ResourceDemandingSEFF) \\
&\lor s.behavior.isKindOf(ForkAction)) \\
&+\#visits(StopAction\ s| \\
&s.behavior.isKindOf(ResourceDemandingSEFF) \\
&\lor s.behavior.isKindOf(ForkAction))
\end{aligned}
$$

$$
X_{C_{\text{entry/exit}}}(S) = \begin{aligned}
&2*\#(StartAction\ s| \\
&s.behavior.isKindOf(ResourceDemandingSEFF) \\
&\lor s.behavior.isKindOf(ForkAction))
\end{aligned}
$$

$$
TER_{C_{\text{entry/exit}}} = \frac{X_{C_{\text{entry/exit}}}(S,T)}{X_{C_{\text{entry/exit}}}(S)}
$$

(6.8)

$TER_{C_{\text{entry/exit}}}$ can go down during execution if behaviors are forked. $TER_{C_{\text{entry/exit}}} = 1$ implies that the execution of a test has come to an end. The denominator ensures that each specified StartAction is at least covered once and each execute StartAction is terminated by a StopAction. Palladio ensures that there are only pairs of these actions.

An illustrating example is the specification with the sequence StartAction, Loop(frequency=2: ForkAction(Asynchronous(StartAction, StopAction))), and StopAction. Figure 6.7 shows the values of $TER_{C_{\text{entry/exit}}}$ during a possible execution. T1 shows that uncovered specification are identified correctly. The difference between T4 and T5 shows how the value can go down if new behaviors are forked. T6 shows that the

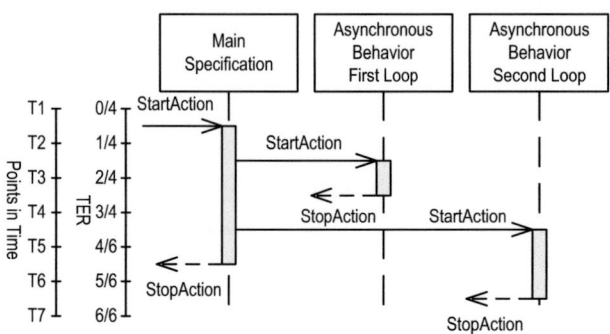

Figure 6.7.: Values of $TER_{C_{entry/exit}}$ for the Illustrating Example.

case is considered that asynchronous behaviors end later than the behavior from which they are started.

$C_{call\ spec}$ and $C_{call\ obs}$ do not subsume $C_{entry/exit}$ because $TER_{C_{entry/exit}}$ are not equal to 1, $TER_{C_{call\ spec}}$ is equal to 1, and $TER_{C_{call\ obs}}$ is equal to 1 for the most simple Palladio specification and no test execution. $C_{entry/exit}$ does not subsume $C_{call\ spec}$ and $C_{call\ obs}$ because $TER_{C_{entry/exit}}$ is equal to 1, $TER_{C_{call\ spec}}$ is not equal to 1, and $TER_{C_{call\ obs}}$ is not equal to 1 for the specification with the sequence StartAction, BranchAction(Guarded-BranchTransition(true, StartAction, StopAction), Guarded-BranchTransition (false, StartAction, InternalAction (ResourceDemand (1)), StopAction), and the StopAction and one test execution.

$|C_{entry/exit}|_L$ is equal to 1 as a valid specification must have exactly one entry point (StartAction) and one exit point (StopAction). Listing 6.3 describes $|C_{entry/exit}|_U$. Lines 3 to 7 reflect that behaviors, which specify the behavior for an operation, must be visited once. Other behaviors do not have to be visited. Line 13 reflects that parameter can be chosen specifically to enter a parameter-dependent branch and the branch only has to be entered if it contains an exit point. Line 15 reflects that probabilistic branches require a number of tests to visit them at least once for a given confidence. The branch only has to be visited if it contains an exit point. Line 19 reflects that a loop must be visited if it contains an exit point. The loop frequency can be probabilistic and the confidence level must be taken into account. Line 23 reflects that each asynchronous forked behavior must be visited at least once, as it contains an exit point. Line 25 reflects that the synchronized forked behaviors can contain exit points. Line 29 reflects that for each entry to a behavior all actions in the behavior are visited once and this offset must be compensated when iterating over all actions.

6.3.2.4. Decision Coverage

This section describes and defines the decision coverage criterion for single decisions in Palladio. This criterion belongs to the criteria with respect to covered nodes and edges.

Decision coverage requires that each decision, at which the control-flow branches, must have evaluated to any possible outcome (true and false) at least once. A formal specification in Z is given in [VB08].

$C_{decision}$ coverage for Palladio is defined taking parametric (Guarded-BranchTransition) and probabilistic (ProbabilisticBranchTransition) control-flow decisions into account. The frequencies of loops and forked behaviors are not regarded as there are no decisions involved for specifications. This criterion uncovers decisions which did not evaluate to all possible outcome at least once.

Listing 6.3: Algorithm for $|C_{entry/exit}|_U$

```
1  function CEntryExitTests(ResourceDemandingBehaviour b,
       Confidence alpha) : int
2      int req;
3      if b hasType ResourceDemandingSEFF
4          req = 1;
5      else
6          req = 0;
7      endif
8      do for Action a in b
9          if a hasType BranchAction
10             int breq = 0;
11             do for BranchCondition c in a
12                 if c hasType GuardedBranchCondition
13                     breq += CEntryExitTests(c.behavior);
14                 else //ProbabilisticBranchCondition
15                     breq = max(breq, MinRequiredTests(c.
       probability, alpha) * CEntryExitTests(c.behavior));
16                 endif
17             enddo
18         elseif a hasType LoopAction
19             breq += CEntryExitTests(a.behavior) *
       MinRequiredTests(probability(a.frequency > 0), alpha)
       ;
20         elseif a hasType ForkAction
21             do for ResourceDemandingBehaviour fb in a
22             if fb.behavior = a
23                 breq += max(1,CEntryExitTests(fb));
24             else
25                 breq += CEntryExitTests(fb);
26             endif
27             enddo
28         endif
29         req += max(0, breq - min(req,1));
30     enddo
31     return req;
32 endfunction
```

$$X_{C_{\text{decision}}}(S, T) = \frac{\#visited(ProbabilisticBranchTransition)}{+\#visited(GuardedBranchTransition)}$$

$$X_{C_{\text{decision}}}(S) = \frac{\#(ProbabilisticBranchTransition)}{+\#(GuardedBranchTransition)} \quad (6.9)$$

$$TERC_{\text{decision}} = \frac{X_{C_{\text{decision}}}(S, T)}{X_{C_{\text{decision}}}(S)}$$

C_{decision} does not subsume $C_{\text{entry / exit}}$ as for the most simple Palladio specification $TERC_{\text{de- cision}} = 1$ without being visited at all. At least one visit is required for $TERC_{\text{entry/exit}}$. C_{decision} does not subsume $C_{\text{call spec}}$ or $C_{\text{call obs}}$ as the specification with the sequence of StartAction, InternalAction with resource, hardware and infrastructure demand, ExternalCallAction, and StopAction does not need to be visited for $TERC_{\text{decision}} = 1$. $C_{\text{entry/exit}}$, $C_{\text{call spec}}$, and $C_{\text{call obs}}$ do not subsume C_{decision} as $TERC_{\text{decision}} \neq 1$ if one of the branches is not taken while the others are equal to 1 for the specification with the sequence StartAction, Branch(ProbabilisticBranchTransition(StartAction, StopAction), ProbabilisticBranchTransition(StartAction, StopAction)), and StopAction and one test execution.

$|C_{\text{decision}}|_L$ equals 0 for the most simple Palladio specification as it does not contain any decisions. Listing 6.5 describes $|C_{\text{decision}}|_U$. Lines 8 and 10 reflect that each branch should be tested at least once. Line 15 reflects that a loop must be covered in order to cover actions contained in its body. Lines 17 to 19 reflect that all forked behaviors must be covered and coverage of each ResourceDemandingBehaviour may require different parameter values.

165

Listing 6.4: Algorithm for $|C_{\text{decision}}|_U$

```
1  function CDecisionTests(ResourceDemandingBehaviour b,
       Confidence alpha) : int
2      int req = 0;
3      do for Action a in b
4          if a hasType BranchAction
5              int breq = 0;
6              do for BranchCondition c in a
7                  if c hasType GuardedBranchCondition
8                      breq += max(1,CDecisionTests(c.
   behavior));
9                  else //ProbabilisticBranchCondition
10                     breq += MinRequiredTests(c.probability
   , alpha) * max(1, CDecisionTests(c.behavior));
11                 endif
12             enddo
13             req += max(0, breq -min(req,1));
14         elseif a hasType LoopAction
15             req += CDecisionTests(a.behavior) *
   MinRequiredTests(probability(a.frequency > 0), alpha)
   ;
16         elseif a hasType ForkAction
17             do for ResourceDemandingBehaviour fb in a
18                 req += CDecisionTests(fb);
19             enddo
20         endif
21     enddo
22     return req;
23  endfunction
```

6.3.2.5. Probabilistic Decision Coverage

This section describes and defines the probabilistic decision coverage criterion for single decisions in Palladio. This criterion belongs to the criteria with respect to covered nodes and edges. It is the only criterion which requires statistical hypothesis testing due to the probabilistic nature of the decision specification. The definition of the criterion uses the terms introduced in section 2.2. The other criteria do not require to test probabilities, which allows making decisions without statistical testing.

There are no pre-existing definition of probabilistic decisions coverage on the code level, as decisions on this level always depend on parametric values. These values may be generated by a (pseudo) random number generator but the decision itself remains deterministic.

$C_\text{probabilistic decision}$ coverage for Palladio is defined for probabilistic control-flow decisions and is based on statistical hypothesis testing. It focusses on the aspect if all probabilistic decisions have been visited often enough during an execution to reason about the accuracy of the branch probability taking the validation limits on hypothesis testing into account. These limits can be provided with the HypothesisBasedSimpleTestPlan element of a TBValidationQuality (see figure 6.5).

In Palladio, probabilistic decisions can be made within BranchAction elements. Each single possible outcome of a decision is modeled with a ProbabilisticBranchTransition. Each transition has a probability and all probabilities for the same BranchAction sum up to 1. Statistical hypothesis testing is used for the probabilities. The tested hypothesis are $H_0 : p_\text{impl} = p_\text{spec}$ and $H_1 : p_\text{impl} \neq p_\text{spec}$, where p_impl denotes the behavior of the implementation and p_spec denotes the probability of the specification. This maps to a Bernoulli experiment, where a success denotes taking the branch and a failure not taking the branch. The sample size n is calculated based on the significance level α and the power of at least $1 - \beta$ against given alternatives. The alternatives are created based on the maximal allowed deviations in the accuracy statements for the decision. The resulting thresholds for lower and upper probability values are denoted p_lt and p_ut with $p_\text{lt} < p_\text{spec} < p_\text{ut}$. If one of the threshold probabilities lies outside the interval $[0,1]$ then p_spec is only compared with the other threshold. If both threshold probabilities lie outside the interval $[0,1]$ then either 0 or 1 is used as threshold, depending which is farther away from p_spec. The statistic must explicitly lie within or outside the confidence interval $[F^{-1}(\alpha/2, n, p_\text{spec}), F^{-1}(1 - \alpha/2, n, p_\text{spec})]$ and outside the intervals if the probability alternatives are considered. The sample size is the smallest n for which $F^{-1}(1 - \beta, n, p_\text{ut}) + 1 <= F^{-1}(\alpha/2, n, p_\text{spec})$ and

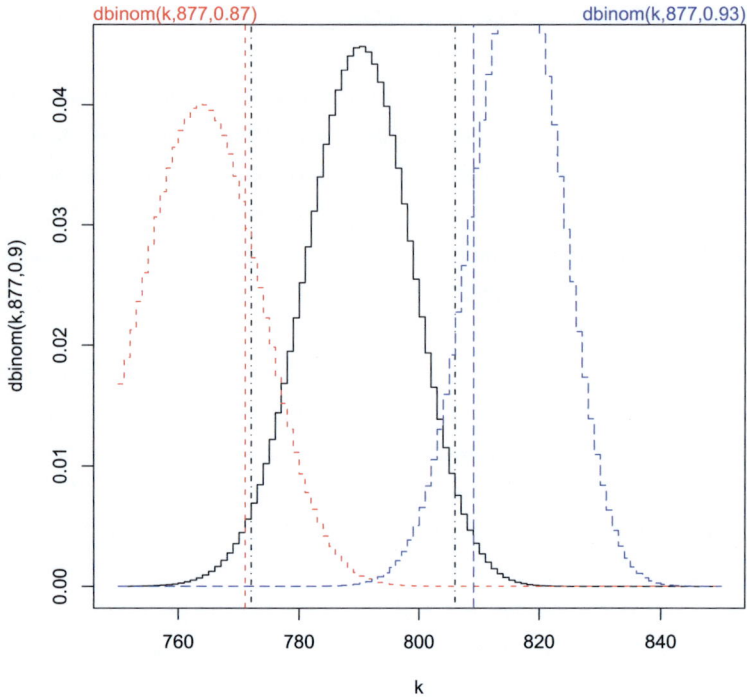

The distribution for p_{lt} is shown with short red dashes. The 0.8-quantile is marked with a vertical line. The distribution for p_{spec} is shown with a solid black line. The 0.025- and 0.975-quantile are marked with vertical lines. The distribution for p_{ut} is shown with blue long dashes. The 0.2-quantile is marked with a vertical line.

Figure 6.8.: Example Statistic Distribution Functions and Acceptance Thresholds

$F^{-1}(1 - \alpha/2, n, p_{\text{spec}}) + 1 <= F^{-1}(\beta, n, p_{\text{ut}})$ hold. Adding 1 to the boundaries ensures the definite assignment for values on the interval thresholds.

Figure 6.8 visualizes the distribution functions for the statistic value k, p_{spec} equal to 0.9, an allowed absolute deviation of 3%, α equal to 0.05, and β equal to 0.2. The statistic is with 80% probability lower than the red dashed vertical line on the left if the probability would be p_{lt}. The statistic is with 95% probability between the black solid vertical lines if the probability would be p_{spec}. The statistic is with 80% probability high than the blue long dashed vertical line if the probability would be p_{ut}. The distance of 1 making the assignment definite can be seen between the red dashed and black solid line at the left side. This positive distance does not exists for n less than 877. Hence, the sound evaluation of the hypothesis if specified and implemented probability are equal requires at least a sample size of n equal to 877. If the BranchAction containing the ProbabilisticBranchTransition with $p_{transition[1]}$ equal to 0.9 has two other transitions with probabilities of $p_{transition[2]}$ equal to 0.01 and $p_{transition[3]}$ equal to 0.09, then the BranchAction must be visited at least $\max\{n(transition[1]), n(transition[2]), n(transition[3])\} = \max\{877, 197, 812\} = 877$ times to reason about all transitions. This results in the following TER definition.

$$X_{C_{\text{probabilistic decision}}}(S,T) =$$

$$sum(ProbabilisticBranchTransition\ t$$
$$|\#visits(t.branchAction) >= n(t)$$
$$\wedge F^{-1}(\alpha/2, \#visits(t), t.probability) \leq \#visits(t)$$
$$\wedge \#visits(t) \leq F^{-1}(1 - \alpha/2, \#visits(t), t.probability))$$
$$+ sum(BranchAction\ b$$
$$|b.transition.typeOf(ProbabilisticBranchTransition)$$
$$\wedge \#visits(b) \geq max\{n(b.transition)\})$$

$$X_{C_{\text{probabilistic decision}}}(S) =$$

$$\#(ProbabilisticBranchTransition)$$
$$+ \#(BranchAction\ b$$
$$|b.transition.typeOf(ProbabilisticBranchTransition))$$

$$TER_{C_{\text{probabilistic decision}}} = \frac{X_{C_{\text{probabilistic decision}}}(S,T)}{X_{C_{\text{probabilistic decision}}}(S)}$$

$$(6.10)$$

$C_{\text{probabilistic decision}}$ does not subsume $C_{\text{entry / exit}}$ as for the most simple Palladio specification $TER_{C_{\text{probabilistic decision}}}$ equals 1 without being visited at all. At least one visit is required for $TER_{C_{\text{entry/exit}}}$. $C_{\text{probabilistic decision}}$ does not subsume $C_{\text{call spec}}$ or $C_{\text{call obs}}$ as the specification with the sequence of StartAction, InternalAction with resource, hardware and infrastructure demand, `ExternalCallAction`, and `StopAction` does not need to be visited for $TER_{C_{\text{probabilistic decision}}}$ becoming equal to 1. $C_{\text{probabilistic decision}}$ does not subsume C_{decision} as the Palladio specifications with the sequence of `StartAction, BranchAction(GuardedBranchTransition( Start-Action, StopAction), GuardedBranchTransition( StartAction, StopAction )`, and the `StopAction` does not need to be visited for $TER_{C_{\text{probabilistic decision}}}$ becoming equal to 1. $C_{\text{entry/exit}}$, $C_{\text{call spec}}$, $C_{\text{call obs}}$, and C_{decision} do not subsume $C_{\text{probabilistic decision}}$ as $TER_{C_{\text{probabilistic decision}}}$ is not equal to 1 if both branches of the sequence `StartAction, BranchAction( ProbabilisticBranchTransition( StartAction, StopAction), ProbabilisticBranchTransition( StartAction, StopAction))`, `StopAction` have been visited once but `n(Probabilisic-BranchTransition)` is not reached for one of the branches.

$|C_{\text{probabilistic decision}}|_L$ equals 0 for the most simple Palladio specification as it does not contain any decisions. Listing **??** describes $|C_{\text{probabilistic decision}}|_U$. Line 8 reflects that deterministic branches have to be visited only in case they contain a probabilistic branch. Line 10 reflects that each probabilistic branch must be visited at least with a sample size appropriate to the specified probability. The sample size is the maximum of the previously required visits, the sample size for the specified probability, and the sample size for the specified probability with the additional restriction that there are least `CProbabilisticDecisionTests(c.behavior)` successful visits in case the probability is within the accuracy limits. The maximum function also ensures that the transition requiring the most effort sets the required visits for the `BranchAction`. Line 15 reflects that a loop must be covered in order to cover actions contained in its body. Lines 17 to 19 reflect that all forked behaviors must be covered and coverage of each `ResourceDemandingBehaviour` may require different parameter values and the required number must be added for each behavior.

Listing 6.5: Algorithm for $|C_{\text{decision}}|_U$

```
1  function CProbabilisticDecisionTests(
       ResourceDemandingBehaviour b, Confidence alpha) : int
2      int req = 0;
3      do for Action a in b
4          if a hasType BranchAction
5              int breq = 0;
6              do for BranchCondition c in a
7                  if c hasType GuardedBranchCondition
8                      breq += CProbabilisticDecisionTests(c.
       behavior);
9                  else // ProbabilisticBranchCondition
10                     breq = max(breq, n(c), n(
       CProbabilisticDecisionTests(c.behavior),c));
11                 endif
12             enddo
13             req += max(0, breq -min(req,1));
14         elseif a hasType LoopAction
15             req += CProbabilisticDecisionTests(a.behavior)
       * MinRequiredTests(probability(a.frequency > 0),
       alpha);
16         elseif a hasType ForkAction
17             do for ResourceDemandingBehaviour fb in a
18                 req += CProbabilisticDecisionTests(fb);
19             enddo
20         endif
21     enddo
22     return req;
23 endfunction
```

6.3.2.6. Statement Coverage

This section describes and defines the action coverage criterion for Palladio. This criterion belongs to the criteria with respect to covered nodes and edges.

Statement coverage requires that all code statements are visited. A formal specification in Z is available in [VB08].

C_{action} coverage for Palladio defines that each action contained in a ResourceDemandingBehaviour must be visited. This criterion allows to detect unused actions and unvisited areas within Palladio specifications.

$$X_{C_{\text{action}}}(S,T) = \#visited(AbstractAction)$$

$$X_{C_{\text{action}}}(S) = \#(AbstractAction) \tag{6.11}$$

$$TER_{C_{\text{action}}} = \frac{X_{C_{\text{action}}}(S,T)}{X_{C_{\text{action}}}(S)}$$

C_{action} subsumes $C_{\text{entry/exit}}$ as a specification must at least have the two actions StartAction and StopAction and both are coved if the path from the single entry to the single exit is tested. C_{action} subsumes $C_{\text{call spec}}$ as calls can only be part of Actions and cannot be contained otherwise in specifications. It does not subsume $C_{\text{call obs}}$ as it does not check if specifications contain calls with a frequency greater than 0. $C_{\text{entry/exit}}$, $C_{\text{call spec}}$, and $C_{\text{call obs}}$ do not subsume C_{action} because the specification with the sequence StartAction, Branch(ProbabilisticBranchTransition(StartAction, StopAction), ProbabilisticBranchTransition(StartAction, StopAction)), and StopAction shows $TER_{C_{\text{call obs}}} = TER_{C_{\text{call spec}}} = TER_{C_{\text{entry/exit}}}$ equals 1 after one visit but $TER_{C_{\text{action}}}$ is not equal to 1. C_{action} subsumes C_{decision} as each decision has exactly one ResourceDemandingBehaviour and each ResourceDemandingBehaviour must at least contain a StartAction and StopAction.

C_{decision} does not subsume C_{action} as $TER_{C_{\text{decision}}}$ equals 1 for the specification StartAction and subsequent StopAction but $TER_{C_{\text{action}}}$ equals 0 if the specification is not visited. C_{action} does not subsume $C_{\text{probabilistic decision}}$ as $TER_{C_{\text{probabilistic decision}}}$ is not equal to 1 if all actions of the sequence Start-Action, BranchAction(ProbabilisticBranchTransition(StartAction, StopAction), ProbabilisticBranchTransition(StartAction, StopAction)), StopAction have been visited at least once but n(ProbabilisicBranchTransition) is not reached for one of

173

the branches. $C_{\text{probabilistic decision}}$ does not subsume C_{action} as for the most simple Palladio specification $TER_{C_{\text{probabilistic decision}}}$ equals 1 without being visited at all. At least one visit is required for $TER_{C_{\text{action}}}$

$|C_{\text{action}}|_L$ equals 1 as a valid specification must have at least a StartAction and a StopAction. $|C_{\text{action}}|_U$ is given in listing 6.6. Lines 5 to 13 reflect that actions in each branch must be covered. Line 15 reflects that actions in the body of a loop must be covered. Lines 21 to 23 reflect that each action in a forked behavior must be covered at least once but one test is sufficient to test a sequence of actions which have no control-flow alternative.

6.3.2.7. Branch Coverage

This section describes and defines the branch coverage criterion for Palladio. This criterion belongs to the criteria with respect to covered nodes and edges.

Branch coverage requires that all branches in the control-flow have been visited. A formal specification in Z is given in [VB08].

C_{branch} coverage for Palladio is defined to cover all branches, including forked behaviors. As there is exactly one way to enter a ResourceDemandingBehaviour and ResourceDemandingBehaviour are only used within BranchAction, LoopAction, and ForkAction, it is sufficient to check that every target is visited at least once. This criterion allows to detect unvisited branches in the control-flow of specifications.

Listing 6.6: Algorithm for $|C_{\text{action}}|_U$

```
1  function CActionTests(ResourceDemandingBehaviour b,
       Confidence alpha) : int
2      int req = 0;
3      do for Action a in b
4          if a hasType BranchAction
5              int breq = 0;
6              do for BranchCondition c in a
7                  if c hasType GuardedBranchCondition
8                      breq += CActionTests(c.behavior);
9                  else //ProbabilisticBranchCondition
10                     breq += CActionTests(c.behavior) *
       MinRequiredTests(c.probability, alpha);
11                 endif
12             enddo
13             req += max(0, breq -min(req,1));
14         elseif a hasType LoopAction
15             req += max(0,CActionTests(a.behavior) *
       MinRequiredTests(probability(a.frequency > 0), alpha)
       -min(req,1));
16         elseif a hasType ForkAction
17             do for ResourceDemandingBehaviour fb in a
18                 req += max(0,CActionTests(fb) - min(req,1)
       );
19             enddo
20         endif
21         if req = 0
22             req = 1;
23         endif
24     enddo
25     return req;
26 endfunction
```

$$X_{C_{\text{branch}}}(S,T) = \#visited(ResourceDemandingBehaviour)$$

$$X_{C_{\text{branch}}}(S) = \#(ResourceDemandingBehaviour) \qquad (6.12)$$

$$TER_{C_{\text{branch}}} = \frac{X_{C_{\text{branch}}}(S,T)}{X_{C_{\text{branch}}}(S)}$$

Table 6.2.: Example for Possible Evaluations for Boolean Condition $c(a_1, a_2) = a_1 \wedge a_2$

	(a) Full Evaluation			(b) Short-Circuit Evaluation	
a_1	a_2	$c(a_1, a_2)$	a_1	a_2	$c(a_1, a_2)$
false	false	false	false	–	false
false	true	false	true	false	false
true	false	false	true	true	true
true	true	true			

Control-flow restrictions lead to C_{branch} subsuming C_{action} and vice versa: Visiting all actions means all ResourceDemandingBehaviour have been visited. If all ResourceDemandingBehaviour have been visited, all branches have been visited. ResourceDemandingBehaviour must always contain at least one StartAction and StopAction, which means there is no branch without an action and the criteria are equivalent with respect to subsumption. This equivalence with respect to subsumption implies that C_{branch} has the same subsumption relations to $C_{call\ spec}$, $C_{call\ obs}$, $C_{entry/exit}$, $C_{decision}$, and $C_{probabilistic\ decision}$ as C_{action}. See section 6.3.2.6 for details.

$|C_{branch}|_L$ equals 1 for the most simple Palladio specification. Listing 6.6 describes $|C_{branch}|_U$ as it is equal to $|C_{action}|_U$.

6.3.2.8. Simple Condition Coverage

This section describes and defines the simple condition coverage criterion for Palladio. This criterion belongs to the criteria with respect to the structure of decisions.

Simple condition coverage requires that each evaluated atomic condition of a decision must have had all outcomes at least once (true and false) and that each atomic condition must be evaluated at least once. This means that simple condition coverage differs if full or short-circuit evaluation is applied. For example, complete coverage of the condition $c = (i > 0) \wedge (j > 0)$ with the atoms $a_1 = (i > 0)$ and $a_2 = (j > 0)$ can be achieved with the boolean value pairs $(false, true)$ and $(true, false)$ for full evaluation (see 6.2(a)) but short-circuit evaluation requires testing $(false, -), (true, false)$, and $(true, true)$ (see 6.2(b)). The good thing is that the number of potential evaluations is limited by $n + 1$ for short-circuit evaluations instead of exponentially (2^n) [AOH03], where n is the number of atoms. This coverage is shown to subsume branch coverage in [Lig09, p. 95]. Common conditions leading to control-flow decisions are related to branches or loops.

$C_{simple\ condition}$ coverage for Palladio is defined taking probabilistic branches and loop frequency specifications into account. Each decision of a branch must be visited at least once and the body of each loop must be executed at least once. Additionally, each sequence of actions must be covered at least once in order to to cover decision-free `ResourceDemandingBehaviour`. This allows to check the structural aspects of performance-relevant decisions in the control-flow.

$$c \text{ boolean condition of atoms}$$

$$atoms(c) = (a_1, \ldots, a_n), a_i \in \{true, false\} \text{ for } i \in 1, \ldots, n$$

$$eval(i, a_1, \ldots, a_n, c) = \begin{cases} 1 & \text{if } a_i \text{ is evaluated for } c \\ 0 & else \end{cases}$$

$$visited(c, a_1, \ldots, a_n) : \text{ condition } c \text{ was visited}$$

$$\text{leading to the given evaluation of atoms.}$$

$$simple(c, i) = \begin{cases} 1 & \begin{aligned} & (\ visited(c, a_1, \ldots, a_n) \\ & \wedge eval(i, a_1, \ldots, a_n, c) = 1 \wedge a_i = false) \\ & \wedge (visited(c, a_1, \ldots, a_n) \\ & \wedge eval(i, a_1, \ldots, a_n, c) = 1 \wedge a_i = true\ ) \end{aligned} \\ 0 & else \end{cases}$$

$$simple(c) = \frac{1}{n} \sum_{i=1}^{n} simple(c, i)$$

$$X_{C_{\text{simple condition}}}(S, T) =$$

$$\#visited(ResourceDemandingBehaviour)$$

$$+ \#visited(LoopAction\ l | l.frequency > 0)$$

$$+ \#visited(ProbabilisticBranchTransition)$$

$$+ simple(GuardedBranchTransition.condition\ c)$$

$$X_{C_{\text{simple condition}}}(S) =$$

$$\#(ResourceDemandingBehaviour)$$
$$+\#(LoopAction)$$
$$+\#(ProbabilisticBranchTransition)$$
$$+|atoms(GuardedBranchTransition.condition\ c)|$$

$$TERC_{\text{simple condition}} = \frac{X_{C_{\text{simple condition}}}(S,T)}{X_{C_{\text{simple condition}}}(S)} \qquad (6.13)$$

$C_{\text{simple condition}}$ subsumes C_{branch}. It ensures that the body of a loop is visited. All loops will terminate. If all branch transitions have been taken and each loop has been executed at least once then all simple conditions have been visited. Decision-free specification parts are covered by both due to `ResourceDemandingBehaviour` coverage. C_{branch} does not subsume $C_{\text{simple condition}}$ as the structure of conditions is not addressed by the former. If the same branch contains two `GuardedBranchTransition`, one with the exemplary condition $c = (i > 0) \wedge (j > 0)$ and one with $\neg c$, complete branch coverage can be achieved for example by testing the value pairs $(true, true)$ and $(true, false)$. Complete simple condition coverage is not achieved by these value pairs. $C_{\text{simple condition}}$ subsumes C_{action} but not the other way round because C_{action} and C_{branch} are equal with respect to subsumption. $C_{\text{simple condition}}$ does not subsume $C_{\text{call obs}}$. The specification with the sequence `StartAction`, `InternalAction(` `ParametricResourceDemand( CPU: 0))`, `StopAction` has a TER $C_{\text{simple condition}}$ of 1 but $TERC_{\text{call obs}}$ equals 0 after one test execution. $C_{\text{call obs}}$ does not subsume $C_{\text{simple condition}}$. The specification with the sequence `StartAction, GuardedBranchAction( GuardedBranchTransition` `(c<0: StartAction, StopAction), GuardedBranchTransition(` `c>=0: StartAction, StopAction)), StopAction` has a $TERC_{\text{call obs}}$

of 1 but $TER_{C_{\text{simple condition}}}$ is not equal to 1 after one single test execution. $C_{\text{simple condition}}$ does not subsume $C_{\text{probabilistic decision}}$ as $TER_{C_{\text{probabilistic decision}}}$ is not equal to 1 if both branches of the sequence StartAction, BranchAction(ProbabilisticBranchTransition(StartAction, StopAction), ProbabilisticBranchTransition(StartAction, StopAction)), StopAction have been visited once but n(Probabilisic-BranchTransition) is not reached for one of the branches. $C_{\text{probabilistic decision}}$ does not subsume $C_{\text{simple condition}}$ as $TER_{C_{\text{probabilistic decision}}}$ equals 1 for the sequence with two GuardedBranchTransition and the conditions $c < 0$ and $c > 0$ shown above without being visited at all. At least two visits are required for $C_{\text{simple condition}}$. $C_{\text{simple condition}}$ subsumes $C_{\text{call spec}}$, $C_{\text{entry/exit}}$, and C_{decision} but not the other way around because its relation to C_{action} and the relation of C_{action} to these criteria.

$|C_{\text{simple condition}}|_L$ equals 1 for the most simple Palladio specification. $|C_{\text{simple condition}}|_U$ is given in listing 6.7. Line 8 reflects the complexity of $n + 1$ [AOH03] where n is the number of atoms of a condition c denoted with atoms(c). Lines 10, 13, and 15 reflect that each probabilistic branch and each loop must be covered at least once. Line 18 reflects that each forked behavior must be covered as well.

6.3.2.9. Condition / Decision Coverage

This section describes and defines the condition / decision coverage criterion for Palladio. This criterion belongs to the criteria with respect to the structure of decisions.

Condition / decision coverage extends simple condition coverage and additionally requires that each evaluated condition (atomic or composed) must have had all possible outcomes at least once.

$C_{\text{condition / decision}}$ coverage for Palladio is equal to simple coverage as short-circuit evaluation ensures decision coverage. Hence, it allows to

Listing 6.7: Algorithm for $|C_{\text{simple condition}}|_U$

```
1  function CSimpleConditionTests(ResourceDemandingBehaviour
       b, Confidence alpha) : int
2      int req = 0;
3      do for Action a in b
4          if a hasType BranchAction
5              int breq = 0;
6              do for BranchCondition c in a
7                  if c hasType GuardedBranchCondition
8                      breq += max(atoms(c)+1,
   CSimpleConditionTests(c.behavior));
9                  else //ProbabilisticBranchCondition
10                     breq += max(1,CSimpleConditionTests(c.
   behavior)) * MinRequiredTests(c.probability, alpha);
11                 endif
12             enddo
13             req += max(0, breq-min(req,1));
14         elseif a hasType LoopAction
15             req += max(0,max(1,CSimpleConditionTests(a.
   behavior)) * MinRequiredTests(probability(a.frequency
   > 0), alpha) -min(req,1));
16         elseif a hasType ForkAction
17             do for ResourceDemandingBehaviour fb in a
18                 req += max(0,CSimpleConditionTests(fb) -
   min(req,1));
19             enddo
20         endif
21         if req = 0
22             req = 1;
23         endif
24     enddo
25     return req;
26  endfunction
```

check the structural aspects of performance-relevant decisions as well as implicit control-flow decisions.

$$TER_{C_{\text{condition / decision}}} = TER_{C_{\text{simple condition}}} \qquad (6.14)$$

$C_{\text{condition / decision}}$ is identical to $C_{\text{simple condition}}$ as short-circuit evaluation ensures all possible outcomes of decisions have been evaluated if simple condition coverage is achieved. All relations of $C_{\text{simple condition}}$ hold for $C_{\text{condition / decision}}$.

$|C_{\text{condition / decision}}|_L$ equals 1 for the most simple Palladio specification. $|C_{\text{condition / decision}}|_U$ equals $|C_{\text{simple condition}}|_U$ and is hence available in listing 6.7.

6.3.2.10. minimal multiple condition

This section describes and defines the minimal multiple coverage criterion for Palladio. This criterion belongs to the criteria with respect to the structure of decisions.

Minimal multiple condition coverage extends condition / decision coverage and additionally requires that each composed boolean condition must be evaluated to all possible outcomes at least once. This criterion focuses on the logical structure of the decision. A formal specification in Z is given in [VB08] denoted as Multiple Condition Coverage.

$C_{\text{minimal multiple}}$ coverage for Palladio is taking the whole structure of decisions into account. Short-circuit evaluation means that $C_{\text{simple condition}}$ also covers composed conditions and both criteria are identical. This criterion uncovers unevaluated outcomes of the logical structure of decisions and hints on invariants in the decision.

In the following, the definition for the TER is provided. It uses the additional function *terms* to check which conditions in a composition are *true* or *false*. The function $eval_t$ allows to check if a condition in the composition is evaluated in order to determine the value of the composition. The function $visited_t$ allows to check if a condition was visited while the evaluation of the composed conditions would have been as specified as parameter. The function $simple_t(c,i)$ checks if a composed condition was evaluated at least once with the result of being $true$ as well as $false$. The function $simple_t(c)$ checks if this holds for all composed conditions.

$$terms(c) = (b_1,\ldots,b_n), b_i \in \{true, false\} \text{ for } i \in 1,\ldots,n$$

$$eval_t(i,b_1,\ldots,b_n,c) = \begin{cases} 1 & \text{if } b_i \text{ is evaluated for } c \\ 0 & else \end{cases}$$

$$visited_t(c,b_1,\ldots,b_n) : \text{ condition c was visited}$$
$$\text{leading to the given evaluation of terms.}$$

$$simple_t(c,i) = \begin{cases} 1 & \begin{aligned} &(visited_t(c,b_1,\ldots,b_n) \\ &\wedge eval_t(i,b_1,\ldots,b_n,c) = 1 \wedge b_i = false) \\ &\wedge (visited_t(c,b_1,\ldots,b_n) \\ &\wedge eval_t(i,b_1,\ldots,b_n,c) = 1 \wedge b_i = true) \end{aligned} \\ 0 & else \end{cases}$$

$$simple_t(c) = \frac{1}{n}\sum_{i=1}^{n} simple_t(c,i)$$

$$XC_{\text{minimal multiple}}(S,T) = \begin{aligned} &\#visited(ResourceDemandingBehaviour) \\ &+\#visited(LoopAction\ l|l.frequency > 0) \\ &+\#visited(ProbabilisticBranchTransition) \\ &+simple_t(GuardedBranchTransition.condition\ c) \end{aligned}$$

$$X_{C_{\text{minimal multiple}}}(S) = \begin{aligned} &\#(ResourceDemandingBehaviour)\\ &+\#(LoopAction)\\ &+\#(ProbabilisticBranchTransition)\\ &+|terms_t(GuardedBranchTransition.condition\ c)| \end{aligned}$$

$$TERC_{\text{minimal multiple}} = \frac{X_{C_{\text{minimal multiple}}}(S,T)}{X_{C_{\text{minimal multiple}}}(S)}$$

$$(6.15)$$

$C_{\text{minimal multiple}}$ is identical to $C_{\text{simple condition}}$ because of short-circuit evaluation and although it additionally considers composed conditions within a decision and not only atoms and the final decision. All relations of $C_{\text{simple condition}}$ hold for $C_{\text{minimal multiple}}$.

$|C_{\text{minimal multiple}}|_L$ equals 1 for the most simple Palladio specification. $|C_{\text{minimal multiple}}|_U$ equals $|C_{\text{simple condition}}|_U$ and is hence available in listing 6.7.

6.3.2.11. Modified Condition / Decision Coverage

This section describes and defines the Modified Condition / Decision Coverage (MCDC) coverage criterion for Palladio. This criterion belongs to the criteria with respect to the structure of decisions.

MCDC for short-circuit evaluations requires that each atomic condition must have been evaluated to all possible outcomes and that its outcome influences the overall decision to have all possible outcomes. This means that tests for an atomic condition must have equal values for the other evaluated atomic conditions (see [Lig09, CM94, p. 106] for more details). A formal specification in Z is given in [VB08], a mathematical definition in [AOH03] denoted as Correlated Active Clause Coverage.

$C_{\text{modified condition / decision}}$ coverage for Palladio is focusing on the logical structure of the decisions and that there are no unnecessary conditions. The values of unevaluated conditions are allowed to change, analogous to Masking Modified Condition Decision Coverage.

$$TER_{C_{\text{modified condition / decision}}} = TER_{C_{\text{simple condition}}} \qquad (6.16)$$

$C_{\text{modified condition / decision}}$ subsumes $C_{\text{minimal multiple}}$ as the consequence of showing the influence of each evaluated atomic condition on the overall decision also forces composed conditions to be evaluated and have all possible outcomes at least once. $C_{\text{minimal multiple}}$ subsumes $C_{\text{modified condition / decision}}$ because each atomic condition must be evaluated at least once to true and false and it is only evaluated if it influences the composed conditions and the decision itself due to short-circuit evaluation. $C_{\text{modified condition / decision}}$ does not subsume $C_{\text{call obs}}$ or $C_{\text{probabilistic decision}}$ or the other way around for the same reason as $C_{\text{simple condition}}$. $C_{\text{modified condition / decision}}$ subsumes $C_{\text{call spec}}, C_{\text{entry/exit}}, C_{\text{decision}}, C_{\text{action}}$ and C_{branch} but not the other way around because its relation to $C_{\text{minimal multiple}}$ and the relations of $C_{\text{minimal multiple}}$ to these criteria.

$|C_{\text{modified condition / decision}}|_L$ equals 1 for the most simple possible Palladio specification. The upper bound $|C_{\text{modified condition / decision}}|_U$ is equal to $|C_{\text{simple condition}}|_U$ and hence described in listing 6.7.

6.3.2.12. Reinforced Condition / Decision Coverage

This section describes and defines the Reinforced Condition / Decision Coverage (RCDC) coverage criterion for Palladio. This criterion belongs to the criteria with respect to the structure of decisions.

RCDC refines MCDC and additionally requires that it should be shown (if possible) that the change of an atomic condition does not change the decision output. This should be shown for a resulting value of true and false. Details on the criterion and a formal definition using Z are available in [VB08].

185

$C_{\text{reinforced condition / decision}}$ coverage for Palladio is extending MCDC in order to cover cases in which the decision should not vary if an atomic condition varies. However, this is not always feasible and hard to determine automatically. An example is the decision $d(b_1, b_2) = b_1 \vee b_2$ and how if can be kept to an overall value of $false$.

In the following, the definition for the TER is provided. It uses the additional function $stay_t^x$ to check if each composed condition would have both truth values although the composition truth value stays the same.

$$
stay_t^x(c, i) =
\begin{cases}
1 &
\begin{aligned}
& (visited_t(c, b_1, \ldots, b_n) \\
& \wedge terms(c) = x \\
& \wedge b_i = false \\
& \wedge eval_t(i, b_1, \ldots, b_n, c) = 0)) \\
& \wedge (visited_t(c, b_1, \ldots, b_n) \\
& \wedge terms(c) = x \\
& \wedge (b_i = true \\
& \wedge eval_t(i, b_1, \ldots, b_n, c) = 0)))
\end{aligned} \\
\\
0 & else
\end{cases}
$$

$$
stay_t^x(c) = \frac{1}{n} \sum_{i=1}^{n} stay_t^x(c, i)
$$

$$XC_{\text{reinforced condition / decision}}(S,T) =$$

$$\#visited(ResourceDemandingBehaviour)$$
$$+\#visited(LoopAction\ l|l.frequency > 0)$$
$$+\#visited(ProbabilisticBranchTransition)$$
$$+simple_t(GuardedBranchTransition.condition\ c)$$
$$+stay_t^{true}(GuardedBranchTransition.condition\ c)$$
$$+stay_t^{false}(GuardedBranchTransition.condition\ c)$$

$$XC_{\text{reinforced condition / decision}}(S) =$$

$$\#(ResourceDemandingBehaviour)$$
$$+\#(LoopAction)$$
$$+\#(ProbabilisticBranchTransition)$$
$$+3*|terms_t(GuardedBranchTransition.condition\ c)|$$

$$TER_{\text{reinforced condition / decision}} = \frac{XC_{\text{reinforced condition / decision}}(S,T)}{XC_{\text{reinforced condition / decision}}(S)} \qquad (6.17)$$

$C_{\text{reinforced condition / decision}}$ subsumes $C_{\text{modified condition / decision}}$ due to the refinement relation. $C_{\text{modified condition / decision}}$ does not subsume $C_{\text{reinforced condition / decision}}$ as MCDC does not require to test that the decision stays the same although an atomic condition is changed. $C_{\text{reinforced condition / decision}}$ does not subsume $C_{\text{call obs}}$ or $C_{\text{probabilistic decision}}$ or the other way around for the same reason as $C_{\text{simple condition}}$. $C_{\text{reinforced condition / decision}}$ subsumes $C_{\text{call spec}}, C_{\text{entry/exit}}, C_{\text{decision}}, C_{\text{action}}, C_{\text{branch}}, C_{\text{simple condition}}, C_{\text{condition / decision}}$, and $C_{\text{minimal multiple}}$ but not the other way around. This is the case because its relation to $C_{\text{modified condition / decision}}$ and the relations of $C_{\text{modified condition / decision}}$ to these criteria.

$|C_{\text{reinforced condition / decision}}|_L$ equals 1 for the most simple Palladio specification. The upper bound $|C_{\text{reinforced condition / decision}}|_U$ is based on the algorithm for $|C_{\text{simple condition}}|_U$ given in listing 6.7. It only replaces `atoms(c) + 1` in line 8 by `6 * atoms(c)`. This reflects that up to 6 different tests are necessary to check that the decision stays at its truth value while the condition is at least once *true* and at least once *false* and that the decision changes its truth value when the condition changes [KB05, p. 31]. A condition consists of at least one atom and hence `atoms(c)` ≥ 1 and $|C_{\text{reinforced condition / decision}}|_U \geq |C_{\text{simple condition}}|_U$.

The effort estimation of 6 times the number of atomic conditions was determined by Chilenski and Miller in [CM94]. They also found that weak coupling does not cause problems in practice but strong coupling does. A further discussion including effort estimation of test set size and number of potential test sets for MCDC variants and RCDC is provided by Kapoor and Bowen in [KB05].

6.3.2.13. Multiple Condition Coverage

This section describes and defines the multiple condition coverage criterion for Palladio. This criterion belongs to the criteria with respect to the structure of decisions.

Multiple condition coverage requires that all combinations of atomic conditions must be tested. If short-circuit evaluation is used then some combinations might be equal to others and not all conditions must be evaluated for a decision. Covering these cases can be used to ensure that the specified behavior matches the intended behavior. Additionally note that dependencies between atomic conditions can render some combinations infeasible. For example $c(b_1, b_2) = b_1 \vee b_2 = (ch ==' 1') \vee (ch ==' 2')$

cannot be covered with the atoms $b_1 = b_2 = true$ and ch representing a character.

$C_{\text{multiple condition}}$ coverage for Palladio is taking all combinations of conditions into account. This criterion uncovers invalid realizations of decisions with respect to the intended and specified behavior, unevaluated outcomes of the logical structure of decisions, and hints on invariants in the decision. This definition assumes independence of atomic conditions which means that if there are infeasible combinations full coverage cannot be achieved.

In the following, the definition for the TER is provided. It uses the additional function *complete* to check if all possible truth values of the composed conditions have been tested.

$$complete(c) = visited(c, false, \ldots, false)$$
$$\land visited(c, true, false, \ldots, false)$$
$$\land visited(c, false, true, false, \ldots, false)$$
$$\land visited(c, true, true, false, \ldots, false)$$
$$\land \ldots \land visited(c, true, \ldots, true)$$

$$XC_{\text{multiple condition}}(S,T) =$$

$$\#visited(LoopAction\ l | l.frequency > 0)$$
$$+\#visited(ProbabilisticBranchTransition)$$
$$+complete(GuardedBranchTransition.condition\ c)$$

$$XC_{\text{multiple condition}}(S) =$$

$$\#(LoopAction)$$
$$+\#(ProbabilisticBranchTransition)$$
$$+2^{|atoms(GuardedBranchTransition.condition\ c)|}$$

$$TER_{C_{\text{multiple condition}}} = \frac{XC_{\text{multiple condition}}(S,T)}{XC_{\text{multiple condition}}(S)} \tag{6.18}$$

$C_{\text{multiple condition}}$ subsumes $C_{\text{reinforced condition / decision}}$ as the coverage of all combinations of atomic conditions includes the subset used for RCDC. $C_{\text{reinforced condition / decision}}$ does not subsume $C_{\text{multiple condition}}$ as is shown in the case study [VB08]. It shows the application of RCDC to a decision and requires only 6 out of $2^{13} = 8192$ test cases required for $C_{\text{multiple condition}}$ coverage. $C_{\text{multiple condition}}$ does not subsume $C_{\text{call obs}}$ or $C_{\text{probabilistic decision}}$ or the other way around for the same reason as $C_{\text{simple condition}}$. $C_{\text{multiple condition}}$ subsumes $C_{\text{call spec}}, C_{\text{entry/exit}}, C_{\text{decision}}, C_{\text{action}}, C_{\text{branch}}, C_{\text{simple condition}},$ $C_{\text{condition / decision}}, C_{\text{minimal multiple}},$ and $C_{\text{modified condition / decision}}$ but not the other way around because its relation to $C_{\text{reinforced condition / decision}}$ and the relations of $C_{\text{reinforced condition / decision}}$ to these criteria.

$|C_{\text{multiple condition}}|_L$ equals 0 for the most simple Palladio specification. The algorithm for $|C_{\text{multiple condition}}|_U$ is based on $|C_{\text{simple condition}}|_U$, which is given in listing 6.7. It only replaces `atoms(c)+1` in line 8 by $2^{\texttt{atoms(c)}}$. This reflects that testing all combinations of potential truth values of a decision requires 2^n test cases if it consists of n independent atomic conditions.

6.3.2.14. Structured Path Testing Coverage

This section describes and defines Structure Path Testing (SPT) coverage criteria for Palladio. These criteria belong to the criteria with respect to the coverage sequence. The definitions have been published in [Gro12b] except for the TER and the relation to non-path coverage criteria.

SPT focuses on covering all possible paths but restricts the number of loop frequencies to a given parameter k in order to reduce the overall number of paths. We use the definition of Ntafos [Nta88] for the criterion:

> Structured path testing requires covering all paths P, where P does not contain any subpath p such that P consists of some subpath β, followed by more than k repetitions of p, followed by some subpath γ. The structured path testing criterion is referred to hereafter as spt^k.

C_{spt}^k coverage for Palladio is defined as follows: Let a be an `Abstract-LoopAction` in S, let a^f denote the frequency f of a, let $\Pi = \{\pi\}$ be the set of paths in S, β be a path from the `StartAction` of S to an action a, γ be a path from a to the `StopAction` of S, and $\circ$ denote the control-flow. Then $\Pi_{\text{spt}}^k = \{\pi_1 : (\pi_1 \in \Pi) \wedge (\pi_1 \notin \{\pi_2 : \pi_2 = \beta \circ a^f \circ \gamma, f > k\})\}$ is the set of control-flow paths in the specification S. C_{spt}^k requires covering Π_{spt}^k. $C_{\text{all paths}}$ covers all possible paths including any number of loop frequencies.

$$X_{C_{\text{spt}}}^n(S,T) = |\{\pi \in \Pi_{\text{spt}}^n : visited(\pi) = true\}|$$

$$X_{C_{\text{spt}}}^n(S) = |\Pi_{\text{spt}}^n|$$

$$TER_{C_{\text{spt}}}^n = \frac{X_{C_{\text{spt}}}^n(S,T)}{X_{C_{\text{spt}}}^n(S)}$$

$$TER_{C_{\text{boundary}}} = TER_{C_{\text{spt}}}^0$$

$$TER_{C_{\text{basic paths}}} = TER_{C_{\text{spt}}}^1$$

$$TER_{C_{\text{all paths}}} = TER_{C_{\text{spt}}}^\infty$$

(6.19)

Subsumption of C_{spt}^n to non-Palladio metrics is shown in [YM09, fig. 3] using definitions of [WHH80]. The subsumption for the Palladio metrics is presented in the following.

C_{boundary} does not subsumes $C_{\text{entry/exit}}$ because forked behaviors can lie within loops, which are not executed for boundary coverage, and their StopAction must be covered for $C_{\text{entry/exit}}$ coverage. C_{boundary} does not subsume $C_{\text{call spec}}$, $C_{\text{call obs}}$, C_{decision}, $C_{\text{probabilistic de- cision}}$, C_{action}, C_{branch}, or any of the structure of decision criteria as call specifications, actions, and branches with decisions can lie within the body of loops, which do no have to be executed for C_{boundary}. $C_{\text{call spec}}$, $C_{\text{call obs}}$, $C_{\text{entry/exit}}$, C_{decision}, $C_{\text{probabilistic decision}}$, C_{action}, C_{branch}, or any of the structure of decisions criteria do not subsume C_{boundary} because none of them requires covering loops with a frequency of 0.

$C_{\text{basic paths}}$ subsumes C_{branch} by definition. C_{branch} does not subsume $C_{\text{basic paths}}$ as the boundary conditions of loops does not have to be covered. $C_{\text{basic paths}}$ subsumes $C_{\text{call spec}}$, $C_{\text{entry/exit}}$, C_{decision}, and C_{action} but not the other way around because its relation to C_{branch} and the relations of C_{branch} to these criteria. $C_{\text{basic paths}}$ does not subsume $C_{\text{call obs}}$ as it does not check if specifications contain calls with a frequency greater than 0. $C_{\text{call spec}}$ does not subsume $C_{\text{basic paths}}$ because the most simple Palladio specification has a $TER_{C_{\text{call spec}}}$ of 1 and a $TER_{C_{\text{basic paths}}}$ of 0 if the specification is not tested at all. $C_{\text{basic paths}}$ does not subsume $C_{\text{probabilistic decision}}$ as $TER_{C_{\text{probabilistic decision}}}$ is not equal to 1 if both branches of the sequence StartAction, BranchAction(ProbabilisticBranchTransition(StartAction, StopAction), ProbabilisticBranchTransition(StartAction, StopAction)), StopAction have been visited at least once but n(ProbabilisicBranchTransition) is not reached for one of the branches. The criterion $C_{\text{probabilistic decision}}$ does not subsume $C_{\text{basic paths}}$ as for the most simple Palladio specification $TER_{C_{\text{probabilistic decision}}}$ equals 1 without being visited at all. At least one visit is required for $TER_{C_{\text{basic paths}}}$. $C_{\text{basic paths}}$ does not subsume any of the structure of decisions criteria because only the outcome of decisions is relevant for path coverage but not the structure of the decisions. The structure of decisions criteria do not subsume $C_{\text{basic paths}}$ because none of them requires covering loops with a frequency of 0. $C_{\text{basic paths}}$ subsumes C_{boundary} by definition. C_{boundary} does not subsume $C_{\text{basic paths}}$ because it does not require to cover all loops with a frequency of 1.

$C_{\text{spt}}^n, n \in \mathbb{N}$ subsumes C_{spt}^{n-1} by definition. $C_{\text{spt}}^n, n \in \mathbb{N}_0$ does not subsume C_{spt}^{n+1} because a higher value of n additionally requires to cover all loops with a frequency higher than n, which is not included in C_{spt}^n. $C_{\text{spt}}^n, n \in \mathbb{N}$ subsumes $C_{\text{spt}}^m, m \in \mathbb{N}_0, m < n$ because it subsumes $C_{\text{spt}}^{n-1}, n \in \mathbb{N}_0$ and that criterion subsumes $C_{\text{spt}}^m, m \in \mathbb{N}_0, m < n$. The first step of the induction was shown for $C_{\text{basic paths}} = C_{\text{spt}}^1$ in the last paragraph. $C_{\text{spt}}^n, n \in \mathbb{N}$ subsumes C_{branch} by definition. C_{branch} does not subsume $C_{\text{spt}}^n, n \in \mathbb{N}$ as the boundary conditions of loops do not have to be covered. $C_{\text{spt}}^n, n \in \mathbb{N}$ does not subsumes $C_{\text{call obs}}$ and the other way around because of the same reasons as $C_{\text{basic paths}}$. $C_{\text{spt}}^n, n \in \mathbb{N}$ subsumes $C_{\text{call spec}}, C_{\text{entry/exit}}, C_{\text{decision}}$, and C_{action} but not the other way around because its relation to C_{branch} and the relations of C_{branch} to these criteria. $C_{\text{spt}}^n, n \in \mathbb{N}$ does not subsume $C_{\text{probabilistic decision}}$ as $TER_{C_{\text{probabilistic decision}}}$ is not equal to 1 if both branches of the sequence StartAction, BranchAction(ProbabilisticBranchTransition(

StartAction, StopAction), ProbabilisticBranchTransition(
StartAction, StopAction)), StopAction have been visited at least
once but n(ProbabilisicBranchTransition) is not reached for one of
the branches. Covering the two different paths crossing the transitions once
is sufficient for C_{spt}^n being equal to 1. $C_{\text{probabilistic decision}}$ does not subsume
$C_{\text{spt}}^n, n \in \mathbb{N}$ as for the most simple Palladio specification $TERC_{\text{probabilistic decision}}$
equals 1 without being visited at all. At least one visit is required for
$C_{\text{spt}}^n, n \in \mathbb{N}$. $C_{\text{spt}}^n, n \in \mathbb{N}$ does not subsume any of the structure of decisions
criteria because only the outcome of decisions is relevant for path coverage
but not the structure of the decisions. The structure of decisions criteria do
not subsume $C_{\text{spt}}^n, n \in \mathbb{N}$ because none of them requires covering loops with
a frequency of 0.

$C_{\text{all paths}}$ there must be a number c for a terminating program, which covers all paths. $C_{\text{all paths}}$ then has the same subsumption relation as C_{spt}^c by
definition.

$|C_{\text{spt}}^n|_L$ equals 1 for the most simple ResourceDemandingBehaviour,
as the contained sequence has to be covered once. $|C_{\text{spt}}^n|_U$ is given in listing
6.8. The parameter n is the n from C_{spt}^n. Line 2 reflects that each behavior
is tested at least once. The variable areq reflects the number of control-
flow path alternatives for each action. Line 28 reflects that every path,
including all combinations of control-flow path alternatives, restricted by
the number of loop frequencies, is tested. Lines 9 and 11 reflect that each
branch is taken at least once. Lines 16 to 19 reflect that each loop frequency up to n is tested but the body only influences tests with a frequency
greater than 0. Lines 21 to 23 reflect that each forked behavior is tested
and uses an offset of 1 to compensate that contained behaviors are covered
once for each visit of the current action. Line 26 reflects that any action
beside BranchAction, AbstractLoopAction, and ForkAction is tested
but there are no control-flow alternatives.

Listing 6.8: Algorithm for $|C_{\mathrm{spt}}^{n}|_{U}$

```
 1 function CSPTTests(ResourceDemandingBehaviour b,
      Confidence alpha, int n) : int
 2   int req = 1;
 3   do for Action a in b
 4       int areq = 0; //for this action
 5       if a hasType BranchAction
 6           int breq = 0;
 7           do for BranchCondition c in a
 8               if c hasType GuardedBranchCondition
 9                   breq += max(1,CSPTTests(c.behavior));
10               else // ProbabilisticBranchCondition
11                   breq += max(1,CSPTTests(c.behavior)) *
      MinRequiredTests(c.probability, alpha);
12               endif
13           enddo
14           areq += max(0, breq-min(req,1));
15       elseif a hasType AbstractLoopAction
16           areq += max(0,max(1,CSPTTests(a.behavior)) *
      MinRequiredTests(probability(a.frequency = 0), alpha)
      -min(req,1));
17           do for k = 1 to n
18               areq += max(0,max(1,CSPTTests(a.behavior))
      * MinRequiredTests(probability(a.frequency = k),
      alpha)-min(req,1));
19           enddo
20       elseif a hasType ForkAction
21           do for ResourceDemandingBehaviour fb in a
22               areq += max(1,CSPTTests(fb) - min(areq,1))
      ;
23           enddo
24       endif
25       if areq = 0
26           areq = 1;
27       endif
28       req *= areq;
29   enddo
30   return req;
31 endfunction
```

6.3.2.15. Boundary Interior

This section describes and defines the relaxed basic paths coverage criterion for Palladio, which is analogous to boundary interior criteria for programming languages. This criterion belongs to the criteria with respect to the coverage sequence. The definitions have been published in [Gro12b] except for the TER, the relation to non-path coverage criteria, and the complete algorithm.

Covering all possible frequencies for each loop usually requires prohibitive effort. Loop coverage is therefor often restricted to the following equivalence classes: Covering the boundary condition (no execution of the body), the execution of the interior (at least one execution of the body), and at least two executions of the interior. The latter allows uncovering data anomalies due to the transition from the body to the body, e.g. redefining instead of using variables. See [Lig09, p.117ff] for a more detailed discussion on these anomalies. Boundary interior testing is equivalent to structured path testing with k equal to2.

In Palladio, data anomalies cannot occur due to body execution isolation and do not need to be checked. Hence, boundary interior coverage can be reduced to tests with a frequency of 0 and a frequency of 1. This coverage is equivalent to $C_{\text{basic path}}$.

It is not always feasible that a loop is iterated exactly once and the same error equivalence class is covered for any frequency greater or equal to one. We relax the condition of a loop's frequency f of exactly 1 and only require any frequency $f > 0$. This eases testing but does not require covering all paths up to a given frequency for all loops, which would be equivalent to C_{spt}^c for a constant c representing loop frequencies.

$C_{\text{relaxed basic paths}}$ coverage for Palladio is defined as follows based on the definition of the SPT criterion. Let $\Pi_{\text{rbp}} = \{(\pi_{\text{rbp}} \in \Pi_{\text{spt}}^0) \vee (\exists \pi_{\text{spt}} \in \Pi_{\text{spt}}^0 : \pi_{\text{spt}} = \beta \circ a^0 \circ \gamma, \pi_{\text{rbp}} = \beta \circ a^k \circ \gamma, k \geq 1)\}$. $C_{\text{relaxed basic paths}}$ requires covering Π_{rbp}. This allows detecting loops which always or never execute their bodies in the control-flow of behavior specifications while covering sequence effects between paths.

$$XC_{\text{relaxed basic paths}}(S,T) = |\{\pi \in \Pi_{\text{relaxed basic paths}} : visited(\pi) = true\}|$$
$$XC_{\text{relaxed basic paths}}(S) = |\Pi_{\text{relaxed basic paths}}|$$
$$TERC_{\text{relaxed basic paths}} = \frac{XC_{\text{relaxed basic paths}}(S,T)}{XC_{\text{relaxed basic paths}}(S)}$$

$$(6.20)$$

$C_{\text{relaxed basic paths}}$ does not subsume $C_{\text{call obs}}$ and the other way around because of the same reasons as $C_{\text{basic paths}}$. $C_{\text{relaxed basic paths}}$ subsumes $C_{\text{call spec}}$, $C_{\text{entry/exit}}, C_{\text{decision}}$, and C_{action} but not the other way around because its relation to C_{branch} and the relations of C_{branch} to these criteria. $C_{\text{relaxed basic paths}}$ does not subsume $C_{\text{probabilistic decision}}$ for the same reason as the non-relaxed criterion $C_{\text{all paths}}$, which requires a superset of covered paths. The subsumption relations of the superset also show that $C_{\text{probabilistic decision}}$ does not subsume $C_{\text{relaxed basic paths}}$.

$C_{\text{relaxed basic paths}}$ does not subsume any of the structure of decisions criteria because only the outcome of decisions is relevant for path coverage but not the structure of the decisions. The structure of decisions criteria do not subsume $C_{\text{relaxed basic paths}}$ because none of them requires covering loops with a frequency of 0.

$C_{\text{relaxed basic paths}}$ subsumes C_{branch} and C_{boundary} by its definition. C_{branch} does not subsume $C_{\text{relaxed basic paths}}$ as the boundary conditions do not have to be covered for branch coverage. C_{boundary} does not subsume $C_{\text{relaxed basic paths}}$ because it does not ensure that loops are executed at least once. $C_{\text{relaxed basic paths}}$ does not subsume $C_{\text{basic paths}}$ because it does not require that every loop is iterated with a frequency of exactly one. $C_{\text{basic paths}}$ subsumes $C_{\text{relaxed basic paths}}$ if all loops can be executed with a frequency of 1. If a loop is executed with a frequency of at least 2 then the former does not require coverage but the latter does. $C_{\text{spt}}^m, m \in \mathbb{N}_0, m \geq c$ subsumes $C_{\text{relaxed basic paths}}$ for a constant $c \in \mathbb{N}$ which is the supremum of all minimal required loop frequencies to execute a loop at least once. $C_{\text{relaxed basic paths}}$ does not subsume $C_{\text{spt}}^m, m \in \mathbb{N}_0, m \geq c$ as the latter one can mean some of the loops must be covered more than once although there is one loop which is only covered once (hence the c). $C_{\text{relaxed basic paths}}$ only requires covering each loop at least once (and its boundary condition). $C_{\text{all paths}}$ subsumes $C_{\text{relaxed basic paths}}$ because only a subset of all paths is required. $C_{\text{relaxed basic paths}}$ does not subsume $C_{\text{all paths}}$ because the latter one can mean some of the loops must be covered more than once.

$|C_{\text{relaxed basic paths}}|_L$ equals 1 for the most simple ResourceDemanding-Behaviour, as the path from StartAction to StopAction must be covered. $|C_{\text{relaxed basic paths}}|_U$ is given in listing 6.9. The relaxation with respect to C_{spt}^1 and its algorithm is that each loop is iterated at least once but not for any possible number up to a given n. The lines 17-19 of algorithm $|C_{\text{spt}}^n|_U$ in listing 6.8 are replaced. Listing 6.9 shows the resulting algorithm for $|C_{\text{relaxed basic paths}}|_U$.

6.3.2.16. JJ-Paths

This section describes and defines Jump to Jump Paths (JJ-Paths) coverage criteria for Palladio. These criteria belong to the criteria with respect to the coverage sequence.

JJ-Paths coverage is also known as Linear Code Sequence and Jump (LC-SAJ) coverage. This criterion focuses on covering paths between a point which is the target of a control-flow decision and a point involving a subsequent control-flow decision. As a consequence, such a JJ-Path can lie within the overall control-flow of a path π and does not have to start at the beginning of π nor end at π's end. It is defined in [YM09] as:

> An LCSAJ is a sequence of one or more consecutively numbered basic blocks: $p, (p+1), ..., q$, of a code unit, followed by

Listing 6.9: Algorithm for $|C_{\text{relaxed basic paths}}|_U$

```
1  function CRelaxedBasicPathTests(ResourceDemandingBehaviour
       b, Confidence alpha) : int
2      int req = 0;
3      do for Action a in b
4          int areq = 0; //for this action
5          if a hasType BranchAction
6              int breq = 0;
7              do for BranchCondition c in a
8                  if c hasType GuardedBranchCondition
9                      breq += max(1,CRelaxedBasicPathTests(c
   .behavior));
10                 else //ProbabilisticBranchCondition
11                     breq += max(1,CRelaxedBasicPathTests(c
   .behavior)) * MinRequiredTests(c.probability, alpha);
12                 endif
13             enddo
14             areq += max(0, breq-min(req,1));
15         elseif a hasType LoopAction
16             areq += max(0,max(1,CRelaxedBasicPathTests(a.
   behavior)) * MinRequiredTests(probability(a.frequency
   = 0), alpha)-min(req,1));
17             areq += max(0,max(1,CRelaxedBasicPathTests(a.
   behavior)) * MinRequiredTests(probability(a.frequency
   > 0), alpha)-min(req,1));
18         elseif a hasType ForkAction
19             do for ResourceDemandingBehaviour fb in a
20                 areq += max(1,CRelaxedBasicPathTests(fb) -
   min(areq,1));
21             enddo
22         endif
23         if areq = 0
24             areq = 1;
25         endif
26         req *= areq;
27     enddo
28     return req;
29 endfunction
```

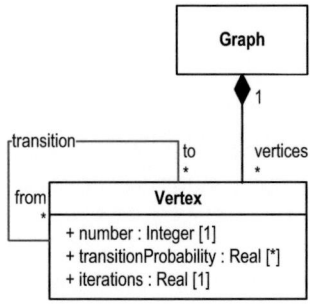

Figure 6.9.: Control-Flow Graph Meta-Model

a control flow jump either out of the code or to a basic block numbered r, where $r \neq (q+1)$, and either $p = 1$ or there exists a control flow jump to block p from some other block in the unit. (A basic block to which such a control flow jump can be made is referred to as a target of the jump.) [...]

Sequences of JJ-Paths of length n are denoted as JJn-Paths ($n \geq 1$, JJ1-Paths=JJ-Paths).

A mapping from Palladio specifications to control-flow graphs is necessary to apply JJ-Paths coverage. We define the following mapping in order to respect the probabilistic as well as parametric dependencies of Palladio specifications while taking actual control-flow decisions into account.

The developed and used meta-model is shown in figure 6.9. The meta-model extends classic control-flow graphs by several properties of vertices. A graph consists of any number of vertices. Each vertex can be be connected to any number of other vertices. The start vertex of the graph is the one with an empty `from` transition relation. It has the `number` 1. The final vertex is the one with an empty `to` transition relation. It has the total number of all vertices in the graph as `number`. The `transitionProbability` specifies the probability of taking the corresponding `to` transition under the assumption that the parameters allow taking the transition. It is necessary

Listing 6.10: Algorithms for calculating the probability to reach a vertex

```
1  function Probability(Vertex v) : Real
2      Real[] probabilities;
3      do for Vertex v in g.vertices
4          do for Vertex target in v.to
5              if target.number > v.number // exclude
                 backward transitions from loops
6                  probabilities[target] += probabilities[v.
                    number] * v.transitionProbability[index of target];
7              endif;
8          enddo
9      enddo
10     return probabilities[v.number];
11 endfunction
```

to determine how many tests are required to cover this control-flow decision with a given confidence. The sum over all `transitionProbability` of a vertex can be unequal to 1 due to parameter-dependent control-flow decisions with different parameter sets for each decision outcome. If only one `to` is defined this is always taken regardless of its `transitionProbability`. This ensures that the probability to reach a vertex for a single test can be calculated as shown in listing 6.10. The attribute `iterations` specifies the mean frequency for visits to that vertex for each visit of the graph's first vertex (if the parameter values allow taking a path which includes the vertex). It allows taking fixed loop frequencies into account for calculating the required tests to cover JJ-Paths. `Iterations` has a default value of 1 if not specified otherwise.

Mapping Palladio specification starts at the `StartAction` of a `ResourceDemandingBehaviour` and continues the sequence of actions until the `StopAction` is mapped. Each action which does not influence the control-flow is directly mapped to a vertex and connected to the mappings of the predecessor and successor actions via the `from` and `to` transitions. Both transition probabilities are 1 as there are no control-flow decisions involved. The `number` of a new mapped vertex is the next integer greater or equal to 1 which has not been assigned to a vertex yet.

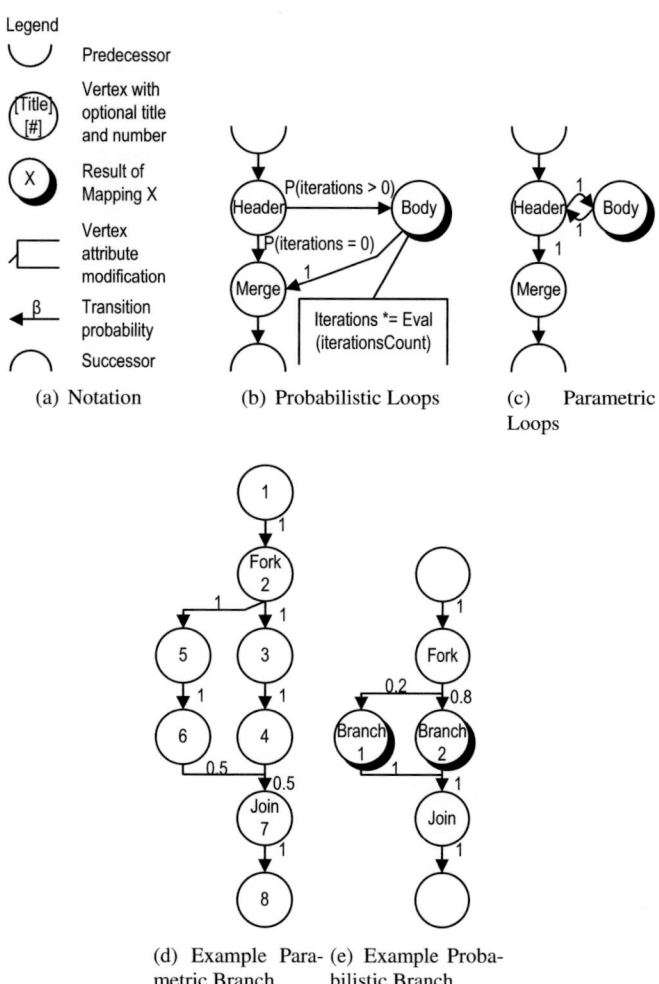

(a) Notation   (b) Probabilistic Loops   (c)   Parametric Loops

(d) Example Para- (e) Example Proba-
metric Branch   bilistic Branch

Figure 6.10.: Mapping of Loops Depending on Frequency Specification and Branch
Examples

An `AbstractLoopAction` with a probabilistic specification of its frequency is mapped to the vertices shown in figure 6.10(b) using the notation depicted in figure 6.10(a). The `Header` vertex represents the decision if the loop's body is visited at least once. If the visit of the loop's body is optional then a transition from the `Header` vertex to the `Merge` vertex is created. Its probability of transition is set to the probability value of not visiting the body. For example, if the specification for the frequency is the probability mass function $\text{pmf}_f = \begin{cases} 0 & 20\% \\ 5 & 80\% \end{cases}$ then the transition probability of `Header` to `Merge` is 0.2. If a visit to the loop's body is mandatory then there is no transition from `Header` to `Merge`. If the loop's body is visited at least once then a transition from `Header` to `Body` is created. The transition probability is set to 1 minus the probability of not visiting the body. The mapping continues with the Palladio specification for the body of the loop. The `iterations` of all vertices which result from that mapping is multiplied with the frequency of the loop. This results in a multiplication of $0 * 0.2 + 5 * 0.8 = 4$ for the given example. This algorithm allows to take into account nested loops. For example the number of `iterations` for the inner body of two nested loops with pmf_f is $4 * 4 = 16$. If the body is never visited then the body's vertices and transition to the body are not created. This mapping ensures that only the decision on visiting the body is included in JJ-Paths on the control-flow graph while taking the frequency for the loop's body into account for calculating the required number of tests for the vertices created for the body.

An `AbstractLoopAction` with a parameter-dependent frequency specification is mapped to the vertices shown in figure 6.10(c). The `Header` vertex represents the decision if the loop's body is visited. There is a transition to the first vertex created for the body and the transition from the last vertex created for the body. Both have a transition probability of 1 (cf. meta-model description). The transition probability from the `Header` vertex to the `Merge` vertex is also 1. This mapping ensures that JJn-Paths cover

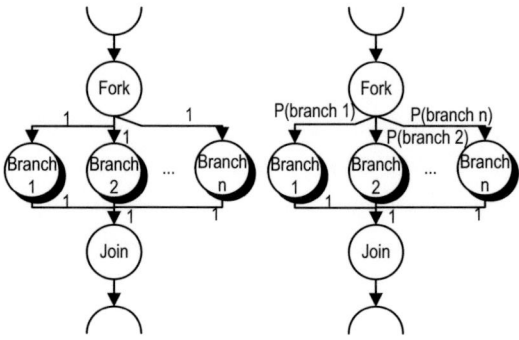

(a) Parameter-Dependent   (b) Probabilistic Branches
Branches and Forks

Figure 6.11.: Mapping of Branches and Forks

each possible loop frequency from 0 to ∞ restricted by the sequence limit n of JJn-Paths.

A GuardedBranchAction with its parametric dependencies is mapped to the vertices shown in figure 6.11(a). The from transition for the first vertex of each mapped branch of a GuardedBranchAction is set to the Fork vertex. All transition probabilities are 1, as the branch selection depends on distinct parameters but the same branch is always taken for that same parameter values. This ensures each branch is covered with different JJ-Paths. The to transition of the last vertex of each mapped branch is set to the Join vertex. The transition probability is $\frac{1}{n}$ as there is no control-flow decision involved but the probability of reaching the Join vertex must be equal to the one of the Fork vertex.

A ForkAction is mapped to the vertices shown in figure 6.11(a). Compared to the mapping of the branch action, all of the branches are always taken. The branches are isolated although there is no decision involved because the parameter set required to test each branch can be different in general. The to transition of the last vertex of each mapped branch is set to the Join vertex. The transition probability is $\frac{1}{n}$ as there is no control-flow decision involved but the probability of reaching the `Join` vertex must be equal to the one of the `Fork` vertex and the entry probability for each branch.

A `ProbabilisticBranchAction` is mapped to the vertices shown in figure 6.11(b). The `to` transition from the `Fork` vertex is set to the first vertex of the mapped branches with the transition probability assigned to that branch. Palladio ensures that all probabilities add up to 1. The `to` transition of the last vertex of each branch is set to the `Join` vertex. A transition probability of 1 is used, as there are no control-flow decisions involved.

The presented mapping covers all meta-model elements of `Resource-DemandingBehavior` specifications, which are relevant for the control-flow. Especially the elements `AbstractLoopAction`, `BranchAction`, and `ForkAction`, which model control-flow decisions, alternatives or concurrent control-flow. This complete mapping supports mapping any Palladio performance specification.

C_{jjpath} coverage for Palladio is based on the defined mapping to control-flow graphs and takes into account all control-flow alternatives including loops. This criterion allows covering different paths in the specification and provides an upper bound for covered paths.

$$X^n_{C_{\text{jjpath}}}(S,T) = \genfrac{}{}{0pt}{}{\text{executed distinct sequences of JJ-Paths}}{\text{of length } m \leq n}$$

$$X^n_{C_{\text{jjpath}}}(S) = \genfrac{}{}{0pt}{}{\text{total number of distinct sequences of JJ-Paths}}{\text{of length } m \leq n} \tag{6.21}$$

$$TER^n_{C_{\text{jjpath}}} = \frac{X^n_{C_{\text{jjpath}}}(S,T)}{X^n_{C_{\text{jjpath}}}(S)} m,n \in \mathbb{N}$$

205

The relation to criteria with respect to visited nodes and edges is comparable to the non-Palladio definitions and is provided in detail in [YM09] and [WHH80]. The results are that $C_{\text{jjpath}}^n, n \in \mathbb{N}$ subsumes C_{branch} but not the other way around. C_{jjpath}^n does not subsume $C_{\text{call obs}}$ and the other way around because of the same reasons as $C_{\text{basic paths}}$. C_{jjpath}^n subsumes $C_{\text{call spec}}, C_{\text{entry/exit}}, C_{\text{decision}}$, and C_{action} but not the other way around because its relation to C_{branch} and the relations of C_{branch} to these criteria. $C_{\text{jjpath}}^n, n \in \mathbb{N}$ does not subsume $C_{\text{probabilistic decision}}$ because the superset C_{jjpath}^∞ is equivalent with respect to subsumption to $C_{\text{all paths}}$ and $C_{\text{all paths}}$ does not subsume $C_{\text{probabilistic decision}}$. $C_{\text{probabilistic decision}}$ does not subsume $C_{\text{jjpath}}^n, n \in \mathbb{N}$ as for the most simple Palladio specification $TER_{C_{\text{probabilistic decision}}}$ equals 1 without being visited at all. At least one visit is required for $C_{\text{jjpath}}^n, n \in \mathbb{N}$.

$C_{\text{jjpath}}^n, n \in \mathbb{N}$ as well as C_{jjpath}^∞ do not subsume any of the structure of decisions criteria because only the outcome of decisions is relevant for path coverage but not the structure of the decisions. The criteria with respect to structure of decisions coverage do not subsume C_{jjpath}^n or C_{jjpath}^∞ because none of them requires covering loops with a frequency of 0.

$C_{\text{jjpath}}^{n+1}, n \in \mathbb{N}$ subsumes C_{jjpath}^n by definition. C_{jjpath}^n does not subsume C_{jjpath}^{n+1} because the sequence of JJ-Paths with length $n+1$ is not tested by the former one. As shown in [YM09] and [WHH80], C_{jjpath}^∞ is equivalent to C_{spt}^∞. The equivalence also implies that C_{boundary}, $C_{\text{basic paths}}$, and C_{spt}^{k+1} are subsumed by C_{jjpath}^∞ but not the other way around. $C_{\text{jjpath}}^k, k \in \mathbb{N}$ does not subsume C_{spt}^0 because the specification with $k+2$ consecutive control-flow alternatives and without loops has JJ-Paths of length $k+1$, which, by definition, do not have to be covered by C_{jjpath}^k but by C_{spt}^0. As $C_{\text{spt}}^n, n \in \mathbb{N}$ includes the requirements for C_{spt}^0 by definition, $C_{\text{jjpath}}^k, k \in \mathbb{N}$ does not subsume $C_{\text{spt}}^n, n \in \mathbb{N}$. $C_{\text{jjpath}}^k, k \in \mathbb{N}$ subsumes $C_{\text{relaxed basic paths}}$ and C_{boundary} if $C_{\text{jjpath}}^k = C_{\text{jjpath}}^\infty$. $C_{\text{spt}}^k, k \in \mathbb{N}$ does not subsume C_{jjpath}^k but C_{spt}^{k+1} does. If a specification contains a body there must be a jump to and from the body. The maximal frequency of the body for C_{jjpath}^k is $k+1$, as the body must be reached using JJ-Paths and a sequence of length k of the JJ-Paths containing the body in the worst case. C_{spt}^k does not cover a frequency of $k+1$. C_{spt}^{k+1} covers all paths up to a frequency of $k+1$ and therefore subsumes C_{jjpath}^k. C_{boundary} does not subsume $C_{\text{jjpath}}^n, n \in \mathbb{N}$ as JJ-Paths can lie within a loop. The equivalence of C_{jjpath}^∞ and C_{spt}^∞ implies that C_{jjpath}^∞ subsumes $C_{\text{boundary}}, C_{\text{basic paths}}$, and $C_{\text{spt}}^{k+1}, k \in \mathbb{N}$. $C_{\text{jjpath}}^k, k \in \mathbb{N}$ does not subsume $C_{\text{all paths}}$ if k is not big enough and C_{jjpath}^k is not equal to C_{jjpath}^∞. $C_{\text{all paths}}$ subsumes $C_{\text{jjpath}}^k, k \in \mathbb{N}$ by definition.

$|C_{\text{jjpath}}^n|_L$ equals 1 for the most simple `ResourceDemandingBehaviour`, as the only possible path must be covered once. $|C_{\text{jjpath}}^n|_U$ can be calculated by the following process. First, a Palladio specification can be mapped to a control-flow graph. Second, the JJ-Path algorithm provided in [YM09] by Yates can be used to determine JJ-Paths in the graph. Third, JJn-Paths are calculated. Finally, the lower and upper bound for the required number of tests can be calculated by the algorithms in listing 6.11. All transformations are realized using QVT Operational [Obj11a] and are available using anonymous SVN access [Gro12d]. The calculation algorithms are described in the following.

The upper bound for the required number of tests (lines 1-11 in listing 6.11) can be estimated by the sum of tests required for each JJn-Path (line 8). If all JJn-Paths start at the first node and end at the final node then the overall required number of test cases is the sum over the test cases (line 8) required for each JJn-Path. The number of required test cases for each path is determined by the probability to follow that path (lines 5-7) in case probabilistic decisions are involved. If JJn-Paths do not start at the first node then additional tests might be necessary to reach the first node of the path (line 4). The example shown in figure 6.10(d) consists of a single parameter-dependent branch. The notation (F-L,J) is used for JJ-Paths and states the first node F, the last node L in a sequence of nodes with consecutive numbers, and the node to which he final jump J is made. The JJ-Paths for the example are (1-2,5), (1-4,7), (5-7,8), and (7-7,8). Its JJ2-Paths are (1-2,5)(5-7,8) and (1-4,7)(7-7,8). Each of the JJ2-Paths requires one test and both must be tested independently, which requires overall two tests for JJ2-Paths coverage.

The lower bound for the required number of tests (lines 13-23 in listing 6.11) can be estimated by the maximum number of tests required for an individual JJn-Path (line 20) out of the JJn-Paths. The function `MinRequiredTestsRaw` is the same as `MinRequiredTests` but without the application of the `ceiling` method. The number of required test cases could be reduced if the part of the graph containing the path is iterated several times for each tests. The number of required test cases for each path must be divided by the minimal number of iterations (line 20, 25-31) over the included vertices. The separation of the number of iterations and the probability allows to ensure that the number of required tests is calculated based on the probability for the path but still allows compensating fixed iteration numbers. If the number of iterations would be included in the probability, a path with probability 0.5 and 2 iterations would have a resulting probability of 1 which prevents taking into account that the path must be tested at least once for a given confidence level greater than 0. The minimal number over all included vertices is required as JJn-Paths can start within a loop with a fixed frequency but its end may be outside of the loop. The example shown in figure 6.10(e) consists of a single probabilistic branch. JJ-Paths and JJ2-Paths are identical to the example with the deterministic branch by construction. The `iterations` for each node are 1, hence the minimum over the iterations of each path is also 1. For a confidence of $alpha = 0.95$, (1-2,5)(5-7,8) requires $\frac{log(1-0.95)}{log(1-0.2)*1} \approx 13.4$ (cf. section 6.3.2.1) test cases and (1-4,7)(7-7,8) requires $\frac{log(1-0.95)}{log(1-0.8)*1} \approx 1.9$ test cases. Using the maximum instead of the sum works because not taking a specific probabilistic branch means that another one is taken in the rest of the cases. As a result, overall $\lceil \frac{log(1-0.95)}{log(1-0.2)*1} \rceil = 14$ test are required in the mean to cover all JJ2-Paths of the specification.

In general, the number of required tests determined by the lower bound is more likely if probabilistic elements outweigh deterministic elements and vice versa.

Malevris shows algorithm adaptation in [Mal04] which addresses infeasible JJ-Paths (e.g. because a certain number of loop frequencies is necessary until a condition is true or conflicting conditions exists, which may change after iterations of the body). The underlying issues cannot arise for Palladio because of loop isolation and because our definition already covers pre-defined number of loop frequencies.

6.3.2.17. Summary

The criteria with respect to covered nodes and edges were presented in the sections 6.3.2.2 to 6.3.2.7. The criteria with respect to the structure of decisions were presented in the sections 6.3.2.8 to 6.3.2.13. Finally, the criteria with respect to the sequence of coverage were presented in the sections 6.3.2.14 to 6.3.2.16.

The subsumption relations described in these sections for the defined coverage criteria are summarized in figure 6.12 and a complete overview on the subsumption relation is given in table 6.3. It is visible that most of the criteria with respect to the structure of decisions are equivalent for Palladio specifications and that these criteria are incomparable to the criteria with respect to the sequence of coverage.

The selection of a criterion involves the covered aspects and the effort for testing. The criteria and their application advantage are summed up in the following for the categories of covered nodes and edges, the structure of decisions, and the sequence of coverage.

Selecting a criterion covering the nodes and edges is recommended in general. This ensures that each performance-relevant block, modeled by an AbstractAction, and the control-flow between these blocks is at least tested once and the general structure of the performance specification is

Listing 6.11: Algorithms for calculating bounds of $|C^n_{jjpath}|_U$

```
 1  function CJJPathsTestsUpper(JJnPath[] paths, Confidence
        alpha) : int
 2      int required = 0;
 3      do for path in paths
 4          Real probability = Probability(path.from);
 5          do for vertex, nextVertex in path
 6              probability *= vertex.transitionProbability[
        index of nextVertex];
 7          enddo;
 8          required += MinRequiredTests(probability, alpha);
 9      enddo
10      return required;
11  endfunction
12
13  function CJJPathsTestsLower(JJnPath[] paths, Confidence
        alpha) : int
14      int required = 0;
15      do for path in paths
16          Real probability = Probability(path.from);
17          do for vertex, nextVertex in path
18              probability *= vertex.transitionProbability[
        index of nextVertex];
19          enddo;
20          required = max(required, MinRequiredTestsRaw(
        probability, alpha) / MinIterations(path));
21      enddo
22      return ceiling(required);
23  endfunction
24
25  function MinIterations(JJnPath path) : real
26      int minIterations = path.from.iterations;
27      do for vertex in path
28          minIterations = min(minIterations, vertex.
        iterations);
29      enddo;
30      return minIterations;
31  endfunction
```

an accurate abstraction. $C_{\text{action}}/C_{\text{branch}}$ provides this general coverage and subsumes the criteria C_{decision} focusing on the decision outcomes, $C_{\text{entry / exit}}$ focusing on the flow into and out of the specification, and $C_{\text{call spec}}$ focusing on calls via required interfaces. The required number of tests grows only linearly with the number of actions in the specification. If the specification contains probabilistic control-flow decisions, $C_{\text{probabilistic decision}}$ allows validating the accuracy of the probabilities for the whole parameter space for which accuracy statements are provided. This reduces the error of invalid probabilities especially if the probability has been identified from a set of observations, which is only a small partition of the parameter space. The number grows linearly with the number of probabilistic decisions in the specification. $C_{\text{call obs}}$ focuses on calls which may but do not have to appear and ensures that each possible call is covered at least once. It extends the general coverage and provides the advantage of checking if the dependency of the number of calls has the right threshold. The required number of tests grows linearly with the number of specified calls.

Selecting a criterion covering the structure of decisions is recommended if the specification contains complex decisions as complex decisions are more likely be faulty. The proportion of the parameter space leading to a certain outcome of a condition within the decision is usually not equal between the conditions. The chance that random testing misses certain parameter combinations, which would influence the decision and the performance-relevant behavior, is higher. This advantage comes at the cost of effort requiring an exponential number of test cases with respect to the number of conditions in a decision if C_{multiple} is used. The criterion closest in the subsumption hierarchy is $C_{\text{reinforced condition / decision}}$, which reduces the effort to 6 times the number of conditions. The next closer criteria in this category are equivalent with respect to subsumption and require only an effort multiplier of 1 for the number of conditions. The trade-off for spending higher effort should honor how the conditions and decisions have been created. For example, if they are taken directly from an implementation without further abstraction then a manual comparison and limited testing on the specification are usually a good trade-off.

Selecting a criterion covering the sequence of coverage is recommended if the specification contains complex sequences of performance-relevant blocks, which involve control-flow decisions. The criteria ensure that the combination of sequential blocks in the specification is accurate. Covering all potential paths in the specification will likely lead to prohibitive effort if the specifications has loops or branches in sequence. The number of potential paths is multiplied by the alternatives of a branch or possible loop frequencies if it occurs as a step in a sequence. $C_{\text{all paths}}$, and the equivalent C_{spt}^{∞} and $C_{\text{jjpath}}^{\infty}$, are the most powerful criteria but have the disadvantage of the required effort, which can grow exponentially. The required number of test cases can be reduced if the parameter value $k \in \mathbb{N}$ for C_{jjpath}^{k} or C_{spt}^{k+1} is reduced. However, the effort will remain exponential and only the overall effort is reduced. $C_{\text{spt}}^{1}/C_{\text{basic paths}}$ reduces the multiplier to 2 for each loop. However, loops with frequencies bigger than 1 (or k in the general case) are not covered. Increasing the k to cover those loops has the disadvantage of the exponentially rising effort. $C_{\text{spt}}^{0}/C_{\text{boundary}}$ has the advantage of covering loops whose body is not visited but this also implies that any behavior within that body is not covered. This is the only criterion of this category which has the disadvantage of not subsuming $C_{\text{action}}/C_{\text{branch}}$ coverage. $C_{\text{relaxed basic paths}}$ is a trade-off between the effort and the covered sequences as it requires loops to be covered with a frequency of 0 as well as with a frequency greater than 0. In contrast to C_{jjpath}^{k} or C_{spt}^{k+1}, it does not require to choose an appropriate parameter and covers the combinations in which some loop bodies are not executed. This should be a good trade-off for most cases, especially because its mitigation of the effect of loop frequencies on the overall effort.

For all criteria, the algorithmic complexity for calculating the lower and upper bounds for the required number of test cases is in $O(n)$ where n is the number of actions contained in a `ResourceDemandingBehaviour` or recursively in the `ResourceDemandingBehaviour` of one of the contained actions.

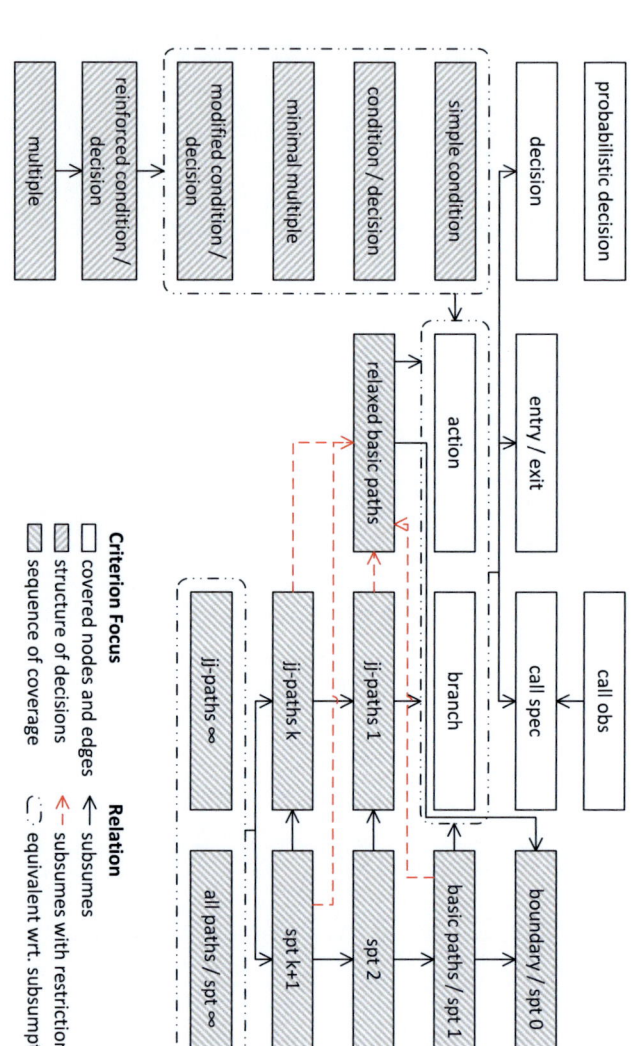

Figure 6.12.: Overview on Criteria Subsumption

Table 6.3.: Summary on Criteria Subsumption

Criterion on the left side has the following relation to the criterion on top:

s subsumes, d does not subsume, $=$ equal with respect to subsumption, $\neq$ incomparable with respect to subsumption. Bold entries are direct relations, the others are indirect relations.

	$C_{\text{call spec}}$	$C_{\text{call obs}}$	$C_{\text{entry/exit}}$	C_{decision}	$C_{\text{probabilistic decision}}$	C_{action}	C_{branch}	$C_{\text{simple condition}}$	$C_{\text{condition / decision}}$	$C_{\text{minimal multiple}}$	$C_{\text{modified condition / decision}}$	$C_{\text{reinforced condition / decision}}$	$C_{\text{multiple condition}}$	C_{boundary}	$C_{\text{basic paths}}$	$C_{\text{spt}}^{k+1}, k \in \mathbb{N}$	$C_{\text{all paths}}$	$C_{\text{relaxed basic paths}}$	C_{jjpath}^{i}	$C_{\text{jjpath}}^{k}, k \in \mathbb{N}$	$C_{\text{jjpath}}^{\infty}$
covered nodes and edges																					
$C_{\text{call spec}}$	=	**s**	≠	≠	≠	≠	≠	≠	≠	≠	≠	≠	≠	≠	≠	≠	≠	≠	≠	≠	≠
$C_{\text{call obs}}$	**d**	=	≠	≠	≠	≠	≠	≠	≠	≠	≠	≠	≠	≠	≠	≠	≠	≠	≠	≠	≠
$C_{\text{entry/exit}}$	≠	≠	=	**s**	≠	s	s	s	s	s	s	s	s	s	s	s	s	s	s	s	s
C_{decision}	≠	≠	=	=	≠	s	s	s	s	s	s	s	s	s	s	s	s	s	s	s	s
$C_{\text{probabilistic decision}}$	≠	≠	≠	≠	=	≠	≠	≠	≠	≠	≠	≠	≠	≠	≠	≠	≠	≠	≠	≠	≠
C_{action}	d	d	s	s	≠	=	=	s	s	s	s	s	s	≠	s	s	s	s	s	s	s
C_{branch}	d	d	s	s	≠	=	=	s	s	s	s	s	s	≠	s	s	s	s	s	s	s
structure of decisions																					
$C_{\text{simple condition}}$	d	d	d	d	≠	d	d	=	=	=	s	s	s	≠	≠	≠	≠	≠	≠	≠	≠
$C_{\text{condition / decision}}$	d	d	d	d	≠	d	d	=	=	=	s	s	s	≠	≠	≠	≠	≠	≠	≠	≠
$C_{\text{minimal multiple}}$	d	d	d	d	≠	d	d	=	=	=	s	s	s	≠	≠	≠	≠	≠	≠	≠	≠
$C_{\text{modified condition / decision}}$	d	d	d	d	≠	d	d	**d**	d	d	=	s	s	≠	≠	≠	≠	≠	≠	≠	≠
$C_{\text{reinforced condition / decision}}$	d	d	d	d	≠	d	d	d	d	d	=	=	**s**	≠	≠	≠	≠	≠	≠	≠	≠
$C_{\text{multiple condition}}$	d	d	d	d	≠	d	d	d	d	d	**d**	=	=	≠	≠	≠	≠	≠	≠	≠	≠
sequence of coverage																					
C_{boundary}	≠	≠	≠	≠	≠	≠	≠	≠	≠	≠	≠	≠	≠	=	s	s	s	s	**s**	s*	s*	s
$C_{\text{basic paths}}$	d	d	d	d	≠	d	d	≠	≠	≠	≠	≠	≠	**d**	=	s	s	**d***	≠	≠	s
$C_{\text{spt}}^{k+1}, k \in \mathbb{N}$	d	d	d	d	≠	d	d	≠	≠	≠	≠	≠	≠	**d**	**d**	=	s	**d***	d	d	s
$C_{\text{all paths}}$	d	d	d	d	≠	d	d	≠	≠	≠	≠	≠	≠	d	d	d	=	d	**d**	**d**	=
$C_{\text{relaxed basic paths}}$	d	d	d	d	≠	d	d	≠	≠	≠	≠	≠	≠	**d**	**s***	s	=	=	**s***	s*	s
C_{jjpath}^{i}	d	d	d	d	≠	d	d	≠	≠	≠	≠	≠	≠	**d***	s	s	**d***	=	=	s	s
$C_{\text{jjpath}}^{k}, k \in \mathbb{N}$	d	d	d	d	≠	d	d	≠	≠	≠	≠	≠	≠	**d***	s*	s*	s	**d***	=	=	s
$C_{\text{jjpath}}^{\infty}$	d	d	d	d	≠	d	d	≠	≠	≠	≠	≠	≠	d	d	d	=	**d**	**d**	**d**	=

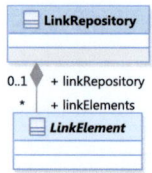

Figure 6.13.: Link Overview

6.4. Link Meta-Model

This section presents the developed meta-model for linking Palladio elements to other meta-models. It is used to map Palladio specifications to implementations, instrumenting the implementation, and gather measurements at runtime. The link meta-model is an annotation or mark meta-model. It allows to annotate Palladio model elements with links to other models without the need to change any of the referred meta-models.

Figure 6.13 shows how links are stored. The storage of the link annotations is independent of the target language, for example Palladio or ByCounter.

The LinkRepository stores a set of links, usually semantically connected. This could be a bundle of links used for a single validation run. The links are stored via the linkElements containment.

The abstract LinkElement is a template for any link between Palladio and another model. It should be specialized through subclasses for each different referred meta-model in order to distinguish the different type of links. The different types are presented in sections 6.4.1 and 6.4.2.

6.4.1. ByCounter Link Meta-Model

This section presents the model-elements for linking Palladio and ByCounter elements. ByCounter is an instrumentation and measurement utility which allows bytecode-exact performance measurements (see also the description at the beginning of section 6.2). More information about By-

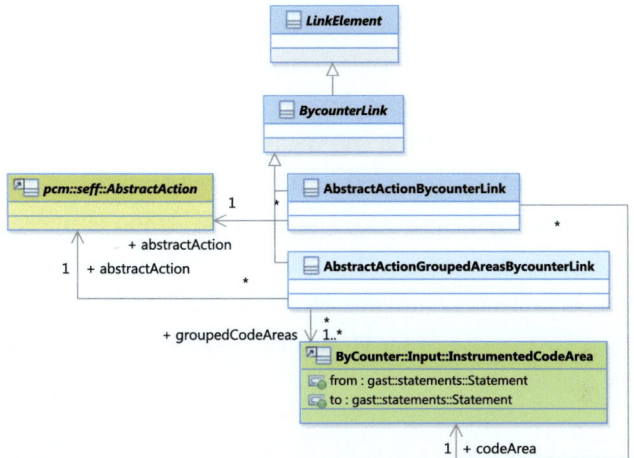

Fully qualified names are provided for external elements. Palladio elements are additionally shown in khaki and ByCounter elements in light green.

Figure 6.14.: Elements Linking Palladio and ByCounter

Counter and the meta-model for its input and output is available at its web page[ByC12].

Figure 6.14 provides an overview about all links to ByCounter model elements.

The abstract `BycounterLink` is used to tag all links to the ByCounter model. Its subclasses are presented in the following.

`AbstractActionBycounterLink` is a link between one `AbstractAc-`tion of a performance specification in Palladio and one `Instrumented-``CodeArea`. This allows mapping instrumented code sections and the performance specification. It is required to compare the actual and specified performance. The first one is an abstraction of the control-flow and the second one an area in the code between two statements. The first is linked via the `abstractAction` reference, the later is linked via the `codeArea` reference.

217

`AbstractActionGroupedAreasBycounterLink` links a single `AbstractAction` with multiple code sections in the implementation. There must be at least one code section in order to distinguish between repeated executions of the whole action and multiple measurements for the same action. It is required if code sections are split into multiple parts and all of these parts belong to one single action. The action is linked via the `abstractAction` reference. All sections are linked via the `groupedCodeAreas` reference. There can be more than one last section in the control-flow, for example if the section starts before a branch and always ends within the branches.

6.4.2. GAST Link Meta-Model

This section presents the model-elements for linking Palladio and General Abstract Syntax Tree (GAST) elements. GAST is a representation of the syntax tree of the implementation. The links allow mapping the elements of performance specifications to the implementation. Its documentation is available in [Q-I08, sections 3.3 and 6.12–6.19].

Figure 6.15 shows the elements which link components and implementation.

The abstract `GastLink` tags all links to the GAST model. Its subclasses are presented in the following.

`ImplementationComponentTypeGastLink` links a single component to all of its Java classes and stores the information necessary to instantiate the component. The component is linked via the `implementationComponentType` reference. It can be either a business or infrastructure component. The Java classes are linked via the `gastClasses` reference. There must be an implementation and, hence, at least one class. Instantiation of the component requires knowledge on how component parameters are set, dependencies to other components are resolved, and dependencies to hardware resources are resolved. The mechanisms for setting component pa-

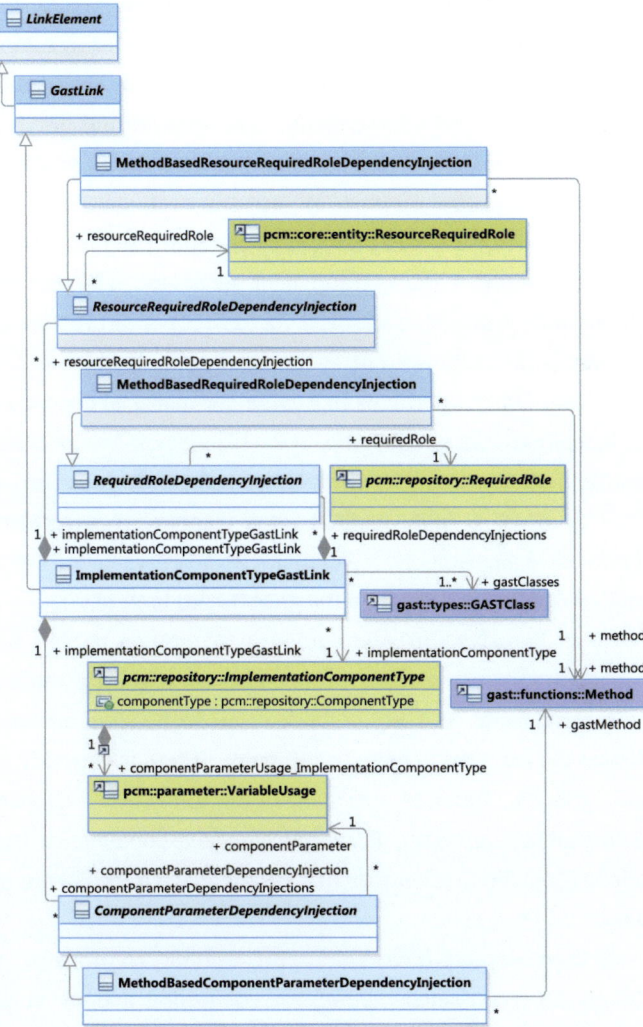

Fully qualified names are provided for external elements. Palladio elements are additionally shown in khaki and GAST elements in light purple.

Figure 6.15.: Elements Linking Palladio Components and Implementation via the GAST Meta-Model

rameters are stored for each parameter via the `componentParameterDependencyInjections` containment. The mechanisms for resolving component dependencies are stored for each parameter via the `requiredRoleDependencyInjections` containment. The mechanisms for resolving resource dependencies are stored for each required resource via the `resourceRequiredRoleDependencyInjection` containment.

The abstract `ComponentParameterDependencyInjection` models the strategy for setting a single component parameter. The parameter for which the strategy is available is linked via the `componentParameter` reference. There is currently just one available algorithm, which is presented in the following. Other algorithms like container-managed dependencies or injection techniques like google guice [Goo12] are possible extensions.

`MethodBasedComponentParameterDependencyInjection` models the technique to use a setter-method for a component parameter. This method must have the component parameter as only parameter. The method in the implementation is linked via the `gastMethod` reference.

The abstract `RequiredRoleDependencyInjection` models the strategy for resolving the dependency of a component requiring another component in a certain role. The required role refers to the required component and is linked via the `requiredRole` reference. There is currently just one available algorithm, which is presented in the following. Comparable to setting component parameters, other algorithms like container-managed dependencies or injection techniques like google guice [Goo12] are possible extensions.

`MethodBasedComponentParameterDependencyInjection` models the technique to use a setter-method for connecting another component to the required role. The method must have the required component's interface as only parameter. The method in the implementation is linked via the `method` reference.

The abstract `ResourceRequiredRoleDependencyInjection` models the strategy for resolving the dependency of a component to a required

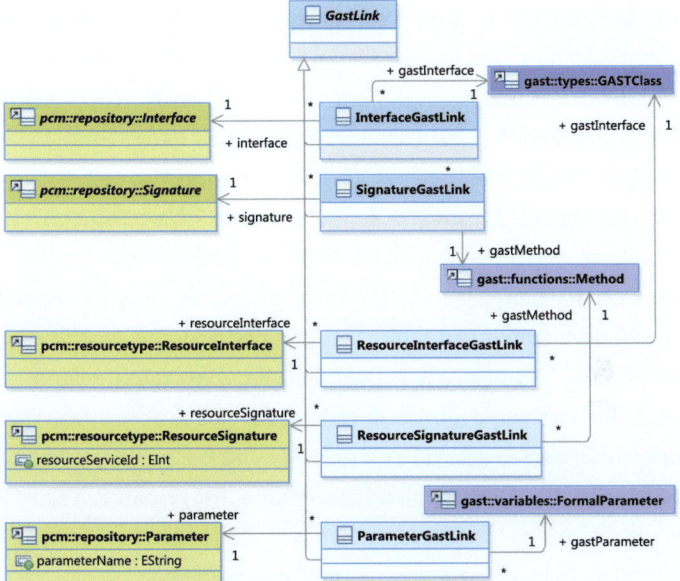

Fully qualified names are provided for external elements. Palladio elements are additionally shown in khaki and GAST elements in light purple.

Figure 6.16.: Elements Linking Palladio Interfaces and Parameters to an Implementation via the GAST Meta-Model

hardware resource. The role of the required resource must be linked via the `resourceRequiredRole` reference. There is currently just one available algorithm, which is presented in the following. The same possible alternatives apply as for the two other presented strategies.

`MethodBasedRequiredRoleDependencyInjection` models the technique to use a setter-method for connecting a required resource to the required role. The method must have the resource's interface as only parameter. The method in the implementation is linked via the `method` reference.

Figure 6.16 shows the elements which link Palladio interfaces and the parameters of their signatures to an implementation.

InterfaceGastLink links a single business or infrastructure interface to the implementing Java interface or a Java class. The business or infrastructure interface is linked via the interface reference. The explicit Java interface or the Java class implementing an implicit interface are linked via the gastInterface reference.

SignatureGastLink links a single signature of a business or infrastructure interface to a single method in the implementation. The signature must be linked separately from the interface as the order of defined signatures and their names can differ between performance specification and implementation. The signature is linked via the signature reference. The method in the implementation is linked via the gastMethod reference.

ResourceInterfaceGastLink links the interface of a resource to the Java interface or class responsible for accessing the resource. The resource interface is linked via the resourceInterface reference. The Java interface or class is linked via the gastInterface reference.

ResourceSignatureGastLink links the signature of a resource interface to the method in the implementation responsible for accessing the resource. Again, signatures must be linked separately as the specified interface may have a different order or a different name than in the implementation. The resource interface is linked via the resourceSignature reference. The method for accessing the resource is linked via the gastMethod reference.

The ParameterGastLink links the parameter within a signature to the parameter of the implementation. As with signatures, the data types, names, and order of parameters between the performance specification and the implementation may be different. This requires explicit links between these elements. The specification's parameter is linked via the parameter reference. The implementation's parameter is linked via the gastParameter reference.

Figure 6.17 shows the elements which link Palladio performance specifications to an implementation.

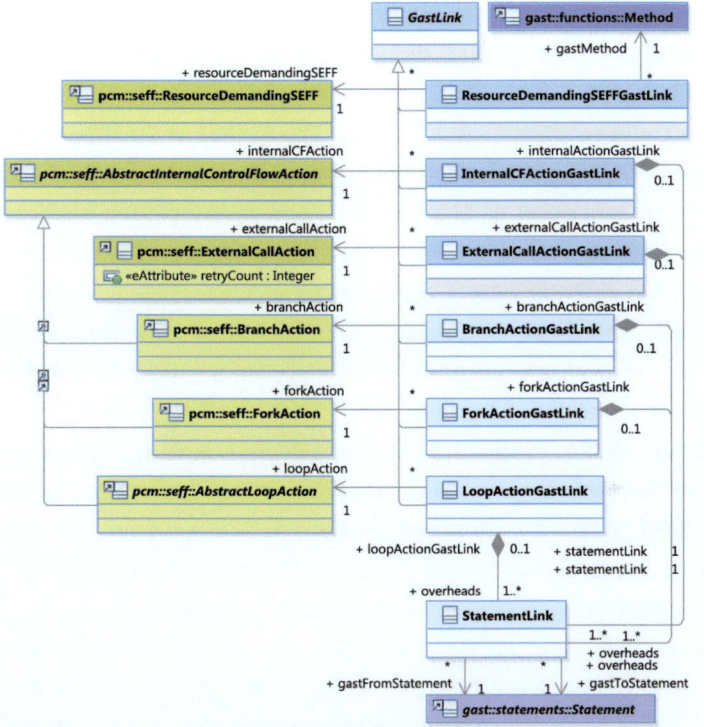

Fully qualified names are provided for external elements. Palladio elements are additionally shown in khaki and GAST elements in light purple.

Figure 6.17.: Elements Linking Palladio Performance Specifications and Implementation via the GAST Meta-Model

`ResourceDemandingSEFFGastLink` links the performance specification for a single business or infrastructure operation with a method in the implementation. A `ResourceDemandingSEFF` element is the behavior abstraction for a single operation of a component's interface. It can be mapped to a method in the component's implementation. It can be used to execute the code which is described by the specification after the component is instantiated. The performance specification is linked via the `resourceDemandingSEFF` reference. The method in the implementation is linked via the `gastMethod` reference. Palladio behavior specifications consist of subclasses of `AbstractActions` describing the performance-relevant behavior of a code section and the control-flow between these actions. The different actions are linked using the following specific links. The most specific link must be used. This allows easy adaption of this meta-model in case a new action is introduced in the specification language and must be handled differently.

`InternalCFActionGastLink` is a generic link to a code section for actions other than the `ExternalCallAction` and for which no explicit link is defined. Examples are `StartAction` and `StopAction`. The behavior specification is linked via the `resourceDemandingSEFF` reference. The code section is linked via the `statementLink` containment.

`StatementLink` models a link to a single code section. The code section is determined by the first and the last statement within that section. There must be at least one statement in the section. This statement can be the first and last at the same time. The first statement is linked via the `gastFromStatement`. The last statement is linked via the `gastToStatement`.

`ExternalCallActionGastLink` links actions which represent calls to required components to a code section. The action is linked via the `ExternalCallAction` reference. The code section is linked via the `statementLink` containment.

`BranchActionGastLink` links actions at which the control-flow follows one of the specified alternatives to one or more code sections. There can be one or more sections depending on the implementation in the code. For example if-then-else-cascades have another representation than switch-statements. Both are still valid models of the behavior. In order to have a precise definition which performance belongs to this action and which to one of the specified alternatives requires allowing more than one code section. The code sections are linked via the `overheads` containment. There must be at least one code section.

`ForkActionGastLink` links actions at which the control flow is split and can be merged again to one or more code sections. There must be at least one code section. There can be more than one section depending on the implementation of the definition of threads and their forking and joining. Only multiple sections allow an accurate measurement of performance caused by the actions. The code sections are linked via the `overheads` containment.

`LoopActionGastLink` links all actions representing a loop in the control-flow to one or more code sections. There must be at least one code section. There can be more than one section depending on the implementation of the loop. For example do-while , for, while-do, and for-each have different representations in the code and are split differently although all have the behavior corresponding to this action. Only multiple sections allow an accurate measurement of all of these cases. The code sections are linked via the `overheads` containment.

The presented meta-model allows linking all parts of Palladio specifications, which are necessary to instantiate, instrument, and measure the performance requests of an implementation of that component. This includes the mapping of the specified control-flow abstraction to the implementation, the interfaces and signatures, and the description of the components and their composed parts. The meta-model is designed extensible and new model elements or dependency resolution techniques are easy to integrate. These extension points were pointed out.

6.5. Validation Results Reporting Meta-Model

This section presents the developed meta-model for reporting results of a test-based validation. Its statements provide formalized means to report and assess success or failure of a test-based validation. The provided information shows errors and allows fault identification. It is suitable for humans as well as programs. It consists of a generic and a language-dependent part. A language-dependent part is developed and shown for Palladio.

The developed meta-model depends on overall five other meta-models: the meta-model for accuracy statements presented in chapter 4, the meta-model for test-based validation presented in section 6.1, the link meta-model presented in section 6.4, the meta-model for ByCounter's input and output available at [ByC12], and the Palladio meta-model presented in section 2.4.

The following are the requirements for reporting validation results. The list additionally shows how this approach addresses each requirement.

1. **No need to modify specification, instrumentation or validation languages.** This approach defines a meta-model which uses existing meta-models and annotates validated specifications with validation results including detailed failure and error messages.

2. **Automated processing of validation information.** The developed meta-model is accessible using EMF. This ensures the conformance with standards and industry-suitable tooling. The defined meta-model elements allow a precise semantic definition and references to elements leading to a validation failure. Validation settings are recorded and can be re-used for subsequent validations.

3. **Viewable by human users.** Human-oriented graphical editors are provided to display model instances. It is ensured by using EMF. Detailed human-readable messages for elements describing validation failures provide convenient access to errors and for fault identification.

This section is structured as follows. Section 6.5.1 describes the language-independent meta-model for reporting results. Section 6.5.2 describes the customizations for a specific modeling language and shows its extensions for reporting validation results of Palladio-based specifications.

6.5.1. Results Meta-Model

This section shows the language-independent meta-model part for reporting results of a test-based validation.

Figure 6.18 shows the elements for storing the result of validation runs.

The RunProtocol stores the result for a single validation run. Its references and attributes are explained in the next two paragraphs.

The validated specification and its tested quality is linked via the qualityAnnotation reference (see section 4.1 for details). The quality of the validation and the validated aspects are linked via the validationQuality reference (see section 6.1 for details). Comparing implementation and specifications requires links between these artifacts. The reference to the link repository is stored via the pcmGastLinkRepository reference (see section 6.4.2 for details). The implementation is measured using ByCounter. This measurement requires setting measurement parameters. These parameters are stored via the bycounterInput reference. The measured code sections are stored in the link repository via the pcmBycounterLinkRepository reference. The raw results with observed bytecode and function call measurements are linked via the executionObservationTrace containment. This documentation allows cross-checking and fault identification based on the raw results reported by By-

227

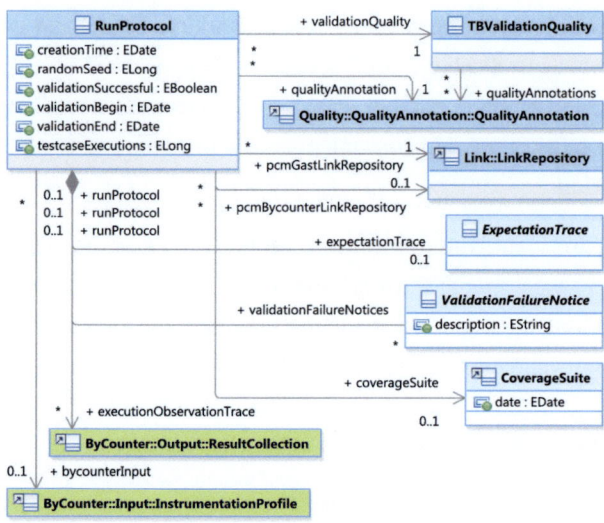

Fully qualified names are provided for external elements. ByCounter elements are additionally shown in light green.

Figure 6.18.: Elements for Storing Validation Run Results

Counter. The measurement-related information helps identifying faults for reported errors and failures (see 2.1 for term definitions). The expectations stated in the specification are linked via the `expectationTrace` containment. Information on experienced failures for unsuccessful validations are stored via the `validationFailureNotices` containment.

Management information for a protocoled validation run is stored in the attributes of the `ProtocolRun`. The validation requires a random number generator to create samples within the parameter space. The random number generator is initialized with the seed provided via the `randomSeed` attribute. The time when the described protocol is created is stored via the `creationTime` attribute. The wall clock times of start and end of the described test-based validation are stored via the `validationBegin` and `validationEnd` attributes. They also provide the timespan required

228

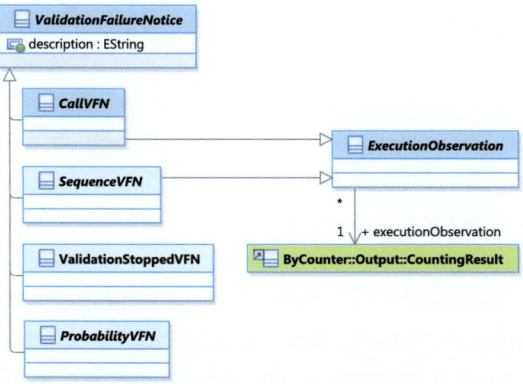

Fully qualified names are provided for external elements. ByCounter elements are additionally shown in light green.

Figure 6.19.: Validation failure notices

for the validation. The number of executed test cases is stored via the testcaseExecutions attribute for statistical and documentation purposes. Finally, the verdict of the validation is stored via the validationSuccessful attribute.

The ExpectationTrace stores the expected behavior during validations including parameter values. The expectations are derived from the tested specification and the test cases. It is an abstract class and must be customized for the parameters and behavior statements of the specification language.

Figure 6.19 shows the elements for stating validation failure notices in a specification language-independent way.

The ValidationFailureNotice stores the information about a validation failure and provides additional details. The attribute description must contain a meaningful messages explaining the error for human readers. The message depends on the specification language in order to help with the interpretation of the message and ease fault identification. It is an abstract class and must be customized for the failure types. The language-independent failure types are as follows.

The abstract element ExecutionObservation is used to mark that other elements provide an execution observation and ensure a single and simple way to access the execution observation linked with a validation failure. An observation can contain bytecode and function call measurements. The observation is linked via the executionObservation reference.

CallVFN models a failure relating to calls or call parameters. It provides information on the error and references the measurements by inheriting from ExecutionObservation. It is an abstract class and must be customized for the call and call parameter types of a specification language.

SequenceVFN models a failure relating to the sequence of behavior statements. It provides information on the error and references the measurements by inheriting from ExecutionObservation. It is an abstract class and must be customized for the behavior statements of a specification language.

ValidationStoppedVFN models that the validation was aborted due to experienced validation failures. These difference between specification and implementation is grave enough that further validation does not provide any benefit. An example for such a case is the use of business operation return parameters in a specification although the implementation does not even issue the call.

ProbabilityVFN models that there was a failure at validating the decision probabilities. It should provide information on the statistic, acceptance thresholds and reference the decision with the invalid probability. It is an abstract class and must be customized for the behavior statements of the specification language.

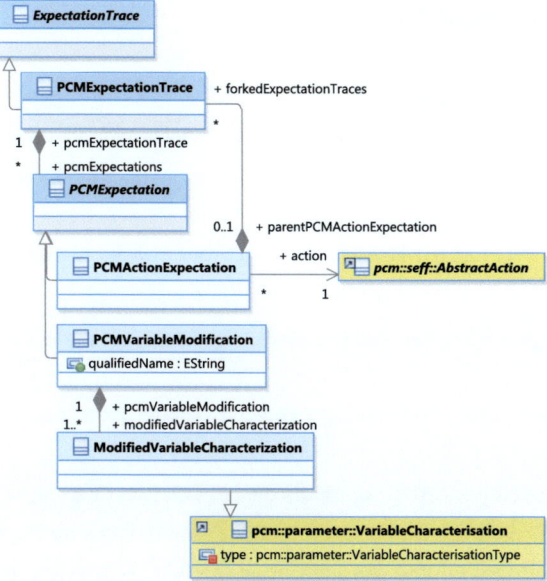

Fully qualified names are provided for external elements. Palladio elements are additionally shown in khaki.

Figure 6.20.: Palladio expectations

6.5.2. Palladio Customizations

This section shows the language-dependent meta-model part for reporting results of a test-based validation. The statements in this section are customized for the Palladio specification language.

Figure 6.20 shows the elements used to state expectations for Palladio.

PCMExpectationTrace stores the trace consisting of a sequence of expectations. It is the result of customizing ExpectationTrace. The single steps are linked via the pcmExpectations containment.

The PCMExpectation models a single expectation. It must be specialized through subclasses for the different types of expectations. For Palladio,

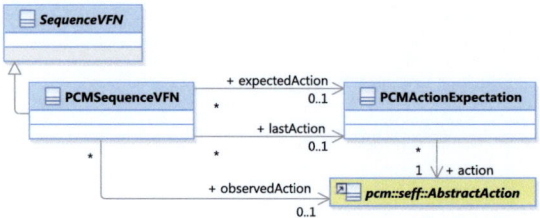

Fully qualified names are provided for external elements. Palladio elements are additionally shown in khaki.

Figure 6.21.: Sequence validation failure notices for Palladio

these are the actions representing expected behavior and parameter modifications.

PCMActionExpectation models the expectation of a single action. The action is linked via the action reference. Palladio has actions, which allow forking synchronized and asynchronous threads. Currently, this behavior is limited to ForkAction instances. The expectation trace for each of the forked threads is linked via the forkedExpectationTraces containment.

PCMVariableModification models the modification of a Palladio variable. The fully qualified name of the variable including its namespace must be provided via the qualifiedName attribute. If it is an unnamed variable then the qualified name must be empty. The value of each variable is described in the Palladio way by providing characterizations of the value. These are stored via the modifiedVariableCharacterization containment.

The ModifiedVariableCharacterization models the characterization for a single characterization type of a variable. It reuses the Variable-Characterization by inheritance but still supports other containment relations.

Figure 6.21 shows the elements for validation failure notices regarding the specified behavior sequence.

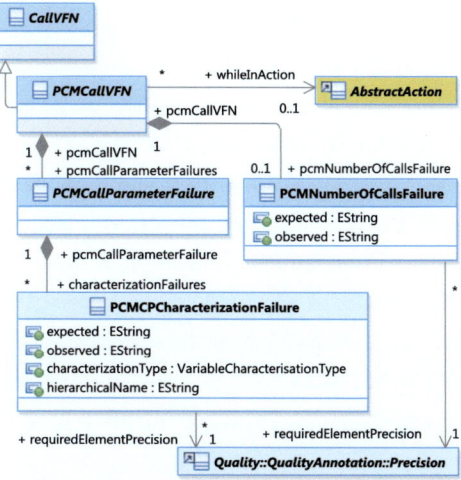

Fully qualified names are provided for external elements. Palladio elements are additionally shown in khaki.

Figure 6.22.: Call validation failure notices for Palladio

The PCMSequenceVFN describes the deviation between the last and expected action on the one hand and the (unexpectedly) observed action on the other hand. It is the result of customizing SequenceVFN. Last and expected action are linked via the lastAction and expectedAction references. If there is no last action, for example because the overall first action is expected, the expected action reference is not used. If there is no expected action, for example because the overall last action in the behavior specification was successfully visited, the last action reference is not used. The unexpectedly observed action is linked via the observedAction reference. It is a direct reference to the action as there is by definition no expectation. If there is an expected action but none is observed, for example because the implementation ends processing, the observed action reference is not used.

Figure 6.22 shows the elements for validation failure notices regarding calls and their parameters.

PCMCallVFN models a failure relating to a call and its call parameters and is the result of customizing CallVFN for Palladio specifications. The position in the specification during validation can be referenced via the whileInAction reference. This aids in identifying the fault, especially of grave differences between specification and implementation. The description of failures for each of the parameters is linked via the pcmCallParameterFailures containment. It is empty if there are no call parameter failures. If the number of expected and observed calls for a type does not match this failure is described via the pcmNumberOfCallsFailure containment. This is an abstract element and must be customized for the different call types of Palladio. This customization is described at the end of this section.

PCMCallParameterFailure models a failure for the value of a single call parameter. The information on the error for this variable is described in the Palladio way by providing information on the error of the characterizations of the value. The information on the error for each characterization is linked via the characterizationFailures containment. This is an abstract element and must be customized for the different parameter types of Palladio. This customization is described together with figure 6.23 later in this section.

PCMCPCharacterizationFailure provides information on the error of the failure of a single characterization of a Palladio parameter. The expected characterization value is stored via the expected attribute in form of a stochastic expression's specification (see section 2.4). The observed characterization value is stored via the observed attribute in form of a stochastic expression's specification. The characterization type its stored via the characterizationType attribute. The qualified name including the namespace is stored via the hierarchicalName attribute. The stipulated precision which makes the error a failure is linked via the requiredElementPrecision reference.

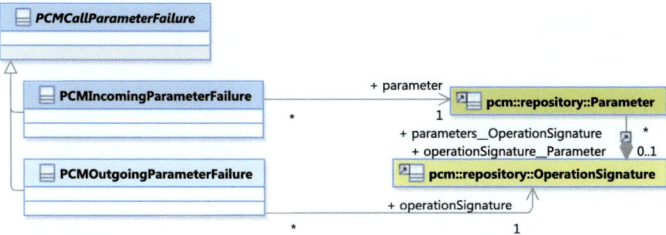

Fully qualified names are provided for external elements. Palladio elements are additionally shown in khaki.

Figure 6.23.: Call parameter failure types for Palladio

PCMNumberOfCallsFailure provides information on the error of failures, where the number of expected and observed calls for a type doesn't match. The expected number of calls is stored via the expected attribute in form of a stochastic expression's specification (see section 2.4). The observed number of calls is stored via the observed attribute in form of a stochastic expression's specification. The stipulated precision which makes the error a failure is linked via the requiredElementPrecision reference.

Figure 6.23 shows the customized elements for the parameter types which can lead to a call parameter failure.

PCMIncomingParameterFailure models the parameter type which is part of the signature of interfaces and is provided as input for an operation or resource access. The parameter is linked via the parameter reference.

PCMOutgoingParameterFailure models the parameter type which is returned by business operations as part of their signature. Palladio provides exactly one implicit parameter per signature. This parameter is linked via the operationSignature reference.

Figure 6.24 shows the customized elements for the call types, which can lead to call validation failure notices.

PCMBusinessCallVFN models calls to business signatures. They can only be specified using ExternalCallAction elements. This action is

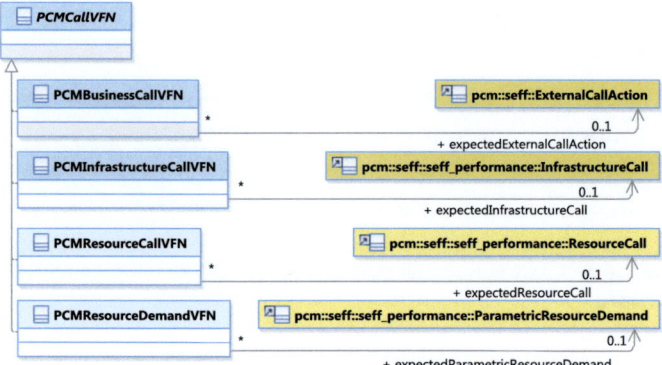

Fully qualified names are provided for external elements. Palladio elements are additionally shown in khaki.

Figure 6.24.: Validation failure notices for the different call types of Palladio

linked via the `expectedExternalCallAction` reference. If there is only an observation but no stated expectation then no action is linked.

`PCMInfrastructureCallVFN` models calls to infrastructure signatures. They can only be specified using `InfrastructureCall` elements. The corresponding element is linked via the `expectedInfrastructureCall` reference. It is only referenced if there is no stated expectation but an observation.

`PCMResourceCallVFN` models calls to resources using explicit interfaces. They can only be specified using `ResourceCall` elements. The corresponding element is linked via the `expectedResourceCall` reference. It is only referenced if there is no stated expectation but an observation.

`PCMResourceDemandVFN` models calls to resources using implicit interfaces. They can only be specified using `ParametricResourceDemand` elements. The corresponding element is linked via the `expectedParametricResourceDemand` reference. It is only referenced if there is no stated expectation but an observation.

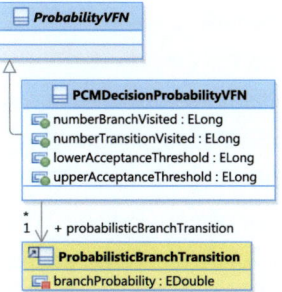

Fully qualified names are provided for external elements. Palladio elements are additionally shown in khaki.

Figure 6.25.: Probability validation failure notices for Palladio

Figure 6.25 shows the elements for validation failure notices regarding decision probabilities.

`PCMDecisionProbabilityVFN` models a failure relating to a branching probability and is the result of customizing `ProbabilityVFN` for Palladio specifications. The transition with the invalid `branchProbability` is referenced via the `probabilisticBranchTransition`. The sample size used for the validation is provided via the `numberBranchVisited` attribute. The statistic for the visits to the transition itself is provided via the `numberTransitionVisited` attribute. The lower and upper acceptance thresholds for the statistic are provided via the `lowerAcceptanceThreshold` and `upperAcceptanceThreshold` attributes.

6.6. Tooling

This section provides an overview on the validation framework developed in this thesis. The framework can be downloaded as eclipse feature from an update site as described on the corresponding web page [Gro13c]. A tailored framework is required to take into account the execution semantics of specification elements and enable comparisons between specification and implementation with respect to the provided accuracy statements.

Existing tools for model-based testing and test value generation based on coverage criteria have limited support for specifications containing both, probabilistic and parametric, dependencies. They have their own specification languages with tailored criteria. Palladio specifications can be mapped and applied to these tools but their criteria and meaning of coverage are not necessarily good matches for Palladio specifications. A case study demonstrating the mapping of Palladio specifications and using built-in criteria with the tool Conformiq Designer is provided by Ernst in [Ern11]. The results show that the tool does not support test case generation for the probabilistic control-flow elements of Palladio and the generated test cases cannot be executed on such specifications.

Figure 6.26 shows the code packages of the core of the validation framework including the management functionality for the packages. The structure and mapping of the packages to the activities of the validation process (see section 6.2) is provided in the following.

The packages are grouped according to their functionality. The `de.fzi.se.validation.testbased` package contains the validation framework. It is controlled via the `ValidationManager`. The functionality of this and the other control elements is explained later in combination with the mapping to the process. The package `execution` contains everything related to the execution of the implementation. It is controlled via the `OUTManager` and controls the measurements of the ByCounter framework (see also the description at the beginning of section 6.2). The package `expectation` contains everything related to specification execution. It is controlled via the `ExpectationManager`. The package `parameters` contains everything related to parameter conversion and generation between the specification language and the implementation. The package `conversion` contains everything related to parameter conversion. The conversion is controlled via the `VariableConversionManager`. The package `generation` contains everything related to goal-oriented parameter value generation. It is controlled via the `SampleManager`. The package `tests` contains jUnit test cases. They ensure that the validation framework works correctly and are used for regression testing. The package `util` contains utility and convenience functions.

The first action of the process, `create default RunProtocol`, is realized by the method `createRunProtocol` of the `ValidationManager`. It requires the quality of the validation, the stipulated accuracy of the specification, and the links between specification and implementation as input. The method returns the corresponding `Prepared RunProtocol`. The main validation loop and the subsequent activities `record stop time` and `update protocol` are coordinated by the method `validate` of the `ValidationManager`. It requires a `Prepared Run Protocol`, adds the validation information to the run protocol. The final `RunProtocol` is available after the method execution is finished.

The loop initialization partition maps as follows. The `instrument` activity maps to the method `instrument` of the `OUTManager`. The initialization of the parameter value generation strategies of the activity `initialize strategies` is controlled by the method `validate` of the `Validation-Manager`. It delegates the generation strategy to the method `createAnd-Register` of the `SampleManager`. The decision `check influence analysis type` is again controlled by the method `validate`. The activity `instantiate` maps to the method `instantiate` of the `OUTManager`. The activity `record start time` is again controlled by the method `validate`.

The loop condition partition maps as follows. The decision `TestExecutionStopStrategy: check condition` and resulting loop iteration or exit is controlled by the method `validate` of the `ValidationManager`.

The body of the loop maps as follows and is controlled by the method `simulateAndValidate` of the `ExpectationManager`. The decision `check influence analysis type` is part of the method. It uses the method `instantiate` of the `OUTManger` if the activity `instantiate` is executed. The activity `initialize component` maps to the method `setObjectParameters` of the `OUTManager`. It is responsible to set the component parameters of the deployed component instance according to the testes specification parameters. This uses the conversion functionality provided by `VariableConversionManager`. The activity `execute and validate test case` maps to the method `execute` of the `OUTManager`. The call parameters are sampled according to the parameter value generation strategy. Samples are drawn using the method `getSample` of the `SampleManager`. The `ExpectationManager` reacts on the measured behavior of the implementation and validates it at runtime. Calls from the implementation to required components are mocked. Return values of these calls which may influence the behavior of the implementation are sampled using the method `getSample` of the `SampleManager`. The method's parameters allow the distinct identification of all calls regardless of their origin. Origins can vary in the issuing threads, actions, and targeted operation of the required interfaces.

After the validation loop, the activities `record stop time` and `update protocol` ensure that the required validation time is properly recorded, the protocol states the correct result, and that the protocol is in a consistent state. These activities are controlled by the method `validate` of the `ValidationManager`. The activity `store protocol` is realized in the `tests` package containing the jUnit regression tests. The protocol and referenced models are bundled and stored together for easy access and assessment.

Validating arbitrary specifications requires the conversion of custom data types used in the implementation or specification. The conversion itself is realized by the `VariableConversionManager`. Implementation data types are converted to specification data types using the method `convert(Object)`. Specification data types are converted using the method `convert(String, PCMParameterValue)`. The data type in the implementation must be provided by its fully qualified textual name. The textual representation is used as decoupling technique. It allows measuring the overhead of data type handling in the implementation. The implementation data type itself must be provided as the same specification data type can be converted to different implementation data types. The list of available converters is provided via the REGISTERED_CONVERTER_CLASSES list. It consists of the fully qualified names of the converters. Again, this decoupling allows taking into account their impact on the performance. The VariableConversionManagerImpl instantiates instrumented versions within the measurement framework. New converters can be provided and added to the converter list programmatically. The converters must provide a default constructor and implement the interface VariableConverter. The method getSupportedTypes provides a list of qualified names of the implementation data types supported by the converter. The method build-From(PCMParameterValue) must provide an instance of the implementation data type based on the given parameter. The method buildFrom(Object) must provide a specification data type based on the given implementation data type instance.

Figure 6.27 shows the code packages related to the coverage criteria.

The package de.fzi.se.validation.effort contains the effort estimation algorithms for the coverage criteria, which were presented in section 6.3.2. The estimations are loosely coupled to the validation. They are available in a standalone fashion. This separation allows criteria selection and effort estimation even without the validation framework in the background. New estimation algorithms can be provided using the extension point mechanism of eclipse. The existing algorithms are implemented as QVTO transformations. They are contained in the qvtoscripts package. QVTO-based estimations are supported by the abstract class AbstractEstimateQVTO, which provides convenient access to the selected specification. The algorithms must be registered at the extension point with the ID de.fzi.se.validation.effort.estimation and implement the interface `IEstimator`. This interface provides programmatic access to configuration options via the method `buildAndSetCustomConfiguration`. This solution supports arbitrary criterion-specific configuration options. The human readable name for the criterion is available via the method `getCriterionName`. The estimation is requested via the method `getEstimation`.

The package `de.fzi.se.pcmcoverage` contains coverage requirement information for Palladio specifications. Coverage requirements are the result of applying a coverage criterion on a specification. They state the elements and the sequence in which they must be covered for that particular specification. The achieved coverage of a validation run for each requirement can be stored and visualized. The package `criteria` contains the algorithms to create the coverage requirements. The package `ui` contains the visualization of fulfilled requirements. The package `example` contains an example demonstrating coverage requirements and their visualization.

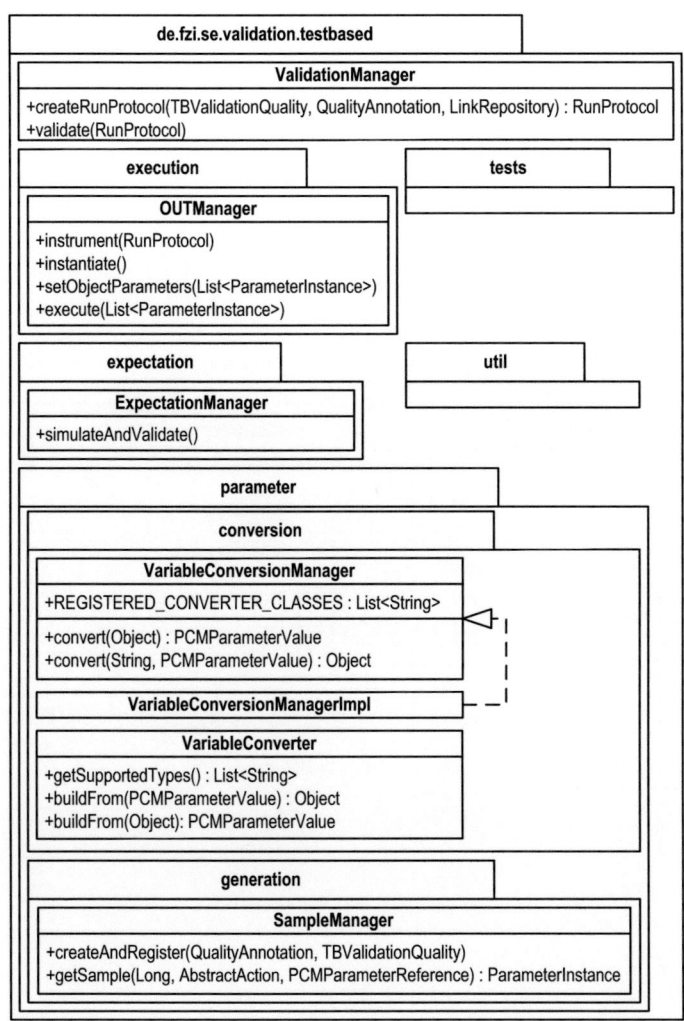

Figure 6.26.: Code Packages and Managers of the Validation Framework

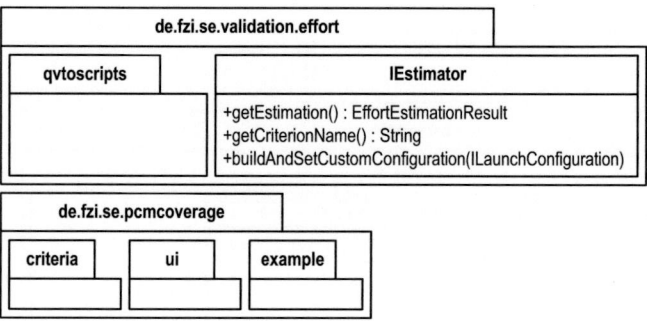

Figure 6.27.: Code Packages for Managing the Coverage Criteria for Palladio

7. Specification Certification

This chapter demonstrates how product certification ensures the trustworthiness of performance specifications. The trust in specifications and their accuracy varies depending on the roles and parties participating in component and system development. Personal or professional relations to creators of specifications and accuracy statements influence appropriate measures for ensuring trust. This chapter shows appropriate measures and their selection for different application scenarios.

Product certification (see also section 1.3.4) for performance specifications is about the confirmation that a given specification with its accuracy statements match the behavior of an implementation. Therefore, the certificate defines which aspects have been validated to which extent. The certificate defined in this thesis (see section 7.2.2) uses the validation and coverage criteria presented in chapter 6 and the accuracy statements presented in chapter 4. The certificate takes into account graduations of the quality of the validation including the covered aspects and the thoroughness of the validation itself.

The certified specifications allow the sound and trustworthy evaluation and selection of components on the architecture level for an envisioned system purely on the base of the specifications and their accuracy statements. Without the presented approach, component evaluation required sharing the implementation in order to assess the quality characteristics of components and their effect on the envisioned system. This need for sharing the implementation for evaluation purposes transferred contained knowledge and IP, for example efficient algorithms and their implementations. The presented certification approach allows to keep knowledge and IP to the component owner until a final acquisition decision has been made. The confidentiality is kept by design and not by complex contracts with regulations and penalties. The certified specifications and their accuracy statements can be distributed freely. This distribution speeds up the evaluation process and requires less contract negotiations without hampering the value for evaluations.

Product certification must be embedded into the component-based development processes used by software engineers for a successful application. This chapter describes how certification of performance specifications can be integrated into own component-based development processes. The defined development process roles point out responsibilities and make the required collaboration explicit. The different roles can span several independent parties. The integration of certification is demonstrated for the Palladio reference development process described in [RBB+11a]. The tailored process is applicable for top-down, bottom-up, and combined development approaches. The development can be restricted to one company or span different companies. The certificates can be used in conjunction with component repositories or on marketplaces. Software engineers gain instructions and an application example, which allows tailoring their own used component-based development processes.

Certificates can be issued by different parties within a component-based development process. As mentioned above, the relation of the parties and their mutual trust plays an important role for trusting issued certificates. The level of trust between the participating parties determines the effort spent to ensure that the specifications and accuracy statements are sound. The assignment of the issuing party therefore affects the evaluation effort and distribution of effort between the parties. The different application scenarios are pointed out and a guideline is provided, which allows to select an appropriate assignment and compare it with assignment alternatives. The guideline points out the evaluation effort share of potential component integrators. This share allows reasoning about the attractiveness of the offered component for `Component Integrators` caused by the necessary evaluation effort. This information is the basis for justified and objective assignment decisions.

The presented work transfers the concept of re-use from components and their implementation to the validation of performance specifications of such components. The maturity of prediction approaches is elevated as the re-use of specifications in different systems and contexts is eased. They can be applied on a broader scale without endangering the quality characteristics of the composed systems or engineering principles. The maturity of Palladio is elevated as the risks are reduced for sound predictions in scenarios with multiple parties and use of marketplaces. The presented work addresses the scientific challenge of certification criteria formulation by defining a performance specification certificate based on the accuracy statements validation meta-model. The workflow for performance specification certification for repositories and marketplaces is addressed by showing the integration of certification in development processes. The adapted component-based development process is addressed by demonstrating the integration of the workflow for the Palladio reference development process.

The certificate defined in this chapter supports performance engineering on the architecture level. It is usable in scenarios with cross-party component (re-)use and component storage in repositories or marketplaces. The soundness of decisions is ensured by trustworthy specifications and quality statements. The certificate eases the assessment of covered aspects and thoroughness of the specification and accuracy statement assessments. Software engineers have a tool at their disposal, which allows integrating certification and quality assurance for performance specifications in their used component-based development process.

This chapter is structured as follows. Section 7.1 shows the generic workflow for certified specifications, which is a basis for tailoring own development processes. It furthermore provides the guideline on selecting the certificate issuing party including an evaluation effort overview for different application scenarios. Section 7.2 demonstrates the integration of certification into the Palladio reference development process and defines a certificate for Palladio.

7.1. Product Certification Process Integration

This section introduces the generic workflow steps and development process roles, which are required to integrate specification certification into own component-based development processes. The steps and roles are introduced in section 7.1. The role responsible for evaluating and certifying the specification and according accuracy statements can be assigned to different parties participating in component development and use. The assignment choices are narrowed down by ensuring trust in the targeted application scenario and provide different advantages and disadvantages. The inherent trade-off decisions are shown and discussed in section 7.1.2.

7.1.1. Integrating Specification Certification into Development Processes

This section provides details on the necessary workflows steps and development process roles for integrating specification certification into own component-based development processes. This development process agnostic part has been published previously in [Gro12c].

The roles and workflow steps are explained in the following and depicted using UML activity diagrams. The necessary knowledge for the different roles and possible interactions are pointed out. The description uses the Proficiency Levels defined in the Architecture Skills Framework of The Open Group Architecture Framework (TOGAF) in [Ope11]. The levels are additionally depicted in table 7.1. The presentation and structure for defining the proficiency levels of the skills desirable by the roles is oriented at the TOGAF Version 9.1.

Table 7.1.: Proficiency Levels as Defined in the Architecture Skills Framework [Ope11]

Level	Achievement	Description
1	Background	Not a required skill, though should be able to define and manage skill if required.
2	Awareness	Understands the background, issues, and implications sufficiently to be able to understand how to proceed further and advise client accordingly.
3	Knowledge	Detailed knowledge of subject area and capable of providing professional advice and guidance. Ability to integrate capability into architecture design.
4	Expert	Extensive and substantial practical experience and applied knowledge on the subject.

This thesis defines the Performance Engineering Skills for specification certification as follows. The skill Performance Modeling is about creating performance specifications for implementations. The skill Accuracy Statements is about creating accuracy statements and the potential calibration of the statements according to the current level of abstraction. The skill Validation and Verification is about testing and ensuring accuracy statements for a specification in a systematic and goal-oriented way. The description focusses on these skills and does not discuss other relevant software development skills. The skills for each role are presented in combination with the description of the role and its interaction with the development process.

The Component Supplier role is responsible for the development and sharing of the component. The role needs Expert proficiency in Performance Engineering in order to create a performance specification for the developed component. The role must have substantial practical experience in creating performance models in order to create and handle the performance model. The role needs Knowledge proficiency in Accuracy

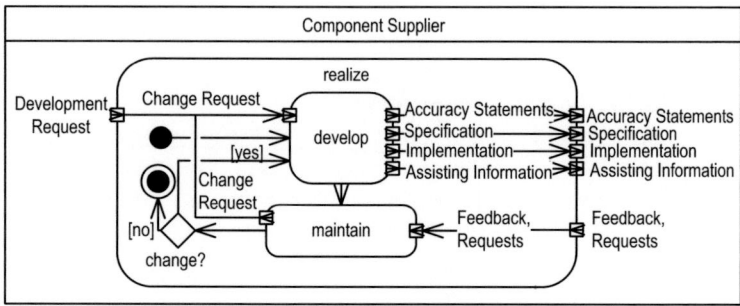

Figure 7.1.: Component Supplier Key Activity Realize

Statements in order to create accuracy statements for the performance model. There must be detailed knowledge about the quality of performance specifications but limited practical experience is sufficient. The role can use white-box information and experience from the development or experience in the component's domain to create the model and statements. The roles needs Awareness proficiency in Validation and Verification in order to ensure that the model and accuracy statements match the behavior of the implementation. The role must know about validation and verification but it is sufficient if it is applied for the developed component and its context. The role can use a constructive approach and own knowledge about the domain and does not require a strong skeptical view point on the model and statements. If no architecture level reasoning is used then this role does not need any proficiencies in Performance Engineering Skills. The role is responsible for the two key activities realize and share. They are described in the following.

The key activity realize models the development including the possible initial creation and maintenance of the component. The activity is depicted in figure 7.1. The activity consists of the activities develop and maintain.

In the activity develop, the implementation for the component is augmented or adapted according to the Change Request. The development of a new implementation for an envisioned component is also regarded as

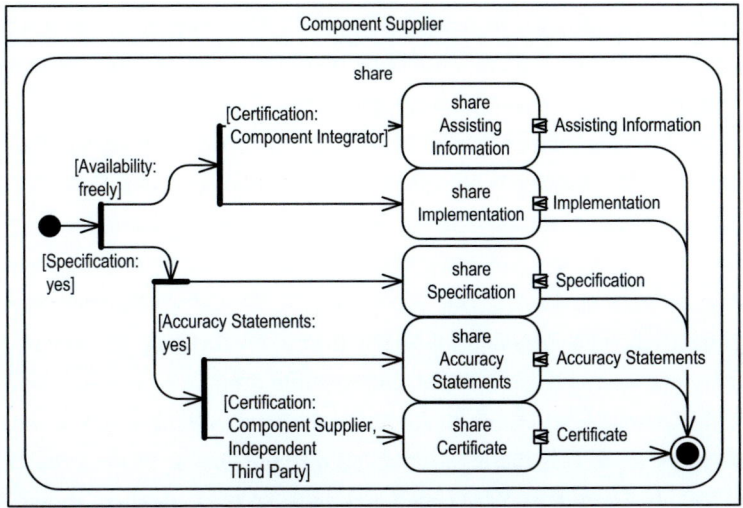

Figure 7.2.: Component Supplier Key Activity Share

a (big) Change Request. After the development, the Implementation of the component, the Specification of the performance model, the corresponding Accuracy Statements, and Assisting Information is available. The Assisting Information provides additional details on the mapping between the performance model and the implementation or how the accuracy statements have been created or tested. This information is not necessary in order to use the component or performance specification but can ease the certification.

In the activity maintain, feedback on the implemented component, its performance specification and accuracy statements is gathered and reviewed. If some of the artifacts should be modified then a Change Request is created. If the maintenance of the component should end without changes than the control flow leaves the realize activity after the change? decision node.

The key activity share models sharing the different possible artifacts before acquisition between the Component Supplier and other participating roles. The activity is depicted in figure 7.2. The Component Supplier must decide, which artifacts should be provided. The guideline presented in chapter 7.1.2 eases making these decisions.

If the implementation should be available freely without restrictions then the implementation is always shared. This sharing is modeled with the share Implementation activity. If certification is used and the Component Certifier roles is assigned to the same party as the Component Integrator then Assisting Information should accompany the implementation. This is modeled with the share Assisting Information activity and eases the certification and required effort.

If the Specification or performance model should be available then it is always shared. This sharing is modeled with the share Specification activity. If Accuracy Statements for the Specification should be provided then they are always shared. This sharing is modeled with the share Accuracy Statements activity. If certification is used and the Component Certifier is assigned to the same party as the Component Supplier or an Independent Third Party then the certificate for the accuracy statements and the specification is shared. This sharing is modeled with the share Certificate activity. The sharing of artifacts ends if one of the artifacts should not longer be shared.

The Component Certifier role is responsible for the certification itself and for verifying the validity of issued certificates. The role needs Knowledge proficiency in Performance Engineering. Detailed knowledge about the performance specification language and possible pitfalls or modeling alternatives is required but it does not have to be extensive and substantial. The role need Expert proficiency in Accuracy Statements in order to assess the validity of accuracy statements. Substantial practical experience and applied knowledge is based for efficiency assessments. The role needs Expert proficiency in Validation and Verification for assessing the correctness of provided accuracy statements and specification and implementation. Extensive and substantial practical experience

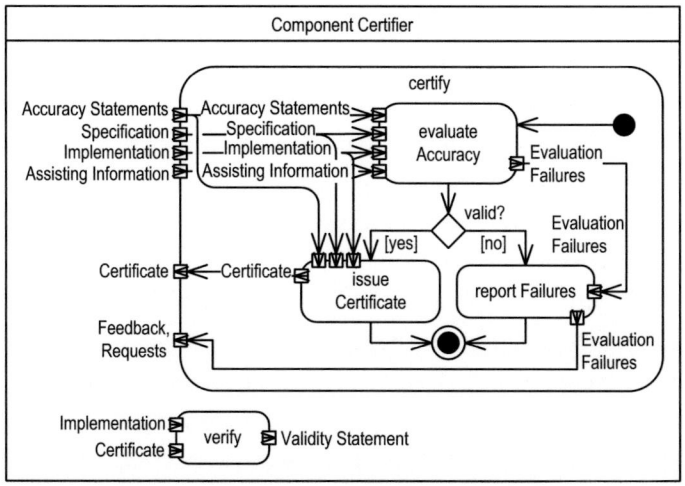

Figure 7.3.: Component Certifier Key Activities

is required for a thorough and goal-oriented assessment leading to issuing a certificate. If no architecture level reasoning is used then this role is omitted. It does not need any proficiencies in Performance Engineering Skills.The roles is responsible for the two key activities certify and verify. They are described in the following.

The key activity certify models the certification of a given specification, accuracy statements, and implementation of a component. The activity is depicted in figure 7.3. The activity consists of the activities evaluate Accuracy, issue Certificate, and report Failures.

In the activity evaluate Accuracy, the given Specification and Accuracy Statements are verified with respect to the given Implementation optionally using Assisting Information. The role scrutinizes the available Additional Information if it poses a danger for the verification. The Accuracy Statements are assessed and evaluated in an objective and goal-oriented way. The goals are provided by the definition of the certificate. A test suite is used to evaluate the correctness of the statements. The verification adheres to the PECT development process defined by Hissam et al. in [HMSW02] and presented in section 3.3. The result after running the test suite is a list of `Evaluation Failures` or the assertion of the validity of the provided statements. The decision node `valid?` models the decision depending on this validity.

In the activity `issue Certificate`, the certificate for the given `Accuracy Statements` and `Implementation` is created. The `Specification` is included as it is referenced from the `Accuracy Statements`. The `Accuracy Statements` contain an additional checksum allowing to check if a `Specification` and given `Accuracy Statements` belong together. This eases the validation if the specifications are merged and composed into a single system. A fingerprint of the `Implementation` used in the certification must be stored in the certificate as well. This allows checking if an appropriate `Implementation` is provided after acquisition for an issued `Certificate`. The result is the `Certificate`. The authenticity of the `Certificate` can be ensured by digital signatures and a Public Key Infrastructure (PKI), for example by using the OpenPGP Message Format [CCD+07].

In the activity `report Failures`, the failures occurred during the evaluation are processed and reported to the role requesting the certificate. Additional information on alternatives for preventing the failures with changes to the `Specification` or `Accuracy Statements` can be provided together with the `Feedback`. The processed `Evaluation Failures` are reported as `Feedback` and potential change `Requests`.

The key activity `verify` models the verification of a given `Certificate` and `Implementation` of a component. The activity is depicted in figure 7.3. The authenticity of the `Certificate` and the issuing party can be checked using digital signatures and a PKI. The activity allows to check if a `Certificate` and the contained `Accuracy Statements` were certified using the given `Implementation`. It can also be used to check if there was an `Implementation` at the time of certification. This means that the statements and specification can be used for reasoning on the architecture level and that a fitting implementation can be acquired. The fingerprint of the Implementation can be provided, if necessary, by means of a hash value of an archive containing the implementation. This allows protecting the IP and verifying the certificate. The Validity Statement provides information on the validity of the given information or verification failures.

The Component Integrator role is responsible for the selection and integration of components into an envisioned system. The role needs Awareness proficiency in Performance Modeling. The role must be aware of the general features of performance modeling and able to interpret if using models is applicable and helpful in the given situation. It does not require detailed knowledge on model creation or the ability to guide and consult others on performance modeling. The role needs Awareness proficiency in Accuracy Statements. The role must be aware of the limitations and able to interpret the implications of given accuracy statements. The role does not have to change or improve accuracy statements but should be able to make what-if analyses. The role must reason on component selection and the degree of fulfillment of quality requirements for the envisioned system. The role needs Background proficiency in Validation and Verification in order to trust the certification. Background knowledge allows judging what is checked during a certification. However, the result of the certification is important and not the certification process. If the role does not use Specifications and Accuracy Statements to reason on the architecture level then it does not require any proficiency in Performance Modeling and Accuracy Statements but Expert proficiency in Validation and Verification. The latter is required in order to make sound decision based on component implementations integrated into complex systems. The role is responsible for the key activity integrate / update, which is described in the following.

The key activity integrate / update models the selection, integration and updating of components for an envisioned system. It serves the

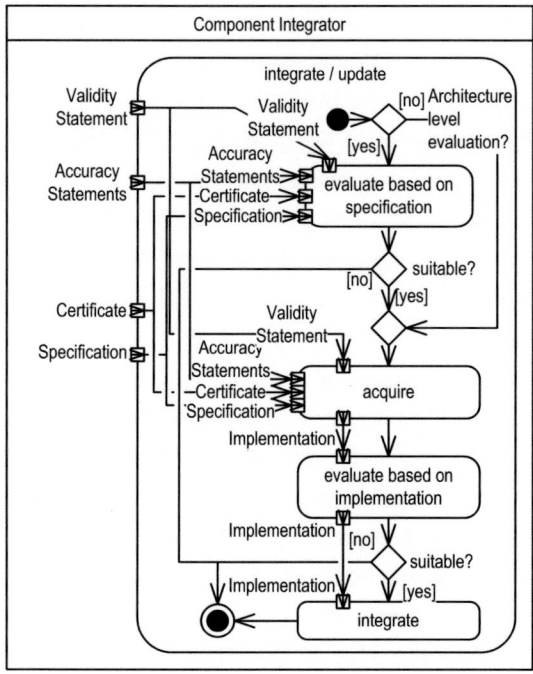

Figure 7.4.: Component Integrator Key Activities

evaluation if a new or updated component is appropriate for the system and worth the integration effort. The activity is depicted in figure 7.4. It consists of the activities `evaluate based on specification`, `acquire`, `evaluate based on implementation`, and `integrate`. These activities are described in the following. If the decision on component selection should use evaluations on the architecture level these are made in the next step. Otherwise, the step is skipped. This is modeled with the `Architecture level evaluation?` decision node.

In the activity `evaluate based on specification`, the role analyses on the architecture level how the component would influence the behavior of the envisioned system. This requires the performance `Specification` and should be accompanied by `Accuracy Statements`, a `Certificate`,

Table 7.2.: Performance Engineering Skills Overview for Roles

Notation: with / without use of architecture level evaluations.

Roles	Component Supplier	Component Certifier	Component Integrator
Performance Engineering Skills			
Performance Modeling	4 / -	3 / -	2 / -
Accuracy Statements	3 / -	4 / -	2 / -
Validation and Verification	2 / -	4 / -	1 / 4

and the `Validity Statement` as verification result. If the component is not suitable and selected for the system then the integration is finished. This is modeled with the `suitable?` decision node. If the component is suitable then the integration continues on the implementation level.

In the activity `acquire`, the implementation is acquired from the Component Supplier. This may range from creating and using customized contracts to downloading a freely available source code archive. A provided `Implementation` is verified to match the provided `Certificate`, `Specification`, and `Accuracy Statements`. This verification results in the `Validity Statement`. This part can be skipped if there was no evaluation on the architecture level. The result and output is the `Implementation` corresponding to the provided `Specification` and `Accuracy Statements`.

In the activity `evaluate based on implementation`, the component is prototypically integrated into the system and the properties of the system are evaluated. This evaluation can require a lot of effort if there was no evaluation on the architecture level in order to ensure quality properties of the system in a sound way. If the component is not suitable then the integration is finished. Otherwise, the control flow continues with the `integrate` activity. This is modeled with the `suitable?` decision node.

In the activity `integrate`, the component is finally fully integrated and embedded into the envisioned system.

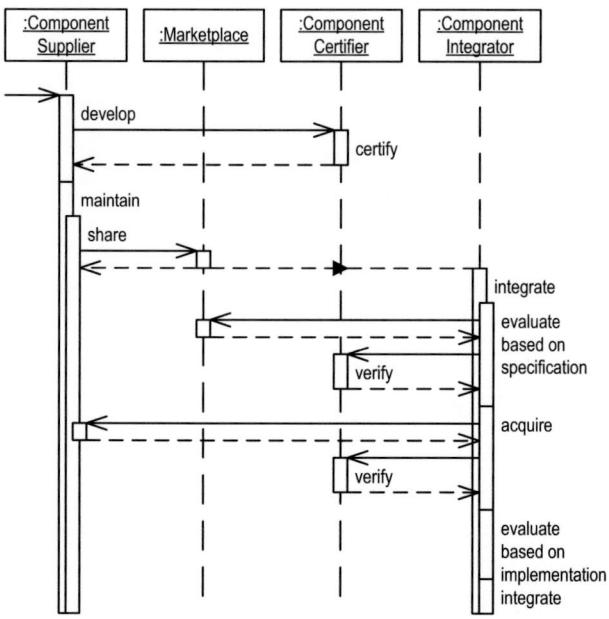

Figure 7.5.: Workflow Steps Interaction Application Example

The presented `Performance Engineering Skills` definitions for the different roles are summarized in table 7.2.

An example for the interaction between the roles and their workflow steps is provided in figure 7.5. A `Component Supplier` starts to `develop` a component. The component and developed performance specifications and accuracy statements are sent to the `Component Certifier`. The `Component Certifier` checks and certifies the provided information successfully. The `Component Supplier` continues with the `maintenance` activity and `shares` the component using a `Marketplace`. The implementation is not shared freely. It is transferred after contracting and acquisition directly between `Component Supplier` and `Component Integrator`. The certificate is additionally used to demonstrate that the `Component Supplier` cares about performance and is able to create accurate specifications. An interested `Component Integrator` can get the `Specification` and `Accuracy Statements` from the `Component Supplier` directly or from the `Marketplace`. The `Component Integrator` gets the information for architecture level evaluations from the `Marketplace` and verifies the certificate. The evaluation is successful. The `Component Integrator` acquires the implementation from the `Component Supplier` and `verifies` that it matches the information used for the evaluation. The evaluation continues on the implementation level. The evaluation is successful and the component is finally integrated into the system of the `Component Integrator`.

This section introduced the three different `Performance Engineering Skills` and the necessary certification process roles `Component Supplier`, `Component Certifier`, and `Component Integrator`. The necessary skills for each roles were defined and explained. Workflow steps for the different roles were described in detail an an application example showed their possible interaction in a marketplace scenario. The workflow steps are a basis for integrating certification into own development processes.

7.1.2. Certifier Party Selection

This section presents the guideline for selecting the certificate issuing party while maintaining trust in the certificate. It points out the different application scenarios and corresponding evaluation effort distribution for the participating roles. The guideline has been published previously in [Gro12c]. It supports the identification of possible alternatives and shows assignment consequences. The consequences allow reasoning about the attractiveness of an offered component for other parties and for making justified trade-off decisions. The value of specification and accuracy statement certification should be considered separately for each quality characteristic. The information provided in this section is also valid for quality characteristics other than performance.

The issuer of a certificate must be trusted in order to take advantage of certification. The issue with trust, as Meyer pointed out in [MMS98], is that it is very subjective and hard to state in general. For the presented process integration, the main influence on trust is the trust relation between Component Supplier and Component Integrator. A component can be integrated by more than one Component Integrator, for example if it is distributed via marketplaces. The trust relationship is considered individually for each possible Component Integrator.

In theory, the Component Certifier can be combined with the party of the Component Supplier or the Component Integrator, it can be assigned to an independent third party, or it can be omitted if no certification is used.

If the Component Supplier self-certifies the specification then a conflict of interest is likely as the Component Supplier may be interested in providing whitewashed information. The implementation remains at the party of the Component Supplier only for the first alternative. It must be shared temporarily with the independent third party in the second alternative.

If an independent third party is responsible for certification then Component Supplier and Component Integrator have to trust this party in order to realize the advantages. The independent Component Certifier should only use necessary information for the certification in order to ensure the correctness of the evaluation result.

If Component Integrator and Component Certifier belong to the same party then it is assumed that the Component Supplier assists in the specification and accuracy statement certification by providing test suites and/or links between implementation and specification. This assisting information eases the evaluation if the specification and given accuracy statements are correct for the provided tests. In this case, the Component

Integrator does not need to infer a specification and according accuracy statements in order to use architecture-level prediction approaches.

The alternative without a certificate of the specification and accuracy statements does not require an issuing party or information assisting in the certification.

The trust in a certificate is also affected by the characteristics of the available and applied assessment tools and techniques. For example, security assessments of components according to standards like the Common Criteria [Comer] usually require manual inspections and automated support is limited. Automation does not only speed up assessments but also ensures objectivity and reproduces the same results. The accuracy statement validation approach presented in chapter 6 is such an automated tool. This kind of trust in a certificate is strongly connected with the definition of the certificate itself. It is not affected by the assignment of the Component Certifier as long as the person having the certifier role can apply the tool or technique correctly.

In general, Component Supplier and Component Certifier require the evaluation effort once per release of the component. If Component Supplier and Component Certifier belong to the same party then they can re-use information and benefit from synergy effects. The Component Integrator requires the evaluation effort each time a new released component is assessed for acquisition. If the Component Integrator uses the specification in the envisioned system outside of its provided accuracy statements then corresponding accuracy statements must be evaluated and certified.

The need for taking into account the effort was also identified by Overhage and Thomas in [OT04]. They identified that:

> Although component testing may well be an integral part of the suitability assessment process, it should not primarily be used to determine component characteristics, but rather to validate them - otherwise, the total assessment costs will quickly

exceed any savings that are achieved by component reuse and COTS (commercial-off-the-shelf) based software engineering in general is likely to fail. [OT04]

The following guideline shows the different alternatives and how this issue can be taken into account.

The assignment on the issuing party on the Component Suppliers side requires a trade off between the need to keep knowledge and IP to the Component Supplier until a final acquisition decision is made, the evaluation effort and attractiveness for Component Integrators , and the competitive advantage of demonstrating the quality characteristic management capabilities by providing specifications and accuracy statements.

The application scenario of certification depends on the availability of accuracy statements, implementation and the mutual trust between Component Supplier and Component Integrator. Using a specification without accuracy statements increases the risks for acquisition decisions but matches the current practice in industry. The implementation can either be freely available or protected by the Component Supplier until an acquisition decision is made and contracts are signed. Specifications and accuracy statements are values for freely available implementations as well as they allow decision making on the architecture-level and can reduce the evaluation effort. The mutual trust between Component, Supplier an Component Integrator can either be weak or strong.

The guideline consists of a two step selection process for the assignment. First, the application scenario is narrowed down. Second, the trade-off for evaluation effort distribution is considered and the issuing party assigned. The guideline is shown in table 7.3. The thorough evaluation and certification of a specification and its accuracy statements is assumed to take increase effort. The shift of the evaluation effort is discussed in the following.

Independent third party certification requires a thorough validation by the Component Certifier, which restricts reusing information created

Table 7.3.: Overview of Evaluation Effort Shift Between Roles for Issuing Parties

Evaluation Effort +: low, ++: moderate, +++:increased, ++++: high, +++++: very high

Accuracy Statements (Availability)	Implementation	Mutual Trust	Evaluation Effort at Component			Issuing Party
			Supplier	Certifier	Integrator	
yes	after Acquisition	weak	++	+++		independent third party
yes	after Acquisition	strong		+++		self (Supplier = Certifier)
yes	freely	weak	++	+++		independent third party
				+++	+	self (Supplier = Certifier)
			+++		++	assisted (Integrator = Certifier)
yes	freely	strong	+++			none
			+++		+++	none, assisted (Integrator = Certifier)
no	freely, after Acquisition	weak			+++++	none
no	freely, after Acquisition	strong			++++	none

by the Component Supplier. The Component Supplier must prepare the certification but does not need to execute it himself. This involves only moderate effort. Component Integrators can trust the specification and accuracy statements and do not require own evaluation effort.

Self certification allows information reuse as Component Supplier and Component Certifier are at the same party. Their white-box knowledge on the component and eases the identifying and addressing potential accuracy deviation risks. If there is only weak mutual trust then the accuracy statements should be ensured by a test sample requiring low effort at the Component Integrator. Otherwise, the Component Integrator does not need evaluation effort.

Assisted certification requires a thorough evaluation of specification and accuracy statements by the Component Supplier. The information assisting in checking the correctness of the accuracy statement must be additionally provided. Overall, increased evaluation effort is required. If the Component Integrator does not trust the provided specification and accuracy statements then using the assisting information for an own evaluation requires moderate effort. If there is mutual trust, the Component Integrator does not need to spend evaluation effort.

Without certificates, the Component Integrator must spend at least increased evaluation effort if he does not trust provided the specification and accuracy statements. The required evaluation effort is high if there are no accuracy statements available and they must be identified and created first. The effort can be very high if there are no accuracy statements available and there is only weak trust in the correctness of the specification itself.

This section discussed the trade-offs inherent to assigning certificate issuing parties. The presented guideline narrows down the selection for given application scenarios. Its application allows risk estimation and ensuring that Component Supplier and Component Integrator trust the provided specification and accuracy statements.

7.2. Palladio Specification Certification

This section describes how certification can be integrated with the Palladio approach. It demonstrates the integration of the generic workflow steps presented in section 7.1.1 in the Palladio reference development process. This integration is presented in section 7.2.1. Furthermore, a certificate for Palladio specifications is defined. The definitions states, which aspects have to be covered to which extent in order to receive a valid certificate. It allows users to reasons about the quality of the validation and verification during the certification and estimate if it is sound enough for their use case. The definition is provided in section 7.2.2.

7.2.1. Product Certification Aware Palladio Development Process

This section shows the integration of the generic workflow steps in the Palladio reference development process. Section 2.5 provides details on the pre-existing reference development process. The resulting adapted process supports certification. This section presents the properties of the pre-existing process from a certification and validation and verification viewpoint. It shows the existing gaps towards integrating certification and adapts the workflow step from section 7.1 to the process in order to close these gaps. Finally, it presents the adapted reference process taking into account certification.

This paragraphs describes the properties of the pre-existing reference process from a certification and validation and verification viewpoint. The process has a single Component Repository in which all component implementations and specifications are stored. It does not take into account that there may be different levels of trust and multiple repositories, which may contain different descriptive information on the same component. The QoS Analyst is responsible for assessing the soundness of specifications (see description about the QoS Analysis workflow in section 2.5). It is not described how the QoS Analyst can achieve this, especially if only specifications are provided by a third party, which is interested in selling its component instead of its competitors. The process model focusses on the development and composition of a system and does not distinguish to which party the persons belong, which have a certain role. As a consequence, the presentation does not support or require the differentiation from which party a component's specification or implementation come. There is no distinguished activity or role suggesting or fostering certification. Overall, the pre-existing process assumes a strong trust in specifications in the repository but provides no explicit means to back this trust.

The integration of specification certification in the reference development process is oriented at the order of presentation of roles, workflow steps and activities in section 7.1. Figures 7.7 to 7.10 show the final version of the process after all adaptations.

The Component Supplier maps to the roles Software Architect and Component Developer. The former is responsible for the system and composition. The latter is responsible for the development of a single component. Component Developers can develop components for a marketplace without a prior request of Software Architects.

The key activity realize and the input artifacts Development Requests and Change Requests are already covered on a more fine granular scale by explicitly elicited requirements and subsequent design and implementation workflows. The artifacts Implementation and Specification map to the artifacts of the same name. New output artifacts are Accuracy Statements and Assisting Information. Both stem from the develop activity. The required adaptations are discussed together with the mapping of that activity.

The activity develop within the key activity realize maps to the component development share of the Provisioning workflow presented together with the Specification workflow (see figure 2.14). In order to reduce misunderstanding between the different types of specifica-

Table 7.4.: Artifact Terms and Operators used in this Chapter and the Process Model

Usage example: a specification artifact containing requirements and functional specifications is denoted Spec(R,F). If such an artifacts flows between activities always in connection with an architecture and may flow together with assets then it is denoted Spec(R,F) + Architecture +| Assets.

Term / Operator	Meaning
Spec(R)	Requirement specifications.
Spec(F)	Functional specifications.
Spec(I)	Interface specifications. Also denoted as Interfaces in the pre-existing process. Interfaces are first class entities and can exists without components or implementations using them.
Spec(D)	Dependency specifications.
Spec(B)	Behavior specifications: denoted as QoS-relevant information in the pre-existing process and Specification in section 7.1.1.
Spec(Ac)	Accuracy Statements.
Spec(As)	Assisting Information.
Architecture	Architecture including all available Information on the specifications of the composed components. Excludes specifications of the QoS of the environment and the usage model.
Assets	Information on interfaces and components. Includes all different specification types and the implementation.
+	Binary operator modeling a mandatory and-relation of artifacts.
+|	Binary operator modeling an optional and-relation of artifacts.
		Binary operator modeling an exclusive or-relation of artifacts.

tion artifacts for a component, the terms and operators presented in table 7.4 are used from now on. The mapping requires an extension of the QoS Property Specification activity. This activity must additionally process Accuracy Statements and Assisting Information beyond pure behavior specifications. These type of specifications are strongly linked with implementations. These artifacts need to be consistent at the end of a component's development and multiple steps back and forth between the activities QoS Property Specification and Component Implementation are likely. The artifacts must flow in both ways and be updated accordingly. Hence, the Component Implementation activity additionally provides Spec(Ac,As) beyond the Implementation + Spec(R,F,I,D) +| Spec(B) artifacts in the pre-existing process as output.

The activity maintain within the key activity realize maps to the flow back and forth between the activities and workflows for different process iterations and phases. The iterations are controlled by the management instead of the development process and not discussed for the development process.

The key activity share maps to the artifact flow between the activity Component Implementation and the Component Repository. The pre-existing transition does neither allow to respect the availability of the implementation nor the decisions involved in sharing. Hence, the new activity Component Sharing is introduced. It uses the outputs of the activity Component Implementation as input. It ensures that the assets are stored in appropriate repositories or marketplaces. Examples are provided together with the summary of the adapted process. It provides the Available Assets for the Component Identification activity of the Specification workflow instead of the Component Implementation activity in the pre-existing process. Available Assets denote the assets, which can be accessed by the party identifying components. If that party can only access public component repositories or marketplaces then the assets in protected component repositories of other parties remain unavailable. Figures 7.8 and 7.9 in the summary section further down give an impression, which information is available in which repository depending if the implementation is available freely or not. See also the documentation of the key activity share in section 7.1.1 and the guideline for party selections including the different decision options in section 7.1.2. The key activity share allows sharing Certificates. Requesting a certificate requires the Implementation and according Spec(B,Ac,As). Because of the strong link of specifications with the implementation the request for the Certificate is additionally assigned to the activity Component Implementation. An equally suitable alternative would be an assignment to the activity QoS Property Specification. The disadvantage of that alternative is that it is in front of the activity Component Implementation in the usual control flow. The selected solution adds the possibility to optionally transfer a requested Certificate from the activity Component Implementation to the activity Component Sharing. The resulting process integration including issuing the certificate is described together with the key activity certify of the Component Certifier later in this section.

The Component Certifier can not be mapped to the pre-existing process. The role is added.

The key activity certify is added to the process under the name Component Certification for the role Component Certifier due consistency with the naming scheme of the pre-existing process. The purpose of the key activity is described in section 7.1.1 and not repeated at this point. Its input artifacts are the Implementation, behavior Specification, Accuracy Statements and Assisting Information. Its output artifact is either the Certificate or the report with the Evaluation Failures. The activity is connected with the Component Implementation activity. This is sufficient for certifying that the developed implementation and specifications are accurate. The added activity is part of the `Provisioning` workflow.

The key activity `verify` is added to the process under the name `Certificate Verification` for the role `Component Certifier` due to consistency with the naming scheme of the pre-existing process. The purpose of the key activity is described in section 7.1.1. Its mandatory input artifacts are the `Certificate` and the `Accuracy Statements`. Its optional input artifact is the `Implementation`. The `Implementation` allows checking if the supplied implementation was used for the certification or is a different one. The output artifact is a `Validity Statement`. The activity is connected with the activity `Component Identification`. This allows to check for all `Available Assets` containing `Certificates` if the provided `Accuracy Statements` are valid. The activity is part of the `Specification` workflow.

The `Component Integrator` maps to the `Software Architect`, `System Deployer`, `Domain Expert`, and `QoS Analyst`. It involves the selection of components in the `Specification` workflow. The involvement continues through the `QoS Analysis`, `Provisioning` and `Assembly` workflows. The final integration decision is in the `Test` workflow and includes the verification that the selected component fulfills the requirements.

The key activity `integrate / update` is distributed over the workflows listed for the `Component Integrator`. It addresses the evaluation and selection of a single component within a system. The aspect of individual component selection is contained within activities of the workflows and mapped directly to the activities. The mapping is discussed for each activity allowing a better understanding. The input artifacts of the behavior `Specifications`, the `Accuracy Statements`, the `Certificates`, and `Validity Statements` are required for certified specification. The pre-existing process additionally supports system development without behavior specifications and certificates. Preserving this property renders all input artifacts optional in the general case. Furthermore, the types of assets for each component can differ even within the same system. For example, certificates may suffice for externally supplied components while the availability of behavior specifications, accuracy statements, and assisting information is sufficient for self-developed components. The adapted process will show the general solution with optional artifacts although the use of them is highly recommended.

The decision node `Architecture level evaluation?` maps to not spending effort or leaving out the activities `Interoperability Check` and `Certificate Verification` in the `Specification` workflow and the whole `QoS Analysis` workflow. The transition can be regarded as if going directly from the activity `Component Specification` in the `Specification` workflow to the `Provisioning` workflow. The activities in the `Provisioning` workflow do not have to provide behavior specifications, accuracy statements, assisting information, or certificates. This information is simply not used in the non-architecture level evaluation case. As a consequence, there is nothing done in the `QoS Property Specification` activity, all output artifacts of that activity are optional.

The activity `evaluate based on specification` maps exactly to the activities and workflow left out if there is no architecture level evaluation. In the `Component Identification` activity of the `Specification` workflow, the `Available Assets` containing `Certificates` are verified. The certified assets have to contain a behavior `Specification`, `Accuracy Statements`, `Certificate`, and `Validity Statement`, which are the input artifacts of the activity. With this input information, invalid assets can be identified and excluded from the evaluation and integration into the system. If an asset does not contain behavior specifications, their creation can be initiated from the `Component Specification` activity as part of the `Provisioning` workflow. The evaluation on the architecture level itself maps to the `QoS Analysis` workflow. The `System Deployer` identifies the necessary environment of the system and allocates the component instances of the system into the environment. This results in Deployment Diagrams and the Deployment-Annotated Architecture. The Domain Expert analyses the usage of the system in different Scenarios and provides detailed Usage Models of the system. The QoS Analyst ensures that behavior specifications exist for all QoS Requirements and QoS Metrics and metric thresholds are defined based on the Business Requirements. QoS Analysts integrate the behavior specifications of composed components and system-external services, the Usage Model, and the Deployment-Annotated Architecture into an Annotated Architecture. The soundness of the specifications and their accuracy is additionally verified in the Component Integration activity of the Specification workflow if certificates are used. Otherwise, a validation of the behavior specifications and accuracy statements is necessary. Validation approaches like the one presented in chapter 6 can be used for this purpose. Assisting information linked with the component in the architecture can aid this purpose. The Annotated Architecture and Usage Model describe all influence factors of a system and the QoS of the system can be evaluated. This system information is combined with information on QoS Metrics, which allows reasoning about the satisfaction of requirements, and transformed into a QoS Evaluation Model. This model is evaluated in the last activity and the Results for the QoS Metrics are used by the Software Architect to reason about the architecture in the Component Identification activity in the Specification workflow.

The decision node suitable? maps to the decision about component selection and is part of the reasoning on the architecture in the Component Identification activity in the Specification workflow. If a component is not suitable then it is removed from the architecture and further considerations. Otherwise, it is kept in the architecture.

The activity acquire maps to component acquisitions after make-or-buy decisions in the Provisioning workflow. In case of a buy-decision, if a behavior Specification, Accuracy Statements, or Certificate have been used for the reasoning then these should be used to request the fitting implementation. The `Implementation`, behavior `Specification`, and `Accuracy Statements` can be verified with the activity `Certifi-cate Verification` of the `Component Certifier`. In case of reusing an own component, it can be directly retrieved from the appropriate repository. In case of creating a new component, the activities for developing a new component come into play.

The activity `evaluate based on implementation` maps to the `As-sembly` and `Test` workflow. The implementation of the components is assembled and deployed to a test system. The fulfillment of the system's requirements is verified by testing in the `Test` workflow.

The decision node `suitable?` maps to the decision about component selection and is part of the reasoning after comparing requirements and component as well as system properties. As for the pre-existing process, the test evaluation results are fed back to other workflows. If a component is not suitable then it is removed from the architecture. A new architecture must be designed and the process continues in the `Component Identification` activity in the `Specification` workflow.

The activity `integrate` maps to keeping components in the architecture if their evaluation based on the implementation was successful. They are integrated and delivered to the customer as part of the `Tested System` in the `Deployment` workflow.

The process taking specification certification into account is shown with all adaptation in the following. The terms and operators shown in table 7.4 are used instead of the terms and operators of the pre-existing process. Further renaming is discussed together with the presented share of the process.

Figure 7.6 shows the adapted process model. The workflow-level is equal to the pre-existing process. An incorrectly missing artifact flow from `Business Requirements` to the `QoS Analysis` workflow was added. The `Architecture` can additionally flow to the `Specification` work-flow. This models that the architecture is kept and may be adapted if the

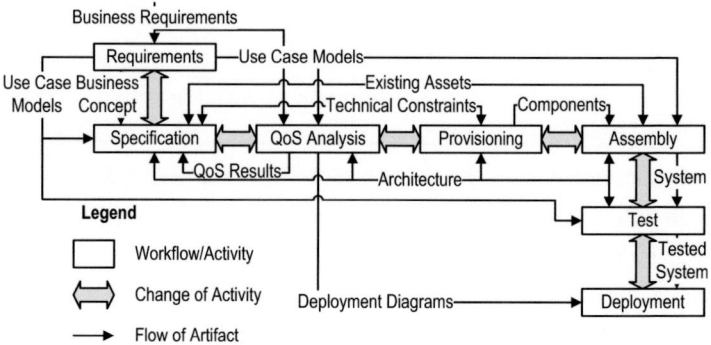

Figure 7.6.: Process Model Taking Into Account Specification Certification

Table 7.5.: Roles for the Process Taking Into Account Specification Certification

Notation: * marks roles, which are unmodified and inherited from the RUP.

Role
Component Developer
Software Architect
System Deployer
Domain Expert
Component Certifier
Test Engineer*
System Integrator*
Integration Tester*
System Tester*

change from activity is from a later workflow. An example for this situation is if a component is identified as not suitable in the Test workflow and needs to be replaced by another one. The roles used in the adapted process are shown in table 7.5. They have been introduced above or are unmodified roles from [CD03], which are described in detail in [JBR99].

Figure 7.7 shows the adapted Specification workflow. The Component Identification activity can now access all available instead of all existing assets. The architecture is usually designed in several iterations,

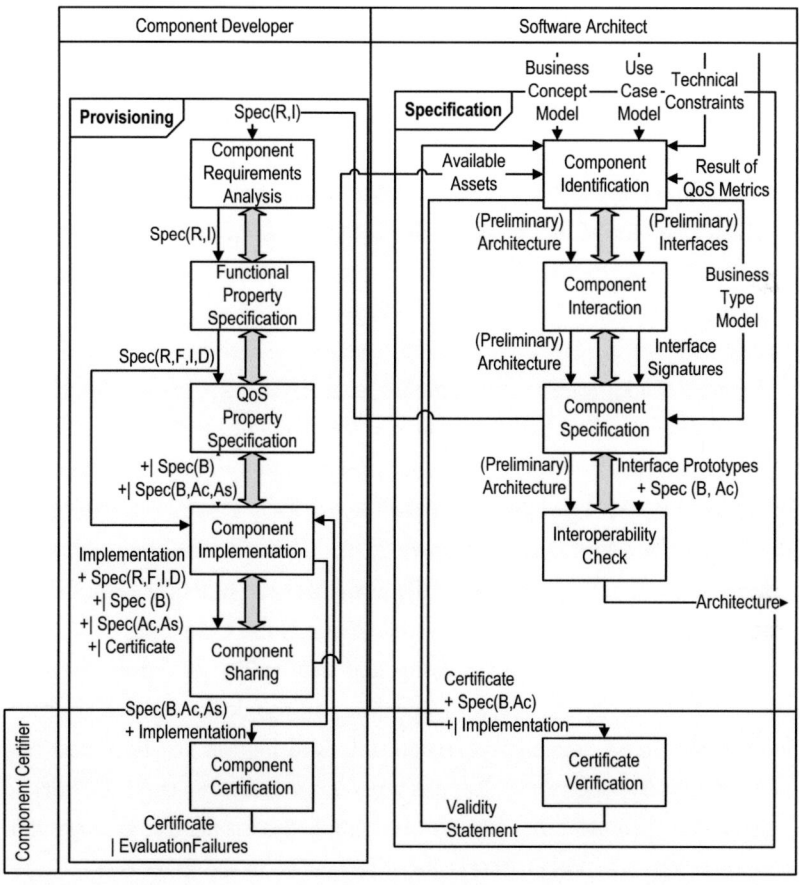

The Provisioning workflow is partially shown to ease differentiation and show interactions for new developed components.

Figure 7.7.: Specification Workflow Taking Into Account Specification Certification

which may involve later workflows. Different component selection techniques can be applied, for example based on quality models like in Andreou and Tziakouris's approach presented in [AT07], Saaty's generic Analytic Hierarchy Process [Saa08], or gap analysis as proposed by [CD03]. The selection technique is not constrained by the adapted process. The term (Preliminary) Architecture is used instead of Initial Component Specs & Architecture in order to reduce misunderstandings and point out the potential iterative aspect. Interfaces, Signatures, and Spec(B, Ac) are also part of the architecture. They are additionally shown as artifact flow besides the architecture in the figure to point out, which information must be specifically provided for the next activity. The Certificate Verification is part of the Specification workflow.

Figure 7.7 additionally shows the Provisioning workflow with respect to the development of new components. The flow of artifacts is more precise in the adapted version. For example, QoS-relevant Information is replaced by +| Spec(B) +| Spec(B,Ac,As). Component Sharing is a part of the Provisioning workflow. The effect of the introduced Component Sharing activity on the availability of assets is described for freely available and unavailable specifications in the following.

Figure 7.8 shows the distribution and availability of information for freely available specifications. Depending on the decisions, which information should be created and shared, this information can be stored into a Protected Component Repository or a Marketplace / Public Component Repository. The information in the former one is only available to selected parties, whereas the information in the latter one is freely available. Usually, the same information will be shared in this scenario, but in theory some of it may be held back. For example, the original requirements may not influence the later use of the component and can be stored in the protected repository for documentation and backup purposes.

Figure 7.9 shows the distribution and availability of information for specifications, which are not freely available. The Implementation and, op-

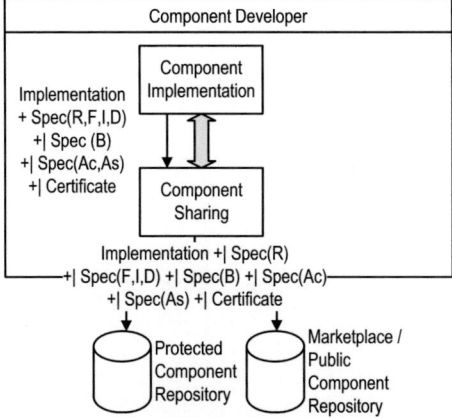

Figure 7.8.: Activity Component Sharing of the Specification Workflow for Freely Available Implementations

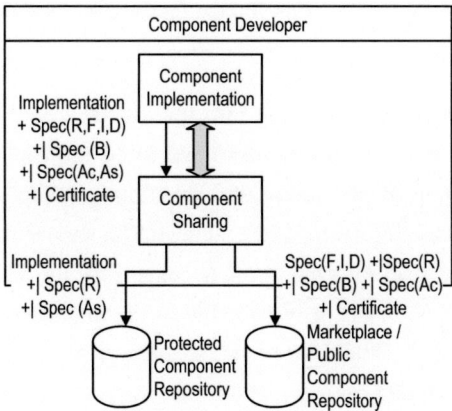

Figure 7.9.: Activity Component Sharing of the Specification Workflow for Non-Freely Available Implementations

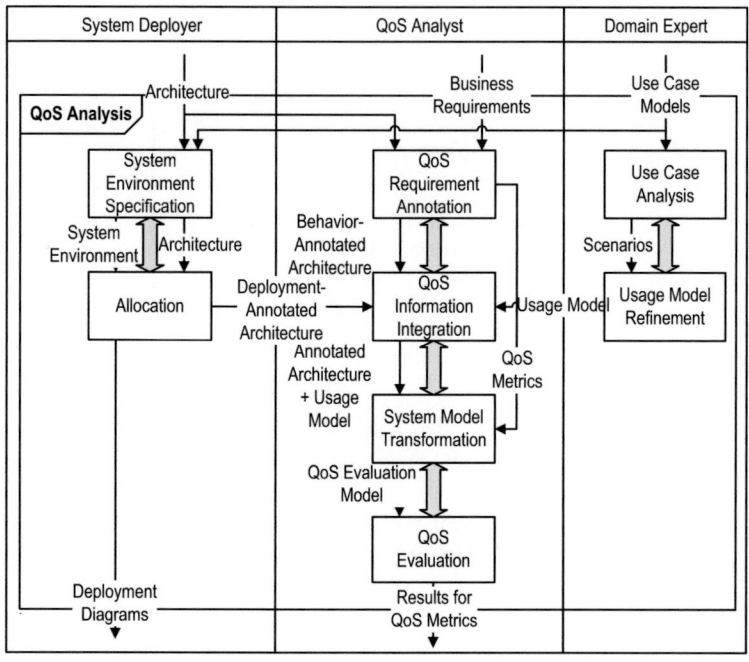

Figure 7.10.: QoS Analysis Workflow Taking Into Account Specification Certification

tionally, requirements and assisting information are stored in the protected repository. The requirements do not have to be protected per se but do not necessarily help in evaluating and selecting a component. Only the information relevant for evaluation and selection should be shared in this scenario. The assisting information is necessary for the verification of behavior specifications but is only valuable in combination with the implementation. Hence, it should be stored together with the implementation. The information shared on the marketplace supports the identification of the component. If specification and certificates are used then even the architecture level evaluation and selection are supported without sharing the implementation and contained knowledge and IP.

Figure 7.10 shows the adapted `QoS Analysis` workflow. The terms used for the QoS information regarding the different influence factors on a system and component is more precise. `Annotated Architecture` contains all necessary annotations and consists of the `Behavior-Annotated Architecture` and `Deployment-Annotated Architecture`. The `Accuracy Statements`, which can be connected with the components in the architecture, improve reasoning about the accuracy effects on the overall prediction. This can indicate if behavior specifications are used outside of the boundaries for which accuracy statements are provided and aid in risk assessment. The `Certificates` of components in the architecture reduce the effort for reasoning about the soundness of accuracy statements. Otherwise, validation approaches like the one presented in chapter 6 can be used to verify accuracy statements.

This section showed the necessary adaptations for including specification certification into the Palladio reference development process. It discussed the mapping of the process agnostic roles, activities and artifacts to the process and introduced terms and operators for precise descriptions of artifact flows. The adaptation were summarized and the resulting new process was presented. Adapted terms were referenced easing the comparison between the pre-existing and the adapted process. Additionally, the distribution of information to protected and public repositories or marketplaces was discussed for two scenarios, which differ in the degree of protection of the implementation.

7.2.2. Palladio Certificate

This section defines a certificate for Palladio performance specifications. It states which aspects of a specification are validated and verified and it states the extent of the checks. The knowledge about these aspects allows reasoning if the quality of the checks is adequate for the intended use case. It permits comparability between results of independent certifiers by providing a common set of requirements. However, an evaluation is limited to the evaluated QoS, for example performance, and users should check if the other properties of the certified component fits their use case.

The certification requirements are stated for general specifications and are analogous to the definition of the Protection Profile (PP) in the Common Criteria [Comer, sec. 9.3]. Their application on a selected specification is analogous to a Security Target (ST), and the validation and verification itself represents the evaluation on the Target Of Evaluation (TOE). The separation between the level of PP and ST is not necessary as there is no human intervention required to generate the ST.

The Palladio certificate is based on the test-based validation of specifications presented in chapter 6.

The Palladio certificate requires that an implementation has been successfully validated against a given specification with its accuracy statements and a given validation quality. The validation quality is part of the certificate and represents the predefined assurance levels of rigor and detail of the validation. This stating of the coverage requirements and covered aspects supports reasoning on the confidence of the result taking into account the intended composition of the specification. The available performance-oriented testing strategies and their configuration options are presented in section 6.3.2 in detail.

The Palladio certificate consists of an archive containing the validation quality information in a single `TBValidationQuality` element, which was presented in section 6.1, the validated accuracy statements as `QualityAnnotation` element, which was presented in section 4.1, a fingerprint of the implementation, and the specification itself including its required architecture specifications, for example interfaces, parameters, and required roles. The integrity and authenticity of the archive can be ensured using signatures and a PKI. The specification itself is referenced from the accuracy statements and its integrity is additionally ensured by a checksum (see `ServiceSpecification` in section 4.1). This integrity check includes ensuring the integrity of the architectural specifications for data types, parameters and required roles. This solution provides the advantage that different component specifications can be merged into a single architecture specification and the authenticity check still provides the same result. The certificate is not needed for this simple check.

Issued certificates and fingerprints for the corresponding implementations must be stored by the Component Certifier in order to allow their verification. Additionally, a certificate revocation list should be considered in case an issued certificate needs to be invalidated.

8. Evaluation

This chapter describes the evaluation of the solutions described in this thesis. Chapter 4 describes the solutions for the Accuracy Statements, chapter 5 for Accuracy Effects on Overall Prediction, chapter 6 for Accuracy Validation, and chapter 7 for Specification Certification. The evaluation itself is based on several experiments, which in turn utilize overall three systems for experimentation. The systems cover a realistic industrial use case as well as technology demonstrations for further remaining features of the presented solutions. This chapter shows the derivation of experiments for the research questions, the goal and setting for each experiment, discusses the experiment execution, and presents the evaluation results.

The chapter is structured as follows. Section 8.1 describes derivation of experiments and the goals and validation of the experiments. Section 8.2 describes the common aspects of the three different experiment systems in detail, which are used for the experiments. Section 8.3 demonstrates the application of the solutions proposed in this thesis and shows the results for each experiment. Section 8.4 summarizes the evaluation results and found evidence.

8.1. Experiments

The experiments serve to evaluate if the overall aim, the contributions, and questions raised in the introduction are addressed. Accordingly, the experiments are derived from the goal, contributions, and questions. The experiments are presented in separate sections for each work area. This eases reasoning on goals, the success in reaching them, and the differentiation of aspects in need of coverage.

The aim and contributions were initially introduced and explained in section 1.3 and are repeated in the following for the reader's convenience. The aim of the thesis is advancing cross-party component-based engineering by improving the evaluation of appropriate use of performance specifications and increasing the trustworthiness in predictions, especial if specifications are reused during the lifecycle of a system.

The contributions towards this aim were listed in section 1.4 and are as follows.

C1 Performance engineering can be used in scenarios with cross-party component repositories or marketplaces. The trustworthy specifications allow exploiting the benefits of architecture level performance predictions without reducing the quality of the evaluation and selection of components.

C2 Reproducible and more reliable validation results. Automated validation and formalized coverage criteria reduce human validation errors and ensure a sound validation.

C3 Faster validation by higher degree of automation.

C4 Reduced effort for specification creation by lowering bar for correct reuse of existing specifications.

C5 Better architectural decisions, especially on the selection of components, based on the knowledge of error margins of predictions due to specification inaccuracies.

C6 Reduced effort of performance engineers required for validation and evaluation of specifications.

C7 Software architects need less performance engineering interpretation knowledge when using architecture level predictions. Results are easier to interpret, inappropriate specifications are easier identified and the understanding of validated aspects is more precise with the criteria.

The raised questions were shown in table 1.1. Their mapping to the work areas was shown in table 1.2. They are repeated in the following for the readers convenience together with their directly related work area.

Q1 Are the targeted implementations appropriately described by the specifications? This relates to Accuracy Validation. Sections 8.1.3 discusses the derived experiments.

Q2 Which accuracy does each specification have? This relates to Accuracy Statements and Accuracy Validation. Sections 8.1.1 and 8.1.3 discuss the derived experiments.

Q3 Is the accuracy of each specification valid for the propagated usage profile? This relates to Accuracy Effects on Overall Prediction. Section 8.1.2 discusses the derived experiments.

Q4 How trustworthy are the statements about targeted implementation and accuracy? This relates to Accuracy Validation and Specification Certification. Sections 8.1.3 and 8.1.4 discuss the derived experiments.

Q5 What is the effect of the accuracies of the composed components on the overall prediction? This relates to Accuracy Effects on Overall Prediction. Section 8.1.2 discusses the derived experiments.

The following sections discuss the evaluation scope and derive experiments for each work area.

8.1.1. Accuracy Statements

The evaluation of providing a suitable answer to question Q2 requires that users can specify the accuracy of a specification. The applicability and

285

whether the input can be acquired and stated is evaluated. In specifications, the control-flow and resource demand is usually an abstraction and approximation of the implemented behavior in order to reduce the complexity. Depending on the measurement method, individual measurements are subject to relative and absolute deviation thresholds. Users must be able to specify this deviation. For ensuring proper component descriptions, it must be ensured that users can specify that there are no calls to required components other than the specified ones.

Experiment E1 checks the hypothesis if statements can be made for all influence factors of a Palladio specification. The completeness should be shown via all representations of these factors in the Palladio meta-model.

Experiment E2 checks the hypothesis if statements for Palladio specifications can be made, which are exact matches of the implemented behavior of a component. The considered influence factors are the resource demand in bytecode instructions and calls to business components. This allows demonstrating the general applicability while limiting the complexity for presentation and comprehension.

Experiment E3 checks the hypothesis if statements for Palladio specifications can be made, which deviate from the implemented behavior of a component in the relative amount of the resource demand but are exact matches with respect to calls to required components. The considered influence factors are the resource demand in bytecode instructions and calls to business components. The relative deviation is set to 10%, which allows abstractions but is significantly lower than the bound of 30% acceptable error proposed by Menasce in [MA01] for predictions in software engineering. This allows demonstrating the general applicability while limiting the complexity for presentation and comprehension.

Experiment E4 checks the hypothesis if statements for Palladio specifications can be made, which deviate from the implemented behavior of a component with respect to the resource demand and are are exact matches with respect to calls to required components. The considered influence factors are the resource demand in processing units and calls business components. The calls to business components are exact matches. The relative deviation for the resource demand is set to 10%, the absolute deviation to 3 processing units. This deviation allows to take the precision and resolution of processing unit measurement into account. Additionally, it allows to hide small performance effects in the abstraction and ease specification creation. This allows demonstrating the general applicability while limiting the complexity for presentation and comprehension.

The combination of the experiments E2, E3, and E4 ensures that evidence is provided if all different deviation types can be specified successfully.

The evaluation of providing a suitable answer to contribution C4 requires assessing if the accuracy for a specification is valid for the intended use case or if there are additional constraints. A common constraint is the range of parameters, as this allows reducing the validation effort. The range specification should support nominal and ordinal scales in order to reflect the meaning of parameter values.

Experiment E5 checks the hypothesis if parameter space limitations can be stated for each parameter type in Palladio. The completeness should be shown via all data type modeling elements in the Palladio meta-model.

Experiment E6 checks the hypothesis if a range of explicitly stated parameter values can be specified by users for Palladio specifications. This ensures that limitations for nominal parameters can be specified. Only one nominal parameter type is considered. This allows demonstrating the general applicability while limiting the complexity for presentation and comprehension.

Experiment E7 checks the hypothesis if parameter intervals can be stated as parameter space limitations by users for Palladio specifications. This ensures that limitations for ordinal parameters can be specified. Only one ordinal parameter type is considered. This allows demonstrating the general applicability while limiting the complexity.

The combination of the experiments E6 and E7 ensures that evidence is provided that specification for all different types of parameters can be provided.

8.1.2. Accuracy Effects on Overall Prediction

The evaluation of providing a suitable answer to question Q3 requires reporting if the propagation of the usage profile leads to using a specification outside of parameter ranges with accuracy statements. Users are typically interested in knowing the parameter values leading to the failure in order to validate the specification in the experienced range.

Experiment E8 checks the hypotheses if the use of inappropriate Palladio specifications is recognized and if the defaulting parameter values are reported correctly by the approach. A specification which is only valid in a fraction of the propagated usage profile according to its accuracy statements is created for that purpose. It is checked if the inappropriate use is recognized and if the user is informed about the parameter values causing the failure.

The evaluation of providing a suitable answer to question Q5 requires showing the added value by margins for a prediction taking into account the propagated usage profile as well as the specifications and their accuracy. The tested hypothesis is if deviations of the composed specifications do provide valuable information even in simple cases with equal and low deviation for all specifications when compared to applying the accuracy on an undeviated result on real-world systems.

Experiment E9 checks this hypothesis and that the approach provides the information on the margins to the user for predictions using Palladio. The resource demand of the specifications are allowed to have a limited relative deviation of 10%. The predictions including the accuracy influence analysis are compared against applying the deviation on the prediction result for undeviated specifications and possible consequences for decision making are discussed.

The evaluation of providing a suitable answer to contribution C4 requires that incorrect Palladio specification (re-)uses are recognized and reported to the user. The user only has to create or validate specifications if they are incorrectly used and not always upfront. Experiment E8 provides the required information and ensures that users can act according to the given situation.

The evaluation of providing a suitable answer to contribution C5 requires showing the margins around an undeviated prediction help decision making. Experiment E9 can provide the required evidence that margins are provides and gives an example how decision making benefits from the information about the margins.

The evaluation of providing a suitable answer to contribution C7 requires showing that the interpretation of predictions is eased. Experiment E9 demonstrates that the effect of inaccuracies on an overall prediction is hard to estimate for human users and how the knowledge eases the interpretation. Experiment E8 can provide the evidence that inappropriate specifications are easier identified as only incorrectly used specifications are reported.

8.1.3. Accuracy Statement Validation

The evaluation of providing a suitable answer to contribution Q1 requires knowing if a specification and given quantitative accuracy statements describe an implementation or the observed deviation exceeds these quantitative thresholds. The evaluations show that the approach correctly identifies accurate and inaccurate specifications accordingly.

Experiment E10.1 checks the hypothesis if an accurate Palladio specification is correctly identified as such. Experiment E10.2 checks the hypothesis if an inaccurate Palladio specification is correctly identified as such.

Both use a complex and realistic specification and the $C_{\text{relaxed basic paths}}$. Implementation and specification differ in the issued resource demand. The specification is accurate for the relative deviation threshold used in experiment E3. It is inaccurate if no deviation is allowed (see experiment E2). The examples demonstrate the applicability in practice, provide evidence that failures are identified correctly, and the power of the approach presented in chapter 6.

Experiment E11.1 checks the hypothesis if an accurate Palladio specification with probabilistic control-flow decisions is correctly identified as such. The implemented and specified branching probability for a control-flow decision with three alternatives is 1% for alternative A, 90% for alternative B, and 9% for alternative C. The accuracy of experiment E2 without allowing deviations is used. Experiment E11.2 checks the hypothesis if an inaccurate Palladio specification is correctly identified as such. The specified probabilities are 10% (A), 80% (B), and 10% (C). This specification is compared against the implementation of experiment E11.1. The examples focus on providing evidence on the correct identification and demonstrate how probabilistic branches are checked and how these specific results are interpreted. The accuracy of experiment E2 without allowing deviations is used. Experiment E11.3 check the hypothesis that the approach identifies inappropriate testing as such. It demonstrates the risks of partition-based random testing and how the approach supports risk identification. It uses the implementation and specification of experiment E11.1 but requires only one test case, which is not enough to ensure that all branches are covered at least once. The accuracy of experiment E2 without allowing deviations is used.

Experiment E12.1 checks the hypothesis if an accurate specification using multithreading is correctly identified as accurate. The specification contains asynchronous and synchronized forked threads ensuring all different types of concurrency are handled correctly. Experiment E12.2 checks the hypothesis if an inaccurate specification is correctly identified. In contrast to experiment E12.1, an asynchronously forked thread and a calculation after a thread synchronization have an inaccurate behavior description. For both, the accuracy of experiment E2 without allowing deviations is used. The validation uses partition-based random testing. The examples focus on demonstrating how multithreaded implementation are checked and provides evidence that inappropriate specifications are identified correctly.

The evaluation of providing a suitable answer to contribution Q2 requires showing that existing statements can be checked and their validity ensured. All experiments derived for question Q1 also provide answers to this question if all validations of the specified accuracies are successful.

The evaluation of providing a suitable answer to contribution Q4 requires reasoning about the covered aspects of a verification and the thoroughness of the verification. This includes selecting an appropriate coverage criterion. The assessment of coverage-based verification risks is demonstrated in example E11.3. Knowing about the criteria and their implied coverage of aspects together with their appropriateness allows assessing their trustworthiness. Consequently, the experiments for appropriateness also address the trustworthiness.

Experiment E13 checks the hypothesis that calculations of the test set size are supported for complex systems and the provided information aids in criterion selection. It uses a complex and realistic specification as basis and shows the size complexity for the specified criteria, which aid in making a trade-off decision between test effort and verified aspects. The effect of probabilistic modeling on the size complexity is shown using a different version of the specification. This version uses fixed probability distributions instead of the parametric dependencies.

The evaluation of providing a suitable answer to contribution C2 requires showing that a verification run is reproducible and can be repeated with the same input values. This allows an independent verification of test runs. The degree of automation and formalized coverage criteria ensures that no aspects, which should be checked are left out. The experiments E10.1, E10.2,

E11.1, and E11.2 use coverage criteria as verification stop conditions and document the applicability. The experiment E11.3 shows how coverage analyses for tests with non-criteria stop conditions help in identifying un-covered aspects, as they can pose a danger to reproducibility.

Experiment E14 checks the hypothesis if the testing framework is able to repeat validation runs if the behavior of the implementation is the same. This ensures the verifiability of validation results by independent parties. The result of experiment E10.1 is compared with a repetition of that exper-iment using the same settings.

The evaluation of providing a suitable answer to contribution C3 requires showing that there is less time required for the validation. The higher de-gree of automation compared to manual validation for parameter value se-lection reduces the overall necessary amount of time and is covered by experiment E15.

The evaluation of providing a suitable answer to contribution C6 requires showing the degree of automation for the validation.

Experiment E15 checks the hypothesis if the required input for the ap-proach can be provided and that less human intervention is required than with a manual validation. The experiments provides evidence which in-formation must be supplied by users and which parts are automated. It demonstrates if users only have to specify parameter constraints for the va-lidation and don't have to determine appropriate parameter input values for testing.

The evaluation of providing a suitable answer to contribution C7 requires showing that the interpretation and validation requires less knowledge than a manual non-criteria based validation. The interpretation is already ad-dressed in the experiments E8 and E9. The use of formalized criteria in-stead of fuzzy definitions or pure experience-based test selection requires less background knowledge to reason about the aspects, which are covered with certainty. Their limited number eases keeping them in mind. Their categorization and the subsumption relation further eases comparisons between different criteria. The degree of automation in the validation framework reduces the need to contest validations. Experiment E15 addresses the degree of automation. The degree of automation further eases reasoning on the quality of tests because reasoning can remain on the criteria level instead of the test execution and individual parameter value level. Hence, successful evaluation of experiments E8, E9, and E15 provides evidence for the fulfillment of contribution C7.

8.1.4. Specification Certification

The evaluation of providing a suitable answer to contribution Q4 requires confidence that the adapted development process allows creating certified specifications. The applicability of the adapted development process and whether the input and output artifacts are available is demonstrated.

Experiment E16 checks the hypothesis if the adapted development process is applicable for offering components. The flow of artifacts and activities for certification should be shown for the development of a new component. The use of the guideline should be demonstrated to decide on certifier party selection. This scenario addresses the development of a component, which should be offered on a marketplace. The experiment provides evidence that the process is applicable.

Experiment E17 checks the hypothesis if the adapted development process is applicable for selecting offered components. The flow of artifacts should be shown for the evaluation and selection of a component. The experiment should show if a component can be successfully acquired for a system if a certificate is used. The experiment is based on the results of experiment E16.

Experiments E16 and E17 should provide evidence in combination that the adapted development process is applicable.

The evaluation of providing a suitable answer to contribution C1 requires showing that the development process successfully covers evaluations on the architecture level without having the implementation of a component. Experiment E16 demonstrates that a certificate can be issued and the experiments shown in section 8.1.3 ensure the trustworthiness. Experiment E17 demonstrates the selection itself. If these experiments are successful they provide evidence that the contribution is fulfilled.

The evaluation of providing a suitable answer to contribution C6 requires showing that performance engineers require less effort for the evaluation of a specification. Experiment E17 can provide evidence that there is no effort necessary to validate the specification if a certificate is used and the specification is correctly used. This would be a reduced effort and provide evidence that the contribution is fulfilled.

8.2. Systems for Experimentation

This section introduces and describes the systems used in the experiments. There are overall three experiment systems. The first example system is the Common Component Modelling Example (CoCoME), which represents an industrial use-case and is a benchmark for prediction approaches. It is used as running example but does not cover all aspects, which the approach presented in this thesis supports. Therefore, two additional example systems focus on highlighting selected features. The second example system is the Probabilistic Modeling Example (PME), which is a technology demonstrator showing how probabilistic control-flow decisions are handled and validated. The last example system is the Multithreaded Modeling Example (MME), which is a technology demonstrator showing how multithreaded specifications are handled and validated.

Each example system is described in a separate section. These sections introduce the systems from high-level descriptions down to the behavior of the implementation. They describe the use case and origin of the example as well as the implemented and specified architecture and participating components. This includes the presentation of different versions of

Table 8.1.: Relations of Experiments, Question, Contributions, and Systems

Notation: X means a an experiment uses a system or addresses a question or contribution.

	Q1	Q2	Q3	Q4	Q5	C1	C2	C3	C4	C5	C6	C7	CoCoME	PME	MME
E1	X												-	-	-
E2	X												X		
E3	X												X		
E4	X												X		
E5	X												X		
E6							X						X		
E7							X						X		
E8			X				X				X		X		
E9				X						X		X	X		
E10.1	X		X			X							X		
E10.2	X		X			X							X		
E11.1	X		X			X								X	
E11.2	X		X			X								X	
E11.3	X		X			X								X	
E12.1	X		X												X
E12.2	X		X												X
E13			X										X		
E14						X							X		
E15							X		X				X		
E16			X			X							X		
E17			X			X				X			X		

the specifications and discussing their differences, where such versions are required for the experiments. They are for example required in order to show that a fault in a specification leads to a failure and that this is identified correctly only for the faulty version by the presented approach. Table 8.1 provides an overview on the relation of experiments to systems and the addressed questions and contributions.

This section is structured as follows. Section 8.2.1 describes the Co-CoME experiment system. Section 8.2.2 describes the PME experiment system. Section 8.2.3 describes the MME experiment system.

8.2.1. Common Component Modelling Example (CoCoME)

This section provides an overview on CoCoME and introduces the relevant aspects for the experiments in more detail. The CoCoME is a benchmark for comparing component-based modeling and prediction approaches. The approaches KobrA, Rich Service, rCOS, CoIn, AutoFocus, Java/A, Boxes, GCM, DisCComp, Palladio, KLAPER, SOFA, and Fractal were initially benchmarked in 2007. The application results are documented in the book about CoCoME by Rausch et al. [RRMP08]. Later, it was used for the approaches JCoBox and ABS. In the European research project SLA@SOI, it was supplemented by Web-Service interfaces and a management infrastructure for Software as a Service (SaaS) deployments including a Service Level Agreement negotiation and monitoring framework. This environment also features a BPEL-Engine for the Payment Service and supports multi-tenant installations [RG11]. The most recent implementation is available at [WB11].

CoCoME as a system supports selling products in a supermarket chain, which has a common headquarter and any number of stores. Its functionality covers back-office store keeping as well as the actual exchange of products and money at the front desk. It is a distributed system with servers and clients at the headquarter as well as the individual stores. It features a diverse environment from enterprise servers to embedded scanner devices at the stores. The stores are equipped with multiple cash desk lines with scanners, displays, printers, and card readers. The stores are linked directly with the headquarter and banks in order to allow customers to buy their products in cash or via credit cards. A detailed introduction to the system is provided by Herold et al. in [HKW$^+$08].

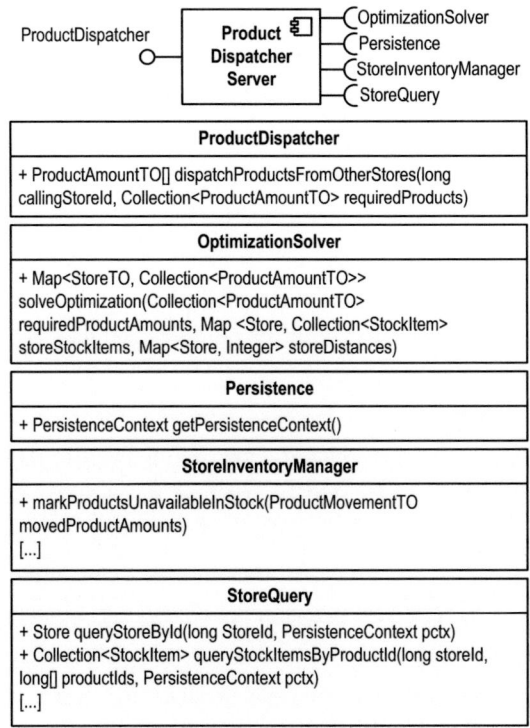

ProductDispatcher

Product **Dispatcher** **Server**

- OptimizationSolver
- Persistence
- StoreInventoryManager
- StoreQuery

ProductDispatcher
+ ProductAmountTO[] dispatchProductsFromOtherStores(long callingStoreId, Collection<ProductAmountTO> requiredProducts)

OptimizationSolver
+ Map<StoreTO, Collection<ProductAmountTO>> solveOptimization(Collection<ProductAmountTO> requiredProductAmounts, Map <Store, Collection<StockItem> storeStockItems, Map<Store, Integer> storeDistances)

Persistence
+ PersistenceContext getPersistenceContext()

StoreInventoryManager
+ markProductsUnavailableInStock(ProductMovementTO movedProductAmounts) [...]

StoreQuery
+ Store queryStoreById(long StoreId, PersistenceContext pctx) + Collection<StockItem> queryStockItemsByProductId(long storeId, long[] productIds, PersistenceContext pctx) [...]

Figure 8.1.: Implementation of the CoCoME

The section of CoCoME used in the experiments is the main part of use case 8 (UC 8): product exchange among stores. The use case models the cost-effective exchange of products between stores if one of the stores runs low on a product. It is selected as it contains a complex specification featuring nested branches and loops and a single operation controls the use case, which eases understanding the scenario. The following provides details on the respective implementation. In addition, the implemented jUnit test cases for the experiments are available at [Gro13d]. The implemented behavior is discussed together with the specification, which is an exact match of the component's behavior.

Figure 8.1 provides an overview on the relevant section of the implementation of the CoCoME. The selected section consists of a single component. The component `ProductDispatcherServer` provides the business interface `ProductDispatcher`, which allows to exchange products cost-efficiently between stores of an enterprise. The operation `dispatchProductsFromOtherStores` is responsible for the planning and implementation of the exchange. It requires the identifier of the store requesting the product and the information on the required products and their quantity as input parameters. It returns a list of the products and their quantity, which are shipped to the requesting store.

The component requires the business interface `OptimizationSolver`, which encapsulates the functionality for optimizing the costs of an exchange based on the geographic location of the stores. The interface has the single operation `solveOptimization`. The operation requires the information on the exchanged products, the availability of products at the stores and the distance between the stores, and the geographic distance between the stores. The operation provides a list of stores and the quantity of shipped products for each product and store. The component requires the business interface `Persistence`, which allows accessing the persistent state of business objects. The interface has the single operation `getPersistenceContext`. The operation provides a context, which allows the access to the business objects. The component requires the business interface `StoreInventoryManager`, which is responsible to manage the inventory of a store. The interface has 11 operations, of which only the operation `markProductsUnavailableInStock` is used. This operation requires information on the products and their quantity, which are marked unavailable and scheduled to be removed from the inventory of the store. The component requires the business interface `StoreQuery`, which groups functionality for queries to the inventory of a store. The interface has 12 operations, of which only the operations `queryStoreById` and `queryStockItemsByProductId` are used. The

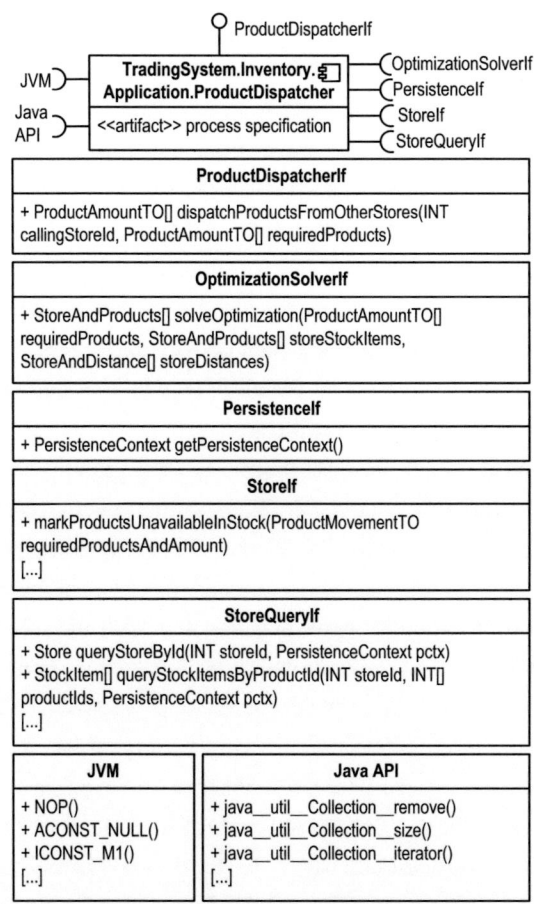

Figure 8.2.: Specification for the CoCoME

operation `queryStoreById` requires the identifier of a store and access to the business objects. It provides the business object for the store. The operation `queryStockItemsByProductsId` requires the identifier of a store, the identifiers for each product, and access to the business objects. It provides information on the available quantity of each product at the provided store.

Figure 8.2 provides an overview on the Palladio specification for the Co-CoME. The specified component `TradingSystem.Inventory.Application.ProductDispatcher` maps to `ProductDispatcherServer`.

The specified component has two additional interfaces: `JVM` and `Java API`. These are infrastructure interfaces, which separate the runtime container from the business implementation. They allow easy redeployment on the model level. The behavior specifications for the infrastructure components describe the performance effect in the hardware environment and allow decoupling the business logic from performance measurements. The `JVM` interface contains operations for all bytecode instructions, the `Java API` for calls targeted at the API of Java.

Provided and required business interfaces map directly, the specifications have the additional ending `If`. The specified data types used in the signature of the operations are abstractions of the real data types. Palladio does no differentiate between arrays and collections. The respective data types are `CollectionDataTypes` and denoted with the additional ending `[]`. in Palladio. The Palladio data type `INT` maps to `int` as well as `long`. Palladio has no explicit data type for `Map`. `CompositeDataTypes` with inner declarations representing a single entry in the map with key and value is added as well as a `CollectionDataType`, which contains all entries. Examples are `StoreAndProduct[]` instead of `Map<Store, Collection<ProductAmountTO> >` or `StoreAndDistance[]` instead of `Map<Store, Integer>`. The specified behavior for operation `dispatchProductsFromOtherStores` matches the implementation. The behavior is presented in the following. Section B.1 shows the complete Palladio representation for this example including the mapping to the implementation. In addition, the specifications are available at [Gro13d].

Figure 8.3 shows the specified behavior using an UML activity diagram for operation `dispatchProductsFromOtherStores`. The process is described in the following. First, access to the business objects is established in the call to operation `getPersistenceContext` of the required

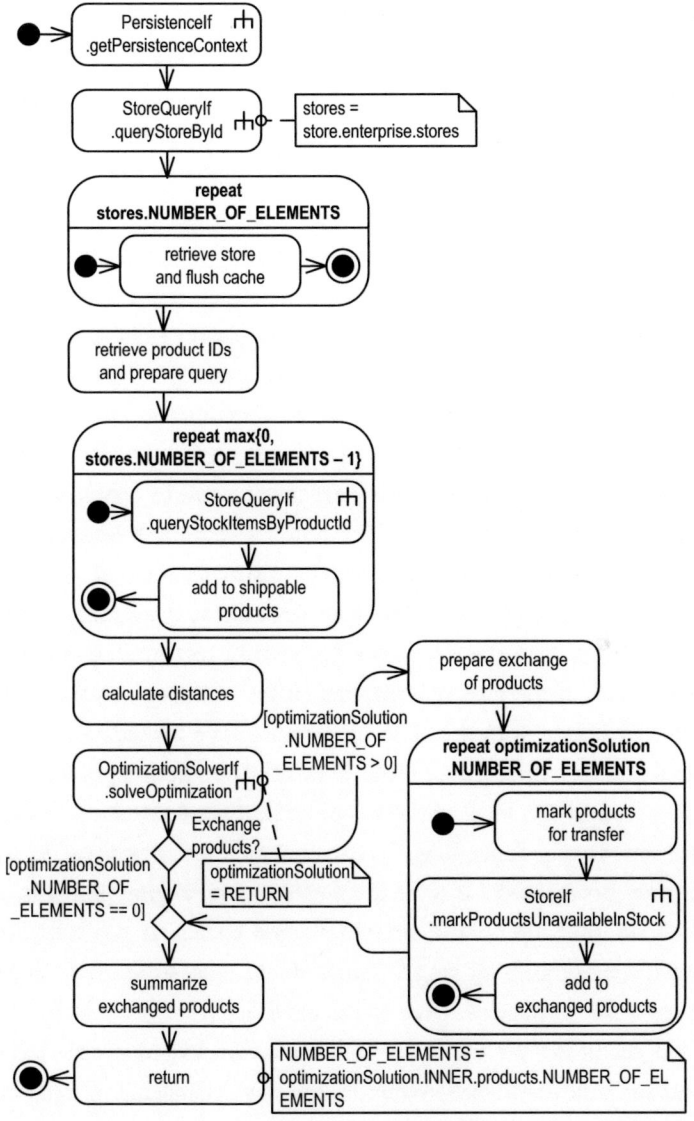

Figure 8.3.: Performance Behavior Specification for Operation dispatchProductsFromOtherStores of TradingSystem.Inventory.Application.ProductDispatcher

component with the interface `PersistenceIf`. Next, the set of all stores belonging to the same enterprise as the store requiring the products is requested. This is realized with an call to operation `queryStoreById` of the required component with the interface `StoreQueryIf`. The relevant aspects of the provided business object are stored in the local variable `stores`. Next, the cache of available products is flushed for all stores of the enterprise in `retrieve store and flush cache`. Next, the unique identifiers of all required products are determined and the query for the available quantity of the products is prepared in `retrieve product IDs and prepare query`. Next, the available quantity of shippable products is request for each store beside the current store in `repeat max{0, stores.NUMBER_OF_ELEMENTS - 1}`. Within this loop, the quantity of the products is requested from the store using a call to operation `queryStockItemsByProductId` from the required interface `StoreQueryIf`. Finally, the results are collected and stored to an internal list of shippable products in `add to shippable products`. Next, the geographical distance between the stores is calculated in `calculate distances` as preparation of the cost optimization of the exchange. Next, the optimization is started with a call to operation `solveOptimization` of the required interface `OptimizationSolverIf`. The solution provided by the call is stored in the local variable `optimizationSolution`. Next, the control flow is split depending if products should actually be exchanged in `Exchange products?`. If there are no stores exchanging products, nothing is done until the control flow is merged again. If products are exchanged, a preprocessing step is required and represented with `prepare exchange of products`. Next, the products from each store are exchanged according the the optimization solution in `foreach store in optimizationSolution`. Within the loop, the exchange is prepared in `mark products for transfer`. Next, the products are marked for shipment using a call to operation `markProductsUnavailableInStock`. Finally, the successful transfer is noted in `add to exchanged products`.

Then, the control flow merges at the unnamed decision node. Next, a summary of all exchanged products is created in `summarize exchanged products`. Finally, the returned performance-relevant information is set in `return`. In this case, the `NUMBER_OF_ELEMENTS` of the return data type `ProductAmountTO[]` is set to the number of products marked for exchange by the optimization solution. Please note that the resource demand in bytecode instructions and the detailed assignment of input parameters in Palladio is show in section B.1 but not depicted in figure 8.3 due to brevity. Examples for resource demand specifications using bytecode instructions are provided in the following sections for the other systems for experimentation.

The Palladio specification of the process states that the resource demand contains `3 + 12 * stores.NUMBER_OF_ELEMENTS ALOAD` instructions. However, the implementation issues only `3 + 11 * stores.stores.NUMBER_OF_ELEMENTS` instructions. This is an acceptable deviation if 10% relative deviation are allowed but will lead to a validation error if no deviation is allowed and the number of stores is greater or equal to 1.

Figure 8.4 shows a probabilistic version of the behavior specification using an UML activity diagramm for operation `dispatchProductsFromOtherStores`. This behavior is equal to the non-probabilistic one except that the specification of the branch is changed from a deterministic dependency on a parameter to a probabilistic specification. The probability p_E for exchanging products is calculated based on the propagated usage profile for the deterministic version and is equal to 0.01. The probability p_{NE} for no product exchange is determined in the same way and equal to 0.99.

A Palladio model for predictions was developed by Krogmann for Co-CoME as part of the original benchmark effort [KR08b]. In the original usage model and requirements of CoCoME, customers bought 1 product with a probability of 30%, 8 products with a probability of 10%, 15 products (15%), 25 products (%15), 50 products (%20), or 75 products (%10). 20 cash desk lines were open in parallel and a new customer arrived 11.25s

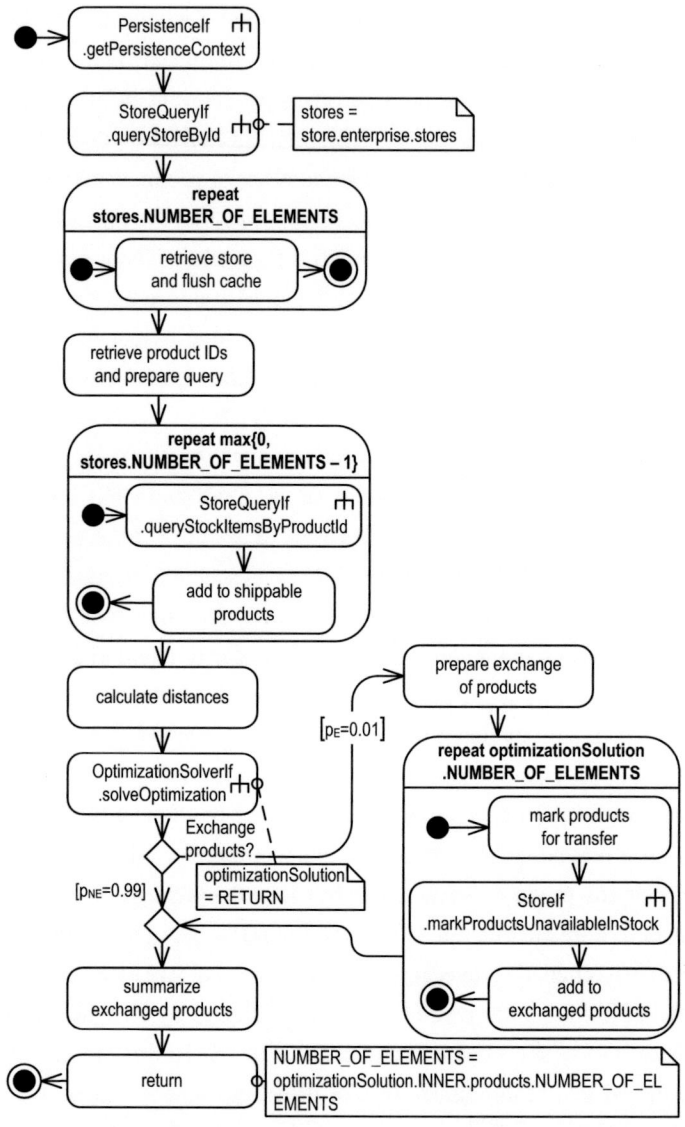

Figure 8.4.: Probabilistic Performance Behavior Specification for Operation dispatchProductsFromOtherStores of TradingSystem.Inventory.Application.ProductDispatcher

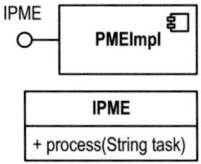

Figure 8.5.: Implementation of the PME

after the last customer was finished. The version for the latest Palladio meta-model uses the same settings and describes an enterprise with two stores, where each enterprise or store has a client and server environment. This model is used for predictions and available at [Gro13d].

8.2.2. Probabilistic Modeling Example (PME)

This section presents the PME. The PME is a technology demonstrator with non-deterministic control-flow decisions. It is used to demonstrate the validation capabilities for probabilistic control-flow decisions. This section describes the implementation, the available Palladio specifications, and their difference.

Figure 8.5 provides an overview on the implementation of the PME. The example consists of a single component. The component PMEImpl provides the business interface IPME, which allows to work on tasks. The operation process represents a simplified version operating on encoded task descriptions. Section B.2 shows the complete Java implementations for this example as reference. In addition, the code including automated jUnit test cases for the validation is available at [Gro13b]. The implemented behavior is discussed together with the specification, which is an exact match of the component's behavior.

Figure 8.6 shows the available Palladio specifications for the PME. The specified interface IPME maps directly to the implementation. The specified component PME has a single performance specification for the operation process. The specified behavior matches the implementation. The

305

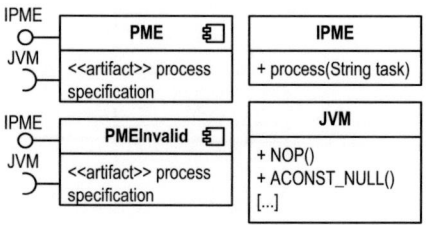

Figure 8.6.: Specifications for the PME

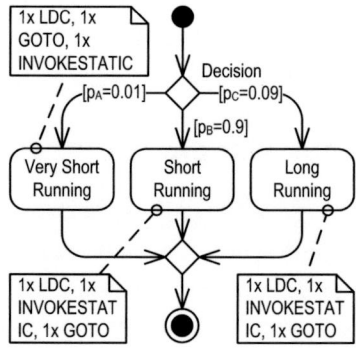

Figure 8.7.: Performance Behavior Specification for Operation process of PME

specified component PMEInvalid has a single performance specification. It deviates from the implementation. The specified components have the additional infrastructure interface JVM, which describes the performance effect in the hardware environment and allows decoupling the business logic from performance measurements. The JVM interface contains operations for all bytecode instructions. The specified behaviors are presented in the following. Section B.2 shows the complete Palladio representations for this example including the mapping to the implementation. In addition, the specifications are available at [Gro13b].

Figure 8.7 shows the specified behavior and resource demand using an UML activity diagram for component PME. The resource demand in bytecode instructions is linked to the activity via notes. The decision node

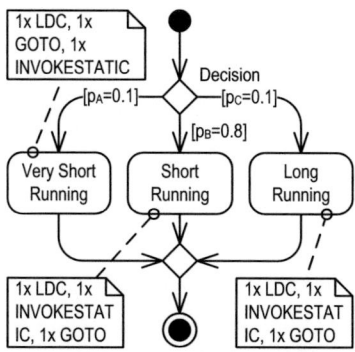

Figure 8.8.: Performance Behavior Specification for Operation process of PMEInvalid

Decision models a probabilistic decision between the three alternatives A,
B, and C. Alternative A is taken with probability $p_A = 0.01$, Alternative B
with $p_B = 0.9$, and alternative C with $p_C = 0.09$. The control flow follows
only one of the alternatives for each entry to the decision node. The activity Very Short Running models tasks with very short execution time.
The implementation is kept minimal for the technology demonstration and
waits for a period of 15 ms. This requires only 3 bytecode instructions.
1 time the LDC, 1 time the GOTO, and 1 time the INVOKESTATIC instruction. The activity Short Running models tasks with a short execution
time. The implementation for Short Running waits for 0.2 s. It requires
the same bytecode instructions as the activity in alternative A. The activity Long Running models tasks with a long execution time. The implementation for Long Running waits for 3 s. It requires the same bytecode
instructions as the activities in the alternatives A and B. The control flow
continues after the branch at the merge node and the operation process is
finished.

Figure 8.8 shows the specified behavior and resource demand using an
UML activity diagram for component PMEInvalid. The resource demand
in bytecode instructions is linked to the activity via notes. It differs from the

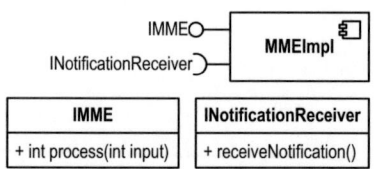

Figure 8.9.: Implementation of the MME

specified behavior for component PME at three points. First, the probability for alternative A is $p_A = 0.1$ instead of $p_A = 0.01$. Second, the probability of alternative B is $p_B = 0.8$ instead of $p_B = 0.9$. Last, the probability of alternative C is $p_C = 0.1$ instead of $p_C = 0.09$.

8.2.3. Multithreaded Modeling Example (MME)

This section presents the MME. The MME is a technology demonstrator using asynchronous and synchronized threads. It is used to demonstrate the validation capabilities in multithreaded environments. This section describes the implementation, the available Palladio specifications, and their difference.

Figure 8.9 provides an overview on the implementation of the MME. The example consists of a single component. The component MMEImpl provides the business interface IMME, which allows to process data. The operation process represents a simplified version operating on integer data. The MME requires the business interface INotificationReceiver, which will receive a notification about the processing. The operation receiveNotification represents the information flow. Parameters are omitted to reduce complexity and focus on multithreading issues. Section B.3 shows the complete Java implementations for this example as reference. In addition, the code including automated jUnit test cases for the validation is available at [Gro13a]. The implemented behavior is discussed together with the specification, which is an exact match of the component's behavior.

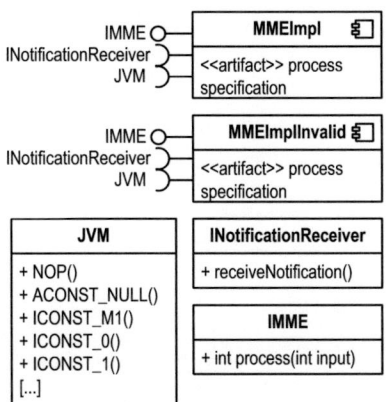

Figure 8.10.: Specifications for the MME

Figure 8.10 shows the available Palladio specifications for the MME. The interfaces IMME and INotificationReceiver are mapped directly. The specified component MMEImpl has a single performance specification for the operation process. This component has the same name as the implementation because the specification is an exact match of the behavior of the implementation. The specified component MMEImplInvalid also has a single performance description for the operation process. The specified components have the additional infrastructure interface JVM, which describes the performance effect in the hardware environment and allows decoupling the business logic from performance measurements. The JVM interface contains operations for all bytecode instructions. The specification of the behavior for the operation of MMEImplInvalid deviates from the behavior of the implementation. The specified behavior is presented in the following. Section B.3 shows the complete Palladio representations for this example including the mapping to the implementation. In addition, the specifications are available at [Gro13a].

Figure 8.11 shows the specified behavior and resource demand using an UML activity diagram for component MMEImpl. The resource demand

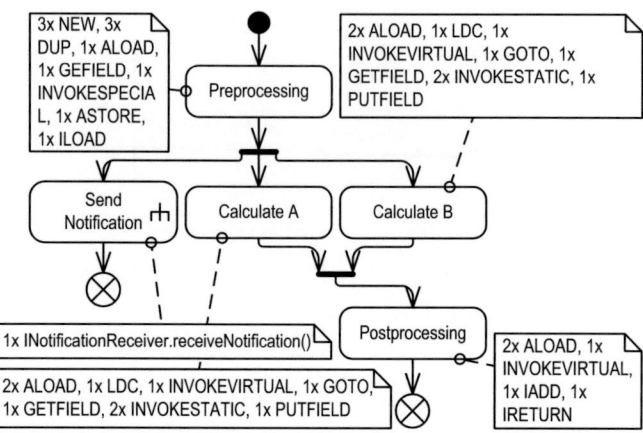

Figure 8.11.: Performance Behavior Specification for Operation process of MMEImpl

in bytecode instructions is linked to the activity via notes. The activity Preprocessing models input validity checks and required preparations. The implementation is kept minimal for the technology demonstration and only 11 bytecode instructions are required within the activity. 3 times the NEW instruction, 3 times the DUP instruction, and so forth. After this preparation, an asynchronous thread is started, which is responsible to deliver the notification. This notification should not influence the processing itself and is part of the Send Notification activity. This activity requires solely a call to the operation receiveNotification and an unspecified amount of bytecode instructions to prepare the call. The processing itself requires the activities Calculate A and Calculate B, which can run in parallel. The implementations for these activities request different types of random numbers and wait for 2 (8) seconds for Calculate A (Calculate B). The resulting 9 bytecode instructions do not show this difference. Each of these activities runs in an own thread and they are synchronized before the control flow continues. The Postprocessing activity is responsible to combine the results of the preceding activities and provide the final pro-

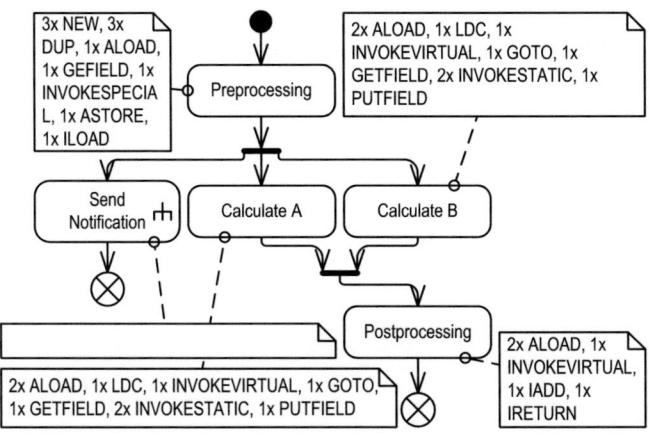

Figure 8.12.: Performance Behavior Specification for Operation process of MMEImplInvalid

cessed data. The implementation adds the numbers and returns them. This results in overall 5 bytecode instructions.

Figure 8.12 show the specified behavior and resource demand for component MMEImplInvalid using an UML activity diagram. The resource demand in bytecode instructions is linked to the activity via notes. It differs from the specified behavior for component MMEImpl at two points. First, there is no resource demand specified for the activity Send Notification. Second, 0 instead of 1 IRETURN bytecode instruction is specified in Postprocessing. Instructions with a frequency can but do not have to be specified. A call frequency of 0 is equal to leaving out this part of the specification.

8.3. Application and Experimental Results

This section provides details on the settings and results for the experiments based on the experiment systems presented in the previous sections.

311

Table 8.2.: Overview on Validation Strategies for the Experiments

Notation: E means the experiment uses a system and exact accuracy statements. R means the experiment uses a system and (only) a relative deviation. A means the experiment uses a system with absolute and relative deviation.

	CoCoME	PME	MME	Validation Strategy / Stop Criterion
E2	E			
E3	R			
E4	A			
E8	E			
E9	R			
E10.1	R			Relaxed Basic Paths
E10.2	E			Relaxed Basic Paths
E11.1		E		Hypothesis-based Probabilistic Branch Testing
E11.2		E		Hypothesis-based Probabilistic Branch Testing
E11.3		E		Random (1)
E12.1			E	Random (1)
E12.2			E	Random (1)
E14	E			Relaxed Basic Paths

Different validation strategies and accuracy statements are used in the experiments. Table 8.2 shows the experiments in which specifications are validated and provides an overview on the used accuracy statements and validation strategies.

This section presents the experiments structured by area of work and increasing order.

8.3.1. Accuracy Statements

Experiment E1 addresses that accuracy statements can be provided for all influencing factors of a Palladio specification. The influence factors are 1) the configuration and state of the model, 2) the behavior of required

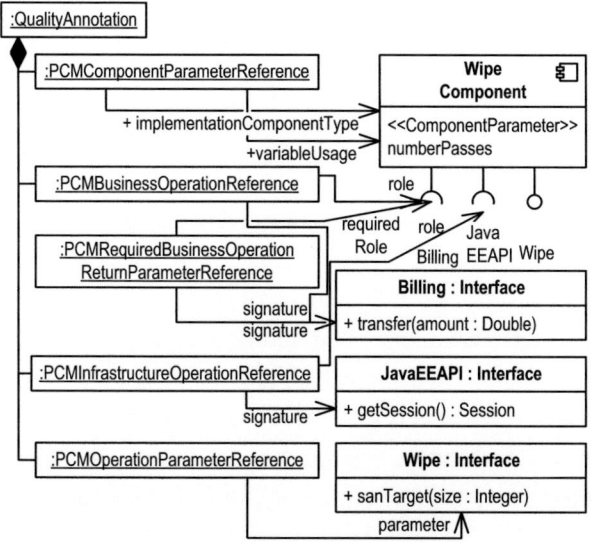

Figure 8.13.: Examples for Accuracy Statements Addressing the Influence Factors

services, 3) the system environment, and 4) the usage profile. Each factor is addressed in a separate paragraph in the following.

In Palladio, the configuration is modeled with component parameters. Accuracy statements can use `PCMComponentParameterReference` instance for specifying the limits on the parameter space. Figure 8.13 shows an example of an accuracy statement for the component parameter `number-Passes` of a component for wiping data securely.

In Palladio, required services or components are modeled via component external calls. These can be business or infrastructure calls. Figure 8.13 shows an example of an accuracy statement for the required operation `transfer` of the business component `Billing` and the required operation `getSession` of the infrastructure component `JavaEEAPI`. Only business component calls can return values. The limitations for these values can be stated using `PCMRequiredBusinessOperationReturnParameter-Reference`.

In Palladio, the system environment can be accessed via calls to explicit and implicit hardware interfaces. The system environment decides when a call is finished. However, there are no return parameters involved. Therefor, only the accuracy of calls made to the environment must be specified using PCMRE elements.

In Palladio, the usage profile is propagated using parameters, which are available in behavior specifications. Figure 8.13 shows an example of an accuracy statement for the parameter `size` of the provided interface `Wipe`.

The experiment could show that accuracy statements can be provided for all meta-model elements in Palladio representing the influence factors. Showing the completeness is successful and the hypothesis is confirmed.

Experiment E2 addresses that accuracy statements can be provided for specifications, which are exact matches of the implemented behavior. The application is shown representatively for infrastructure resource demand and calls to business components.

The accuracy statements are provided for the operation `dispatchProductsFromOtherStores` of component `TradingSystem.Inventory.Application.ProductDispatcher` and shown in figure 8.14. The number of calls to required business components as well as the call parameters for these calls are exact matches. This is represented by the `PCMRECategory` instance for the category `Component`. This solution could be applied likewise to the categories `Resource`, `Infrastructure`, or `ComponentInternal`. It is shown for the category `Infrastructure`, which describes resource demand in bytecode instruction. The category `ResourceDemand` is a special case and its handling shown in experiment E4. This covers all categories.

The experiment shows that statements for Palladio specifications exactly describing implementations can be made. The hypothesis is confirmed.

Experiment E3 addresses that accuracy statements can be provided for specifications, which deviate in the relative amount of resource demand but are exact descriptions of calls to business components.

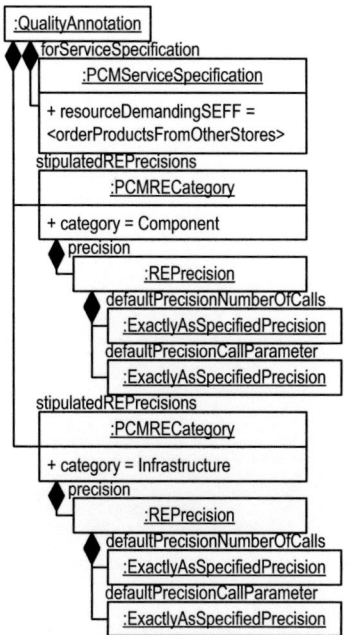

Figure 8.14.: Examples for Accuracy Statements Describing Exactly Matching Specifications

The accuracy statements are provided for the operation `dispatchProductsFromOtherStores` of component `TradingSystem.Inventory.Application.ProductDispatcher` and shown in figure 8.15. As in the previous experiment, the calls to required business components and their call parameters are exact matches. In contrast, the resource demand in bytecode instructions is allowed to deviate up to 10%. The parameters passed to the few bytecode instructions requiring performance-relevant parameters, for example `newarray`, are assumed to be exact matches in the experiment. This experiment shows that inaccuracies due to the level of abstraction with relative errors can be stated correctly.

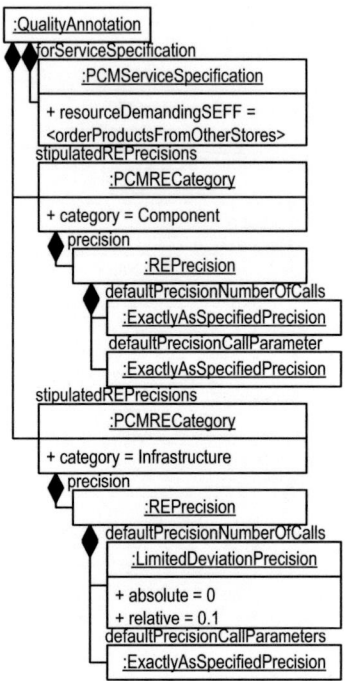

Figure 8.15.: Examples for Accuracy Statements Describing Specifications with Allowed Relative Deviations

The experiment shows that statements for Palladio specifications describing implementations with relative deviations can be made. The hypothesis is confirmed.

Experiment E4 addresses that accuracy statements can be provided for specifications, which are created based on measurements with precision and resolution limitations. The statements are provided for a precision of ±10% and a resolution of 3 processing units.

The accuracy statements are provided for the operation dispatchProductsFromOtherStores of component TradingSystem.Inventory. Application.ProductDispatcher and shown in figure 8.16. As in the previous experiments, the calls to required business component and their

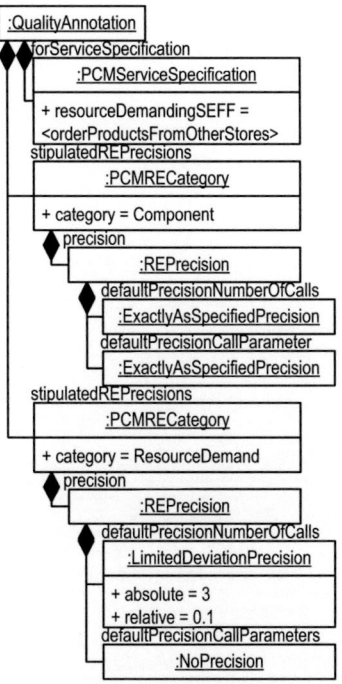

Figure 8.16.: Examples for Accuracy Statements Describing Specifications with Allowed Absolute and Relative Deviations

call parameters are exact matches. In contrast, the resource demand is specified using processing units and calls over implicit interfaces. The category for this kind of resource demand is ResourceDemand. For this category, only a precision for the number of calls can be provided as there are no call parameters. The call parameter precision must be set to NoPrecision. The precision and resolution limitation can be provided as depicted using the attributes absolute and relative.

The experiment shows that statements for Palladio specifications describing implementations with absolute and relative deviations can be made. The hypothesis is confirmed.

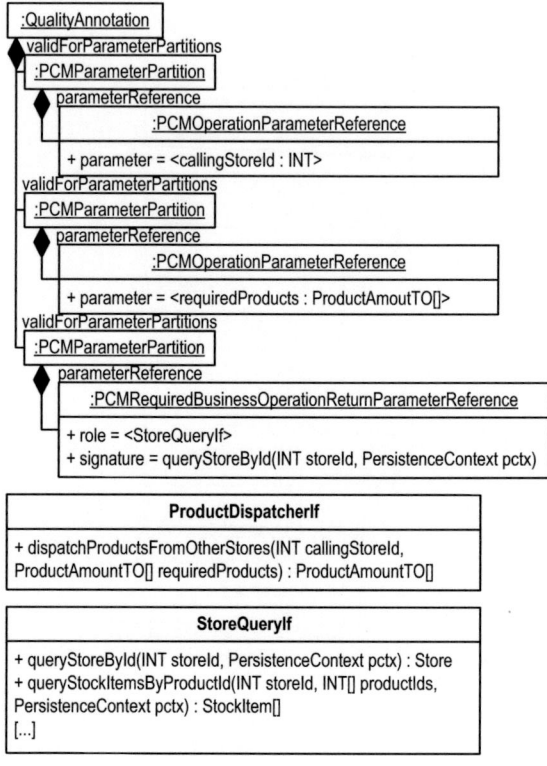

Figure 8.17.: Examples for Accuracy Statements Describing Palladio Parameter Types

The confirmation of the hypotheses of experiments E2, E3, and E4 provides evidence that accuracy specifications can be provided for all different deviation types.

Experiment E5 addresses that parameter space limitations can be stated for each parameter data type in Palladio. These types are `PrimitiveDataType`, `CollectionDataType`, and `CompositeDataType`.

The accuracy statements are provided for the operation `dispatchProductsFromOtherStores` of component `TradingSystem.Inventory.Application.ProductDispatcher` and shown in figure 8.17. The parameter `callingStoreId` of this operation is a `PrimitiveDataType` and has the concrete data type `INT`. The parameter `requiredProducts` of this operation is a `CollectionDataType` and has the concrete data type `ProductAmountTO[]`. The parameter returned by a call to the business operation `queryStoreById` of the interface `StoreQueryIf` is a `CompositeDataType` and has the concrete data type `Store`. It must be referenced via the `role` and `signature` because of the meta-model structure of Palladio. The interface is additionally depicted in the figure. This shows that all data types can be referenced. This means by construction that all concrete data types can be referenced as well. Providing and limiting the parameter space for characterizations of these parameters is demonstrated in the experiments E6 and E7.

The experiment could show that accuracy statements can be provided for all meta-model elements in Palladio representing parameter type definitions. Showing the completeness is successful and the hypothesis is confirmed.

Experiment E6 addresses statements for parameter ranges of ordinal and nominal parameter characterizations.

The accuracy statements are provided for the operation `dispatchProductsFromOtherStores` of component `TradingSystem.Inventory.Application.ProductDispatcher` and shown in figure 8.18. The parameter range for the parameter returned from calls to operation `queryStoreById` of interface `StoreQueryIf` is limited to the values `Karlsruhe` and `Stuttgart` for the characterization `VALUE` for the inner declaration `location` of the concrete data type `Store`. The definitions of the concrete data type `Store` and the interface `StoreQueryIf` are additionally depicted in the figure. The data type `Store` describes a single store. This description includes the `tradingEnterprise` to which the store belongs, the unique identifier `id` of the store, the `location` of the store, and the name of the store. Each of these descriptions has a concrete data type and can be characterized according to its data type using the appropri-

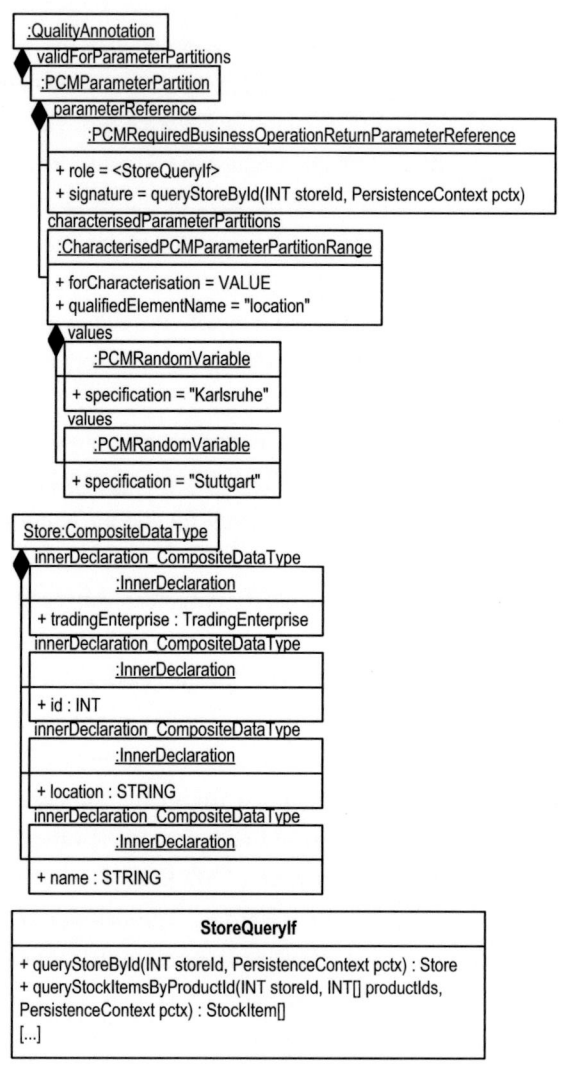

Figure 8.18.: Examples for Parameter Range Specifications in Accuracy Statements

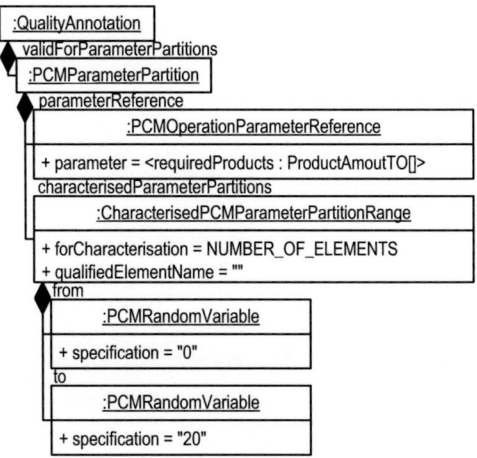

Figure 8.19.: Examples for Parameter Range Specifications in Accuracy Statements

ate `qualifiedElementName` and `forCharacterization` attributes. For nominal parameter characterizations, the enumeration of values is the only possibility to limit the validity. For ordinal parameter characterizations, value intervals can be specified, which partition the parameter space.

The experiment shows that parameter range limitations for the accuracy of Palladio specifications can be made. The hypothesis is confirmed.

Experiment E7 addresses statements for value intervals of ordinal parameter characterizations.

The accuracy statements are provided for the operation `dispatchPro-ductsFromOtherStores` of component `TradingSystem.Inventory.Application.ProductDispatcher` and shown in figure 8.19. The accuracy statements limit the accuracy for the characterization `NUMBER_OF_E-LEMENTS` of the operation's input parameter `requiredProducts` to the interval [0,20].

The experiment shows that parameter interval limitations for the accuracy of Palladio specifications can be made. The hypothesis is confirmed.

The confirmation of the hypotheses of experiments E6 andE7 provides evidence that specifications for all different types of parameters can be provided.

8.3.2. Accuracy Effects on Overall Prediction

Experiment E8 addresses the reporting of specifications which are outside for a prediction outside of the parameter space for which accuracy statements are available.

The accuracy statements for all components in CoCoME state in this experiment that all categories are exactly as specified. The statements are valid in the whole possible parameter space of the components. The only exemption is that the statement for the characterization `NUMBER_OF_ELE-MENTS` of the parameter `requiredProducts` of the operation `dispatch-ProductsFromOtherStores` of the component `TradingSystem.Inventory.Application.ProductDispatcher` is only valid in the interval [0,20]. This represents that the specification has only be validated for this limited parameter space.

A prediction of CoCoME with enabled accuracy influence analysis gathering 1000 samples of customers leads to the failure report shown in figure 8.20. 1000 samples are selected to reduce the effect of outliers and have a good approximation of the resulting distribution. It is reported that extrapolation is used and the result is accordingly endangered. It becomes obvious, that the validity of the specification should be checked. At least for the experienced values of 25, 50, and 75 (further down in the list shown in the figure). The UUIDs of the model elements at which the failure for a parameter was detected are additionally reported to ease cause identification. This shows how the risk caused by the use of invalid specifications can be considered for decision making. The precision in this experiment is 1 as all reported failures are failures. The recall is 1 as only and all failures have been reported.

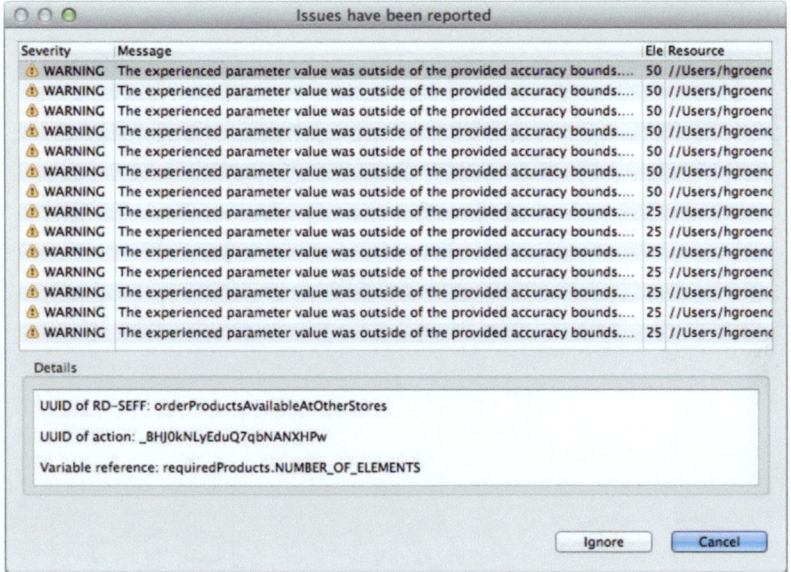

Figure 8.20.: Screenshot of Range Failure Report

The experiment shows that the inappropriate use of a specification within a system is identified and reported correctly. Both hypotheses are confirmed.

Experiment E9 addresses the capability of the approach to report margins for the prediction based on accuracy statements. The reported margins are compared with estimated margins based on calculating the deviation on the prediction result for undeviated specifications. The propagation effect and possible consequences for decision making are discussed based on these results.

The accuracy statements for all components state that all categories are exactly as specified but the ResourceDemand allows a relative deviation of 10% and no absolute deviation. This represents that the resource demand statements for the processor are specified with an accuracy of ±10%.

Customer Usage Profile

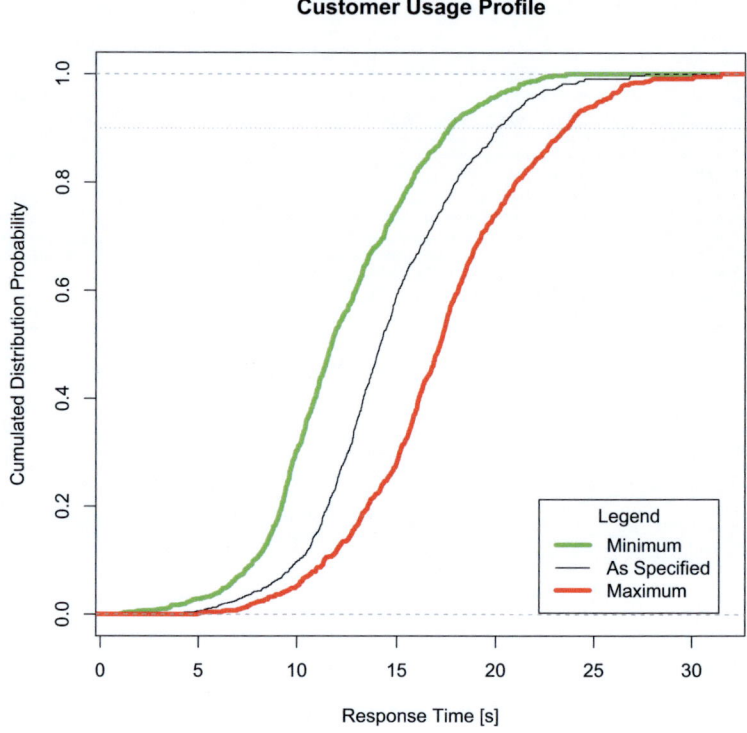

Figure 8.21.: Cumulative Distribution of the Response Time of Customer Interactions with Accuracy Influence Analysis

A prediction of CoCoME with enabled accuracy influence analysis gathering 1000 samples of customers leads to the cumulative distribution of the customer's interaction response time depicted in figure 8.21. 1000 samples are selected to reduce the effect of outliers and have a good approximation of the resulting distribution. The cumulative distribution function allows identifying the response time for a given share of interactions. This is commonly used in service level agreement management. As an example, the values of the 90% quantile are examined more closely. This quantile is marked with a dotted line in the figure. The response times are approxi-

Customer Usage Profile

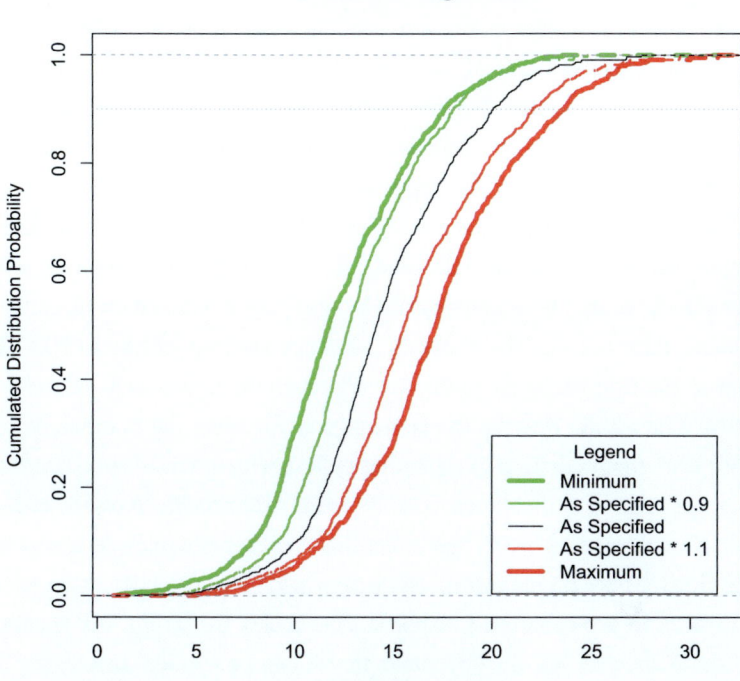

Figure 8.22.: Comparison of Accuracy Influence Analysis and Modified Average Result

mately 17.6 (`Minimum`), 20.1 (`As Specified`), and 23.6 (`Maximum`). The resulting relative deviation with respect to `As Specified` is approximately 12.4% (`Minimum`) and 17.3% (`Maximum`). These deviations are above a deviation of $\pm 10\%$ and a result of resource contention, delay and mutual influence effects in general. Without the influence analysis, a response time of 20.1s could have been assured. With the influence analysis, a response time below 23.6s can be assured taking into account the accuracy assuming that Palladio makes correct predictions. The correctness of Palladio predictions is not part of this thesis but has been shown previously.

The results of the accuracy influence analysis are compared to the results of As Specified after taking into account a deviation of $\pm 10\%$ in figure 8.22. The response times of the 90% quantile are approximately 18.1 (As Specified * 0.9) and 22.1 (As Specified * 1.1). As can be seen in the trend of the distribution function, the contention effects are not equally distributed but the size of the gap between a prediction with deviated values and the modified average result varies. This shows that even in such a simple case of 10% resource demand deviation in general the mutual influence effects cannot be approximated by applying the deviation directly on an undeviated result. The accuracy influence analysis allows to take into account the features of the prediction approach to include such effects correctly. The results provide the advantage of knowing the margins, which result from the prediction of a running system with deviated specifications. This eases risk identification and assessment. Additionally, it can be used in what-if-analyses to identify the effect that a higher accuracy of composed specifications has on the result, which allows to focus (re-)validation effort. Compared to pre-calculated response time tables for sizing, the accuracy influence analysis has the advantage that it can be applied exactly for the intended usage and environment of the system.

The experiment shows that the accuracy analysis provides valuable information even in simple cases when compared to applying the accuracy on an undeviated result in real-world systems. The applicability and identification of margin was successfully shown. The hypothesis is confirmed.

8.3.3. Accuracy Statement Validation

Experiment E10.1 addresses the reliable identification of accurate complex and realistic specifications using path coverage. The experiment uses the system CoCoME and validates the specification for operation dispatch-ProductsFromOtherStores of the component TradingSystem.Inven-

`tory.Application.ProductDispatcher` against the implementation `ProductDispatcherServer`.

The accuracy statements for the specification state that the resource demand in bytecode instructions may deviate up to 10%. An absolute deviation is not allowed. Implicit `ResourceDemand` is not validated. The other categories are stated to behave exactly as specified. The chosen parameter space limitations are as follows.

The `NUMBER_OF_ELEMENTS` of the input parameter `requiredProduct` is either 1, 2, or 30. Business calls to the operation `queryStoreId` of the required `StoreQueryIf` return a `NUMBER_OF_ELEMENTS` of either 0, 1, or 3. Business calls to the operation `solveOptimization` of the required `OptimizationSolverIf` return a `NUMBER_OF_ELEMENTS` of 0 or 3 and a `NUMBER_OF_ELEMENTS` for `INNER.products` of 0 or 4. The `TYPE` of the component parameter `dataInstance` is set to `NO_HIBERNATE` as only the component itself without the database access via Hibernate should be validated. Business calls to the operation `getPersistenceContext` of the required `PersistenceIf` return a `TYPE` of `NONE`, which allows to resolve required component dependencies in the implementation of Co-CoME. The operation `queryStockItemsByProductId` of the required `StoreQueryIf` returns a `NUMBER_OF_ELEMENTS` of 0 or 30.

The `TBValidationQuality` states that a coverage driven test strategy with the criterion $C_{\text{relaxed basic paths}}$ is used for the validation. Random testing is used and the internal state is not analyzed. The coverage requirements for this criterion and the specification lead to overall 13 different paths. However, not all of these paths are feasible. The feasibility is discussed next. An overview on the paths with respect to the visited loops in the specification is given in table 8.3. The second loop in the specification cannot be covered more often than the first one, which excludes the paths with the number 3, 4, and 5. The third loop is part of a branch, which restricts the number of possible loop iterations to values greater or equal to 1. This excludes the paths with the numbers 1, 4, 8, and 11.

Table 8.3.: Feasibility of Relaxed Basics Paths in Operation dispatchProductsFromOtherStores

Notation: 0 means a loop is not iterated, 1 means a loop is iterated at least once, and
- means that the loop is not visited in the control flow.

Paths #	Loop 1	Loop 2	Loop 3	Feasible
0	0	0	-	Yes
1	0	0	0	No
2	0	0	1	Yes
3	0	1	-	No
4	0	1	0	No
5	0	1	1	No
6	1	0	-	Yes
7	1	0	1	Yes
8	1	0	0	No
9	1	0	1	Yes
10	1	1	-	Yes
11	1	1	0	No
12	1	1	1	Yes

The attribute ignoreNumberOfCoverageRequirements of the strategy
CoverageDriven is set to 6 to reflect the number of infeasible paths. The
test set size estimation for this settings is 12.

The RunProtocol resulting from the validation shows that the validation
was successful. Overall, 11 tests were executed. The random generation of
input values and skipping of infeasible paths allows that 11 instead of 12
test cases are sufficient. The precision in this experiment is 1 as all reported
failures are failures. The recall is 1 as all contained failures have been
reported.

The experiment shows that accurate specifications are successfully identified as such. The hypothesis is confirmed.

Experiment E10.2 addresses the reliable identification of inaccurate complex and realistic specifications using path coverage. The experiment uses
the same system and implementation as experiment E10.1.

The accuracy statements for the specification state that the resource demand in bytecode instructions behave as specified and may not deviate. Implicit ResourceDemand is not validated. The other categories are stated to behave exactly as specified. The chosen parameter space limitations are identical to experiment E10.1.

The TBValidationQuality is identical to the one of experiment E10.1.

The RunProtocol resulting from the validation shows that the validation was not successful. Overall, 7 tests were executed. The random generation of input values and skipping of infeasible paths allows that 7 instead of 12 test cases are sufficient. There are overall 2 validation failure notices. Both report that the number of specified and observed bytecode instruction did not match for the activity calculate distances. Both report that 27 ALOAD instructions were expected but only 25 were observed. More details and an example for such failure notices are provided in combination with experiment E12.2. The coverage information observed during validation and stored with the run protocol shows that all feasible coverage requirements have been met. The precision in this experiment is 1 as all reported failures are failures. The recall is 1 as only and all failures have been reported.

The experiment shows that inaccurate specifications are successfully identified as such. The hypothesis is confirmed.

Experiment E11.1 addresses the reliable identification of specifications with accurate decision probability descriptions. The experiment uses the system PME and validates the specifications of component PME against the implementation PMEImpl.

The accuracy statements for the specification of the operation process state that the probability of all decisions do not have an absolute deviation of more that 3%.

The TBValidationQuality states that random testing and the HypothesisBasedFixedSamplePlan testing strategy with the parameter alpha equal to 0.05 and beta equal to 0.2 is used for the validation. This

329

requires 877 tests in order to fulfill the sample size requirements for the specified probabilities.

The RunProtocol resulting from the validation shows that the validation was successful. The coverage of BranchActions and ProbabilisticBranchTransitions contained via the CoverageSuite shows that TER $C_{\text{probabilistic decision}}$ equals 1. Additionally, the contained expectations via the PCMExpectationTrace and observed measurements via the ResultCollection show that specified and implemented behavior match for all branches. The precision in this experiment is 1 as all reported failures are failures. The recall is 1 as all contained failures have been reported. These values are above the expected values for the precision of $\frac{1-\alpha}{1-\alpha+\beta} = \frac{0.95}{1.15} \approx 0.8$ and the recall of $1 - \alpha$, which is equal to 0.95. This deviation between a single observation and the expected values of a sufficiently large number of repetitions is consistent with the acceptable hypothesis testing errors of Type I and Type II.

The experiment shows that accurate probabilistic specifications are successfully identified as such. The hypothesis is confirmed.

Experiment E11.2 addresses the reliable identification of specifications with inaccurate decision probability descriptions. The experiment uses the system PME and validates the specifications of component PMEInvalid against the implementation PMEImpl.

The accuracy statements for the specification of the operation process are equal to experiment E11.1 and state that the probability of all decisions do not have an absolute deviation of more that 3%.

The TBValidationQuality states that random testing and the HypothesisBasedFixedSamplePlan testing strategy with the parameters alpha equal to 0.05 and beta equal to 0.2 is used for the validation. This requires 1466 tests in order to fulfill the sample size requirements for the specified probabilities.

The validation failures and transition coverage from the resulting RunProtocol is depicted in figure 8.23 and shows that the validation was

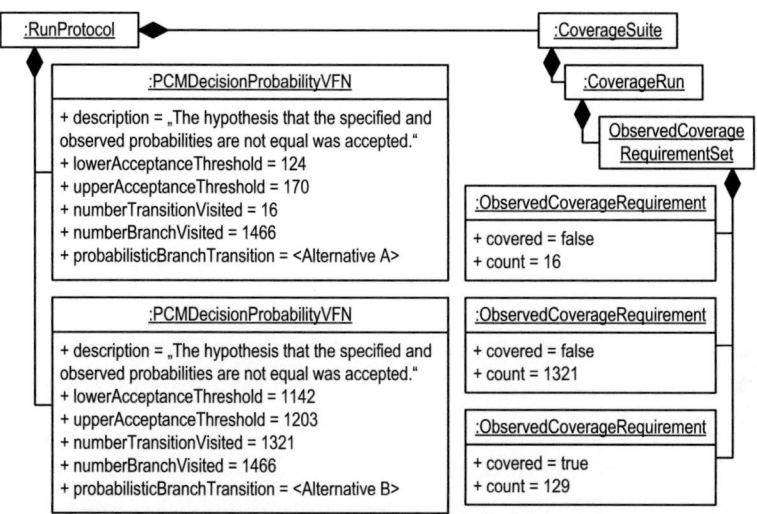

Figure 8.23.: Validation Failure Notices and Transition Coverage for PMEInvalid

not successful. There are overall 2 validation failure notices. The first shows that the probability of `Alternative A` was not valid for the provided accuracy statements. The hypothesis that the specified and observed probability are within an absolute deviation of 3% was rejected at a confidence level of 0.05 and a power of 0.8. Testing the hypothesis of `Alternative B` requires a minimal sample size of 1466. This results in acceptance threshold of 1142 and 1203. The acceptance thresholds for `Alternative A` and `Alternative C` are calculated for the statistic based on 1466 samples, although 877 samples would be sufficient. This results in a lower acceptance threshold of 124 and an upper acceptance threshold of 170. This means that the statistic of 16 for`Alternative A` is outside the thresholds and the statistic of 129 for `Alternative C` within. Hence, thy hypothesis holds for `Alternative C`. The relation of `numberTransitionVisited` to `numberBranchVisited` for the different transitions ($\frac{16}{1466} \approx 1.1\%$, $\frac{1321}{1466} \approx 90.1\%$, $\frac{129}{1466} \approx 8.8\%$) allows reasoning about the experienced probability and can help in improving the specification. Experiments E11.1 and E11.2 show that failures are identified correctly and give an impression how the information in the failure notices eases the interpretation and specification improvement. The precision in this experiment is 1 as all reported failures are failures. The recall is 1 as only and all failures have been reported. As for experiment E11.1, these values are above the expected values of approximately 0.8 for the precision and 0.95 for the recall. This deviation between a single observation and the expected values of a sufficiently large number of repetitions is consistent with the acceptable hypothesis testing errors of Type I and Type II.

The experiment shows that inaccurate probabilistic specifications are successfully identified as such. The hypothesis is confirmed.

Experiment E11.3 addresses how the coverage criteria support risk identification. The experiment uses the implementation and specification of experiment E11.1. However, the experiment uses only a fixed amount of tests and does not validate the decision probabilities.

The accuracy statements for the specification of the operation `process` are equal to experiment E11.1 and state that the probability of all decisions do not have an absolute deviation of more that 3%.

The `TBValidationQuality` states that random testing is used with a minimal number of test cases of 1. Coverage is observed for the criterion C_{action}.

The `RunProtocol` resulting from the validation shows that the validation was successful. The achieved coverage of the tests of the validation run for criterion C_{action} is depicted in figure 8.24. As can be seen, only `Alternative B` is visited and the other two remain unvisited and are not validated. $TER_{C_{action}}$ is 0.5 as 6 out of the 12 `AbstractAction` elements are covered. This coverage information eases the reasoning and identification of untested parts of the specification. The precision in this experiment is 1 as all reported failures are failures. The recall is 1 as all contained failures have been reported.

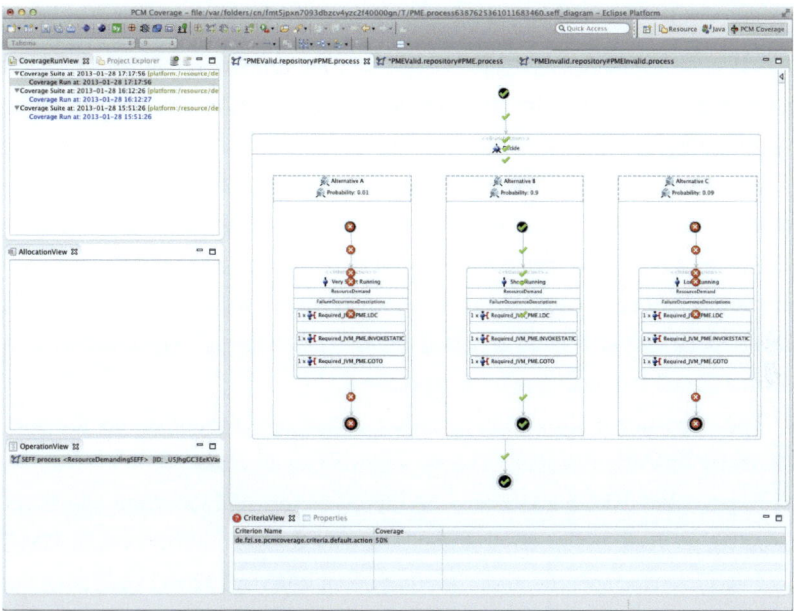

Figure 8.24.: Screenshot of the Achieved Coverage for PME in Experiment E11.3

The experiment shows that the achieved coverage is identified correctly and users are able to see that covering C_{action} failed. The hypothesis is confirmed.

Experiment E12.1 addresses the identification of accurate specifications for multithreading environments. It uses the experiment system MME and validates the specifications of component MME against the implementation MMEImpl.

The accuracy statements for the specification of the operation process state that calls to business components and infrastructure calls are exactly as specified. The constraints for the input parameter input of the operation process restrict the validity to the VALUE characterization and the interval $[-10, 1000000]$. The interval was chosen arbitrarily, other values work as well.

The `TBValidationQuality` states that a single random test without internal state influence analysis is used for the validation. A single test is sufficient in this case, as all parts of the specification are covered if the specification itself is covered.

The `RunProtocol` resulting from the validation shows that the validation was successful. The contained expectations via the `PCMExpectation-Trace` and observed measurements via the `ResultCollection` additionally show that specified and implemented behavior match. The precision in this experiment is 1 as all reported failures are failures. The recall is 1 as all contained failures have been reported.

The experiment shows that accurate concurrent specifications are successfully identified as such. The hypothesis is confirmed.

Experiment E12.2 addresses the identification of inaccurate specifications for multithreading environments. It uses the experiment system MME and validates the specifications of component `MMEImplInvalid` against the implementation `MMEImpl`. The accuracy statements and validation quality are equal to the ones used for experiment E12.1.

The `RunProtocol` resulting from the validation shows that the validation was not successful. There are overall 5 validation failure notices. The first four report validation failures while in the specified activity `Send Notification`. For bytecode instructions, they report that unspecified calls for the instructions `ALOAD`, `GETFIELD`, and `INVOKEINTERFACE` occurred, which is outside of the stated accuracy threshold. For business calls, they report that an unspecified call to `INotificationRequired.receiveNotification()` occurred. The last validation failure notice reports that the observed (1 time) and specified (0 times) number of bytecode instructions for `IRETURN` within the activity `Postprocessing` is exceeding the deviation threshold. This shows that all faults were identified and reported correctly. Additionally, the expectations show that all threads in the specification were validated. The information on the activity eases correlation and the information on the observed and specified number eases

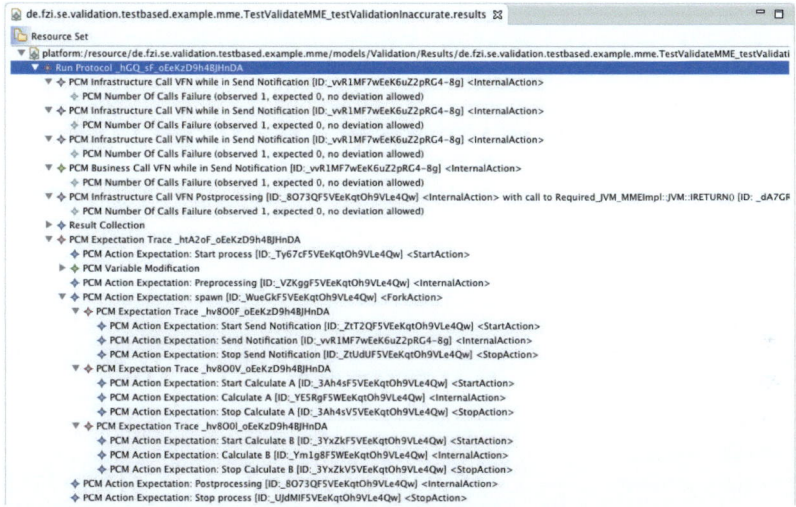

Figure 8.25.: Screenshot of the Validation Result for MMEImplInvalid

fault identification. See figure 8.25 for a screenshot of the structure of the validation result. Experiments E12.1 and E12.2 show that failures are identified correctly and the additional information eases the interpretation. The precision in this experiment is 1 as all reported failures are failures. The recall is 1 as only and all failures have been reported.

The experiment shows that inaccurate concurrent specifications are successfully identified as such. The hypothesis is confirmed.

Experiment E13 addresses the support for validation criterion selection and the effect of probabilistic modeling on the test set size for a validation. First, the criterion selection based on test set size estimations is shown for the behavior specification of operation dispatchProductsFromOther-Stores. Second, the estimated test set size estimations are compared to the probabilistic version of dispatchProductsFromOtherStores.

For both specifications, the accuracy statements state that the probability of all decisions does not have an absolute deviation of more that 3%. The TBValidationQuality states that the HypothesisisBasedFixedSample-

Table 8.4.: Overview on Test Set Size Estimations for Specification of Operation dispatchProductsFromOtherStores

Notation: For C_{jjpath}^1 , a range with lower and upper bounds for the test set size is provided. See section 6.3.2.16 for details on the bound estimations.

Criterion	Test Set Size Estimation	Confidence Level
$C_{\text{call spec}}$	1	0.9
$C_{\text{call obs}}$	66	0.9
$C_{\text{entry/exit}}$	1	0.9
C_{decision}	2	0.9
$C_{\text{probabilistic decision}}$	0	0.95 ($\beta = 0.2$)
C_{action}	2	0.9
C_{branch}	2	0.9
$C_{\text{simple condition}}$	4	0.9
$C_{\text{condition / decision}}$	4	0.9
$C_{\text{minimal multiple}}$	4	0.9
$C_{\text{modified condition / decision}}$	4	0.9
$C_{\text{reinforced condition / decision}}$	4	0.9
$C_{\text{multiple condition}}$	4	0.9
$C_{\text{relaxed basic paths}}$	12	0.9
C_{spt}^3	80	0.9
C_{jjpath}^1	1..18	0.9

Plan testing strategy with alpha equal to 0.05 and beta equal to 0.2 is used for the estimations. The other test set sizes are estimated with a confidence level of 0.9.

Table 8.4 shows the test set size estimations for the upper bounds. Covering all specified calls only requires one test case, as the branch decision in the specifications has only one branch with call specifications. The specification has only one entry and exit point and covering those requires one test. Covering the decisions requires covering both branches of the branch decision and, hence, two tests. Action or branch coverage also requires to take both branches of the branch decision in order to cover all actions resulting in overall 2 required tests. The remaining criteria for covered nodes and edges not subsumed by other criteria are probabilistic decision and observed calls coverage. Covering probabilistic decisions does not require a test, as the specification does not have probabilistic decisions. Covering the observed calls requires 66 tests. The structure of decision criteria require 4 tests each, as both branches consist of a single condition, which must be covered for all possible truth values. The interdependency between the outcome of the branch decision specifications in this special case (inverse) is not taken into account for bound estimation, hence 4 and not 2 is reported to ensure coverage. Regarding the sequence of coverage requires more tests. Covering the relaxed basic paths requires 12 tests, covering jj-path[1] between 1 and 18, and spt[3] already 80 tests.

Selecting a criterion should include the subsumption relations, an overview is provided in figure 6.12). Looking at the figures in general, relatively few tests allow covering complex criteria and no criterion requires prohibitive effort for automated validation. Hence, the criterion choice is not severely limited by the test set size. The overall amount of time required for the validation can be guesstimated based on the average run-time for a few number of random validation executions and the number of estimated test cases. The probabilistic decision criterion is already covered and does not even need to be checked. Relaxed basic paths coverage requires only 12 tests and subsumes action coverage. The other path criteria do not add significant advantages but require more tests. The criteria with respect to the structure of decisions could be checked as well. Call observation coverage can require more tests but subsumes only the specified calls. A good solution for the validation is the selection of the criterion relaxed basic paths and the additional observation of the coverage of the criteria multiple and call observations. If the tests for relaxed basic paths already include the criteria then they are valid as well without requiring additional effort. Evaluating the achieved coverage can provide additional insights on (un-)covered parts of the specification.

Table 8.5 shows the test set size estimations for the upper bounds of the probabilistic specification of the operation `dispatchProductsFromOth-`

Table 8.5.: Overview on Test Set Size Estimations for the Probabilistic Specification of Operation dispatchProductsFromOtherStores

Notation: For C^1_{jjpath} , a range with lower and upper bounds for the test set size is provided. See section 6.3.2.16 for details on the bound estimations.

Criterion	Test Set Size Estimation	Confidence Level
$C_{\text{call spec}}$	1	0.9
$C_{\text{call obs}}$	66	0.9
$C_{\text{entry/exit}}$	1	0.9
C_{decision}	232	0.9
$C_{\text{probabilistic decision}}$	368	0.95 ($\beta = 0.2$)
C_{action}	232	0.9
C_{branch}	232	0.9
$C_{\text{simple condition}}$	233	0.9
$C_{\text{condition / decision}}$	233	0.9
$C_{\text{minimal multiple}}$	233	0.9
$C_{\text{modified condition / decision}}$	233	0.9
$C_{\text{reinforced condition / decision}}$	233	0.9
$C_{\text{multiple condition}}$	233	0.9
$C_{\text{relaxed basic paths}}$	932	0.9
C^3_{spt}	3760	0.9
C^1_{jjpath}	0..935	0.9

erStores. The criteria specified calls, observed calls, and entry/exit have the same estimations, as they are not influenced by the probabilistic decision. Covering the branch decision with the probability p_E equal to 0.01 at least once with a confidence level of 0.9 requires approximately 230 tests, which can be seen in the estimations for the other criteria. The test set size estimations for these criteria are significantly larger in general compared to the specification with the deterministic decision. The criterion probabilistic decision allows to check the branch decision probabilities. The hypothesis for p_E is compared with 0.04, and the hypothesis for p_{NE} with 0.96. Although 368 tests are required, the validation ensures that the specified probability is within the allowed deviation. This criterion should be validated in addition to the criteria discussed for the deterministic version. If the guesstimated required run-time is too high, alternatives with a lower confidence level or a modified version of the specification, which is easier to validate, can be analyzed using the validation effort estimation.

The experiment shows that test set sizes can be calculated and how they aid in criterion selection. The hypothesis is confirmed.

Experiment E14 addresses the reproducibility of validation results, which allows independent verification of validation runs.

This experiment is a repetition of experiment E10.2. It uses the same settings. The only difference is that this experiment is initialized with the random number seed stored in the run protocol of E10.2.

The comparison of the expectations shows that the experiment is repeatable and the same results are provided. The expectations are compared as they contain all provided parameter values and the sequence of covered elements in the specification. The jUnit test case for this experiment is available at [Gro13d]. As long as the behavior of the implementation is the same, the expectations must remain the same if the same random number seed used. The precision in this experiment is 1 as all reported failures are failures. The recall is 1 as all contained failures have been reported.

The experiment shows the validation framework support repeating validations and allows the verification of validations by independent parties. The hypothesis is confirmed.

Experiment E15 addresses the provisioning of information required from users of the validation approach. The required information, the evaluation if this information is only required for the approach presented in this thesis, and the support in the eclipse IDE provided to users of the approach are presented in the following. At the end, the discussed information and consequences for the applicability are summarized.

Users need to provide the specification and the implementation, as well as information on the quality of the specification and the mapping between specification and implementation. Specification and implementation must exist regardless of the approach for a validation. The quality of the specification must be stated using the accuracy statements. The information on the quality must also exist regardless of the approach for a validation. Stating the information with accuracy statements is supported using graphical editors and the EMF. Additionally, the file creation wizard `Quality model with default values` for the batch generation of accuracy statements for all specifications in a repository is provided integrated into the eclipse Integrated Development Environment (IDE). The hierarchical organization of statements for the different categories eases making general statements about the accuracy while allowing deviations for certain elements. The mapping between specification and implementation must exist regardless of the approach for a validation if the performance effect for elements of a specification are compared to the implementation. The approach presented in this thesis provides a customized editor for the mapping with user friendly labels for the mapped elements. The implementation is mapped via a model of the abstract syntax tree of the implementation. This model can be generated fully automatically using the feature Structural Investigation of Software Systems (SISSy) [Q-I11].

Users need to select, which aspects of the specification should be covered. Users either have to create tests manually and ensure all aspects are properly covered or they can use coverage criteria and test set generation tools. Manual tests and tested aspects are hard to verify by third parties without additional documentation. This approach supports the estimation of test set sizes via the `Validation Effort Estimation` run configuration for given specifications and eases the selection of coverage criteria. It can generate a test set and validate the coverage for the selected criterion automatically. There is no additional documentation necessary. The observed coverage for the criteria during the validation can be additionally visualized graphically on the specification itself via the `PCM Coverage` perspective.

Users need to provide data type converters between the specification and implementation data types. Converters must exist if data samples should be created automatically, for example to select random samples from a huge parameter space. A manual specification of explicit values and test cases has the drawback that these values are not chosen arbitrarily and should not be used for certifying that implementation and specification match. The approach presented in this thesis already provides data converters for all primitive data types in Palladio as well as for the data types related to the validated partition of CoCoME. It is extensible and additional converters can be easily plugged in. The execution of the validation itself is fully automated for the approach presented in this thesis. The results contain the expectations, observations, and - if occurred - validation failures easing reasoning about the success, fault identification, and specification improvement.

The consequences for the applicability of the approach presented in this thesis summarized from the discussion above are that it does not require more information than alternatives. The provisioning of the information by users is feasible and the feedback provided by the approach eases selecting validation settings. The automation of the validation itself requires less human interaction and improves the validation process.

The experiment shows that the input can be provided successfully and that less human intervention is required when compared to a manual validation. The hypothesis is confirmed.

8.3.4. Specification Certification

Experiment E16 shows the applicability and addresses the flow of artifacts and the sequence of activities for the adapted and certification-aware development process. The order of workflows and activities is described in the following with a focus on the adapted process steps.

The applicability is shown for the development of a solution, which provides cost-efficient shipping of products between stores of an enterprise and should be sold via marketplaces. This decision is an outcome of the Requirements workflow. The Business Concept and the related Use

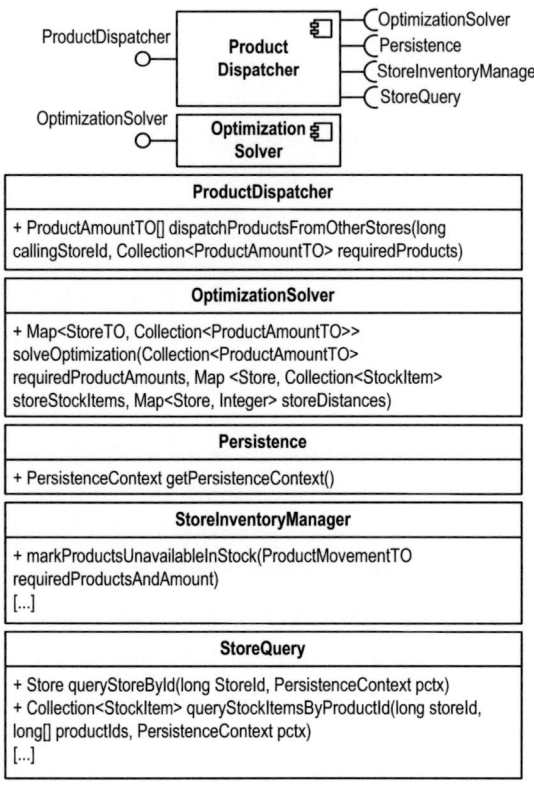

Figure 8.26.: (Preliminary) Architecture Artifact as Output of the Activity Component Specification

Case Models are additional outcomes of the workflow. The workflow is not described in detail, as section 7.2.1 did not introduce any changes.

In the Specification workflow, the Available Assets are checked if the Business Concept and Use Case Models are already (partially) supported by existing components. There are no Technical Constraints or Results of QoS Metrics yet. An analysis showed that the ProductDispatcher interface is used in many shop solutions and its use eases integration into existing shop systems. The realization of the solution requires access to information about the stores and their inventory as well as the layout of the enterprise. The design rationale to separate data queries and data modifying operations is applied. The interfaces `Persistence`, `StoreQuery`, and `StoreInventoryManager` are therefore set as required interfaces. The decision is made that the cost optimization algorithm is realized as an own component in the solution in order to improve maintenance and testing. The `(Preliminary) Architecture` of the solution is determined in the `Component Specification` activity and depicted in figure 8.26. The development of both components of the solution is realized in different `Provisioning` workflows by subcontractors. Only the flow for developing the `ProductDispatcher` component is described in detail for brevity.

In the `Provisioning` workflow, the `Requirements` and `Interfaces` are refined in the activity `Component Requirement Analysis`. The specification of the implementation's required functionality and final component dependencies are set in the activity `Functional Property Specification`. An early estimation of the behavior and performance of the component is created in the activity `QoS Property Specification`. This information is used in the `Specification` workflow in the background in the activity `Interoperability Check`. The analysis shows that the development can continue with the implementation. This is realized in the activity `Component Implementation` of the `Provisioning` workflow.

The guideline for the `Certifier` party selection is used in the `Component Implementation` activity in order to identify the best opportunity to market the solution. The decision is made as follows. It is a requirement that the solution should be sold in marketplaces and the implementation and contained knowledge should be protected. This limits the possible selection alternatives to the ones stating `after Acquisition` for the availability of the implementation. It is assumed that previously unrelated companies will look for the solution in the marketplaces. This means that only weak mutual trust can be assumed. The attractiveness of the offer for these companies is assumed to be correlated with the effort required for testing. Therefore, from the two remaining alternatives none and independent third party the latter one is selected. This also implies that Accuracy Statements must be shared and Assisting Information must be created during development.

In parallel to the component development in the activity Component Implementation, the QoS Analysis Workflow ensures that the System Environment Specification matches the state of the development and that Behavior annotations are added as soon as parts of the implementation are mature. Combining these results from the business perspective of the activity Usage Model Refinement with the Annotated Architecture allows to check the QoS Metrics derived from the requirements and reason on requirement fulfillment.

The development results in the specifications shown in experiment E10.2 for Behavior, Accuracy Statements, and Assisting Information. The failure in the Accuracy Statements identified in the experiment has not yet been identified by the developers. The specifications and implementation are passed to the activity Component Certification and consequently results in Evaluation Failures. The certification report allows the identification of the fault and leads to the creation of the information presented for experiment E10.1, which passes validation and certification. In the Component Sharing activity, the developed artifacts are transferred from the subcontractor to the original company and stored in their own protected Repository.

The component and information is used to check the interoperability in the Specification workflow and enables entering the activity QoS Evaluation in the QoS Analysis workflow. The architecture level evaluation shows that the initial requirements are met. The workflow continues with composing the solution in the Assembly workflow

In the `Test` and `Deployment` workflows, the composition is tested and it is ensured that the requirements are met by the implemented system. However, these are just test implementation as the solution should be integrated into existing enterprise systems and sold on marketplaces. After this quality assurance is completed successfully, the `Functional`, `Interface`, `Dependency`, `Behavior` specification as well as the `Accuracy State-ments` and the `Certificate` are published in the marketplaces.

Summarizing, it can be seen that not every activity is required for a specific product and many activities can run in parallel or iteratively after increments of the solution become available. The constructive part of the development process is applicable (type II validation, [BR08b]) and supports protecting implementation knowledge and IP. The selection part is discussed in the next experiment.

The experiment shows that the adapted process is applicable for offering components. The hypothesis is confirmed.

Experiment E17 shows the applicability of the architecture-based component evaluation and selection for the adapted process.

An enterprise selling products in different shops is interested in improving its efficiency by allowing to transfer products directly between shops instead of via a central warehouse. The current software solution does not support this request. The new solution should provide a decreased time until an exchanged product is available at a store and run within the current hardware environment without endangering the SLA for the IT management services provided for each shop.

This new `Business Requirement` is used in the `Requirements` Work-flow to derive a `Business Concept` and `Use Case Models`.

In the `Specification` workflow, the `Available Assets` from mar-ketplaces are identified in the `Component Identification` activity. Assume that different possible alternatives are identified, one of them the result from experiment E16. Assume further, that this is the only one with `Behavior` specifications and a `Certificate` for its accuracy. Architecture-level analysis of requirement fulfillment is selected as this reduces the evaluation time and does not require to build a test system. If a good solution is found, it is kept and the other alternatives are discarded. The `Provisioning` workflow is not needed at this point. The validity of the `Certificate` is checked successfully in the `Certificate Validation` activity. A `(Preliminary) Architecture` is sketched, which describes the current component-based system after integrating the component. The interoperability check is successful and the architecture is analyzed.

In the `QoS Analysis` workflow, the `Domain Expert` derives the `Usage Model` for the new system in the activities `Use Case Analysis` and `Usage Model Refinement`. The `Business Requirements` and `Deployment-Annotated Architecture` are used to reason about the `QoS Metrics` and the fulfillment of the requirements. The final `QoS Evaluation` activity shows that the solution fulfills the requirements and the SLA are met. The implementation of the component is acquired. That the implementation is a match for the specifications and accuracy statements is ensured by a transition to the activity `Certificate Validation` and a verification of the correctness.

In the `Assembly` workflow, the system is assembled according to the architecture. The fulfillment of the analyzed QoS properties is assured in the `Test` workflow. The final solution is put into production in the `Deployment` workflow.

Summarizing, selecting components on the architecture-level taking into account QoS requirements without implementation is applicable and supported by the adapted process. Invalid certificates would be identified before the specifications are used and decisions are made. The implementation needs only to be transferred if a decision has been made.

The experiment shows that the adapted process is applicable for the evaluation and selection of offered components. The hypothesis is confirmed.

8.4. Discussion of Results

8.4.1. Internal Validity

All experiments using a prediction or executing a validation were designed in a way that only one independent variable has been modified when compared to another experiment in order to ensure distinct causal conclusions between independent and dependent variables. For example, any experiment with a successful validation of a specification goes along with another experiment showing an unsuccessful validation with only one modified variable. All experiments showing the completeness via elements of the Palladio meta-model were carefully reviewed. Literature references to the meta-model definitions were provided allowing independent verification. The design of the experiments ensured that the outcome for repetitions of the experiments is the same or at least has a high confidence level in the probabilistic case. The information contained in the validation results provides means to check the covariation of cause and effect as well as exclude alternative explanations. This additional information was carefully reviewed. The results and test cases used to generate them are made publicly available in combination with the systems for experimentation. The automated prediction or validation itself rules out any experimenter bias. The random numbers used to generate parameter samples are drawn using the pseudo random number generator provided by Java, which has been thoroughly tested. A detailed discussion for each area of work follows.

The completeness of the accuracy statements with respect to the influencing factors has been shown in experiment E1. The capability of the approach presented in this thesis for expressing relative and absolute deviation thresholds for the precision of the number of calls as well as the call parameters for all influencing factors has been demonstrated in the experiments E2, E3, and E4. This ensures that the accuracy of specifications can be stated successfully and is applicable. These experiments provide evidence that question Q2 is answered successfully for the area accuracy statements.

The capability of limiting accuracy statements for each parameter type has been shown in experiment E5. This ensures the completeness with respect to parameter types. The support for nominal and ordinal parameter limitations as well as a user convenient specification has been shown in the experiments E6 and E7. These experiments provide evidence that contribution C4 is addressed successfully for the area of accuracy statements.

The capability to identify threats to the validity of overall predictions based on the accuracies of the composed specifications has been shown in experiment E8. This experiments also demonstrated how the feedback provided by the approach allows eliminating the faults in a goal-oriented way. The experiment provides evidence that question Q3 is answered and contribution C4 is addressed successfully for the area accuracy effects on overall prediction. The achieved improvement for decision making when taking into account the accuracies of the composed specification has been shown in experiment E9. The experiment also demonstrated the added value of margins calculated by the approach presented in this thesis in contrast to direct modifications of undeviated results. The experiment provides evidence that questions Q5 is answered and contributions C5 and C7 are addressed successfully for the area accuracy effects on overall prediction.

The applicability and correctness of accuracy statement validation has been shown on different systems and with different characteristics in the experiments E10.1, E10.2, E11.1, E11.2, E11.3, E12.1, and E12.2. Experiments E12.1 and E12.2 focussed on concurrent specifications. The validation of decision probabilities has been demonstrated in the experiments E11.1, E11.2, and E11.3 on probabilistic specifications. The verifiability of the validation using the defined coverage criteria has been shown in experiment E11.3. The applicability on realistic and complex specifications as well as implementations has been focussed in the experiments E10.1 and E10.2. These experiments have shown the versatile applicability. The experiments provide evidence that questions Q1, Q2, and Q4 are answered successfully for the area statement validation. The applicability and correctness of coverage criteria as stop conditions has been shown in the experiments E10.1, E10.2, E11.1, and E11.2. The applicability of the criterion selection support has been shown in experiment E13. The reproducibility of validation runs has been shown in experiment E14. The experiments provide evidence that contribution C2 is addressed successfully for the area statement validation. The acquisition of required input and time for the evaluation has been discussed in experiment E15. This experiment also shows the ease of reasoning addressed by the provided degree of automation. The experiment provides evidence that contributions C3 and C6 are addressed successfully for the area statement validation. The reduced effort for the interpretation of validation results compared to manual non-criteria-based validations has been shown in the experiments E8 and E9. The experiments provide evidence that contribution C7 is addressed successfully for the area statement validation.

The applicability of the adapted development process taking into account specification certification has been shown in the experiments E16 and E17. These experiments also show the process' support for architecture-level reasoning without acquired component implementations. The latter one has also shown the reduced effort of component integrators for checking the validity of specifications if certificates are available. The experiments provide evidence that question Q4 is answered and contributions C1 and C6 are addressed successfully for the area specification certification.

Summarizing, all experiments confirmed the hypotheses. The experiments were derived in section 8.1 in order to answer the questions and address the contributions for each area of work. This provides evidence that the approach provides answer to all posed questions and addresses all contributions successfully.

8.4.2. External Validity

The accuracy statements consider all influencing factors, which are currently used in the specification languages identified in the surveys of Becker et al. [BGMO06] and Koziolek [Koz10]. The applicability for Palladio has been shown, which considers all of these influencing factors. The transfer to other specification languages should be possible without having to modify the customizable meta-model.

The accuracy statements support the indirect description of complex parameter data types, which is used in Palladio. This includes nominal and ordinal numerical data types, strings, and composed data types. Other languages are likely to have a similar set of elements or less complexity. The actual value description is part of the customizable meta-model and a transfer should be possible without having to modify the customizable meta-model.

The accuracy statements support relative as well as absolute deviation thresholds. This specification of accuracy for elements of a behavior specification limits the allowed deviation without enforcing an additional assumption on the probability of experiencing an error. If such an assumption exists and is valid then it could be applied on the specification for the number of calls or call parameters in the first place. This would provide a more accurate description and reduce the need for such an error probability function. Hence, the provided accuracy statements are adequate and likely cover specifications beyond the validated Palladio specifications.

The effect of inaccuracies on the overall prediction has been shown for the case that all composed specifications have the same accuracy. The added value and contribution could be even shown for this simple case. It could be further shown that the validations support different accuracy statements for the experiments. The validation is designed for and supports different accuracy statements within the same composed system. The application and exploitation of the contributions for more complex cases is straight forward although it was not explicitly validated in the experiments.

The developed heuristic for the minimal and maximal margins does not guarantee to find minimal or maximal values by design although the assumptions were checked with a survey on published case studies. However, the trade-off allows to apply the accuracy influence analysis even in the case if a single prediction run takes a few minutes or more execution time. Otherwise, a full search of the parameter space would lead to prohibitive effort in that case. Especially for highly parameterized specifications with several influencing factors. A partitioned search reduces the number of runs but requires assumptions on the error distribution. If such a distribution would be known then the specification could be improved instead of applying this function. The heuristic can be applied in general although it was only validated in the experiment systems. Threats on the outcome can be identified easily in the specifications if negatively correlated dependencies to input parameters exist.

The handling and validation of probabilistic decision specifications has been shown using the technology demonstrator PME. The demonstrator showed reduced complexity in resource demand and control-flow constructs besides the probabilistic decisions. However, each branch was validated at least once besides the validation of the branch probabilities. The applied validation framework was identical to the one applied to more complex use cases. The application and exploitation of contributions should be straight forward for complex specifications.

The handling and validation of concurrent behavior specifications has been shown using the technology demonstrator MME. The demonstrator showed reduced complexity in resource demand and control-flow constructs besides the specification of concurrent behavior. However, each concurrent behavior and the sequence was validated at least once. The applied validation framework was identical to the one applied to more complex use cases. The application and exploitation of contributions should be straight forward for complex specifications.

The handling and validation of a complex specification on a benchmark and industrial use case was shown in the running example taken from the CoCoME system. The selected part uses all different parameter data types, makes use of external service parameter dependencies for its internal control-flow, and shows a complex and nested control-flow in general. The application and exploitation of the contributions should be straight forward on other real-world systems.

Exploiting the presented contribution of accuracy statement validation for other prediction approaches than Palladio requires adapting the accuracy statements, coverage criteria, and expectations in the run protocol. The meta-models were designed for customizability and oriented at the general patterns used in component-based prediction approaches and specification languages. Although the applicability has been demonstrated for Palladio the explicit considerations in the design should allow the transfer to other specification languages and prediction approaches as well.

Adapting a development process to take into account specification certification has been shown for the Palladio development process. The developed template was designed for process-agnostic support. The integration in other component-based development processes should be possible as well.

9. Conclusion

This chapter concludes the thesis. Section 9.1 summarizes the contributions of the presented approach and the validation results and describes the benefits for software architects and performance engineers. Section 9.2 discusses the assumptions and limitations. Finally, section 9.3 provides a perspective on short-term and long-term work.

9.1. Summary

The contributions of this thesis were provided in the four different area of work accuracy statements, accuracy effects on overall prediction, accuracy statement validation, and specification certification. In combination, they ensure that the goal of evaluating the appropriate use of performance specifications is reached. The main conceptual and technical contributions are summarized for each are of work in the following.

Accuracy Statements The thesis provided a formalization for stating the accuracy of performance specifications in form of a meta-model. The meta-model consists of a generic and language-independent part. The abstractions in the generic part are independent of a certain specification language and provide a template, which can be extended for different languages. The generic part provides a common vocabulary and ensures that statements can be made for all influence factors. The presented customization for the specification language of Palladio shows that even complex parameter descriptions like the characterizations in Palladio are supported. The tailoring and application also showed the capability for making statements about platform-independent parameterized specifications, which may contain concurrent, probabilistic and deterministic parts. Accuracy statements for required elements can be provided on several levels for each influence factor, which allows the easy specification of default values as well as fine-granular specifications for each individual target. The presented approach allows automated processing of the accuracy information and bundling accuracy statements with specifications but does not require modifications of the performance specification language itself.

Accuracy Effects on Overall Prediction The presented method allows analyzing the influence of the accuracies of composed specifications on an overall prediction. It determines best and worst case margins around predictions and supports reasoning if the accuracy of the prediction is appropriate for making an architectural decision. Threats based on the intra- and extrapolation of the resource demand and propagation of the usage profile in specifications as well as mitigation actions were identified. The heuristic to determine only the best and worst case deviations for all specifications was selected based on a survey of resource demand relations in case studies with academical as well as industrial focus and based on the run-time of prediction runs. The heuristic's advantage in pruning the analysis effort from hundreds or thousands to three times of a prediction without influence analysis allows using simulation-based solvers. These solver require less assumptions than analytical solvers, have the ability to predict arbitrary distribution functions including performance peaks, and provide more accurate distribution functions for real-world systems. This allows overall predictions in several minutes for typical applications and in-depth analysis on the architecture level. The heuristic was integrated into the Palladio prediction process and complemented by the ability to report threats on the prediction based on the actual use of the specification in a composition. These threat reports include failure details like experienced parameter values without accuracy information and allows what-if-analyses for modified accuracy statements as well as goal-oriented re-validation of specifications.

Accuracy Statement Validation The introduced meta-model for test-based validations allows stating the quality and validated aspects. The defined strategies for the generation of parameter values, the stop condition, the internal state influence analysis strategy, or the probability validation can be easily adapted if new validation algorithms should be supported and be re-used in combination with these new algorithms. The presented test-based validation process is based on exact measurements of the resource demand in bytecode instructions. This reduces the overall number of required tests heavily and allows omitting the necessity for test repetitions in identical scenarios in order to reduce measurement errors. The process shows the flow of artifacts in the process and defines component initialization and measurement points precisely. The validation of performance specifications is backed by the definition of performance-oriented coverage criteria. These criteria cover all aspects of Palladio specifications including concurrent, probabilistic as well as deterministic, and platform-independent elements. Thus, the criteria allow taking into account the full semantics of the Palladio specification language and their effect on covered aspects and mutual coverage. The thesis provided definitions for 13 unparameterized criteria and the two parameterized criteria $C_{\mathrm{spt}}^{k_1}$ and $C_{\mathrm{jjpath}}^{k_2}$ in the three categories covered nodes and edges, structure of decisions, and sequence of coverage. The criterion $C_{\mathrm{probabilistic\ decisions}}$ specifically targets statistical hypothesis testing of probabilistic decisions. It showed their relation to existing criteria on code level, their covered aspects as well as mutual coverage and expected test set sizes. Reasoning about the test set size supports selecting validation criteria and make trade-off decisions between the effort and quality of the validation. The introduced meta-models for linking Palladio specifications with the implementation and the measurement framework ByCounter were shown in detail and support the traceability and the verification of validation results. The presented meta-model for validation results is designed with the same rationale in mind as the accuracy statements meta-model and consists of a generic, specification language independent, part and a customized extension for Palladio specifications. This common vocabulary eases result interpretation for different languages. The results link all required information on measurements, expectations and validation failure notices. Especially, the validation failure notices contain user-oriented descriptions as well as links to all elements leading to a failure. This supports automated and manual fault identification likewise and is a base for goal-oriented improvement of accuracy statements or specifications. The last contribution for this area of work is an overview on the implemented automated validation framework.

Specification Certification   A novel approach for the protection of knowledge and IP contained in implementations and the use of specifications in protected repositories as well as open marketplaces has been presented. The approach is based on product certification of specifications and can be applied for distributed development in time or space well as across different parties. Certification ensures the soundness of the specifications and their accuracies. Prediction approaches with influence analysis allow trustworthy reasoning on the suitability of components and the quality properties of composed systems. The analysis of required adaptations of existing component-based software engineering processes for incorporating the use of certified specifications lead to the definition of the roles Component Supplier, Component Certifier, and Component Integrator including their key activities and required performance engineering skills. The assignment of these roles to parties can differ and a guideline was provided for certifier party selection. The guideline takes into account the need for protection of the implementation, the mutual trust between Component Supplier and Component Integrator as well as the distribution of evaluation effort between the roles and the use of accuracy statements. The guideline supports trade-off decisions between these degrees of freedom and the selection of the appropriate assignment for each component and usage context. The adaptations were applied on the RUP-based pre-existing development process for Palladio. The resulting certification aware process was presented in detail from the process model down to activities, participating roles, and storage of artifacts in protected component repositories or open marketplaces. A definition of the Palladio certificate, its contents, and mechanisms to ensure its integrity were provided.

The evaluation confirmed that the accuracy statement language was complete with respect to the influence factors. The accuracy influence analysis showed the inappropriate (re-)use of specifications and the support of error margins for decision making. The evaluation showed a heavy variation of the deviation and that the 90% quantile of a prediction can be about 17% off even if a constant and low deviation of the resource demand of 10% in the specifications is assumed. The evaluation of the accuracy statements validation showed that all failures in specifications were identified correctly and no false positive were identified. They further showed that results are reproducible and verifiable by independent parties if the same specification, accuracy statements and validation quality is used. It has been shown that component certificates allow the successful sharing, evaluation, and

357

selection of a component in a public marketplace scenario in which the implementation and the contained knowledge and IP is protected.

The benefits resulting from these contributions for software architects and performance engineers are as follows.

Performance engineers benefit from stating and validating the accuracy of specifications on the component level. They need to be less involved in the actual validation and require less effort due to the automated validation including implementation instrumentation, the actual measurements, and the comparison of the specified and measured behavior. The reproducibility of validation results increases the trustworthiness and verifiability. The coverage criteria ensure the ability for systematic testing of selected aspects. Coverage measurements ensure that nothing is missed and the omission of single elements due to human errors is eliminated by the automated validation.

Software architects and performance engineers benefit from the definition of coverage criteria, which allows discussing about the covered aspects and is a basis for optimizing test sets. Software architects and engineers can use the coverage criteria to agree on a higher level on covered aspects reducing the need to discuss performance validation details and test sets. The documentation of a specification's accuracy supports re-use of the specification at a later point in time as well as by different parties. On the one hand, the knowledge is persisted and transferred between participating persons. On the other hand, the knowledge can be used for assessing if the accuracies fits the expectations and context.

Software architects require less proficiency in performance testing and can concentrate on architecture-level analyses. They benefit from the knowledge about the appropriate use of specifications in composed systems and the quality of overall predictions. They are notified of inappropriate re-use and threats to the validity of a prediction, for example because specifications are used with a usage profile for which no accuracy statements are available. The provided information supports goal-oriented (re-)validation of modified specifications or modified accuracy statements. What-if-analyses with modified accuracy statements and their effect on an overall prediction allow assessing if improving the accuracy of one or more specifications has the desired effect. The accuracy statements and threat identification supports the correct re-use of specifications. Thus, the approach can reduce the need for creating new specifications or validating a specification again only to be sure it is appropriate for the current context. Software architects can incorporate the error margins of predictions due to specification inaccuracies into their decision making and are less likely to make wrong decisions.

Performance engineering in general benefits from the trustworthy specifications as architecture level performance analyses can be applied in scenarios across parties without endangering the quality of the evaluation or selection decision while protecting the knowledge and IP in implementations. Previous restrictions are mitigated and the shown benefits can be realized in scenarios with protected component repositories as well as public marketplaces. The integration of certification into own development processes is eased by the provided templates or using the certificate-aware development process for Palladio directly. Results are easier to interpret, inappropriate specifications are easier identified and the understanding of validated aspects is more precise with the presented approach. Overall, this shows that the aim of this thesis to improve the evaluation of the appropriate use of performance specifications has been reached.

9.2. Assumptions and Limitations

This section points out and discusses assumptions and limitations of the approach presented in this thesis.

Availability of Implementation The approach assumes that an implementation is available for the validation, which is not true in the whole lifecycle. Specifications without according implementations can be used in early design stages for the relative ranking of different design alternatives. They can be based on inaccurate estimations and still lead to an equivalent ranking compared to implemented system. However, predicting absolute performance values requires the accurate description of an implementation. The implementation is the responsible artifact determining the performance-related behavior, besides the influence factors with separate specification, and the assumption of its availability is not a strong one for actual behavior comparisons.

Availability of Mapping Between Specification and Implementation The approach assumes that a mapping between the elements of a validated specification and the corresponding implementation exists. This is not a hard assumption as a mapping is also required for determining the measured sections and instrumenting the implementation if the approach is not used. A mapping on the level of actions in Palladio is required in order to ensure that the order and number of component-external calls can be validated. This approach does not require a more detailed mapping.

Noise-free Measurements The validation approach builds specifically on the ability of measurement frameworks to determine resource demands without noise or acquisition errors. This property is provided for implementations using hardware-independent programming languages with intermediate languages by design, for example Java with its bytecode or Microsoft's .NET with its Common Intermediate Language. This separation also eases the use of specifications for predictions in different hardware environments. Detailed information about the prediction of and for platform-independent specifications is provided by Kuperberg in his PhD thesis [Kup10], which is also based on ideas for platform-specific calibration of specifications presented by Wu in [WW04]. Implementations in C, C++, ObjectiveC,

Ada, Fortran, Python, or PHP are typically directly compiled for binary platforms but approaches like LLVM [LA04] allow addressing this issue. Gartner already identified in 2009 that the prevailing categories of application server architectures are .NET and Java EE and that they dominate the mainstream application server market [NPI09]. The trend for job positions regarding development languages also shows that languages with intermediate language are widespread and have a positive growth, while the other languages are tending to stagnate [Dia12]. This job trend may be even stronger if only business software and no software for embedded devices with their serious restrictions are regarded. This shows that the assumption of using a programming language with an intermediate language is not a strong one for business systems. Furthermore, this assumption is only required for the validation and is not required for the accuracy influence analysis, which allows taking into account inaccurate measurements due to noise. In general, intermediate languages allow noise-free measurements, which makes this a weak assumption.

Manual Specification of Limitations for Accuracy Statements

The presented approach assumes that software architects or performance engineers provide the limits for accuracy statements. There is no explicit support for determining these limits besides reporting inappropriate use and experienced values if a specification is used in a prediction with parameter values for which no accuracy statements are available. The approach ensures that threats for predictions are identified but judging about appropriate limits depends on the context, intended use of the specifications, and acceptable validation effort. These decisions require reasoning and the integration of software architects and performance engineers is considered a weak assumption.

Resource Demand Extremum at Accuracy Boundaries The accuracy influence analysis heuristic assumes that the worst-case deviation for a single specification can be observed at the boundaries for which accuracy statements exist. This assumption has been accepted after analyzing the usual behavior of case studies in the survey described in section 5.2. The survey has shown that higher parameter values usually corresponds with higher resource demands. The fulfillment of this assumption can be easily checked on composed specifications and threats for prediction results are thus easy to identify. This assumption is only used for the accuracy influence analysis heuristic.

Handling Software Resources Software resource validation is currently limited to ensuring the accuracy of the corresponding bytecode instructions for acquiring and releasing the resources, which follows the concept of monitors. Higher-order constructs may be built on this basis and might require measuring additional parameters. However, Palladio does not know such constructs and, in general, the possibility for specifying synchronized concurrent behavior in combination with arbitrary explicit resource and infrastructure component access makes it very likely that a semantically equivalent behavior to the construct can be specified. This limitation is therefore seen as minimal.

Approximation of Test Set Sizes The algorithms for the test set size estimations do not necessarily find the lowest possible bounds. They do not take all constraints into account, which are imposed by the structure of the specification and the assignment of parameters within the specification. This limitation does not impede calculations and comparison for common cases and is therefor seen as possible improvement and weak limitation.

Focus on Accuracy Influence The accuracy influence analysis is limited to the influence of the accuracy of composed specifications and does not address the prediction approach with respect to handling influence factors, resource consumption, or contention itself. These factors are inherent to the selected prediction approach and solver. The approach for accuracy influence analysis does show how overall predictions can deviate if the accuracy of the specifications varies within their specified accuracy boundaries. This limitation does not affect the validation of performance specifications, which can ensure that the deviation is below given boundaries.

Analysis of Internal State The internal state influence analysis strategy ReuseInstanceISIA is implemented and incorporated in the process definition in section 6.2 but has not been evaluated. Furthermore, Palladio specifications have the underlying assumption that components have no additional state beyond the behavior specification and configuration settings. A component having internal state would violate this assumption and threaten the trustworthiness of predictions. By design, no property of such a specification has a lower or higher probability for experiencing internal state and coverage or goal-oriented testing is difficult. Alternatives to test-based validation can provide advantages with respect to the overall effort and the precision and recall. An example for such an alternative are code reviews. A manual analysis of the systems for experimentation showed that they do not have an internal state beyond configuration settings. Analyzing the internal state during validation is therefore regarded as weak limitation.

Coverage Criteria for Reliability An extension of Brosch [Bro12] for analyzing the reliability of component-based systems was included recently in Palladio. This extension introduces additional meta-model elements and reliability-related information. Reliability-ori-

363

ented coverage criteria could be defined to take these into account. However, a test-based validation of reliability is essentially limited by the necessary effort to cases with relatively low reliability requirements from 10^{-2} to 10^{-4} failures per hour [Lap95, GPT01]. Furthermore, techniques like software reliability growth models are often applied although their underlying assumptions are violated and the significance of predictions results is threatened for business software [BKH09]. Transferring reliability estimates and software defect prediction models between projects has been identified as seriously challenging and can threaten results [ZNG$^+$09]. Using historic defect information from the same software leads to precision and recall values below 80% even with state of the art metrics and different sampling strategies [PH11]. Taking into account this information, it remains questionable if a test-based validation of reliability is desirable and the best way to proceed. This limitation does not affect the validation of specifications focussing on performance.

9.3. Perspectives on Future Work

This section discusses ideas and open issues for short-term as well as long-term future work. The amount of conceptional work and in-depth analysis of concepts has a bigger share for long-term future work.

The perspective on short-term future work is as follows.

Coverage Criteria for Event-Based Systems Rathfelder developed an extension of Palladio for modeling and predicting the performance of event-based systems, which has been recently included and is described in [Rat13]. This extension introduces additional meta-model elements in order to ease the modeling for users. These additional elements are transformed into pre-existing elements and are hence compatible with the approach presented in this thesis. An analysis of the semantics of these added elements should be made and it should be checked if the existing coverage criteria should be adapted or new ones should be defined in order to reflect their meaning.

Integrated Certification Tool Support Issuing, signing and verifying Palladio certificates is currently not fully automated and supported by customized tools. A user-friendly reference implementation could ease the application and make the approach more attractive for the industry.

Handling Software Resources A survey and analysis of software resource handling in real-world systems allows identifying worthwhile additional higher-order constructs, which might provide advantages to users if they could be modeled more easily. However, this is mainly a question of the specification language and the mapping of specification language elements to the implementation than an extension of the validation approach.

Improve Internal State Analyses An approach to analyze if the implementation of components is influenced by internal state could be developed. If no guarantees can be provided a heuristic could be devised, which points to areas more or less likely to show internal state, and a goal-oriented validation could be applied.

Support Noised Measurements The validation framework could be extended to support noised measurements. Noise distribution assumptions and statistical analysis for repetitions with the exact same set of parameters can be used to determine the most likely resource demand including a confidence interval. However, the number of required tests will rise significantly in order to reduce errors of Type I. The noise distribution assumption must be carefully validated for each context. Measurement on the fine-granular level will be harder to measure and must take into account warm-up, tear-down, and instrumentation effects. This increases the likeliness of accepting an in-

365

correct resource demand value only to validate a platform-dependent specification.

Sequential Test Plans for Hypothesis Tests The simple test plan for $C_{\text{probabilistic decision}}$ could be replaced by a sequential test plan. This would allow faster results in case the specified probabilities are invalid.

Intermedia Language Support Resource demand measurement could be extended to further intermediate languages than Java and its byte-code. Candidates are Microsoft's .NET with its Common Intermediate Language and the LLVM. LLVM is an intermediate language, state-of-the-art compiler infrastructure, and run-time environment. LLVM originates from the University of Illinois at Urbana-Champaign and has been started as a research project on program analysis [LA04]. LLVM supports a variety of programming languages including C, C++, ObjectiveC, Ada, Fortran, Python, or PHP. The most promising and interesting candidate for an extension is LLVM as it allows measuring code from languages, which are usually compiled for a specific target platform only. This effort should be accompanied by an in-depth analysis of the run-time of single LLVM instructions on specific platforms. Combining these platform-dependent specifications and the platform-independent specifications allows reasoning about the performance on that platform. The approach of Kuperberg for these platform-dependent measurements based on Java is presented in his PhD thesis [Kup10] and can be transferred to other languages as well.

Infeasible Testing Requirements Handling The identification of infeasible testing requirements could be supported by symbolic execution and constraint solving algorithms. This would further improve automated test generation and execution if a coverage driven test strategy is used.

The perspective on long-term future work is as follows.

Application to further Prediction Approaches   The specification language independent parts of the accuracy statements, the link meta-model, and the validation results meta-model could be applied on a broader scale to further prediction approaches. Coverage criteria for the specification languages of these new approaches should be devised and tailored to the elements and their semantics. This step is likely to require a big share of conceptual effort. If a further approach has a corresponding development process then it should be adapted to be certification-aware.

Test-based Validation for Embedded Systems Embedded systems usually have strong restrictions with respect to the available resources. These restrictions impede measurements on the running implementation, even if hardware-in-the-loop approaches are used. Emulating the environment does not guarantee that the identical behavior is shown in the real environment and may take significantly more time than direct execution. The processing of real-time data with hard deadlines poses an additional obstacle for the instrumentation and measurements.

Large-Scale Validation A broad application of the approach on real-world systems by people from academia as well as industry is desirable. Additional experiments and experience reports could lead to improved validation failure notices. It would require a lot of effort but guide further development effectively and enable the identification of new research topics, which are relevant for the industry as well.

Specification Construction Performance specifications are often created using reconstruction or reverse engineering techniques. They allow reducing the specification effort and probability for error. However, neither all performance-relevant aspects can be extracted successfully nor are they needed depending on the level of abstraction. An example for such an behavior specifications extraction approach is provided by Krogmann [KKR10]. Resulting specifications are currently not annotated with accuracy informations and may contain heuristic estimations of the behavior shown in test cases. Unbiased generation or selection of test cases is rarely addressed. Incorporating accuracy considerations into these techniques and storing the accuracy information depending on the used heuristic could ease the creation of accuracy statements. Furthermore, the mapping between the specification and the implementation is often not stored in order to ease subsequent validation if manual adaptations are applied to the specification. Addressing these issues could improve the quality of the specifications, reduce the required human effort for creating the specifications, and ease the validation.

Test Set Optimization The currently available and implemented strategies generate samples randomly within the parameter space included in the validation. Developing test set optimization algorithms could decrease the number of required tests for full coverage, especially for complex and nested specifications tested with a huge parameter space and an advanced path coverage criterion. These algorithms must be able to reflect the complexity and constraints expressed in the parameter assignment language, which means that complex mathematical calculations and the parameter characterization must be considered for Palladio. At the same time, the algorithms for test set size estimation could be improved by taking the additional constraints into account.

Embedding Accuracy in the Lifecycle The handling and necessity of quality and especially performance requirements and the accuracy of specifications in requirements engineering has not been adopted to its full extend in the industry yet [BSGR$^+$12]. An in-depth analysis considering the whole lifecycle of components could identify the critical points and allow focussing future research.

A. Checksum Calculation Algorithm

Listing A.1: Validation Utilities - Checksum Calculation

```
1  /**
2   *
3   */
4  package de.fzi.se.quality.util;
5
6  import java.util.Arrays;
7  import java.util.List;
8
9  import de.fzi.se.quality.qualityannotation.
       ServiceSpecification;
10
11 /**Contains general utilities used for the validation of
       performance specifications.
12  * Provides checksum calculation algorithms.
13  *
14  * @author groenda
15  */
16 public class ValidationUtilities {
17     /** List of available data type converters. */
18     public static List<SpecificationChecksumCalculator>
       calculators =
19             Arrays.asList((SpecificationChecksumCalculator
       ) new Checksum_PCM_10());
20
21     /**Calculates the checksum for the given specification
       with a calculator for the given identifier.
22      * @param specification The performance specification.
23      * @param algorithmIdentifier The unique identifier
       for the algorithm.
```

```
24       */
25       public static long calculate(ServiceSpecification
         specification, String algorithmIdentifier) {
26           for (SpecificationChecksumCalculator calculator :
         calculators) {
27               if (calculator.identify().equals(
         algorithmIdentifier)) {
28                   return calculator.calculate(specification)
         ;
29               }
30           }
31           throw new IllegalArgumentException("There was no
         algorithm known for the provided identifier. The
         identifier was " + algorithmIdentifier);
32       }
33
34       /**Updates the checksum for the given specification
          using a calculator for the given identifier.
35        * @param specification The performance specification.
36        * @param algorithmIdentifier The unique identifier
          for the algorithm.
37        */
38       public static void update(ServiceSpecification
         specification, String algorithmIdentifier) {
39           for (SpecificationChecksumCalculator calculator :
         calculators) {
40               if (calculator.identify().equals(
         algorithmIdentifier)) {
41                   calculator.update(specification);
42                   return;
43               }
44           }
45           throw new IllegalArgumentException("There was no
         algorithm known for the provided identifier. The
         identifier was " + algorithmIdentifier);
46       }
47   }
```

Listing A.2: Validation Utilities - Checksum Calculation Interface

```
1  /**
2   *
3   */
4  package de.fzi.se.quality.util;
5
6  import de.fzi.se.quality.qualityannotation.
       ServiceSpecification;
7
8  /**Interface for algorithm which calculate the checksum
       for a given specification.
9   * @author groenda
10  *
11  */
12 public interface SpecificationChecksumCalculator {
13
14     /**Calculates the checksum for the provided
           specification.
15      * Throws a runtime exception if the calculation fails
           , e.g. the specification language is not supported.
16      * @param specification The performance specification.
17      */
18     public long calculate(ServiceSpecification
           specification);
19
20     /**
21      * @return The unique identifier for this algorithm.
22      */
23     public String identify();
24
25     /**Updates the checksum of the provided specification.
26      * Throws a runtime exception if the calculation fails
           , e.g. the specification language is not supported.
27      * @param specification The performance specification.
28      */
29     public void update(ServiceSpecification specification)
           ;
30 }
```

Listing A.3: Validation Utilities - Checksum Calculation Algorithm for Palladio

```
 1  /**
 2   *
 3   */
 4  package de.fzi.se.quality.util;
 5
 6  import java.io.StringWriter;
 7  import java.util.ArrayList;
 8  import java.util.logging.Logger;
 9  import java.util.zip.CRC32;
10  import java.util.zip.Checksum;
11
12  import de.fzi.se.quality.qualityannotation.
         PCMServiceSpecification;
13  import de.fzi.se.quality.qualityannotation.
         ServiceSpecification;
14  import de.uka.ipd.sdq.pcm.core.entity.ResourceRequiredRole
         ;
15  import de.uka.ipd.sdq.pcm.parameter.VariableUsage;
16  import de.uka.ipd.sdq.pcm.repository.CollectionDataType;
17  import de.uka.ipd.sdq.pcm.repository.CompositeDataType;
18  import de.uka.ipd.sdq.pcm.repository.DataType;
19  import de.uka.ipd.sdq.pcm.repository.
         InfrastructureRequiredRole;
20  import de.uka.ipd.sdq.pcm.repository.
         InfrastructureSignature;
21  import de.uka.ipd.sdq.pcm.repository.InnerDeclaration;
22  import de.uka.ipd.sdq.pcm.repository.OperationRequiredRole
         ;
23  import de.uka.ipd.sdq.pcm.repository.OperationSignature;
24  import de.uka.ipd.sdq.pcm.repository.Parameter;
25  import de.uka.ipd.sdq.pcm.repository.PassiveResource;
26  import de.uka.ipd.sdq.pcm.repository.PrimitiveDataType;
27  import de.uka.ipd.sdq.pcm.repository.RequiredRole;
28  import de.uka.ipd.sdq.pcm.repository.Signature;
29  import de.uka.ipd.sdq.pcm.repository.util.RepositorySwitch
         ;
30  import de.uka.ipd.sdq.pcm.resourcetype.ResourceSignature;
```

```
31 import de.uka.ipd.sdq.pcm.seff.ResourceDemandingSEFF;
32
33 /**
34  * Checksum calculation algorithm for PCM.
35  *
36  * @author groenda
37  * @version 1.0
38  *
39  */
40 public class Checksum_PCM_10 implements
          SpecificationChecksumCalculator {
41     /** Logger for this class. */
42     public static final Logger logger = Logger.getLogger(
          Checksum_PCM_10.class.getCanonicalName());
43     /** Identifier for version 1.0 of the PCM checksum
          calculation algorithm. */
44     public static final String CHECKSUM_PCM_10_IDENTIFIER
          = "PCM 1.0";
45     /**
46      * Separator character for the same hierarchy level.
          Improves readability
47      * for humans. Technically not necessary.
48      */
49     protected static final String SEPARATOR = "_";
50     /**
51      * Separator character for the opening a new hierarchy
          level. Improves
52      * readability for humans. Technically not necessary.
53      */
54     protected static final String
          SEPARATOR_HIERARCHY_START = "(";
55     /**
56      * Separator character for closing a hierarchy level.
          Improves readability
57      * for humans. Technically not necessary.
58      */
59     protected static final String SEPARATOR_HIERARCHY_END
          = ")";
60
```

```
61      /** String converter for data types. */
62      private final DataTypeConverter dataTypeConverter =
        new DataTypeConverter();
63
64      @Override
65      public void update(ServiceSpecification specification)
        {
66          Long checksum = calculate(specification);
67          specification.setChecksum(checksum);
68          specification.setChecksumAlg(
        CHECKSUM_PCM_10_IDENTIFIER);
69      }
70
71      @Override
72      public long calculate(ServiceSpecification
        specification) {
73          if (!(specification instanceof
        PCMServiceSpecification)) {
74              throw new IllegalArgumentException(
75                      "This algorithm can only calculate
        checksums for PCM service specifications. The
        provided specification type must be
        PCMServiceSpecification.");
76          }
77          Checksum checksum = new CRC32();
78          checksum.reset();
79          ResourceDemandingSEFF rdseff = ((
        PCMServiceSpecification) specification)
80                  .getResourceDemandingSEFF();
81          // Provided interface must stay the same
82          updateChecksumWithSignature(checksum,
83                  rdseff.getDescribedService__SEFF());
84          // Component parameter and component parameter
        must stay the same
85          for (VariableUsage usage : rdseff
86                          .
        getBasicComponent_ServiceEffectSpecification()
```

```
87                      .
       getComponentParameterUsage_ImplementationComponentType
       ( ) ) {
88             updateChecksum ( checksum ,
89                     " ComponentParameter " + PCMUtil .
       getQualifiedName ( usage ) ) ;
90         }
91     for ( PassiveResource passiveResource : rdseff
92                      .
       getBasicComponent_ServiceEffectSpecification ( )
93             . getPassiveResource_BasicComponent ( ) ) {
94             updateChecksum ( checksum , passiveResource .
       eClass ( ) . getName ( )
95                     + SEPARATOR + passiveResource . getId ( )
       + SEPARATOR
96                     + passiveResource . getEntityName ( ) ) ;
97         }
98     // Required interface identifiers and operation
       parameters must stay the
99     // same
100    for ( RequiredRole requiredRole : rdseff
101                      .
       getBasicComponent_ServiceEffectSpecification ( )
102            . getRequiredRoles_InterfaceRequiringEntity
       ( ) ) {
103            updateChecksum ( checksum , requiredRole . eClass ( )
       . getName ( )
104                    + SEPARATOR + requiredRole . getId ( ) ) ;
105        if ( requiredRole instanceof
       OperationRequiredRole ) {
106            OperationRequiredRole
       operationRequiredRole = ( OperationRequiredRole )
       requiredRole ;
107            updateChecksum ( checksum , SEPARATOR
108                    + operationRequiredRole
109                      .
       getRequiredInterface__OperationRequiredRole ( )
110                      . getId ( ) +
       SEPARATOR_HIERARCHY_START ) ;
```

```
111                    for (Signature signature :
        operationRequiredRole
112                         .
        getRequiredInterface__OperationRequiredRole()
113                         .getSignatures__OperationInterface
        ()) {
114                        updateChecksumWithSignature(checksum,
        signature);
115                    }
116                    updateChecksum(checksum,
        SEPARATOR_HIERARCHY_END);
117            } else if (requiredRole instanceof
        InfrastructureRequiredRole) {
118                    InfrastructureRequiredRole
        infrastructureRequiredRole = (
        InfrastructureRequiredRole) requiredRole;
119                updateChecksum(
120                        checksum,
121                        SEPARATOR
122                            + infrastructureRequiredRole
123                         .
        getRequiredInterface__InfrastructureRequiredRole()
124            .getId() + SEPARATOR_HIERARCHY_START);
125                    for (Signature signature :
        infrastructureRequiredRole
126         .getRequiredInterface__InfrastructureRequiredRole()
127         .getInfrastructureSignatures__InfrastructureInterface
        ()) {
128                        updateChecksumWithSignature(checksum,
        signature);
129                    }
130                    updateChecksum(checksum,
        SEPARATOR_HIERARCHY_END);
131            } else {
132                throw new IllegalArgumentException(
133                    "Required roles of the component
        containing the specification may only have operation
        and infrastructure required roles. Experienced role
        was:"
```

```
134                          + requiredRole.eClass().
      getName());
135          }
136        }
137        for (ResourceRequiredRole rrRole : rdseff
138   .getBasicComponent_ServiceEffectSpecification()
139   .getResourceRequiredRoles__
      ResourceInterfaceRequiringEntity()) {
140          updateChecksum(checksum, SEPARATOR + rrRole.
      getId()
141                      + SEPARATOR_HIERARCHY_START);
142          for (ResourceSignature resourceSignature :
      rrRole
143                      .
      getRequiredResourceInterface__ResourceRequiredRole()
144                      .
      getResourceSignatures__ResourceInterface()) {
145              updateChecksumWithSignature(checksum,
      resourceSignature);
146          }
147          updateChecksum(checksum,
      SEPARATOR_HIERARCHY_END);
148        }
149        // Specified behavior must stay the same
150        ActionChecksumSwitch checksumSwitch = new
      ActionChecksumSwitch(checksum);
151        checksumSwitch.doSwitch(rdseff);
152        return checksum.getValue();
153   }
154
155   /**
156    * Updates the checksum with details about the
      signatures.
157    *
158    * @param checksum
159    *            The checksum.
160    * @param signature
161    *            The signature.
162    */
```

```
163    protected void updateChecksumWithSignature(Checksum
       checksum,
164            Signature signature) {
165        if (signature instanceof OperationSignature) {
166            OperationSignature operationSignature = (
       OperationSignature) signature;
167            for (Parameter parameter : operationSignature
168                    .getParameters__OperationSignature())
       {
169                updateChecksum(
170                        checksum,
171                        parameter.getParameterName()
172                            + SEPARATOR
173                            + dataTypeConverter.
       getUniqueIdentifier(parameter
174                                                      .
       getDataType__Parameter()));
175            }
176            if (operationSignature.
       getReturnType__OperationSignature() != null) {
177                updateChecksum(checksum,
178                        dataTypeConverter.
       getUniqueIdentifier(operationSignature
179                                              .
       getReturnType__OperationSignature()));
180            }
181        } else if (signature instanceof
       InfrastructureSignature) {
182            for (Parameter parameter : ((
       InfrastructureSignature) signature)
183                                          .
       getParameters__InfrastructureSignature()) {
184                updateChecksum(
185                        checksum,
186                        parameter.getParameterName()
187                            + SEPARATOR
188                            + dataTypeConverter.
       getUniqueIdentifier(parameter
```

```
189                                                 .
         getDataType__Parameter ( ) ) ) ;
190              }
191           } else {
192              throw new IllegalArgumentException (
193                      "Only signature of operation and
         infrastructure interfaces can be processed. Provided
         type was : "
194                          + signature . eClass ( ) . getName ( )
         ) ;
195           }
196      }
197
198      /**
199       * Updates the checksum with details about the
         signatures .
200       *
201       * @param checksum
202       *            The checksum .
203       * @param signature
204       *            The signature .
205       */
206      protected void updateChecksumWithSignature ( Checksum
         checksum ,
207              ResourceSignature signature ) {
208           updateChecksum ( checksum ,
209                  Integer . toString ( signature .
         getResourceServiceId ( ) ) + SEPARATOR ) ;
210           if ( signature . getParameter__ResourceSignature ( ) !=
         null ) {
211              updateChecksum (
212                      checksum ,
213                      signature .
         getParameter__ResourceSignature ( )
214                          . getParameterName ( )
215                          + SEPARATOR
216                          + dataTypeConverter .
         getUniqueIdentifier ( signature
```

```
217                                              .
          getParameter__ResourceSignature ()
218                                              .
          getDataType__Parameter ()));
219           }
220       }
221
222       @Override
223       public String identify () {
224           return CHECKSUM_PCM_10_IDENTIFIER;
225       }
226
227       /**
228        * Updates checksum with the given string.
229        *
230        * @param checksum
231        *               Checksum generator and storage.
232        * @param string
233        *               String used to update the checksum.
234        */
235       public static void updateChecksum (Checksum checksum,
          String string) {
236           byte[] byteArray = string.getBytes ();
237           checksum.update (byteArray, 0, byteArray.length);
238       }
239
240
241       /**
242        * Converts data types to strings for the checksum
          calculations. Unique
243        * identifiers and names are included.
244        *
245        * @author groenda
246        *
247        */
248       private class DataTypeConverter extends
          RepositorySwitch <String> {
249           /** List of data types handled in a conversion.
          Allows to track recursive definitions. */
```

```
250        protected ArrayList<DataType> handledDataTypes;
251
252        /**Calculates and returns the unique string for
           the data type.
253         * @param dataType The data type.
254         * @return The unique string.
255         */
256        public String getUniqueIdentifier(DataType
           dataType) {
257            handledDataTypes = new ArrayList<DataType>();
258            return doSwitch(dataType);
259        }
260
261        @Override
262        public String caseCollectionDataType(
           CollectionDataType object) {
263            if (handledDataTypes.contains(object)) {
264                return object.eClass().getName() +
           SEPARATOR + object.getId() + SEPARATOR + object.
           getEntityName();
265            }
266            handledDataTypes.add(object);
267            String result = object.eClass().getName() +
           SEPARATOR + object.getId()
268                + SEPARATOR + object.getEntityName()
269                + SEPARATOR_HIERARCHY_START
270                + doSwitch(object.
           getInnerType_CollectionDataType())
271                + SEPARATOR_HIERARCHY_END;
272            handledDataTypes.remove(object);
273            return result;
274        }
275
276        @Override
277        public String caseCompositeDataType(
           CompositeDataType object) {
278            if (handledDataTypes.contains(object)) {
```

```
279                     return object . eClass () . getName () +
            SEPARATOR + object . getId () + SEPARATOR + object .
            getEntityName () ;
280                 }
281                 handledDataTypes . add ( object ) ;
282                 StringWriter result = new StringWriter () ;
283                 result . append ( object . eClass () . getName () +
            SEPARATOR
284                         + object . getId () + SEPARATOR + object .
            getEntityName () ) ;
285                 for ( InnerDeclaration declaration : object
286                         . getInnerDeclaration_CompositeDataType
            () ) {
287                     result . append ( SEPARATOR + declaration .
            getEntityName ()
288                             + SEPARATOR_HIERARCHY_START
289                             + doSwitch ( declaration .
            getDatatype_InnerDeclaration () )
290                             + SEPARATOR_HIERARCHY_END) ;
291                 }
292                 handledDataTypes . remove ( object ) ;
293                 return result . toString () ;
294             }
295
296         @Override
297         public String casePrimitiveDataType (
            PrimitiveDataType object ) {
298             handledDataTypes . add ( object ) ;
299             String result = object . eClass () . getName () +
            SEPARATOR
300                         + object . getType () . getValue () +
            SEPARATOR
301                         + object . getType () . getLiteral () ;
302             handledDataTypes . remove ( object ) ;
303             return result ;
304         }
305
306         @Override
307         public String caseDataType ( DataType object ) {
```

```
308                 throw new IllegalArgumentException(
309                     "The provided data type is not
            supported by this implementation. The data type was "
310                         + object.eClass().getName());
311             }
312         }
313
314 }
```

Listing A.4: Validation Utilities - Checksum Calculation Algorithm for Palladio Specifications

```
 1 /**
 2  *
 3  */
 4 package de.fzi.se.quality.util;
 5
 6 import java.util.zip.Checksum;
 7
 8 import de.uka.ipd.sdq.pcm.core.PCMRandomVariable;
 9 import de.uka.ipd.sdq.pcm.parameter.
          VariableCharacterisation;
10 import de.uka.ipd.sdq.pcm.parameter.VariableUsage;
11 import de.uka.ipd.sdq.pcm.seff.AbstractAction;
12 import de.uka.ipd.sdq.pcm.seff.AbstractBranchTransition;
13 import de.uka.ipd.sdq.pcm.seff.
          AbstractInternalControlFlowAction;
14 import de.uka.ipd.sdq.pcm.seff.AcquireAction;
15 import de.uka.ipd.sdq.pcm.seff.BranchAction;
16 import de.uka.ipd.sdq.pcm.seff.CollectionIteratorAction;
17 import de.uka.ipd.sdq.pcm.seff.ExternalCallAction;
18 import de.uka.ipd.sdq.pcm.seff.ForkAction;
19 import de.uka.ipd.sdq.pcm.seff.ForkedBehaviour;
20 import de.uka.ipd.sdq.pcm.seff.GuardedBranchTransition;
21 import de.uka.ipd.sdq.pcm.seff.InternalAction;
22 import de.uka.ipd.sdq.pcm.seff.InternalCallAction;
23 import de.uka.ipd.sdq.pcm.seff.LoopAction;
24 import de.uka.ipd.sdq.pcm.seff.
          ProbabilisticBranchTransition;
```

```
25  import de.uka.ipd.sdq.pcm.seff.ReleaseAction;
26  import de.uka.ipd.sdq.pcm.seff.ResourceDemandingBehaviour;
27  import de.uka.ipd.sdq.pcm.seff.SetVariableAction;
28  import de.uka.ipd.sdq.pcm.seff.StartAction;
29  import de.uka.ipd.sdq.pcm.seff.StopAction;
30  import de.uka.ipd.sdq.pcm.seff.seff_performance.
        InfrastructureCall;
31  import de.uka.ipd.sdq.pcm.seff.seff_performance.
        ParametricResourceDemand;
32  import de.uka.ipd.sdq.pcm.seff.seff_performance.
        ResourceCall;
33  import de.uka.ipd.sdq.pcm.seff.util.SeffSwitch;
34
35  /**
36   * Builds the checksum for the content of an action.
        Structure and
37   * performance-relevant behavior differences lead to a
        different checksum,
38   * entity name and identifier changes don't.
39   *
40   * @author groenda
41   *
42   */
43  public class ActionChecksumSwitch extends SeffSwitch<
        Boolean> {
44      /** Checksum generator used to calculate the checksum.
         */
45      private Checksum checksum;
46
47      /**
48       * Initializes the checksum calculator switch.
49       *
50       * @param checksum
51       *              Instance of the checksum generator.
52       */
53      public ActionChecksumSwitch(Checksum checksum) {
54          this.checksum = checksum;
55      }
56
```

```
57    /**
58     * Updates the checksum with the information that the
       provided action is
59     * next in the order.
60     *
61     * @param action
62     */
63    protected void updateChecksumWithOrder(AbstractAction
      action) {
64        Checksum_PCM_10.updateChecksum(checksum,
      Checksum_PCM_10.SEPARATOR
65                + action.eClass().getName());
66    }
67
68    /**
69     * Updates the checksum with the specifications for
       the provided variable
70     * usage.
71     *
72     * @param variableUsage
73     *            The usage.
74     */
75    protected void updateChecksumWithVariableUsage(
      VariableUsage variableUsage) {
76        Checksum_PCM_10.updateChecksum(
77                checksum,
78                Checksum_PCM_10.SEPARATOR_HIERARCHY_START
79                    + PCMUtil.getQualifiedName(
      variableUsage));
80        for (VariableCharacterisation varChar :
      variableUsage
81                .getVariableCharacterisation_VariableUsage
      ()) {
82            Checksum_PCM_10
83                .updateChecksum(
84                    checksum,
85                    Checksum_PCM_10.SEPARATOR
86                        + varChar.getType().
      getLiteral()
```

```
87                                          +  "="
88                                          +
         toUnformattedSpecification(varChar
89                 .getSpecification_VariableCharacterisation
         ()));
90          }
91       Checksum_PCM_10.updateChecksum(checksum,
92              Checksum_PCM_10.SEPARATOR_HIERARCHY_END);
93    }
94
95    /**
96     * Updates the checksum with the information on
         internal resource demand for
97     * {@link AbstractInternalControlFlowAction}s.
98     *
99     * @param action
100    *           The action.
101    */
102   protected void updateChecksumWithAICFACalls(
103           AbstractInternalControlFlowAction action) {
104       for (InfrastructureCall infrastructureCall :
         action
105                .getInfrastructureCall__Action()) {
106          Checksum_PCM_10.updateChecksum(checksum,
         Checksum_PCM_10.SEPARATOR
107                + infrastructureCall.
         getSignature__InfrastructureCall()
108                      .getId());
109          Checksum_PCM_10.updateChecksum(checksum,
         Checksum_PCM_10.SEPARATOR
110                + infrastructureCall.
         getRequiredRole__InfrastructureCall()
111                      .getId());
112          Checksum_PCM_10.updateChecksum(
113                checksum,
114                Checksum_PCM_10.SEPARATOR
115                      + toUnformattedSpecification(
         infrastructureCall
```

```
116                                          .
            getNumberOfCalls__InfrastructureCall ()));
117            for (VariableUsage variableUsage :
            infrastructureCall
118                      . getInputVariableUsages__CallAction ())
            {
119                  updateChecksumWithVariableUsage (
            variableUsage );
120            }
121        }
122        for (ResourceCall resourceCall : action.
            getResourceCall__Action ()) {
123            Checksum_PCM_10. updateChecksum ( checksum ,
            Checksum_PCM_10. SEPARATOR
124                        + resourceCall.
            getSignature__ResourceCall (). getId ());
125            Checksum_PCM_10. updateChecksum ( checksum ,
            Checksum_PCM_10. SEPARATOR
126                        + resourceCall.
            getResourceRequiredRole__ResourceCall ()
127                            . getId ());
128            Checksum_PCM_10. updateChecksum (
129                    checksum ,
130                    Checksum_PCM_10. SEPARATOR
131                        + toUnformattedSpecification (
            resourceCall
132                                          .
            getNumberOfCalls__ResourceCall ()));
133            for (VariableUsage variableUsage :
            resourceCall
134                      . getInputVariableUsages__CallAction ())
            {
135                  updateChecksumWithVariableUsage (
            variableUsage );
136            }
137        }
138        for (ParametricResourceDemand demand : action
139              . getResourceDemand_Action ()) {
140            Checksum_PCM_10
```

```
141                        . updateChecksum (
142                            checksum ,
143                            demand . eClass ( ) . getName ( )
144                + Checksum_PCM_10 . SEPARATOR
145                + demand .
         getRequiredResource_ParametricResourceDemand ( )
146                        . getId ( )
147                + Checksum_PCM_10 . SEPARATOR
148                + demand .
         getRequiredResource_ParametricResourceDemand ( )
149                        . getEntityName ( )
150                + Checksum_PCM_10 . SEPARATOR_HIERARCHY_END
151                + toUnformattedSpecification (demand
152                        .
         getSpecification_ParametericResourceDemand ( ) ) );
153            }
154    }
155
156    /**
157     * Returns  a  textual  representation  stripped  of
        whitespace  and  formatting
158     * characters .
159     *
160     * @param  specification
161     *            The  specification .
162     * @return  Stripped  text .
163     */
164    protected  String  toUnformattedSpecification (
        PCMRandomVariable  specification )  {
165        return  specification . getSpecification ( ) . replaceAll
        ( " [\ t \n\ f \r \u000B ]" ,
166            "" ) ;
167    }
168
169    @Override
170    public  Boolean  caseResourceDemandingBehaviour (
171            ResourceDemandingBehaviour  object )  {
172        Checksum_PCM_10 . updateChecksum ( checksum ,
```

```
173                    Checksum_PCM_10.SEPARATOR_HIERARCHY_START)
       ;
174        AbstractAction action = PCMUtil.getInitialAction(
       object);
175        while (action != null) {
176            Checksum_PCM_10.updateChecksum(checksum,
       Checksum_PCM_10.SEPARATOR
177                    + action.eClass().getName());
178            doSwitch(action);
179            action = action.getSuccessor_AbstractAction();
180        }
181        Checksum_PCM_10.updateChecksum(checksum,
182                Checksum_PCM_10.SEPARATOR_HIERARCHY_END);
183        return true;
184    }
185
186    @Override
187    public Boolean caseStartAction(StartAction object) {
188        updateChecksumWithOrder(object);
189        updateChecksumWithAICFACalls(object);
190        return true;
191    }
192
193    @Override
194    public Boolean caseStopAction(StopAction object) {
195        updateChecksumWithOrder(object);
196        updateChecksumWithAICFACalls(object);
197        return true;
198    }
199
200    @Override
201    public Boolean caseInternalAction(InternalAction
       object) {
202        updateChecksumWithOrder(object);
203        updateChecksumWithAICFACalls(object);
204        return true;
205    }
206
207    @Override
```

```
208    public Boolean caseInternalCallAction(
       InternalCallAction object) {
209        updateChecksumWithOrder(object);
210        updateChecksumWithAICFACalls(object);
211        doSwitch(object.
       getCalledResourceDemandingInternalBehaviour());
212        return true;
213    }
214
215    @Override
216    public Boolean caseExternalCallAction(
       ExternalCallAction object) {
217        updateChecksumWithOrder(object);
218        Checksum_PCM_10.updateChecksum(checksum,
       Checksum_PCM_10.SEPARATOR
219                + object.getCalledService_ExternalService
       ().getId()
220                + Checksum_PCM_10.SEPARATOR + object.
       getRole_ExternalService()
221                + Checksum_PCM_10.
       SEPARATOR_HIERARCHY_START + "Input=");
222        for (VariableUsage variableUsage : object
223                .getInputVariableUsages__CallAction()) {
224            updateChecksumWithVariableUsage(variableUsage)
       ;
225        }
226        Checksum_PCM_10.updateChecksum(checksum,
       Checksum_PCM_10.SEPARATOR
227                + "Output=");
228        for (VariableUsage variableUsage : object
229                .getReturnVariableUsage__CallReturnAction
       ()) {
230            updateChecksumWithVariableUsage(variableUsage)
       ;
231        }
232        Checksum_PCM_10.updateChecksum(checksum,
233                Checksum_PCM_10.SEPARATOR_HIERARCHY_END);
234        return true;
235    }
```

```
236
237     @Override
238     public Boolean caseSetVariableAction(SetVariableAction
            object) {
239         updateChecksumWithOrder(object);
240         updateChecksumWithAICFACalls(object);
241         for (VariableUsage variableUsage : object
242                 .getLocalVariableUsages_SetVariableAction
        ()) {
243             updateChecksumWithVariableUsage(variableUsage)
        ;
244         }
245         return true;
246     }
247
248     @Override
249     public Boolean caseAcquireAction(AcquireAction object)
            {
250         updateChecksumWithOrder(object);
251         updateChecksumWithAICFACalls(object);
252         Checksum_PCM_10.updateChecksum(checksum, object
253                 .getPassiveresource_AcquireAction().getId
        ());
254         return true;
255     }
256
257     @Override
258     public Boolean caseReleaseAction(ReleaseAction object)
            {
259         updateChecksumWithOrder(object);
260         updateChecksumWithAICFACalls(object);
261         Checksum_PCM_10.updateChecksum(checksum, object
262                 .getPassiveResource_ReleaseAction().getId
        ());
263         return true;
264     }
265
266     @Override
267     public Boolean caseLoopAction(LoopAction object) {
```

```
268            updateChecksumWithOrder(object);
269            updateChecksumWithAICFACalls(object);
270            Checksum_PCM_10.updateChecksum(
271                    checksum,
272                    Checksum_PCM_10.SEPARATOR
273                            + toUnformattedSpecification(
        object
274                                    .
        getIterationCount_LoopAction()));
275            doSwitch(object.getBodyBehaviour_Loop());
276            return true;
277        }
278
279        @Override
280        public Boolean caseCollectionIteratorAction(
           CollectionIteratorAction object) {
281            updateChecksumWithOrder(object);
282            updateChecksumWithAICFACalls(object);
283            Checksum_PCM_10.updateChecksum(checksum,
           Checksum_PCM_10.SEPARATOR
284                    + object.
           getParameter_CollectionIteratorAction()
285                            .getParameterName());
286            doSwitch(object.getBodyBehaviour_Loop());
287            return true;
288        }
289
290        @Override
291        public Boolean caseBranchAction(BranchAction object) {
292            updateChecksumWithOrder(object);
293            updateChecksumWithAICFACalls(object);
294            int i = 0;
295            for (AbstractBranchTransition abt : object.
           getBranches_Branch()) {
296                Checksum_PCM_10.updateChecksum(checksum,
           Checksum_PCM_10.SEPARATOR
297                        + Integer.toString(i++) +
           Checksum_PCM_10.SEPARATOR
298                        + abt.eClass().getName());
```

```
299              if (abt instanceof GuardedBranchTransition) {
300                  GuardedBranchTransition gbt = (
     GuardedBranchTransition) abt;
301                  Checksum_PCM_10
302                      .updateChecksum(
303                          checksum,
304                          Checksum_PCM_10.SEPARATOR
305                  + toUnformattedSpecification(gbt
306                      .
     getBranchCondition_GuardedBranchTransition())));
307              } else if (abt instanceof
     ProbabilisticBranchTransition) {
308                  ProbabilisticBranchTransition pbt = (
     ProbabilisticBranchTransition) abt;
309                  Checksum_PCM_10.updateChecksum(
310                          checksum,
311                          Checksum_PCM_10.SEPARATOR
312                  + Double.toString(pbt.
     getBranchProbability())));
313              } else {
314                  throw new IllegalArgumentException(
315                      "Branch transition must be guarded
     or probabilistic. Exprienced type: "
316                          + abt.eClass().getName());
317              }
318              doSwitch(abt.
     getBranchBehaviour_BranchTransition());
319          }
320          return true;
321      }
322
323      @Override
324      public Boolean caseForkAction(ForkAction object) {
325          updateChecksumWithOrder(object);
326          updateChecksumWithAICFACalls(object);
327          int i = 0;
328          for (ForkedBehaviour behavior : object
329              .
     getAsynchronousForkedBehaviours_ForkAction()) {
```

395

```
330              Checksum_PCM_10. updateChecksum (checksum,
         Checksum_PCM_10 . SEPARATOR
331                  + Integer . toString ( i++ ) +
         Checksum_PCM_10 . SEPARATOR
332                  + "Asynchronous");
333          doSwitch ( behavior );
334      }
335      i = 0;
336      for ( ForkedBehaviour behavior : object
337              . getSynchronisingBehaviours_ForkAction ()
338              .
         getSynchronousForkedBehaviours_SynchronisationPoint ()
         ) {
339          Checksum_PCM_10. updateChecksum (checksum,
         Checksum_PCM_10 . SEPARATOR
340                  + Integer . toString ( i++ ) +
         Checksum_PCM_10 . SEPARATOR
341                  + "Synchronized");
342          doSwitch ( behavior );
343      }
344      for ( VariableUsage variableUsage : object
345              . getSynchronisingBehaviours_ForkAction ()
346              .
         getOutputParameterUsage_SynchronisationPoint ()) {
347          updateChecksumWithVariableUsage ( variableUsage )
             ;
348      }
349      return true ;
350  }
351 }
```

The listings A.1 and A.2 show how checksum calculation algorithm are provided to developers. The first shows the API, the second the interface each algorithm must implement.

The listings A.3 and A.4 show the implemented algorithm for the calculation of the checksum of Palladio performance specifications. Internally, the CRC32 algorithm provided with Java is used to calculate hash values.

B. Systems for Experimentation

This section presents additional details on the systems used for experimentation and complements the information provided in section 8.2.

First, section B.1 provides details on the CoCoME. Section B.2 provides details on the PME. Last, section B.3 provides details on the MME.

B.1. Common Component Modelling Example (CoCoME)

This chapter shows the Palladio specifications and implementations for the CoCoME example. Showing the specifications allows comparing the given UML diagrams to the Palladio models. This section also presents the mapping between specifications and implementation, which is used in the experiments.

This section is structured as follow. First, it shows the specifications. Then, it shows the mapping between specifications and implementation. The implementation is available at [WB11].

Figure B.1 shows the component specification of `TradingSystem.Inventory.Application .ProductDispatcher` in Palladio. Figures B.2 to B.7 show the performance specification for its operation `dispatchProductsFromOtherStores`. Figures B.8 to B.13 show the version in which the deterministic branch decision is replaced by a probabilistic branch decision (compare figures B.5 and B.11).

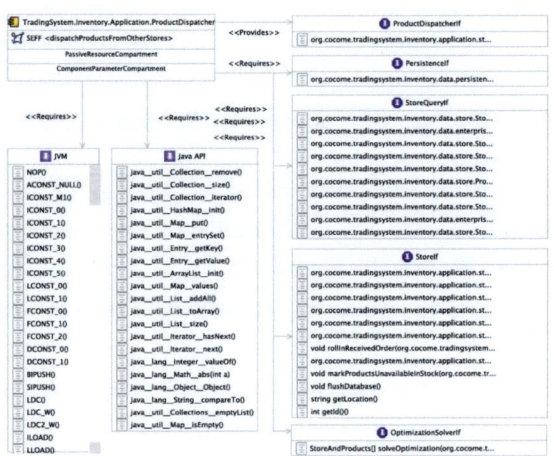

Figure B.1.: Component TradingSystem.Inventory.Application.ProductDispatcher and its Provided and Required Roles

Figure B.2.: Specification for Operation dispatchProductsFromOtherStores of Component CoCoME (Part 1 of 6)

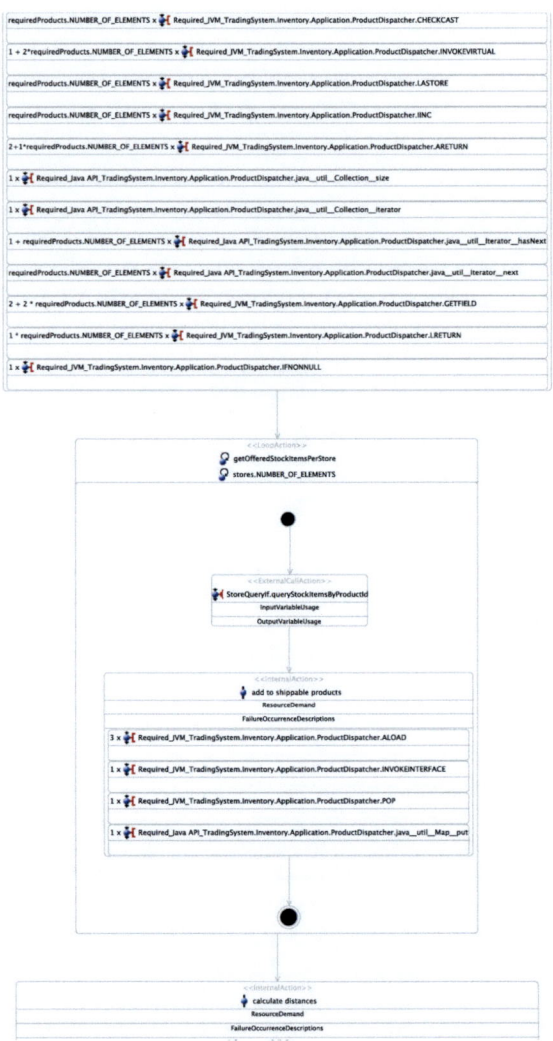

Figure B.3.: Specification for Operation dispatchProductsFromOtherStores of Component CoCoME (Part 2 of 6)

Figure B.4.: Specification for Operation dispatchProductsFromOtherStores of Component CoCoME (Part 3 of 6)

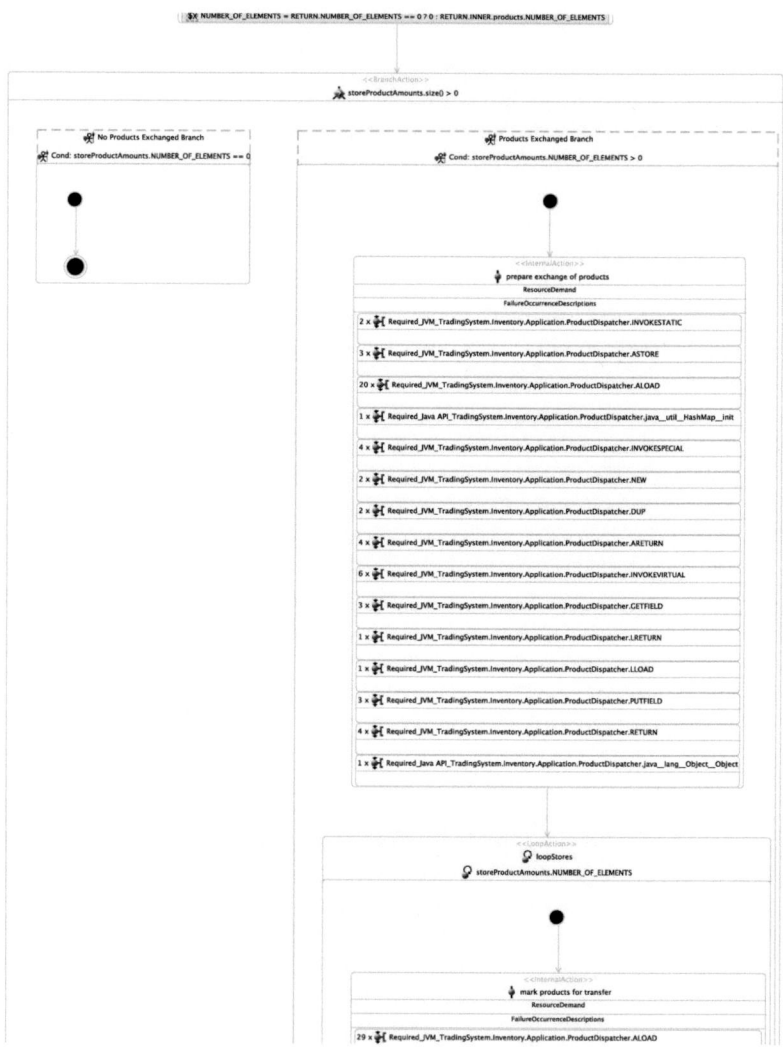

Figure B.5.: Specification for Operation dispatchProductsFromOtherStores of Component CoCoME (Part 4 of 6)

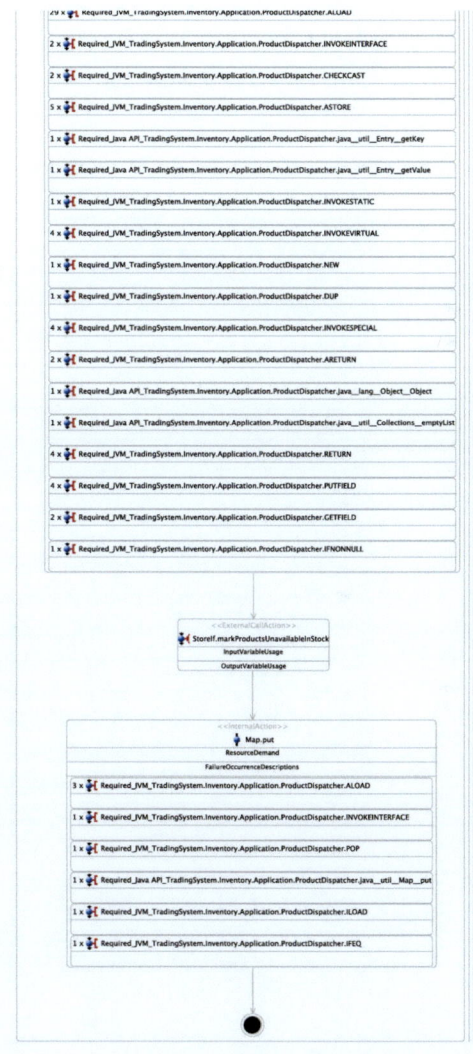

Figure B.6.: Specification for Operation dispatchProductsFromOtherStores of Component CoCoME (Part 5 of 6)

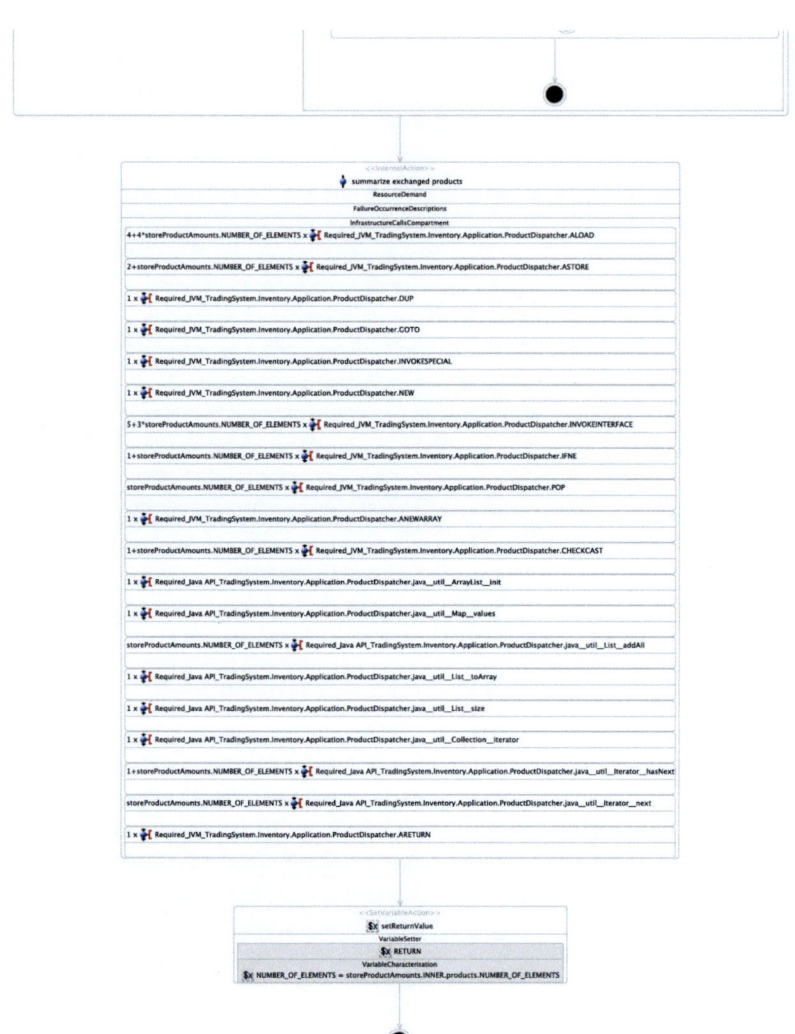

Figure B.7.: Specification for Operation dispatchProductsFromOtherStores of Component CoCoME (Part 6 of 6)

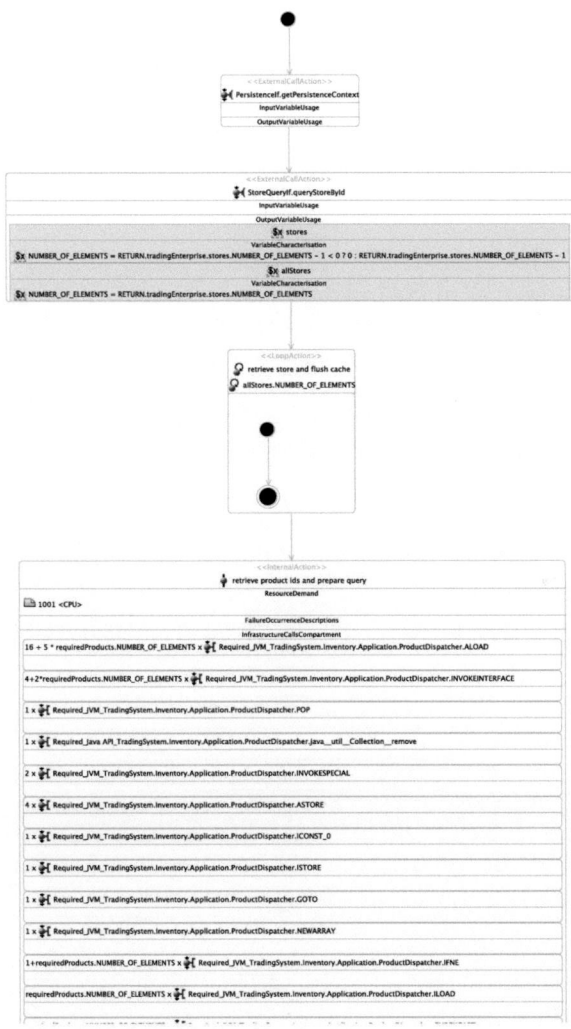

Figure B.8.: Probabilistic Specification for Operation dispatchProductsFromOther-Stores of Component CoCoME (Part 1 of 6)

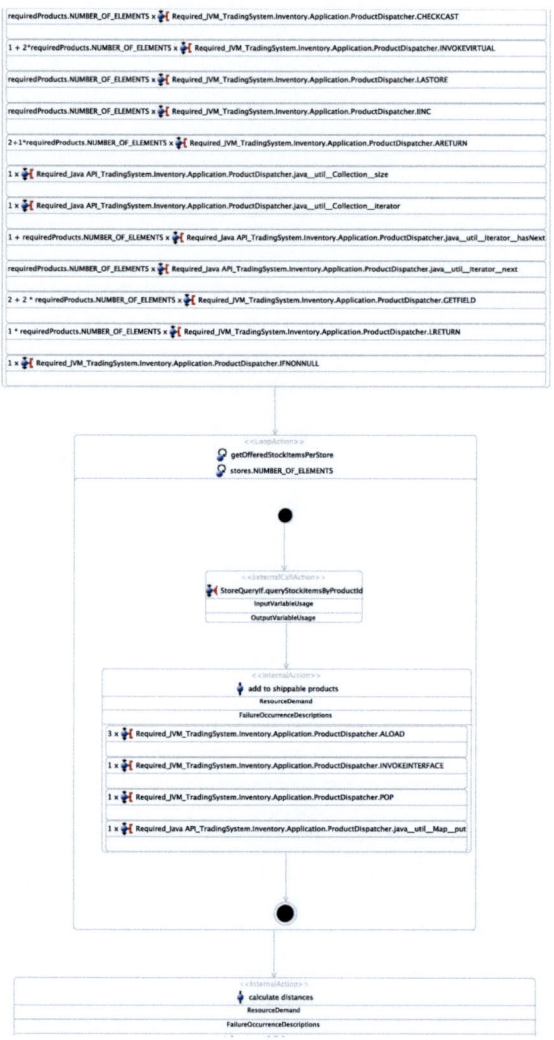

Figure B.9.: Probabilistic Specification for Operation dispatchProductsFromOther-
Stores of Component CoCoME (Part 2 of 6)

Figure B.10.: Probabilistic Specification for Operation dispatchProductsFromOtherStores of Component CoCoME (Part 3 of 6)

Figure B.11.: Probabilistic Specification for Operation dispatchProductsFromOtherStores of Component CoCoME (Part 4 of 6)

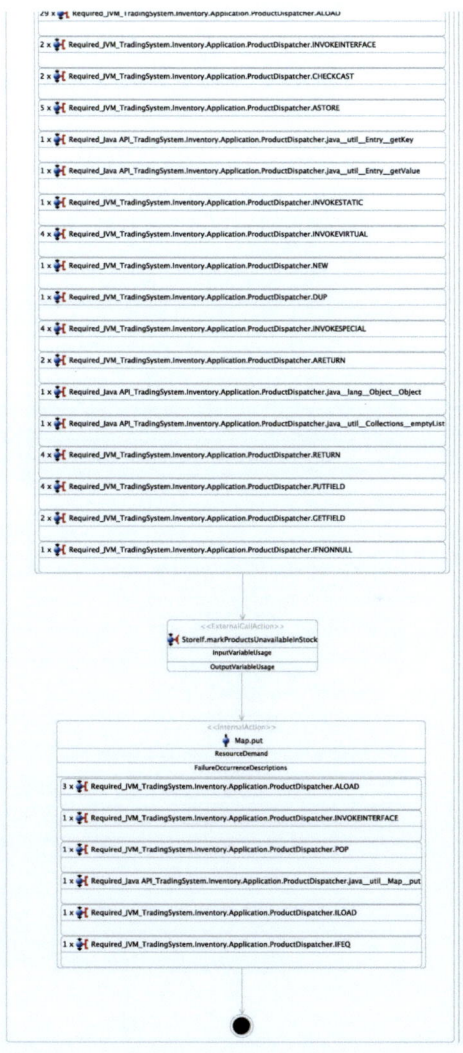

Figure B.12.: Probabilistic Specification for Operation dispatchProductsFromOtherStores of Component CoCoME (Part 5 of 6)

Figure B.13.: Probabilistic Specification for Operation dispatchProductsFromOtherStores of Component CoCoME (Part 6 of 6)

Listing B.1: Mapping of CoCoME and Implementation

```
1  Specification
2      Implementation
3
4  TradingSystem.Inventory.Application.ProductDispatcher
5      org.cocome.tradingsystem.inventory.application.
       productdispatcher.ProductDispatcherServer, org.cocome
       .tradingsystem.inventory.data.store.Store, org.cocome
       .tradingsystem.inventory.data.store.
       FillTransferObjects, org.cocome.tradingsystem.util.
       java.Maps, org.cocome.tradingsystem.inventory.
       application.store.ProductAmountTO, org.cocome.
       tradingsystem.inventory.application.store.ProductTO,
       org.cocome.tradingsystem.inventory.application.store.
       StoreTO, org.cocome.tradingsystem.inventory.data.
       persistence.PersistenceContext, org.cocome.
       tradingsystem.inventory.application.store.
       ProductMovementTO
6      Component Parameter 'dataInstance' via 'org.cocome.
       tradingsystem.inventory.data.DataFactory.
       setDataInstance(final Data dataInstance)'
7      Required Role 'PersistenceIf' via Method 'de.fzi.se.
       validation.testbased.example.cocome.conversion.
       SettableData.setPersistence(Persistence persistence)'
8      Required Role 'StoreQueryIf' via Method 'de.fzi.se.
       validation.testbased.example.cocome.conversion.
       SettableData.setStoreQuery(StoreQuery storeQuery)'
9      Required Role 'EnterpriseQueryIf' via Method 'de.fzi.
       se.validation.testbased.example.cocome.conversion.
       SettableData.setEnterpriseQuery(EnterpriseQuery
       enterpriseQuery)'
10     Required Role '
       Required_OptimizationSolver_TradingSystem.Inventory.
       Application.ProductDispatcher' via Method 'org.
       cocome.tradingsystem.inventory.application.
       productdispatcher.ProductDispatcherServer.
       setOptimizationComponent(OptimizationSolver
       optimizationComponent)'
```

```
11      Required  Role  ' StoreIf '   via  Method  ' org . cocome .
        tradingsystem . inventory . application . productdispatcher
        . ProductDispatcherServer . setStoreInventoryManager (
        StoreInventoryManager  storeInventoryManager ) '
12
13  OptimizationSolverIf
14      org . cocome . tradingsystem . inventory . application .
        productdispatcher . OptimizationSolver
15  PersistenceIf
16      org . cocome . tradingsystem . inventory . data . persistence .
        Persistence
17  StoreQueryIf
18      org . cocome . tradingsystem . inventory . data . store .
        StoreQuery
19  EnterpriseQueryIf
20      org . cocome . tradingsystem . inventory . data . enterprise .
        EnterpriseQuery
21  StoreIf
22      org . cocome . tradingsystem . inventory . application . store .
        StoreInventoryManager
23  Java API :: java__util__ArrayList__init
24      java . util . ArrayList . ArrayList ()
25  Java API :: java__util__Collection__iterator
26      java . util . Collection . iterator ()
27  Java API :: java__util__Collection__remove
28      java . util . Collection . remove ( Object  arg0 )
29  Java API :: java__util__Collection__size
30      java . util . Collection . size ()
31  Java API :: java__util__Iterator__hasNext ()
32      java . util . Iterator . hasNext ()
33  Java API :: java__util__Iterator__next ()
34      java . util . Iterator . next ()
35  Java API :: java__util__List__addAll
36      java . util . List . addAll ( Collection  arg0 )
37  Java API :: java__util__List_size ()
38      java . util . List . size ()
39  Java API :: java__util__List__toArray ()
40      java . util . List . toArray ( Object []  arg1 )
41  Java API :: java__util__Entry__getKey ()
```

```
42      java.util.Entry.getKey()
43 Java API::java__util__Entry__getValue()
44      java.util.Entry.getValue()
45 Java API::java__util__Map__entrySet()
46      java.util.Map.entrySet()
47 Java API::java__util__HashMap__init
48      java.util.HashMap.HashMap()
49 Java API::java__util__Map__put()
50      java.util.Map.put(Object key, Object value)
51 Java API::java__util__Map__values()
52      java.util.Map.values()
53 OptimizationSolverIf::solveOptimization(java.util.
        Collection<ProductAmountTO> requiredProducts,
        StoreAndProducts storeStockItems, StoreAndDistances
        storeDistances)
54      org.cocome.tradingsystem.inventory.application.
        productdispatcher.OptimizationSolver.
        solveOptimization(Collection <ProductAmountTO>
        requiredProductAmounts, Map <Store, Collection <
        StockItem>> storeStockItems, Map <Store, Integer>
        storeDistances)
55 StoreQueryIf::queryStockItemsByProductId(INT storeId, long
        [] productIds, org.cocome.tradingsystem.inventory.
        data.persistence.PersistenceContext pctx)
56      org.cocome.tradingsystem.inventory.data.store.
        StoreQuery.queryStockItemsByProductId(long storeId,
        long [] productIds, PersistenceContext pctx)
57 Java API::java__lang__Integer__valueOf()
58      java.lang.Integer.valueOf(int arg)
59 StoreQueryIf::getLocation()
60      org.cocome.tradingsystem.inventory.data.store.Store.
        getLocation()
61 StoreQueryIf::getId()
62      org.cocome.tradingsystem.inventory.data.store.Store.
        getId()
63 Java API::java__lang_Math_abs()
64      java.lang.Math.abs(int arg0)
65 Java API::java__lang__Object__Object()
66      java.lang.Object.Object()
```

```
67  Java  API :: java__lang__String__compareTo ()
68       java . lang . String . compareTo ( String  arg0 )
69  Java  API :: java__util_Collections__emptyList ()
70       java . util . Collections . emptyList ()
71  StoreIf :: markProductsUnavailableInStock ( org . cocome .
         tradingsystem . inventory . application . store .
         ProductMovementTO  requiredProductsAndAmount )
72       org . cocome . tradingsystem . inventory . application . store .
         StoreInventoryManager . markProductsUnavailableInStock (
         ProductMovementTO  movedProductAmounts )
73  Java  API :: java__util_Map_isEmpty ()
74       java . util . Map . isEmpty ()
75
76  TradingSystem . Inventory . Application . ProductDispatcher ::
         dispatchProductsFromOtherStores ( INT  callingStoreId ,
         java . util . Collection <ProductAmountTO>
         requiredProducts )
77       org . cocome . tradingsystem . inventory . application .
         productdispatcher . ProductDispatcherServer .
         dispatchProductsFromOtherStores ( final  long
         callingStoreId ,  final  Collection <ProductAmountTO>
         requiredProducts )
78  getPersistenceContext <ExternalCallAction>
79       org . cocome . tradingsystem . inventory . application .
         productdispatcher . ProductDispatcherServer :  line  71
80  queryStoreById <ExternalCallAction>
81       org . cocome . tradingsystem . inventory . application .
         productdispatcher . ProductDispatcherServer :  line  77
82  retrieve  store  and  flush  cache <LoopAction>
83       org . cocome . tradingsystem . inventory . application .
         productdispatcher . ProductDispatcherServer :  lines
         148 − 152
84  retrieve  products  ids  and  prepare  query <InternalAction>
85       org . cocome . tradingsystem . inventory . application .
         productdispatcher . ProductDispatcherServer :  lines
         90 − 127
86  getOfferedStockItemsPerStore <LoopAction>
```

87   org.cocome.tradingsystem.inventory.application.
      productdispatcher.ProductDispatcherServer: lines
      309−318
88 queryStockItemByProductId <ExternalCallActionY
89   org.cocome.tradingsystem.inventory.application.
      productdispatcher.ProductDispatcherServer: lines
      313−315
90 add to shippable products <InternalAction>
91   org.cocome.tradingsystem.inventory.application.
      productdispatcher.ProductDispatcherServer: line 317
92 calculate distances <InternalAction>
93   org.cocome.tradingsystem.inventory.application.
      productdispatcher.ProductDispatcherServer: lines
      338−345
94 solveOptimization <ExternalCallAction>
95   org.cocome.tradingsystem.inventory.application.
      productdispatcher.ProductDispatcherServer: lines
      129−133
96 storeProductAmounts.size() > 0 <BranchAction>
97   org.cocome.tradingsystem.inventory.application.
      productdispatcher.ProductDispatcherServer: lines
      95−104
98   No Products Exchanged Branch <GuardedBranchTransition>
99   org.cocome.tradingsystem.inventory.application.
      productdispatcher.ProductDispatcherServer: lines
      100−101
100   Products Exchanged Branch <GuardedBranchTransition>
101   org.cocome.tradingsystem.inventory.application.
      productdispatcher.ProductDispatcherServer: line 103
102 loopStores <LoopAction>
103   org.cocome.tradingsystem.inventory.application.
      productdispatcher.ProductDispatcherServer: lines
      193−207
104 Map.put <InternalAction>
105   org.cocome.tradingsystem.inventory.application.
      productdispatcher.ProductDispatcherServer: lines
      204−206
106 markProductsUnavailableInStock <ExternalCallAction>

415

```
107      org.cocome.tradingsystem.inventory.application.
         productdispatcher.ProductDispatcherServer: line 237
108  mark products for transfer <InternalAction>
109      org.cocome.tradingsystem.inventory.application.
         productdispatcher.ProductDispatcherServer: lines
         197-235
110  prepare exchange of products <InternalAction>
111      org.cocome.tradingsystem.inventory.application.
         productdispatcher.ProductDispatcherServer: lines
         100-191
112  summarize exchanged products <InternalAction>
113      org.cocome.tradingsystem.inventory.application.
         productdispatcher.ProductDispatcherServer: lines
         280-289
114  setReturnValue <SetVariableAction>
115      org.cocome.tradingsystem.inventory.application.
         productdispatcher.ProductDispatcherServer: line 106
```

The mapping between the structural and behavioral aspects of specification CoCoME and the implementation is shown in listing B.1.

B.2. Probabilistic Modeling Example (PME)

This chapter shows the Palladio specifications and implementations for the PME example. Showing the specifications allows comparing the given UML diagrams to the Palladio models and to the implementation. This section also presents the mapping between specifications and implementation, which is used in the experiments.

This section is structured as follow. First, it shows the specifications. Second, it shows the implementation. Last, it shows the mapping between specifications and implementation.

Figure B.14 shows the component specification of PME in Palladio. Figure B.15 shows the performance specification for its operation process. Figure B.16 shows the component specification of PMEInvalid in Pal-

416

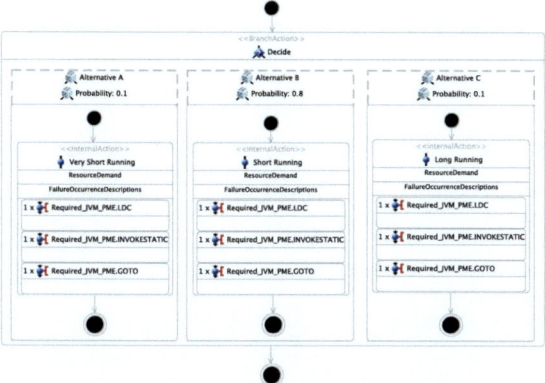

Figure B.14.: Specification for Operation process of Component PMEInvalid

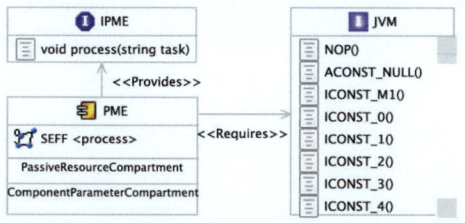

Figure B.15.: Component PME and its Provided Role

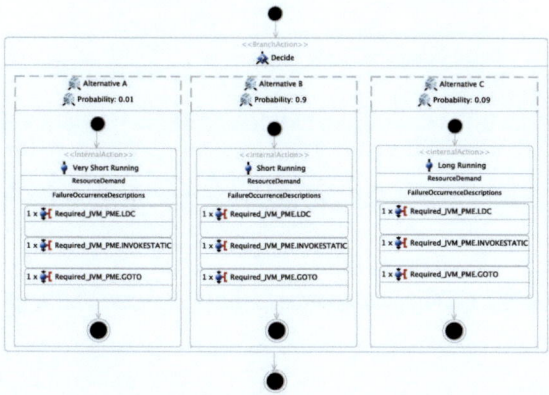

Figure B.16.: Specification for Operation process of Component PME

Listing B.2: Implementation of the Interface IPME

```
1  /**
2   *
3   */
4  package de.fzi.se.validation.testbased.example.pme;
5
6  /**Provided component interface for the Probabilistic
         Modeling Example (PME).
7   * Demonstrates the validation feature if probabilistic
         control-flow decisions
8   * are involved.
9   * @author groenda
10  *
11  */
12 public interface IPME {
13
14     /**Operation for working on a provided task.
15      * @param task Encoded task description.
16      */
17     void process(String task);
18
19 }
```

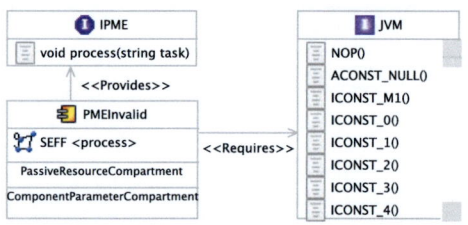

Figure B.17.: Component PMEInvalid and its Provided Role

ladio. Figure B.17 shows the performance specification for its operation process.

Listing B.3: Implementation of the Component PMEImpl

```
1  /**
2   *
3   */
4  package de.fzi.se.validation.testbased.example.pme;
```

```
5
6  import java.util.Random;
7
8  /**Example implementation for the Probabilistic Modeling
       Example (PME).
9   * See also {@link IPME} for documentation.
10  * @author groenda
11  *
12  */
13 public class PMEImpl implements IPME {
14     /** Probability that alternative A is chosen. */
15     public static final double PROBABILITY_ALTERNATIVE_A =
           0.01;
16     /** Probability that alternative B is chosen. */
17     public static final double PROBABILITY_ALTERNATIVE_B =
           0.90;
18     /** Probability that alternative C is chosen. */
19     public static final double PROBABILITY_ALTERNATIVE_C =
           0.09;
20
21     /** Random number generator used for the decision. */
22     private static final Random rng = new Random(System.
       currentTimeMillis());
23
24     /* (non-Javadoc)
25      * @see de.fzi.se.validation.testbased.example.pme.
       IPME#process(java.lang.String)
26      */
27     @Override
28     public void process(String task) {
29         // activity Decide
30         double random = rng.nextDouble();
31         if (random < PROBABILITY_ALTERNATIVE_A) {
32             try {
33                 // template for activity Very Short
           Running
34                 Thread.sleep(15);
35             } catch (InterruptedException e) {
```

```
36              // no error handling in technology
       demonstration code
37          }
38        } else if (random < PROBABILITY_ALTERNATIVE_A +
       PROBABILITY_ALTERNATIVE_B) {
39          try {
40              // template for activity Short Running
41              Thread.sleep(200);
42          } catch (InterruptedException e) {
43              // no error handling in technology
       demonstration code
44          }
45        } else {
46          try {
47              // template for activity Long Running
48              Thread.sleep(3000);
49          } catch (InterruptedException e) {
50              // no error handling in technology
       demonstration code
51          }
52        }
53      }
54
55  }
```

Listing B.4: Mapping of PME and Implementation

```
1  Specification
2      Implementation
3
4  PME
5      de.fzi.se.validation.testbased.example.pme.PMEImpl,
           java.util.Random, java.lang.Thread, java.lang.System
6
7  PME::process(String task)
8      de.fzi.se.validation.testbased.example.pme.PMEImpl.
           process(String task)
9  Decide <BranchAction>
```

```
10      de.fzi.se.validation.testbased.example.pme.PMEImpl:
        lines 28-30
11 Very Short Running <InternalAction>
12      de.fzi.se.validation.testbased.example.pme.PMEImpl:
        lines 32-37
13 Short Running <InternalAction>
14      de.fzi.se.validation.testbased.example.pme.PMEImpl:
        lines 39-44
15 Long Running <InternalAction>
16      de.fzi.se.validation.testbased.example.pme.PMEImpl:
        lines 46-51
```

Listing B.5: Mapping of PMEInvalid and Implementation

```
1 Specification
2      Implementation
3
4 PMEInvalid
5      de.fzi.se.validation.testbased.example.pme.PMEImpl,
        java.util.Random, java.lang.Thread, java.lang.System
6
7 PMEInvalid::process(String task)
8      de.fzi.se.validation.testbased.example.pme.PMEImpl.
        process(String task)
9 Decide <BranchAction>
10      de.fzi.se.validation.testbased.example.pme.PMEImpl:
        lines 28-30
11 Very Short Running <InternalAction>
12      de.fzi.se.validation.testbased.example.pme.PMEImpl:
        lines 32-37
13 Short Running <InternalAction>
14      de.fzi.se.validation.testbased.example.pme.PMEImpl:
        lines 39-44
15 Long Running <InternalAction>
16      de.fzi.se.validation.testbased.example.pme.PMEImpl:
        lines 46-51
```

Listing B.2 shows the implementation of the interface. Listing B.2 shows the implementation of the component PMEImpl. The mapping between the

421

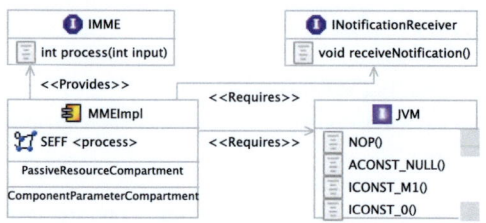

Figure B.18.: Component MMEImpl and Provided and Required Roles

structural and behavioral aspects of specification PME and the implementation is shown in B.4. The mapping between the structural and behavioral aspects of the specification PMEInvalid and the implementation is shown in listing B.5.

B.3. Multithreaded Modeling Example (MME)

This chapter shows the Palladio specifications and implementations for the MME example. Showing the specifications allows comparing the given UML diagrams to the Palladio models and to the implementations. This section also presents the mapping between specifications and implementation, which is used in the experiments.

This section is structured as follow. First, it shows the specifications. Second, it shows the implementation. Last, it shows the mapping between specifications and implementation.

Figure B.18 shows the component specification of MMEImpl in Palladio. Figure B.19 shows the performance specification for its operation process. Figure B.20 shows the component specification of MMEImplInvalid in Palladio. Figure B.21 shows the performance specification for its operation process.

Listing B.6: Implementation of the Interface IMME

```
1  /**
2   *
```

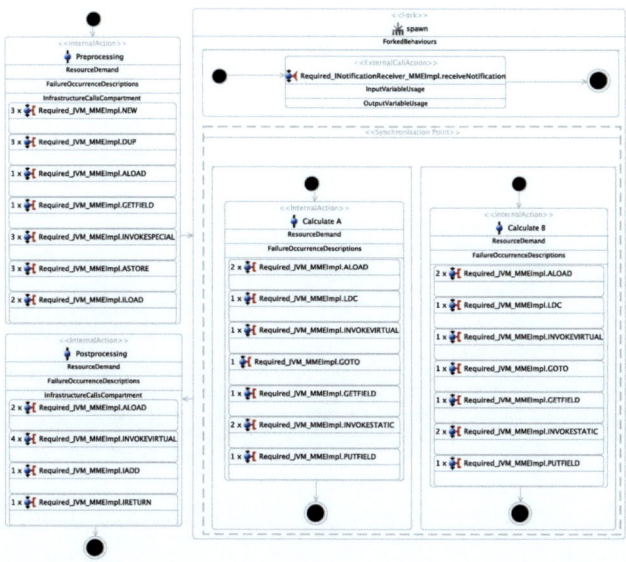

Figure B.19.: Specification for Operation process of Component MMEImpl

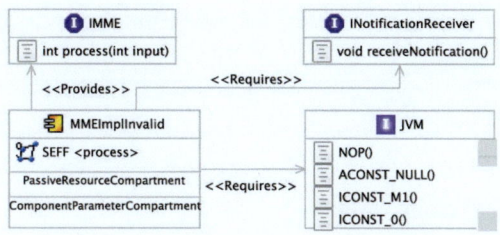

Figure B.20.: Component MMEImplInvalid and Provided and Required Roles

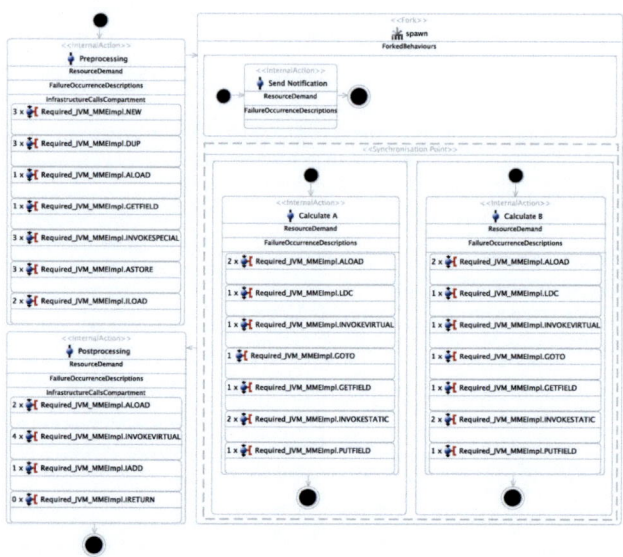

Figure B.21.: Specification for Operation process of Component MMEImplInvalid

```
3    */
4    package de.fzi.se.validation.testbased.example.mme;
5
6    /**Provided component interface for the Multithreaded
          Modeling Example (MME).
7     * Demonstrates the validation feature if multiple threads
          are used. The
8     * performance impact can be determined for synchronized
          and unsynchronized
9     * threads.
10    * @author groenda
11    *
12    */
13   public interface IMME {
14
15       /**Operation for processing data.
16        * @param input The provided input data.
17        * @return The processing result.
```

```
18        */
19        int process(int input);
20
21 }
```

Listing B.7: Implementation of the Interface INotificationReceiver

```
1 /**
2  *
3  */
4 package de.fzi.se.validation.testbased.example.mme;
5
6 /**Interface for receiving a notification.
7  * @author groenda
8  *
9  */
10 public interface INotificationReceiver {
11
12     /**Component-internal processing
13      */
14     void receiveNotification();
15
16 }
```

Listing B.8: Implementation of the Component MMEImpl

```
1 /**
2  *
3  */
4 package de.fzi.se.validation.testbased.example.mme;
5
6 /**Example implementation for the Multithreaded Modeling
       Example (MME).
7  * See also {@link IMME} for documentation.
8  * @author groenda
9  *
10  */
11 public class MMEImpl implements IMME {
12     /** Component receiving the notification */
13     private INotificationReceiver dependency;
```

```
14
15      /* (non−Javadoc)
16       * @see de.fzi.se.validation.testbased.example.mme.
        ISimple#process()
17       */
18      @Override
19      public int process(int input) {
20          // preprocessing
21          SendNotification sender = new SendNotification(
        dependency);
22          CalculateA calcA = new CalculateA(input);
23          CalculateB calcB = new CalculateB(input);
24
25          // fork threads
26          sender.start();
27          calcA.start();
28          calcB.start();
29          // join on synchronized threads
30          try {
31              calcA.join(); // start calculate A
32              calcB.join(); // start calculate B
33          } catch (InterruptedException e) {
34              // no error handling in technology
        demonstration code
35          }
36
37          // postprocessing
38          return calcA.getResult() + calcB.getResult().
        intValue();
39      }
40
41      /**
42       * @param dependency The dependency to set
43       */
44      public void setDependency(INotificationReceiver
        dependency) {
45          this.dependency = dependency;
46      }
47
```

426

```
48  }
```

Listing B.9: Implementation of Activity Send Notification

```
1  /**
2   *
3   */
4  package de.fzi.se.validation.testbased.example.mme;
5
6  /**Thread sending a possibly long running notification to
        a dependency, which should not run in a main thread
        but asynchronously.
7   * @author groenda
8   *
9   */
10 public class SendNotification extends Thread {
11     private final INotificationReceiver dependency;
12
13     public SendNotification(INotificationReceiver
           dependency) {
14         this.dependency = dependency;
15     }
16
17     @Override
18     public void run() {
19         dependency.receiveNotification();
20     }
21
22 }
```

Listing B.10: Implementation of Activity Calculate A

```
1  /**
2   *
3   */
4  package de.fzi.se.validation.testbased.example.mme;
5
6  import java.util.Random;
7
```

```
 8  /**Template for a possibly long running calculation. The
         result of the calculation is accessible via {@link #
         getResult()}.
 9   * @author groenda
10   *
11   */
12  public class CalculateA extends Thread {
13      /** Random number generator. */
14      private final Random random;
15      /** Result of the calculation. */
16      private Integer result;
17
18      /**Create a new calculation instance.
19       * @param input Input used for the calculation.
20       */
21      public CalculateA(int input) {
22          this.random = new Random(input);
23      }
24
25      @Override
26      public void run() {
27          try {
28              // template for activity
29              Thread.sleep(2000);
30          } catch (InterruptedException e) {
31              // no error handling in technology
         demonstration code
32          }
33          this.result = random.nextInt();
34      }
35
36      /**
37       * @return The result of the calculation.
38       */
39      public Integer getResult() {
40          return result;
41      }
42
43  }
```

Listing B.11: Implementation of Activity Calculate B

```
 1  /**
 2   *
 3   */
 4  package de.fzi.se.validation.testbased.example.mme;
 5
 6  import java.util.Random;
 7
 8  /**Template for a possibly long running calculation. The
        result of the calculation is accessible via {@link #
        getResult()}.
 9   * @author groenda
10   *
11   */
12  public class CalculateB extends Thread {
13      /** Random number generator. */
14      private final Random random;
15      /** Result of the calculation. */
16      private Long result;
17
18      /**Create a new calculation instance.
19       * @param input Input used for the calculation.
20       */
21      public CalculateB(int input) {
22          this.random = new Random(input);
23      }
24
25      @Override
26      public void run() {
27          try {
28              // template for activity
29              Thread.sleep(8000);
30          } catch (InterruptedException e) {
31              // no error handling in technology
        demonstration code
32          }
33          this.result = random.nextLong();
34      }
```

```
35
36     /**
37      * @return The result of the calculation.
38      */
39     public Long getResult() {
40         return result;
41     }
42
43  }
```

Listing B.12: Mapping of MMEImpl and Implementation

```
1  Specification
2      Implementation
3
4  MMEImpl
5      de.fzi.se.validation.testbased.example.mme.MMEImpl, de
       .fzi.se.validation.testbased.example.mme.
       SendNotification, de.fzi.se.validation.testbased.
       example.mme.CalculateA, de.fzi.se.validation.
       testbased.example.mme.CalculateB, java.lang.Thread,
       java.util.Random, java.lang.Integer, java.lang.Long
6  Required_INotificationReceiver_MMEImpl
7      de.fzi.se.validation.testbased.example.mme.MMEImpl.
       setDependency(INotificationReceiver dependency)
8  INotificationReceiver
9      de.fzi.se.validation.testbased.example.mme.
       INotificationReceiver
10
11 MMEImpl::process(int)
12     int de.fzi.se.validation.testbased.example.mme.MMEImpl
       .process(int input)
13 Preprocessing <InternalAction>
14     de.fzi.se.validation.testbased.example.mme.MMEImpl:
       lines 21−23
15 spawn <ForkAction>
16     de.fzi.se.validation.testbased.example.mme.MMEImpl:
       lines 26−35
17 send notification <ExternalCallAction>
```

```
18      de.fzi.se.validation.testbased.example.mme.
        SendNotification: lines 18−20
19 Calculate A <InternalAction>
20      de.fzi.se.validation.testbased.example.mme.CalculateA:
        lines 27−33
21 Calculate B <InternalAction>
22      de.fzi.se.validation.testbased.example.mme.CalculateB:
        lines 27−33
23 Postprocessing <InternalAction>
24      de.fzi.se.validation.testbased.example.mme.MMEImpl:
        line 38
```

Listing B.13: Mapping of MMEImplInvalid and Implementation

```
1 Specification
2      Implementation
3
4 MMEImplInvalid
5      de.fzi.se.validation.testbased.example.mme.MMEImpl, de
        .fzi.se.validation.testbased.example.mme.
        SendNotification, de.fzi.se.validation.testbased.
        example.mme.CalculateA, de.fzi.se.validation.
        testbased.example.mme.CalculateB, java.lang.Thread,
        java.util.Random, java.lang.Integer, java.lang.Long
6 Required_INotificationReceiver_MMEImpl
7      de.fzi.se.validation.testbased.example.mme.MMEImpl.
        setDependency(INotificationReceiver dependency)
8 INotificationReceiver
9      de.fzi.se.validation.testbased.example.mme.
        INotificationReceiver
10
11 MMEImplInvalid::process(int)
12      int de.fzi.se.validation.testbased.example.mme.MMEImpl
        .process(int input)
13 Preprocessing <InternalAction>
14      de.fzi.se.validation.testbased.example.mme.MMEImpl:
        lines 21−23
15 spawn <ForkAction>
```

```
16      de . fzi . se . validation . testbased . example . mme . MMEImpl :
        lines  26−35
17  Send   Notification  <InternalAction>
18      de . fzi . se . validation . testbased . example . mme .
        SendNotification :  lines  18−20
19  Calculate  A  <InternalAction>
20      de . fzi . se . validation . testbased . example . mme . CalculateA :
        lines  27−33
21  Calculate  B  <InternalAction>
22      de . fzi . se . validation . testbased . example . mme . CalculateB :
        lines  27−33
23  Postprocessing  <InternalAction>
24      de . fzi . se . validation . testbased . example . mme . MMEImpl :
        line  38
```

Listings B.6 and B.7 show the implementation of the interfaces. Listing B.8 shows the implementation of the component MMEImpl. Listings
B.9, B.10, and B.11 show the implementations of the activities running
in parallel. The mapping between the structural and behavioral aspects
of specification MMEImpl and the implementation is shown in B.12. The
mapping between the structural and behavioral aspects of the specification
MMEImplInvalid and the implementation is shown in listing B.13.

List of Figures

List of Tables

List of Listings

Acronyms

API	Application Programming Interface.
APPEAR	Analysis and Prediction of Performance for Evolving Architectures.
AQuA	Automatic Quality Assurance.
ByCounter	Bytecode Counter.
CARAT	Component Architectures Analysis Tool.
CB-SPE	Component-Based Software Performance Engineering.
CBML	Component-Based Modeling Language.
CCL	Construction and Composition Language.
CLP	Constraint Logic Programming.
CMMI	Capability Maturity Model Integration.
CMU	Carnegie Mellon University.
CoCoME	Common Component Modelling Example.
COMPAS	Component Performance Assurance Solutions.
COMQUAD	COMponents with QUantiative properties and ADaptivity.

CQML+	Component Quality Modeling Language+.
CSM	Core Scenario Model.
EJB	Enterprise Java Bean.
EMF	Eclipse Modeling Framework.
ETSI	European Telecommunications Standards Institute.
FSM	Finite State Machines.
GAST	General Abstract Syntax Tree.
IDE	Integrated Development Environment.
IP	Intellectual Property.
iSQI	international Software Quality Institute.
JJ-Paths	Jump to Jump Paths.
JVM	Java Virtual Machine.
KAMI	Keep Alive Models with Implementations.
KLAPER	Kernel LAnguage for PErformance and Reliability analysis.
LCSAJ	Linear Code Sequence and Jump.
LTS	Labeled Transition Systems.
MCDC	Modified Condition / Decision Coverage.
MCITP	Microsoft Certified IT Professional.

MME	Multithreaded Modeling Example.
MOSES	MOdel-based SElf-adaptation of SOA systems.
OCL	Object Constraint Language.
OMG	Object Management Group.
PACC	Predictable Assembly from Certifiable Components.
PAD	Performance Antipattern Detection.
Palladio	Palladio Component Model.
PECT	Prediction-Enabled Component Technology.
PKI	Public Key Infrastructure.
PME	Probabilistic Modeling Example.
PP	Protection Profile.
PUMA	Performance by Unified Model Analysis.
QoS	Quality of Service.
QVTO	Operational Query/View/Transformation.
RAQS	Rapid Analysis of Queuing Networks.
RCDC	Reinforced Condition / Decision Coverage.
ROBOCOP	Robust Open Component Based Software Architecture for Configurable Devices Project.
RUP	Rational Unified Process.

SEI	Software Engineering Institute.
SISSy	Structural Investigation of Software Systems.
SLA	Service Level Agreement.
SPE	Software Performance Engineering.
SPICE	Software Process Improvement and Capability Determination.
SPRT	Sequential Probability Ratio Test.
SPT	Structure Path Testing.
ST	Security Target.
StoEx	Stochastic Expression.
SUT	System Under Test.
SVN	Subversion.
SysML	Systems Modeling Language.
TER	Test Effectiveness Ratio.
TOE	Target Of Evaluation.
TOGAF	The Open Group Architecture Framework.
TTCN-3	Testing and Test Control Notation.
UML	Unified Modeling Language.
UML-MARTE	UML Profile for Modeling and Analysis of Real-Time Embedded Systems.
UML-PCM	Performance Context Model.
UML-SPT	UML Profile for Schedulability, Performance, and Time.
WCET	Worst-Case Execution Time.

Glossary

Bytecode Counter

Bytecode Counter is an instrumentation and measurement framework which allows bytecode-precise measurements. It is purely based on Java and does not require changes to the Java Virtual Machine. It is a base for hardware-independent performance measurements. Measurements include bytecode instruction as well as function calls.

Eclipse Modeling Framework

EMF is an open source framework of the eclipse community. It allows to exchange, store, access, display, and modify meta-model instances. The meta-models are described using the Ecore format which is compatible to the Object Management Group (OMG)'s Essential Meta Object Facility (EMOF) standard. Model instances are usually stored using the OMG's XML Metadata Interchange (XMI) standard.

General Abstract Syntax Tree

Model of the syntax tree of an implementation. The GAST used in this thesis was developed as part of the European Project Q-ImPrESS.

PECT

The Prediction Enabled Component Technology was defined by the CMU's SEI and targets the prediction of real time and safety critical system. See also section 3.3.

451

Subversion

Subversion is a version or revision control system for files and directories. It enables storing and comparing file system artifacts including meta-data on changes between different versions. It is a successor of CVS and an alternative to other version control systems like GIT, Perforce, or Visual Source Safe.

Validation

Fulfillment of user needs. Confirmation through objective evidence that a performance specification fulfills user requirements. See also section 1.3.3.

Verification

Fulfillment of specified requirements. Confirmation through objective evidence that specification and implementation are equal with respect to a given definition of quality. See also section 1.3.3.

Bibliography

[AdAdLM05] A. Alvaro, E. de Almeida, and S. de Lemos Meira, "Software component certification: a survey," *31st EUROMICRO Conference on Software Engineering and Advanced Applications*, pp. 106–113, September 2005.

[AdAdLM07] A. Alvaro, E. S. de Almeida, and S. R. de Lemos Meira, "A component quality assurance process," in *Fourth International Workshop on Software Quality Assurance (SOQUA '07)*. New York, NY, USA: ACM, 2007, pp. 94–101.

[AdAM07] A. Alvaro, E. S. de Almeida, and S. L. Meira, "Component quality assurance: Towards a software component certification process," *IEEE International Conference on Information Reuse and Integration (IRI 2007)*, pp. 134–139, August 2007.

[AHM$^+$08] N. Ayewah, D. Hovemeyer, J. D. Morgenthaler, J. Penix, and W. Pugh, "Using static analysis to find bugs," *IEEE Software*, vol. 25, no. 5, pp. 22–29, October 2008.

[ALC07] A. Alvaro, R. Land, and I. Crnkovic, "Software component evaluation: A theoretical study on component selection and certification," Mälardalen University, Technical Report MDH-MRTC-217/2007-1-SE, November 2007. [Online]. Available: http://www.mrtc.mdh.se/index.php?choice=publications&id=1371

[And08]   R. Andrej, "Evaluation des vorhersageverfahrens "palladio" im industriellen kontext der CAS Software AG," Master's thesis, Universität Karlsruhe (TH), July 2008.

[AOH03]   P. Ammann, A. J. Offutt, and H. Huang, "Coverage criteria for logical expressions," in *14th International Symposium on Software Reliability Engineering (ISSRE)*. IEEE Computer Society, 2003, pp. 99–107. [Online]. Available: http://doi.ieeecomputersociety.org/10.1109/ISSRE. 2003.1251034

[Apa]   Apache, "JMeter Website," https://jmeter.apache.org/.

[AT07]   A. S. Andreou and M. Tziakouris, "A quality framework for developing and evaluating original software components," *Information and Software Technology*, vol. 49, no. 2, pp. 122 – 141, 2007. [Online]. Available: http://www. sciencedirect.com/science/article/pii/S0950584906000437

[BB10]   R. Bloomfield and P. Bishop, "Safety and assurance cases: Past, present and possible future – an adelard perspective," in *Making Systems Safer*, C. Dale and T. Anderson, Eds. Springer London, 2010, pp. 51–67. [Online]. Available: http://dx.doi.org/10.1007/978-1-84996-086-1_4

[BCC⁺10]   T. Bureš, J. Carlson, I. Crnković, S. Sentilles, and A. Vulgarakis, "Procom — the progress component model procom - the progress component model reference manual version 1.1," Mälardalen University, Västerås, Sweden, Tech. Rep., June 2010.

[BCdW07]   E. R. V. Bondarev, M. R. V. Chaudron, and P. H. N. de With, "Carat: a toolkit for design and performance analysis of component-based embedded systems," in *Conference on*

Design, Automation and Test in Europe (DATE), R. Lauwereins and J. Madsen, Eds. ACM, 2007, pp. 1024–1029.

[BCLR04]   T. Ball, B. Cook, V. Levin, and S. Rajamani, "Slam and static driver verifier: Technology transfer of formal methods inside microsoft," in *Integrated Formal Methods*, ser. Lecture Notes in Computer Science, E. Boiten, J. Derrick, and G. Smith, Eds. Springer Berlin / Heidelberg, 2004, vol. 2999, pp. 1–20, 10.1007/978-3-540-24756-2_1. [Online]. Available: http://dx.doi.org/10.1007/978-3-540-24756-2_1

[BDIS04]   S. Balsamo, A. Di Marco, P. Inverardi, and M. Simeoni, "Model-Based Performance Prediction in Software Development: A Survey," *IEEE Transactions on Software Engineering*, vol. 30, no. 5, pp. 295–310, May 2004.

[Bec08]   S. Becker, "Coupled model transformations for qos enabled component-based software design," Ph.D. dissertation, Universität Oldenburg, 2008. [Online]. Available: http://docserver.bis.uni-oldenburg.de/publikationen/dissertation/2008/beccou08/beccou08.html

[Bei95]   B. Beizer, *Black box testing : techniques for functional testing of software and systems*. New York [u.a.]: Wiley, 1995.

[BFS05]   A. Belinfante, L. Frantzen, and C. Schallhart, "14 tools for test case generation," in *Model-Based Testing of Reactive Systems*, ser. Lecture Notes in Computer Science, M. Broy, B. Jonsson, J.-P. Katoen, M. Leucker, and A. Pretschner, Eds. Springer Berlin Heidelberg, 2005, vol. 3472, pp. 391–438. [Online]. Available: http://dx.doi.org/10.1007/11498490_18

[BGMO06]   S. Becker, L. Grunske, R. Mirandola, and S. Overhage, "Performance Prediction of Component-Based Systems: A Survey from an Engineering Perspective," in *Architecting Systems with Trustworthy Components*, ser. Lecture Notes in Computer Science, R. Reussner, J. Stafford, and C. Szyperski, Eds.   Springer, 2006, vol. 3938, pp. 169–192.

[BHK11]   F. Brosig, N. Huber, and S. Kounev, "Automated extraction of architecture-level performance models of distributed component-based systems," in *26th IEEE/ACM International Conference on Automated Software Engineering (ASE)*, November 2011, pp. 183–192.

[BJK+05]   M. Broy, B. Jonsson, J.-P. Katoen, M. Leucker, and A. Pretschner, *Model-based Testing of Reactive Systems*, ser. Lecture Notes in Computer Science.   Springer, 2005, vol. 3472.

[BKBR12]   F. Brosch, H. Koziolek, B. Buhnova, and R. Reussner, "Architecture-based reliability prediction with the palladio component model," *IEEE Transactions on Software Engineering*, vol. 38, no. 6, pp. 1319–1339, December 2012.

[BKH09]   A. Beckhaus, L. Karg, and G. Hanselmann, "Applicability of software reliability growth modeling in the quality assurance phase of a large business software vendor," in *33rd Annual IEEE International on Computer Software and Applications Conference (COMPSAC '09)*, vol. 1, July 2009, pp. 209–215.

[BKR09]   S. Becker, H. Koziolek, and R. Reussner, "The Palladio component model for model-driven performance prediction," *Journal of Systems and Soft-*

ware, vol. 82, pp. 3–22, 2009. [Online]. Available: http://dx.doi.org/10.1016/j.jss.2008.03.066

[BM04] A. Bertolino and R. Mirandola, "CB-SPE tool: Putting component-based performance engineering into practice," in *Component-Based Software Engineering*, ser. Lecture Notes in Computer Science, I. Crnkovic, J. A. Stafford, H. W. Schmidt, and K. Wallnau, Eds. Springer Berlin Heidelberg, 2004, vol. 3054, pp. 233–248. [Online]. Available: http://dx.doi.org/10.1007/978-3-540-24774-6_21

[BMdW⁺04] E. Bondarev, J. Muskens, P. de With, M. Chaudron, and J. Lukkien, "Predicting real-time properties of component assemblies: a scenario-simulation approach," in *Proceedings of the 30th Euromicro conference*, September 2004, pp. 40–47.

[Boe06] J. Boegh, "Certifying software component attributes," *IEEE Software*, vol. 23, no. 3, pp. 74–81, June 2006.

[BR08a] G. Balakrishnan and T. Reps, "Analyzing stripped device-driver executables," in *Tools and Algorithms for the Construction and Analysis of Systems*, ser. Lecture Notes in Computer Science, C. Ramakrishnan and J. Rehof, Eds. Springer Berlin / Heidelberg, 2008, vol. 4963, pp. 124–140, 10.1007/978-3-540-78800-3_10. [Online]. Available: http://dx.doi.org/10.1007/978-3-540-78800-3_10

[BR08b] R. Böhme and R. Reussner, *Dependability Metrics: Advanced Lectures [result from a Dagstuhl seminar, October 30 - November 1, 2005]*, ser. Lecture Notes in Computer Science. Springer, 2008, vol. 4909, ch. Validation of Prediction with Measurements, pp. 14–18.

[Bro12]   F. Brosch, "Integrated software architecture-based re-
            liability prediction for it systems," Ph.D. disserta-
            tion, Institut für Programmstrukturen und Datenor-
            ganisation (IPD), Karlsruher Institut für Technologie,
            Karlsruhe, Germany, June 2012. [Online]. Available:
            http://digbib.ubka.uni-karlsruhe.de/volltexte/1000028288

[BSGR⁺12]   R. Berntsson Svensson, T. Gorschek, B. Regnell, R. Torkar,
            A. Shahrokni, and R. Feldt, "Quality requirements in indus-
            trial practice - an extended interview study at eleven compa-
            nies," *IEEE Transactions on Software Engineering*, vol. 38,
            no. 4, pp. 923–935, August 2012.

[ByC12]   "ByCounter Homepage," June 2012. [Online]. Available:
            http://sdqweb.ipd.kit.edu/wiki/ByCounter

[CCD⁺07]   J. Callas, P. Corporation, L. Donnerhacke, I. GmbH,
            H. Finney, D. Shaw, and R. Thayer, "Rfc 4880:
            Openpgp message format," Internet Engineering Task
            Force, Tech. Rep., November 2007. [Online]. Available:
            https://www.ietf.org/rfc/rfc4880.txt

[CCG⁺09]   V. Cardellini, E. Casalicchio, V. Grassi, F. Lo Presti, and
            R. Mirandola, "Qos-driven runtime adaptation of service
            oriented architectures," in *Proceedings of the the 7th joint
            meeting of the European software engineering conference
            and the ACM SIGSOFT symposium on The foundations
            of software engineering*, ser. ESEC/FSE '09.   New York,
            NY, USA: ACM, 2009, pp. 131–140. [Online]. Available:
            http://doi.acm.org/10.1145/1595696.1595718

[CD03]   J. Cheesman and J. Daniels, *UML Components: A Simple
            Process for Specifying Component-based Software*, 2nd ed.,

ser. Component Software Series. Boston, MA, USA: Addison-Wesley, 2003.

[CM94]   J. Chilenski and S. Miller, "Applicability of modified condition/decision coverage to software testing," *Software Engineering Journal*, vol. 9, no. 5, pp. 193–200, September 1994.

[Comer]   "Common criteria specifications cc v3.1 release 4," http://www.commoncriteriaportal.org/cc/, Common Criteria Recognition Agreement Management Committee, 2012 September.

[Con13]   Conformiq. (2013, March) Conformiq website. [Online]. Available: http://www.conformiq.com/

[CSSW01] I. Crnkovic, H. Schmidt, J. Stafford, and K. Wallnau, "4th icse workshop on component-based software engineering: component certification and system prediction," *SIGSOFT Software Engineering Notes*, vol. 26, no. 6, pp. 33–40, Nov. 2001. [Online]. Available: http://doi.acm.org/10.1145/505532.505540

[Dep96]   *Handbook for Reliability Test Methods, Plans, and Environments for Engineering, Development, Qualification, and Production.*, Department of Defense, April 1996.

[Dia12]   R. Diana, "Traditional programming language job trends," *DZone Articles*, August 2012. [Online]. Available: http://java.dzone.com/articles/traditional-programming-1

[DIN05]   DIN, "DIN EN ISO/IEC 17000:2005-03 - conformity assessment – vocabulary and general principles (ISO/IEC 17000:2004); trilingual version EN ISO/IEC 17000:2004," Deutsches Institut für Normung, Tech. Rep., March 2005.

[DM05]   A. Diaconescu and J. Murphy, "Automating the performance management of component-based enterprise systems through the use of redundancy," in *20th IEEE/ACM International Conference on Automated Software Engineering (ASE 2005)*, D. F. Redmiles, T. Ellman, and A. Zisman, Eds. ACM, 2005, pp. 44–53.

[DMM04]   A. Diaconescu, A. Mos, and J. Murphy, "Automatic performance management in component based software systems," in *1st International Conference on Autonomic Computing (ICAC).* IEEE Computer Society, 2004, pp. 214–221.

[DMW⁺95] R. DeMillo, A. Mathur, W. Wong, P. Frankl, and E. Weyuker, "Some critical remarks on a hierarchy of fault-detecting abilities of test methods [and reply]," *IEEE Transactions on Software Engineering*, vol. 21, no. 10, pp. 858–863, October 1995.

[DPPS04]   S. Distefano, D. Paci, A. Puliafito, and M. Scarpa, "Uml design and software performance modeling," in *Computer and Information Sciences (ISCIS 2004)*, ser. Lecture Notes in Computer Science, C. Aykanat, T. Dayar, and I. Körpeoglu, Eds. Springer Berlin Heidelberg, 2004, vol. 3280, pp. 564–573. [Online]. Available: http://dx.doi.org/10.1007/978-3-540-30182-0_57

[DPS11]   S. Distefano, A. Puliafito, and M. Scarpa, "A representation method for performance specifications in uml domain," *Computers in Human Behavior*, vol. 27, no. 5, pp. 1579–1592, 2011, 2009 Fifth International Conference on Intelligent Computing (CIC 2009). [Online]. Available: http://www.sciencedirect.com/science/article/pii/S0747563210003432

[DRP99]   E. Dustin, J. Rashka, and J. Paul, *Automated software test-ing : introduction, management, and performance*, 1st ed. Reading, Mass. [u.a.]: Addison-Wesley, 1999.

[DSP11]   S. Distefano, M. Scarpa, and A. Puliafito, "From uml to petri nets: The pcm-based methodology," *IEEE Transactions on Software Engineering*, vol. 37, no. 1, pp. 65–79, February 2011.

[EFH02]   E. Eskenazi, A. Fioukov, and D. K. Hammer, "Performance prediction for software architectures," in *Proceedings of Workshop on Software Infrastructures for Component-Based Applications on Consumer Devices*, September 2002.

[EFH04]   E. Eskenazi, A. Fioukov, and D. Hammer, "Performance prediction for component compositions," in *Component-Based Software Engineering*, ser. Lecture Notes in Computer Science, I. Crnkovic, J. Stafford, H. Schmidt, and K. Wallnau, Eds. Springer Berlin Heidelberg, 2004, vol. 3054, pp. 280–293. [Online]. Available: http://dx.doi.org/10.1007/978-3-540-24774-6_25

[EGMT09]   I. Epifani, C. Ghezzi, R. Mirandola, and G. Tamburrelli, "Model evolution by run-time parameter adaptation," in *IEEE 31st International Conference on Software Engineering (ICSE 2009)*, May 2009, pp. 111–121.

[Ern11]   D. Ernst, "Test case generation with performance model-based test coverage," Bachelorthesis, Institut für Angewandte Informatik und Formale Beschreibungsverfahren des Karlsruher Instituts für Technologie, May 2011.

[Eur04]   European Telecommunications Standards Institute, "Methods for testing and specification (mts); the testing and test

control notation version 3; part 1: Ttcn-3 core language,"
European Telecommunications Standards Institute, Tech.
Rep. ETSI ES 201 873-1 V4.4.1 (2012-04), April 2004.

[Eur13] ——, "Ttcn-3 tools (academic and commercial)," March
2013. [Online]. Available: http://www.ttcn-3.org/index.
php/tools

[FDT13] FDT Group, "Certification and its benefits," March
2013. [Online]. Available: http://www.fdtgroup.org/
certification-and-its-benefits

[FH12] M. Faber and J. Happe, "Systematic adoption of genetic
programming for deriving software performance curves," in
*Proceedings of the third joint WOSP/SIPEW international
conference on Performance Engineering*, ser. ICPE '12.
New York, NY, USA: ACM, 2012, pp. 33–44. [Online].
Available: http://doi.acm.org/10.1145/2188286.2188295

[FHM+95] G. Franks, A. Hubbard, S. Majumdar, J. Neilson, D. Petriu,
J. Rolia, and M. Woodside, "A toolset for performance
engineering and software design of client-server systems,"
Performance Evaluation, vol. 24, no. 1–2, pp. 117–136,
1995. [Online]. Available: http://www.sciencedirect.com/
science/article/pii/016653169596869T

[FW93] P. Frankl and E. Weyuker, "A formal analysis of the fault-
detecting ability of testing methods," *IEEE Transactions on
Software Engineering*, vol. 19, no. 3, pp. 202–213, March
1993.

[GKS07] P. Graydon, J. Knight, and E. Strunk, "Assurance based development of critical systems," in *37th Annual IEEE/IFIP*

International Conference on Dependable Systems and Networks (DSN '07), June 2007, pp. 347–357.

[GMS07]   V. Grassi, R. Mirandola, and A. Sabetta, "Filling the gap between design and performance/reliability models of component-based systems: A model-driven approach," *Journal of Systems and Software*, vol. 80, no. 4, pp. 528–558, Apr. 2007. [Online]. Available: http://dx.doi.org/10.1016/j.jss.2006.07.023

[Goo12]   "Google guice project website," November 2012. [Online]. Available: https://code.google.com/p/google-guice/

[GPRZ04]   S. Göbel, C. Pohl, S. Röttger, and S. Zschaler, "The comquad component model: enabling dynamic selection of implementations by weaving non-functional aspects," in *Proceedings of the 3rd international conference on Aspect-oriented software development*, ser. AOSD '04. New York, NY, USA: ACM, 2004, pp. 74–82. [Online]. Available: http://doi.acm.org/10.1145/976270.976281

[GPT01]   K. Goševa-Popstojanova and K. S. Trivedi, "Architecture-based approach to reliability assessment of software systems," *Performance Evaluation*, vol. 45, no. 2–3, pp. 179 – 204, 2001, <ce:title>Performance Validation of Software Systems</ce:title>. [Online]. Available: http://www.sciencedirect.com/science/article/pii/S0166531601000347

[Gro09]   H. Groenda, "Certification of software component performance specifications," in *Proceedings of the Fourteenth International Workshop on Component-Oriented Programming (WCOP) 2009*, ser. Interner Bericht, C. Szyperski, R. Reussner, and W. Weck, Eds., no. 2009-11. Karlsruhe, Germany: Fakultät für Informatik, Universität

Karlsruhe, November 2009, pp. 13–21. [Online]. Available: https://research.microsoft.com/en-us/um/people/cszypers/events/wcop2009/WCOP%202009%20Proceedings.pdf

[Gro10]   ——, "Usage profile and platform independent automated validation of service behavior specifications," in *Proceedings of the 2nd International Workshop on the Quality of Service-Oriented Software Systems*, ser. QUASOSS '10. New York, NY, USA: ACM, 2010, pp. 6:1–6:6. [Online]. Available: http://doi.acm.org/10.1145/1858263.1858271

[Gro11a]   ——, "An Accuracy Information Annotation Model for Validated Service Behavior Specifications," in *Proceedings of the thirteenth international conference on Models in software engineering - Models in Software Engineering (MODELS '10)*, ser. Lecture Notes in Computer Science, J. Dingel and A. Solberg, Eds.   Springer Berlin / Heidelberg, 2011, vol. 6627, pp. 369–383, 10.1007/978-3-642-21210-9_36. [Online]. Available: http://dx.doi.org/10.1007/978-3-642-21210-9_36

[Gro11b]   ——. (2011) Palladio transformations for Accuracy Influence Analyses (Anonymous SVN Access). [Online]. Available: https://anonymous:anonymous@svnserver.informatik.kit.edu/i43/svn/code/Palladio/Core/trunk/Accuracy/de.fzi.se.accuracy

[Gro12a]   ——, "Improving performance predictions by accounting for the accuracy of composed performance models," in *Proceedings of the 8th international ACM SIGSOFT conference on Quality of Software Architectures (QoSA)*, ser. QoSA '12.   New York, NY, USA: ACM, June 2012, pp. 111–116. [Online]. Available: http://doi.acm.org/10. 1145/2304696.2304715

[Gro12b] ——, "Path coverage criteria for palladio performance models," in *Proceedings of the 38th EUROMICRO Conference on Software Engineering and Advanced Applications*, ser. SEAA '12, September 2012, pp. 133–137.

[Gro12c] ——, "Protecting intellectual property by certified component quality descriptions," in *Proceedings of the 2012 Ninth International Conference on Information Technology - New Generations*, ser. ITNG '12, B. Verkhovsky and Y. Reddy, Eds. Washington, DC, USA: IEEE Computer Society, April 2012, pp. 287–292. [Online]. Available: http://dx.doi.org/10.1109/ITNG.2012.49

[Gro12d] ——. (2012) Transformations for Criterion Effort Estimations. [Online]. Available: https://anonymous:anonymous@svnserver.informatik. kit.edu/i43/svn/code/Palladio/Addons/Validation/trunk/de. fzi.se.validation.effort.qvtoscripts

[Gro13a] ——. (2013, January) Subversion Repository Location of the Multithreaded Modeling Example (MME). [Online]. Available: https://anonymous:anonymous@svnserver.informatik. kit.edu/i43/svn/code/Palladio/Addons/Validation/trunk/de. fzi.se.validation.testbased.example.mme

[Gro13b] ——. (2013, January) Subversion Repository Location of the Probabilistic Modeling Example (PME). [Online]. Available: https://anonymous:anonymous@svnserver.informatik.

kit.edu/i43/svn/code/Palladio/Addons/Validation/trunk/de. fzi.se.validation.testbased.example.pme

[Gro13c] ——. (2013, March) Test-based validation for palladio specifications web page. [Online]. Available: http://sdqweb. ipd.kit.edu/wiki/TestBasedValidation

[Gro13d] ——. (2013, February) Validation framework junit test cases and specifications for cocome. [Online]. Available: https://anonymous:anonymous@svnserver.informatik.kit. edu/i43/svn/code/CaseStudies/CoCoME2-Instrumented/de. fzi.se.validation.testbased.example.cocome

[GS05] C. Gaston and D. Seifert, "11 evaluating coverage based testing," in *Model-Based Testing of Reactive Systems*, ser. Lecture Notes in Computer Science, M. Broy, B. Jonsson, J.-P. Katoen, M. Leucker, and A. Pretschner, Eds. Springer Berlin Heidelberg, 2005, vol. 3472, pp. 293–322. [Online]. Available: http://dx.doi.org/10.1007/11498490_14

[GZ09] L. Grunske and P. Zhang, "Monitoring probabilistic properties," in *Proceedings of the the 7th joint meeting of the European software engineering conference and the ACM SIGSOFT symposium on The foundations of software engineering*, ser. ESEC/FSE '09. New York, NY, USA: ACM, 2009, pp. 183–192. [Online]. Available: http://doi.acm.org/10.1145/1595696.1595724

[Ham07] G. Hamilton, "Application complexity spurs growth in performance validation market," Yankee Group Research, Inc., Tech. Rep. 4AA1-7656ENW, December 2007.

[Ham09] D. Hamlet, "Tools and experiments supporting a testing-based theory of component composition," *ACM Trans-*

actions on Software Engineering Methodology, vol. 18, no. 3, pp. 12:1–12:41, June 2009. [Online]. Available: http://doi.acm.org/10.1145/1525880.1525885

[HBR⁺10]   N. Huber, S. Becker, C. Rathfelder, J. Scheflinghaus, and R. Reussner, "Performance Modeling in Industry: A Case Study on Storage Virtualization," in *ACM/IEEE 32nd International Conference on Software Engineering (ICSE 2010)*. New York, NY, USA: ACM, May 2010, pp. 1–10.

[HK07]   T. Harmon and R. Klefstad, "A survey of worst-case execution time analysis for real-time java," in *IEEE Parallel and Distributed Processing Symposium*, March 2007, pp. 1–8.

[HKW⁺08]   S. Herold, H. Klus, Y. Welsch, C. Deiters, A. Rausch, R. Reussner, K. Krogmann, H. Koziolek, R. Mirandola, B. Hummel, M. Meisinger, and C. Pfaller, "Cocome - the common component modeling example," in *The Common Component Modeling Example*, ser. Lecture Notes in Computer Science, A. Rausch, R. Reussner, R. Mirandola, and F. Plášil, Eds.   Springer Berlin Heidelberg, 2008, vol. 5153, pp. 16–53. [Online]. Available: http://dx.doi.org/10.1007/978-3-540-85289-6_3

[HMSW01]   S. Hissam, G. Moreno, J. A. Stafford, and K. C. Wallnau, "Packaging predictable assembly with prediction-enabled component technology," Software Engineering Institute at the Carnegie Mellon University, Tech. Rep. CMU/SEI-2001-TR-024, 2001.

[HMSW02]   S. A. Hissam, G. A. Moreno, J. A. Stafford, and K. C. Wallnau, "Packaging predictable assembly," in *Component Deployment*, ser. Lecture Notes in Computer Science, J. Bishop, Ed.   Springer Berlin Heidelberg,

2002, vol. 2370, pp. 108–124. [Online]. Available: http://dx.doi.org/10.1007/3-540-45440-3_8

[HMSW03] S. Hissam, G. Moreno, J. Stafford, and K. Wallnau, "Enabling predictable assembly," *Journal of Systems and Software*, vol. 65, pp. 185–198, March 2003. [Online]. Available: http://portal.acm.org/citation.cfm?id=860119. 860122

[HT90] D. Hamlet and R. Taylor, "Partition testing does not inspire confidence [program testing]," *IEEE Transactions on Software Engineering*, vol. 16, no. 12, pp. 1402–1411, December 1990.

[Hum99] W. S. Humphrey, *Introduction to the Team Software Process*. Addison-Wesley Longman, Amsterdam, September 1999.

[Hum05] ——, *PSP: A Self-Improvement Process for Software Engineers*. Addison-Wesley Longman, Amsterdam, March 2005.

[IEE05] IEEE CS, "Ieee standard for software verification and validation," *IEEE Std 1012-2004 (Revision of IEEE Std 1012-1998)*, pp. 0_1 –110, 2005.

[ISO94] ISO, "Iso/iec 8402:1994 quality management and quality assurance – vocabulary," International Organization for Standardization, Tech. Rep., 1994.

[ISO01] ——, "Iso/iec 9126-1:2001(e) - software engineering – product quality – part 1: Quality model," International Organization for Standardization, Tech. Rep., 2001.

[ISO04]   ——, "Iso/iec 15504-1:2004: Information technology – process assessment – part 1: Concepts and vocabulary," International Organization for Standardization, Tech. Rep. JTC 1/SC 7, 2004.

[ISO08a]   ——, "Iso 9001:2008: Quality management systems – requirements," International Organization for Standardization, Tech. Rep. TC 176/SC 2, 2008.

[ISO08b]   ——, "Iso/iec 12207:2008: Systems and software engineering – software life cycle processes," International Organization for Standardization, Tech. Rep. JTC 1/SC 7, 2008.

[ISO11a]   ——, "Iso/iec 15504-10:2011: Information technology – process assessment – part 10: Safety extension," International Organization for Standardization, Tech. Rep. JTC 1/SC 7, 2011.

[ISO11b]   ——, "Iso/iec 26262-1:2011 - road verhicles – functional safet – part 1: Vocabulary," International Organization for Standardization, Tech. Rep., 2011.

[iSQI13]   international Software Quality Institute. (2013, March) Certificates. [Online]. Available: https://www.isqi.org/en/certificates.html

[JBR99]   I. Jacobson, G. Booch, and J. E. Rumbaugh, *The unified software development process*, 1st ed., ser. Addison-Wesley object technology series.   Addison-Wesley, January 1999.

[JSDH07]   Y. Jarraya, A. Soeanu, M. Debbabi, and F. Hassaine, "Automatic verification and performance analysis of time-constrained sysml activity diagrams," in *14th Annual IEEE*

International Conference and Workshops on the Engineering of Computer-Based Systems (ECBS '07), March 2007, pp. 515–522.

[KB05]   K. Kapoor and J. P. Bowen, "A formal analysis of mcdc and rcdc test criteria: Research articles," *Software Testing, Verification and Reliability*, vol. 15, pp. 21–40, March 2005. [Online]. Available: http://dl.acm.org/citation.cfm? id=1077293.1077294

[KH06]   H. Koziolek and J. Happe, "A QoS Driven Development Process Model for Component-Based Software Systems," in *9th International Symposium on Component-Based Software Engineering (CBSE'06)*, I. Gorton, G. T. Heineman, I. Crnkovic, H. W. Schmidt, J. A. Stafford, C. A. Szyperski, and K. C. Wallnau, Eds., vol. 4063, 2006, pp. 336–343. [Online]. Available: http://sdqweb.ipd.uka. de/publications/pdfs/koziolek2006b.pdf

[KKP+11] R. Kirner, J. Knoop, A. Prantl, M. Schordan, and A. Kadlec, "Beyond loop bounds: comparing annotation languages for worst-case execution time analysis," *Software and Systems Modeling*, vol. 10, pp. 411–437, 2011. [Online]. Available: http://dx.doi.org/10.1007/s10270-010-0161-0

[KKR10] K. Krogmann, M. Kuperberg, and R. Reussner, "Using Genetic Search for Reverse Engineering of Parametric Behaviour Models for Performance Prediction," *IEEE Transactions on Software Engineering*, vol. 36, no. 6, pp. 865–877, 2010. [Online]. Available: http://sdqweb.ipd.kit. edu/publications/pdfs/krogmann2009c.pdf

[KKR11] M. Kuperberg, M. Krogmann, and R. Reussner, "Metric-based Selection of Timer Methods for Accurate Measurements," in *Proceedings of the International Conference on Software Engineering 2011 (ICPE'11), March 14–16, 2011, Karlsruhe, Germany*, 2011.

[Koz08]   H. Koziolek, "Parameter dependencies for reusable performance specifications of software components," Ph.D. dissertation, Universität Oldenburg, 2008. [Online]. Available: http://docserver.bis.uni-oldenburg.de/publikationen/dissertation/2008/kozpar08/kozpar08.html

[Koz10]   ——, "Performance evaluation of component-based software systems: A survey," *Elsevier Performance Evaluation*, vol. 67, no. 8, pp. 634–658, August 2010. [Online]. Available: http://portal.acm.org/citation.cfm?id=1808359.1808729

[Koz11]   A. Koziolek, "Automated improvement of software architecture models for performance and other quality attributes," Ph.D. dissertation, Institut für Programmstrukturen und Datenorganisation (IPD), Karlsruher Institut für Technologie, Karlsruhe, Germany, July 2011. [Online]. Available: http://digbib.ubka.uni-karlsruhe.de/volltexte/1000024955

[KR08a]   H. Koziolek and R. Reussner, "A Model Transformation from the Palladio Component Model to Layered Queueing Networks," in *Performance Evaluation: Metrics, Models and Benchmarks, SIPEW 2008*, ser. Lecture Notes in Computer Science, vol. 5119. Springer, 2008, pp. 58–78. [Online]. Available: http://www.springerlink.com/content/w14m0g520u675x10/fulltext.pdf

[KR08b]   K. Krogmann and R. H. Reussner, *The Common Component Modeling Example*, ser. Lecture Notes in Computer Science. Springer, 2008, vol. 5153, ch. Palladio: Prediction of Performance Properties, pp. 297–326. [Online]. Available: http://springerlink.com/content/63617n4j5688879h/?p=9666cb29a31b453aba8a1ae6ee7831b6&pi=11

[Kru00]   P. Kruchten, *The Rational Unified Process: An Introduction*, 2nd ed., ser. Addison-Wesley object technology series. Boston: Addison-Wesley, 2000.

[Kup10]   M. Kuperberg, "Quantifying and predicting the influence of execution platform on software component performance," Ph.D. dissertation, Karlsruhe Insitute of Technology, November 2010. [Online]. Available: http://digbib.ubka.uni-karlsruhe.de/volltexte/1000023351

[LA04]   C. Lattner and V. Adve, "LLVM: A Compilation Framework for Lifelong Program Analysis & Transformation," in *Proceedings of the 2004 International Symposium on Code Generation and Optimization (CGO'04)*, Palo Alto, California, March 2004.

[LAC08]   R. Land, A. Alvaro, and I. Crnkovic, "Towards efficient software component evaluation: An examination of component selection and certification," *34th Euromicro Conference on Software Engineering and Advanced Applications (SEAA '08)*, pp. 274–281, September 2008.

[Lap95]   J.-C. Laprie, "Dependability of computer systems: concepts, limits, improvements," in *Software Reliability Engineering, 1995. Proceedings., Sixth International Symposium on*, October 1995, pp. 2–11.

[Lav03]   R. M. Laverty, "ROBOCOP — robust open component based software architecture for configurable devices project — deliverable 1.5 – revised specification of framework and models," ROBOCOP Project, Tech. Rep. ITEA PROJECT 00001: ROBOCOP, July 2003. [Online]. Available: http://www.hitech-projects.com/euprojects/ robocop/deliverables_public/robocop_wp1_deliverable15_ 18july2003.pdf

[LGF05]   Y. Liu, I. Gorton, and A. Fekete, "Design-level performance prediction of component-based applications," *IEEE Transactions on Software Engineering*, vol. 31, no. 11, pp. 928–941, November 2005.

[Lig09]   P. Liggesmeyer, *Software-Qualität: Testen, Analysieren und Verifizieren von Software*, 2nd ed.   Spektrum, 2009.

[MA01]   D. A. Menasce and V. Almeida, *Capacity Planning for Web Services: Metrics, Models, and Methods.*   Upper Saddle River, NJ, USA: Prentice Hall PTR, 2001, ch. 3.1: Basic Performance Concepts: Service times at Single Disks and Disk Arrays, pp. 72–90.

[MAD04]   D. A. Menascé, V. A. Almeida, and L. W. Dowdy, *Performance by design : computer capacity planning by example*, 1st ed.   Upper Saddle River, NJ: Prentice Hall PTR, 2004. [Online]. Available: http://digitool.hbz-nrw.de: 1801/webclient/DeliveryManager?pid=3356976

[MAG12]   I. Meedeniya, A. Aleti, and L. Grunske, "Architecture-driven reliability optimization with uncertain model parameters," *Journal of Systems and Software*, vol. 85, no. 10, pp. 2340–2355, 2012. [Online]. Available: http://www. sciencedirect.com/science/article/pii/S0164121212001276

[Mal04]   N. Malevris, "On structurally testing java programs effectively," in *3rd International Symposium on Principles and*

Practice of Programming in Java (PPPJ'04). Trinity College Dublin, 2004, pp. 21–26.

[Mar04] M. Marzolla, "Simulation-based performance modeling of uml software architectures," Ph.D. dissertation, Universita ca foscari di venezia, dipartimento di informatica, February 2004.

[Mee12] I. Meedeniya, "Architecture optimisation of embedded systems under uncertainty in probabilistic reliability evaluation model parameters," Ph.D. dissertation, Faculty of Information and Communication Technologies, Swinburne University of Technology, July 2012.

[Meu95] M. v. d. Meulen, *Definitions for hardware/software reliability engineers*, 2nd ed. Rotterdam: Simtech, 1995.

[Mey03] B. Meyer, "The grand challenge of trusted components," *25th International Conference on Software Engineering*, pp. 660–667, May 2003.

[Mey07] M. B. Meyerhöfer, "Messung und verwaltung von softwarekomponenten für die performancevorhersage," Ph.D. dissertation, University of Erlangen, Juli 2007.

[MH11] P. Merkle and J. Henss, "EventSim – an event-driven Palladio software architecture simulator," in *Palladio Days 2011 Proceedings*, ser. Karlsruhe Reports in Informatics ; 2011,32, S. Becker, J. Happe, and R. Reussner, Eds. Karlsruhe: KIT, Fakultät für Informatik, 2011, pp. 15–22. [Online]. Available: http://digbib.ubka.uni-karlsruhe.de/ volltexte/1000025188

[Mic13]   Microsoft. (2013, January) Microsoft certified it profes-
            sional (mcitp). [Online]. Available: https://www.microsoft.
            com/de-de/business/learning/mcitp.aspx

[MKK11]   P. Meier, S. Kounev, and H. Koziolek, "Automated
            Transformation of Component-based Software Architecture
            Models to Queueing Petri Nets," in *19th IEEE/ACM Inter-
            national Symposium on Modeling, Analysis and Simulation
            of Computer and Telecommunication Systems (MASCOTS
            2013)*, 2011, pp. 339–348.

[MLP+01]   J. Morris, G. Lee, K. Parker, G. A. Bundell, and C. P. Lam,
            "Software component certification," *Computer*, vol. 34,
            no. 9, pp. 30–36, September 2001.

[MM02]   A. Mos and J. Murphy, "A framework for performance
            monitoring, modelling and prediction of component
            oriented distributed systems," in *Proceedings of the 3rd
            international workshop on software and performance*, ser.
            WOSP '02. New York, NY, USA: ACM, 2002, pp.
            235–236. [Online]. Available: http://doi.acm.org/10.1145/
            584369.584403

[MMS98]   B. Meyer, C. Mingins, and H. Schmidt, "Providing trusted
            components to the industry," *Computer*, vol. 31, no. 5, pp.
            104–105, May 1998.

[MN04]   M. Meyerhöfer and C. Neumann, "TESTEJB – a
            measurement framework for ejbs," in *Component-Based
            Software Engineering*, ser. Lecture Notes in Computer
            Science, I. Crnkovic, J. Stafford, H. Schmidt, and
            K. Wallnau, Eds. Springer Berlin Heidelberg, 2004,
            vol. 3054, pp. 294–301. [Online]. Available: http:
            //dx.doi.org/10.1007/978-3-540-24774-6_26

[Mot08]   Motor Industry Software Reliability Association (MISRA), "Guidelines for the use of the c++ language in critical systems," Motor Industry Software Reliability Association, Tech. Rep., June 2008.

[MW08]   T. S. E. Maibaum and A. Wassyng, "A product-focused approach to software certification," *Computer*, vol. 41, no. 2, pp. 91–93, February 2008.

[Mye04]   G. J. Myers, *The art of software testing*, 2nd ed.   Wiley, 2004.

[NPI09]   Y. V. Natis, M. Pezzini, and K. Iijima, "Magic quadrant for enterprise application servers," Gartner, Tech. Rep. G00170610, September 2009.

[Nta88]   S. Ntafos, "A comparison of some structural testing strategies," *IEEE Transactions on Software Engineering*, vol. 14, no. 6, pp. 868–874, June 1988.

[Obj05]   *UML Profile for Schedulability, Performance, and Time, v1.1*, http://www.omg.org/cgi-bin/doc?formal/2005-01-02, Object Management Group Std. formal/05-01-02, Jan 2005. [Online]. Available: http://www.omg.org/cgi-bin/doc?formal/2005-01-02

[Obj11a]   Object Management Group, "Meta Object Facility (MOF) 2.0 Query/View/ Transformation Specification," Object Management Group, Tech. Rep. formal/2011-01-01, January 2011.

[Obj11b]   ——, "UML Profile for MARTE: Modeling and Analysis of Real-Time Embedded Systems - Version 1.1," Object Management Group, Tech. Rep. formal/2011-06-02, June 2011.

[Obj12]   ——, "OMG Systems Modeling Language (OMG SysML)," Object Management Group, Tech. Rep. formal/2012-06-01, June 2012.

[OMG13]   (2013, January). [Online]. Available: http://www.omgmarte.org/

[Ope11]   "Togaf version 9.1: Part vii (architecture capability framework)," http://pubs.opengroup.org/architecture/togaf9-doc/arch/chap52.html, The Open Group, Dezember 2011.

[OT04]   S. Overhage and P. Thomas, "A business perspective on component trading: Criteria, immaturities,and critical success factors," in *Proceedings of the 30th EUROMICRO Conference (EUROMICRO'04)*. Los Alamitos, CA, USA: IEEE Computer Society, 2004, pp. 108–117.

[Par12]   I. Parkes, "Business benefits of service virtualization - study: North america 2012," Coleman-Parkes Ltd. (UK), Weavering, Maidstone, Kent, United Kindowm, Tech. Rep., November 2012.

[PAT12]   D. C. Petriu, M. Alhaj, and R. Tawhid, "Software performance modeling," in *Formal Methods for Model-Driven Engineering*, ser. Lecture Notes in Computer Science, M. Bernardo, V. Cortellessa, and A. Pierantonio, Eds. Springer Berlin Heidelberg, 2012, vol. 7320, pp. 219–262. [Online]. Available: http://dx.doi.org/10.1007/978-3-642-30982-3_7

[PH11]   R. Premraj and K. Herzig, "Network versus code metrics to predict defects: A replication study," in *Proceedings of the 2011 International Symposium on Empirical Software Engineering and Measurement*, ser.

ESEM '11. Washington, DC, USA: IEEE Computer Society, 2011, pp. 215–224. [Online]. Available: http://dx.doi.org/10.1109/ESEM.2011.30

[PM08]   T. Parsons and J. Murphy, "Detecting performance antipatterns in component based enterprise systems," *Journal of Object Technology*, vol. 7, no. 3, pp. 55–90, March 2008. [Online]. Available: http://www.jot.fm/contents/issue_2008_03/article1.html

[PP05]   A. Pretschner and J. Philipps, "10 methodological issues in model-based testing," in *Model-Based Testing of Reactive Systems*, ser. Lecture Notes in Computer Science, M. Broy, B. Jonsson, J.-P. Katoen, M. Leucker, and A. Pretschner, Eds.   Springer Berlin / Heidelberg, 2005, vol. 3472, pp. 11–18, 10.1007/11498490_13. [Online]. Available: http://dx.doi.org/10.1007/11498490_13

[PRQ09]   PRQA, "QA C++ Summary Sheet," http://www.programmingresearch.com/brochures/qacpp.pdf, January 2009.

[PV02]   F. Plasil and S. Visnovsky, "Behavior protocols for software components," *IEEE Transactions on Software Engineering*, vol. 28, no. 11, pp. 1056–1076, November 2002.

[PW04]   D. B. Petriu and M. Woodside, "A metamodel for generating performance models from uml designs," in *UML 2004 - The Unified Modeling Language. Modelling Languages and Applications*, ser. Lecture Notes in Computer Science, T. Baar, A. Strohmeier, A. Moreira, and S. Mellor, Eds.   Springer Berlin Heidelberg, 2004, vol. 3273, pp. 41–53. [Online]. Available: http://dx.doi.org/10.1007/978-3-540-30187-5_4

[Q-I08]   Q-ImPrESS   Consortium.   (2008)   Project   de-
            liverable   d2.1   service   architecture   meta-
            model   (samm).   [Online].   Available: http:
            //www.q-impress.eu/wordpress/wp-content/uploads/
            2009/05/d21-service_architecture_meta-model.pdf

[Q-I11]   ——, "Sissy feature eclipse update site," http://q-
            impress.ow2.org/release, January 2011.

[RAQ04]   (2004) Rapid Analysis of Queueing Systems (RAQS).
            [Online]. Available: http://www.okstate.edu/cocim/raqs/

[Rat13]   C. Rathfelder, "Modelling event-based interactions in
            component-based architectures for modelling event-based
            interactions in component-based architectures for quanti-
            tative system evaluation," Ph.D. dissertation, Fakultät für
            Informatik des Karlsruher Instituts für Technologie (KIT),
            2013.

[RBB+11a]   R. Reussner, S. Becker, E. Burger, J. Happe, M. Hauck,
            A. Koziolek, H. Koziolek, K. Krogmann, and M. Kuper-
            berg, *The Palladio Component Model*.   Fakultät für Infor-
            matik, IPD, 2011, ch. 2.1, pp. 6–15. [Online]. Available:
            http://digbib.ubka.uni-karlsruhe.de/volltexte/1000022503

[RBB+11b]   ——, "The Palladio Component Model," Fakultät für
            Informatik, IPD, Tech. Rep., 2011. [Online]. Available:
            http://digbib.ubka.uni-karlsruhe.de/volltexte/1000022503

[RBKR12]   C. Rathfelder, S. Becker, K. Krogmann, and R. Reussner,
            "Workload-aware system monitoring using performance
            predictions applied to a large-scale e-mail system,"
            in *Proceedings of the Joint 10th Working IEEE/IFIP
            Conference on Software Architecture (WICSA) & 6th*

European Conference on Software Architecture (ECSA), Helsinki, Finland, 2012. [Online]. Available: http://www.wicsa.net/

[RG11]   C. Rathfelder and C. Gärtner, "ORC Deployment Guide," http://sla-at-soi.eu/wp-content/uploads/2011/08/D.B2b-M38-AppendixD-ORC_Deployment_Guide.pdf, July 2011.

[RGR08]   C. Rathfelder, H. Groenda, and R. Reussner, "Software Industrialization and Architecture Certification," in *Industrialisierung des Software-Managements*, G. Herzwurm and M. Mikusz, Eds., vol. P-139. Bonn, Germany: Gesellschaft für Informatik, 2008, pp. 169–180. [Online]. Available: http://subs.emis.de/LNI/Proceedings/Proceedings139/gi-proc-139-013.pdf

[RKE11]   C. Rathfelder, S. Kounev, and D. Evans, "Capacity Planning for Event-based Systems using Automated Performance Predictions," in *26th IEEE/ACM International Conference On Automated Software Engineering (ASE 2011)*, Oread, Lawrence, Kansas, November 2011, pp. 352–361.

[RRMP08]   A. Rausch, R. Reussner, R. Mirandola, and F. Plasil, Eds., *The Common Component Modeling Example: Comparing Software Component Models*, ser. Lecture Notes in Computer Science.   Springer Berlin / Heidelberg, 2008, vol. 5153. [Online]. Available: http://springerlink.com/content/l8t37r41612l/

[RTC92]   *DO-178B, Software Considerations in Airborne Systems and Equipment Certification*, RTCA, Inc. Std., December 1992.

[RZ03]   S. Roettger and S. Zschaler, "Cqml+: Enhancements to cqml," in *Proceedings of the 1st International Workshop on Quality of Service in Component-Based Software Engineering*, June 2003, pp. 43–56.

[Saa08]   T. L. Saaty, *Decision making for leaders : the analytic hierarchy process for decisions in a complex world*, new edition, 5th print ed.   Pittsburgh, PA: RWS Publ., 2008.

[SEI]   SEI, "Official CMMI web site," http://www.sei.cmu.edu/cmmi/.

[SEI13]   (2013, March) Predictability by construction - research. [Online]. Available: http://www.sei.cmu.edu/predictability/research/

[SK06]   E. A. Strunk and J. C. Knight, "The essential synthesis of problem frames and assurance cases," in *Proceedings of the 2006 international workshop on Advances and applications of problem frames*, ser. IWAAPF '06.   New York, NY, USA: ACM, 2006, pp. 81–86. [Online]. Available: http://doi.acm.org/10.1145/1138670.1138683

[SKK+01]   M. Sitaraman, G. Kulczycki, J. Krone, W. F. Ogden, and A. L. N. Reddy, "Performance specification of software components," *SIGSOFT Software Engineering Notes*, vol. 26, no. 3, pp. 3–10, May 2001. [Online]. Available: http://doi.acm.org/10.1145/379377.375223

[Smi90]   C. U. Smith, *Performance Engineering of Software Systems*. Addison-Wesley, 1990.

[Som07]   I. Sommerville, *Software Engineering*, 8th ed.   Pearson Education Ltd., 2007.

[SRA⁺08]   A. Satelli, M. Rooto, T. Andres, F. Campolongo, J. Cariboni, D. Gatelli, M. Saisana, and S.Tarantola, *Global Sensitivity Analysis. The Primer.*   John Wiley & Sons, Ltd, 2008.

[SW03]   C. U. Smith and L. G. Williams, "Best practices for software performance engineering," Performance Engineering Services and Software Engineering Research, Tech. Rep., 2003. [Online]. Available: http://www.perfeng.com/papers/bestprac.pdf

[TMW10]   M. Tribastone, P. Mayer, and M. Wirsing, "Performance prediction of service-oriented systems with layered queueing networks," in *Leveraging Applications of Formal Methods, Verification, and Validation*, ser. Lecture Notes in Computer Science, T. Margaria and B. Steffen, Eds.   Springer Berlin Heidelberg, 2010, vol. 6416, pp. 51–65. [Online]. Available: http://dx.doi.org/10.1007/978-3-642-16561-0_12

[UL07]   M. Utting and B. Legeard, *Practical Model-Based Testing: A Tools Approach.*   500 Sansome Street, Suite 400, San Francisco, CA 9411:   Morgan Kaufmann, 2007. [Online]. Available: http://books.google.de/books?id=8hAGtY4-oOoC

[UPL06]   M. Utting, A. Pretschner, and B. Legeard, "A taxonomy of model-based testing," The University of Waikato, Department of Computer Science, Private Bag 3105, Hamilton, New Zealand, Tech. Rep. 04/2006, April 2006.

[VB08]   S. A. Vilkomir and J. P. Bowen, "From mc/dc to rc/dc: Formalization and analysis of control-flow testing criteria," in

Formal Methods and Testing, ser. Lecture Notes in Computer Science, R. M. Hierons, J. P. Bowen, and M. Harman, Eds., vol. 4949. Springer, 2008, pp. 240–270.

[Voa99] J. Voas, "Certification: reducing the hidden costs of poor quality," *IEEE Software*, vol. 16, no. 4, pp. 22–25, Jul/Aug 1999.

[vV10] E. van Veenendaal, "Standard glossary of terms used in software testing," International Software Quality Testing Board (ISTQB), Tech. Rep. Version 2.1, April 2010.

[Wal45] A. Wald, "Sequential Tests of Statistical Hypotheses," *Annals of Mathematical Statistics*, vol. 16, no. 2, pp. 117–186, Jan. 1945. [Online]. Available: http://dx.doi.org/10.1214/aoms/1177731118

[Wal47] ——, *Sequential Analysis*. New York, NY, USA: Joh Wiley and Sons, 1947.

[Wal03] K. C. Wallnau, "Volume iii: A technology for predictable assembly from certifiable components (pacc)," SEI, CMU, Tech. Rep. CMU/SEI-2003-TR-009, 2003.

[WB11] Y. Welsch and L. Bulej, "CoCoME Website," http://sourceforge.net/apps/trac/cocome/, August 2011.

[WHH80] M. Woodward, D. Hedley, and M. Hennell, "Experience with path analysis and testing of programs," *IEEE Transactions on Software Engineering*, vol. SE-6, no. 3, pp. 278–286, May 1980.

[WHKF12] D. Westermann, J. Happe, R. Krebs, and R. Farahbod, "Automated inference of goal-oriented performance prediction functions," in *Proceedings of the*

27th IEEE/ACM International Conference on Automated Software Engineering, ser. ASE 2012. New York, NY, USA: ACM, 2012, pp. 190–199. [Online]. Available: http://doi.acm.org/10.1145/2351676.2351703

[WI03]   K. C. Wallnau and J. Ivers, "Snapshot of ccl: A language for predictable assembly," Software Engineering Institute at the Carnegie Mellon University, Tech. Rep. CMU/SEI-2003-TN-025, June 2003.

[WMLB11]   A. Wassyng, T. Maibaum, M. Lawford, and H. Bherer, "Software certification: Is there a case against safety cases?" in *Foundations of Computer Software. Modeling, Development, and Verification of Adaptive Systems*, ser. Lecture Notes in Computer Science, R. Calinescu and E. Jackson, Eds. Springer Berlin / Heidelberg, 2011, vol. 6662, pp. 206–227, 10.1007/978-3-642-21292-5_12. [Online]. Available: http://dx.doi.org/10.1007/978-3-642-21292-5_12

[Woo05]   M. Woodside, "A composable performance model for service/resource systems," in *Proceeedings of the 7th Workshop on Performability Modelling of Computer an Communications Systems (PMCCS7)*, September 2005, pp. 88–92.

[WPP+05]   M. Woodside, D. C. Petriu, D. B. Petriu, H. Shen, T. Israr, and J. Merseguer, "Performance by unified model analysis (puma)," in *Proceedings of the 5th international workshop on Software and performance*, ser. WOSP '05. New York, NY, USA: ACM, 2005, pp. 1–12. [Online]. Available: http://doi.acm.org/10.1145/1071021.1071022

[WVCB01]   M. Woodside, V. Vetland, M. Courtois, and S. Bayarov, "Resource function capture for performance aspects of software components and sub-systems," in *Performance Engineering*, ser. Lecture Notes in Computer Science, R. Dumke, C. Rautenstrauch, A. Scholz, and A. Schmietendorf, Eds. Springer Berlin Heidelberg, 2001, vol. 2047, pp. 239–256. [Online]. Available: http://dx.doi.org/10.1007/3-540-45156-0_15

[WW04]   X. Wu and M. Woodside, "Performance modeling from software components," in *Proceedings of the 4th international workshop on software and performance*, ser. WOSP '04. New York, NY, USA: ACM, 2004, pp. 290–301. [Online]. Available: http://doi.acm.org/10.1145/974044.974089

[YM09]   D. F. Yates and N. Malevris, "Inclusion, subsumption, jj-paths, and structured path testing: a redress," *Software Testing, Verification and Reliability*, vol. 19, no. 3, pp. 199–213, 2009. [Online]. Available: http://dx.doi.org/10.1002/stvr.400

[You05]   H. L. S. Younes, "Verification and Planning for Stochastic Processes with Asynchronous Events," Ph.D. dissertation, School of Computer Science, Carnegie Mellon University, Pittsburgh, PA, USA, January 2005.

[ZM03]   S. Zschaler and M. Meyerhoefer, "Explicit modelling of qos-dependencies," in *Proceedings of the 1st International Workshop on Quality of Service in Component-Based Software Engineering*, June 2003, pp. 57–66.

[ZNG+09]   T. Zimmermann, N. Nagappan, H. Gall, E. Giger, and B. Murphy, "Cross-project defect prediction: a large scale experiment on data vs. domain vs. process," in *Proceedings of the the 7th joint meeting of the*

European software engineering conference and the ACM SIGSOFT symposium on the foundations of software engineering, ser. ESEC/FSE '09. New York, NY, USA: ACM, 2009, pp. 91–100. [Online]. Available: http://doi.acm.org/10.1145/1595696.1595713

[ZWL08]   T. Zheng, M. Woodside, and M. Litoiu, "Performance model estimation and tracking using optimal filters," *IEEE Transactions on Software Engineering*, vol. 34, no. 3, pp. 391–406, June 2008.

The Karlsruhe Series on
Software Design and Quality

Edited by Prof. Dr. Ralf Reussner // ISSN 1867-0067

Band 1   **Steffen Becker**
Coupled Model Transformations for QoS Enabled
Component-Based Software Design. 2008
ISBN 978-3-86644-271-9

Band 2   **Heiko Koziolek**
Parameter Dependencies for Reusable Performance
Specifications of Software Components. 2008
ISBN 978-3-86644-272-6

Band 3   **Jens Happe**
Predicting Software Performance in Symmetric
Multi-core and Multiprocessor Environments. 2009
ISBN 978-3-86644-381-5

Band 4   **Klaus Krogmann**
Reconstruction of Software Component Architectures and
Behaviour Models using Static and Dynamic Analysis. 2012
ISBN 978-3-86644-804-9

Band 5   **Michael Kuperberg**
Quantifying and Predicting the Influence of Execution
Platform on Software Component Performance. 2010
ISBN 978-3-86644-741-7

Band 6   **Thomas Goldschmidt**
View-Based Textual Modelling. 2011
ISBN 978-3-86644-642-7

Die Bände sind unter www.ksp.kit.edu als PDF frei verfügbar oder als Druckausgabe bestellbar.

The Karlsruhe Series on Software Design and Quality

Edited by Prof. Dr. Ralf Reussner // ISSN 1867-0067

Die Bände sind unter www.ksp.kit.edu als PDF frei verfügbar oder als Druckausgabe bestellbar.